Ann Baumbach
7-29-05

THE TRIAL OF
IVAN THE
TERRIBLE

THE TRIAL OF
IVAN THE
TERRIBLE

STATE OF ISRAEL VS.
JOHN DEMJANJUK

Tom Teicholz

ST. MARTIN'S PRESS
New York

THE TRIAL OF IVAN THE TERRIBLE. Copyright © 1990 by Tom Teicholz. All rights reserved. Printed in the United States of America. No part of this book may be used or reproduced in any manner whatsoever without written permission except in the case of brief quotations embodied in critical articles or reviews. For information, address St. Martin's Press, 175 Fifth Avenue, New York, N.Y. 10010.

Design by Janet Tingey

Library of Congress Cataloging-in-Publication Data
Teicholz, Tom.
    The trial of Ivan the Terrible: state of Israel vs. John Demjanjuk.
    p. cm.
  ISBN 0-312-01450-3
  1. Demjanjuk, John—Trials, litigation, etc. 2. War crime trials—Jerusalem. 3. Treblinka (Poland: Concentration camp). 4. World War, 1939–1945—Poland—Atrocities. I. Title.
JX5441.D45T45 1988
341.6'9'026856944—dc19   87-28400

10 9 8 7 6 5 4 3 2

Justice, Justice shall ye pursue.
—DEUTERONOMY 16:20

Justice must not only be done, it must be seen
to be done.
—JUSTICE DOV LEVIN, QUOTING A
TALMUDIC SAYING.

Outside: Jerusalem and the moaning of the
Lord's trees, cut down by her enemies in every
generation; clouds heavy with thunders that,
for me, on this night of rain, are tidings from
the mouth of the God of Might to endless
generations.
—URI ZVI GREENBERG

CONTENTS

ACKNOWLEDGMENTS

A first book has many midwives and I would like to thank them all, as best I can.

My friend, Yacov Gur-Arie, first urged me to write a book on this case. In Israel, he helped in every way possible, serving as translator, Israeli clip service, driver—even on occasion loaning me his computer. I can't thank him enough. Dr. Scott Wetzler was this project's earliest enthusiast, my most faithful reader, and of great aid in researching and understanding the relevant psychological issues. Michael Carlisle, my agent, was my advocate, arbitrator, facilitator, and a critical reader. This book marks the culmination of a decade of friendship and professional association. Michael Sagalyn, my editor at St. Martin's, taught me how to write a proposal, and then later taught me many invaluable lessons about writing and about publishing. Thanks, Mike.

To my parents, Bruce and Eva Teicholz, their support and patience was much appreciated. To Debbie and Nuriel Guedalia, thanks for the encouragement, and thanks to "The Bigger Picture."

And to Amy—you have all my love, but let me give some thanks where thanks are due: you "managed the environment," were patient and understanding in many time zones, and helped with the hardest part of the writing—deciding who I was in this ocean of information. I couldn't have done it without you.

It would be hard to thank the State of Israel or the City of Jerusalem enough for the time spent there, but I must—the context was so much a part of the richly rewarding experience. In Israel I found many friends. Those I knew already, Amos and Eva Gur-Arie, Mordechai and Bila Ben-Ari, and Harry and Levana Guedalia and those I met while there: Karin Moses, Ruth, Amos, and Jackie, and everyone at Mishkenot Shaananim, my home away from home. Alan and Nadja Hoffman opened their home to me—the time spent with their family and relatives and the discussions at their table provided insights into Israel and into the case that are reflected in this manuscript.

I owe much to the journalists I befriended at the trial: (alphabetically) Alison Bender, Eric Fettmann, Toby Greenwald, Nancie Katz, Michele Lesie, Ernie Meyer, Ken Myers, Tom Seghev, Gitta Sereny, Amir Shaviv. We sat together for many months in the Binyanei Haooma; and when we met outside, or spoke long-distance, we discussed the minutiae of the trial. This book is but the shadow of their knowledge; an imperfect distillation of our conversations. They paid me the honor of treating me as a colleague. I do not deserve it; but hope still to earn it. Ken Myers, "Mr. Cleveland," always had the deep background; Gitta Sereny was a great resource—and she and Don are great friends; Ken and Michele read the manuscript for accuracy. Thank you.

For their courtesy, I want to thank the court staff, Elizur and Nira, in particular; the judge's clerks; the translators (thanks to Batya Frost, Ruth Levy-Berlowitz, and Miriam Schlesinger); and Translator's Pool for transcripts. For their cooperation, I want to thank the prosecution and defense attorneys (both those in Israel and those in the U.S.). Yossi Hassan, attorney and diplomat, the official spokesperson for the prosecution, is the unsung helper to my work. The account of the trial I have presented does not give him the credit he deserves. I would like as best I can to rectify that here. On a day-to-day basis no one was more important nor more helpful than Yossi in understanding the process unfolding before us and in helping me get access to court documents and interviews.

My time in Israel and my work on this book was enhanced by the pleasure of meeting Herb Krosney and Danny Setton, with whom I worked on a documentary about the case. Though I was their consultant, I felt much more that they were mine.

The following also deserve thanks for their help: Rivka at the Israel Press office; Paul Korda; journalists Mark Gottlieb, Jay Bushinky, Susan Adams; Naomi Godel and Ellen Ben Ze'ev (translators from Hebrew); Mari Langer (translation from German); Susan Bornstein, Johanna Schneller, Natasha Vassiltchikov, Kirk Walsh; Charles Langer, for providing me with a room in New York to write in. Diligent and honest readers: Nessa Rapoport, Mike Wolf, Faye Cone, Gary Finder, and Deborah Solomon—without whom the manuscript would be twice as long and half as good. David Hirshey came through with a last-moment save (and mention); and Carolyn White for her editorial guidance at the crucial stage.

Also thanks to Allen Finkelstein and the law firm of Finkelstein Bruckman Wohl Most & Rothman, who were tremendously supportive of this project (and of me).

There are also certain individuals, who wished to remain nameless, who provided access and information. I will respect your request but, at least, I'd like to thank you. I will always be grateful. And to those who remain nameless through the sin of omission, my apologies—but my thanks as well.

Finally, I was privileged during the course of the trial to meet many Treblinka survivors and their families. They gave of their time and shared of their sorrow. Writing this book, I was acutely aware of their pain. I would like to dedicate this book to them, and if possible, to the memory of all the families that perished there, and to the families that would have been, had there been no Treblinka.

New York
February 1, 1990

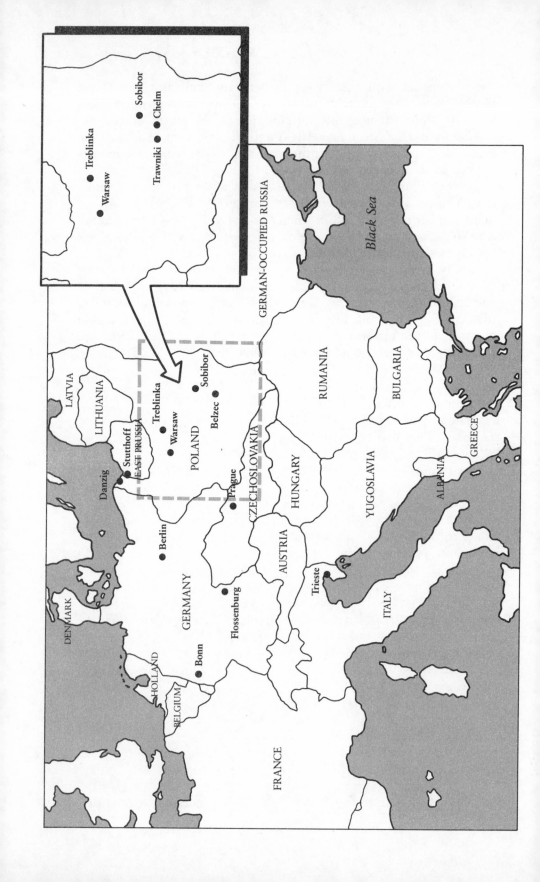

CHAPTER 1

Who Cares?

On Sunday, February 15, 1987, the night before the trial of John Demjanjuk was to begin, a casual canvassing of Jerusalem taxi drivers found they had no opinion about the trial. This was striking because in Israel, everyone has an opinion, on everything. But in the year since Demjanjuk had arrived in custody in Israel from the United States, ambivalence about his trial had permeated the country. Who could say if he was truly guilty? Who cared? Could Israel mount a successful case concerning crimes forty-five years past? Could the memories of Treblinka survivors be trusted? Didn't Israel have more pressing current problems? Why return to Treblinka?

In the United States, public reaction was as curiously low-key—even indifferent—as it was in Israel. The Klaus Barbie trial, to commence that summer in Lyons, held far greater attention. *That* was the important trial. Who was Demjanjuk? A small cog, not a planner; a collaborator, not a German Nazi.

Demjanjuk was alleged to be "Ivan the Terrible," the Ukrainian gas-chamber operator at Treblinka who had, with his own hands, murdered hundreds of thousands of men, women, and children, cruelly, zealously, and with a sadism beyond any bounds. But John Demjanjuk had spent more than thirty years living the successful immigrant's life in the United States, among family, his three children, friends, workers, and fellow congregants who believed in his innocence as fervently as his prosecutors did in his guilt.

On the following morning, Monday, February 16, 1987, his trial attracted as many reporters as spectators. To accommodate security arrangements for Demjanjuk, as well as the public and press, the smaller hall of Jerusalem's convention center—the Binyanei Haooma, or "The Hall of the People"—had been transformed into a courtroom. It was used often as a movie theater.

As you walked into the building, you had to pass a sign, "Box Office for the Performances," that seemed a cynical portent, given the occasion, and the equally resonant, "Deposit Weapons Here." After clearing a metal detector at the door, you registered your passport number with the guards seated inside the hall. In the foyer was a small snack bar; off to the left was a counter where reporters and spectators could pick up, at no charge, Walkman-like gear to listen to the simultaneous translation of the testimony from Hebrew into English. To the far right was the press area, with a separate entrance, pay phones, and long-distance operators.

Israel's ambivalence about the trial was evident in the makeshift quality of some of its arrangements. The judges' dais had been hauled over from Jerusalem District Court; the attorneys' desks had been taken from storerooms. Only Demjanjuk's witness booth was newly constructed. Outside the courtroom, a simple sign had been taped to the wall informing visitors of the do's and don'ts of courtroom etiquette.

A former dressing room, off stage left, had been transmuted into a temporary cell for Demjanjuk. As a safety and security precaution, workers had changed all 220-volt outlets in the room to non-dangerous 24 volts. A bed and table were bolted to the floor, and now a closed-circuit camera enabled police to monitor the room from a separate office in the building. The small hall was being rented from its owner, the Jewish Agency, for $17,000 a month. Arrangements had been made for a three-month lease.

The trapezoid-shaped hall was paneled with blond wood that stretched to a high ceiling of large acoustical tiles. Seating for three hundred was provided; benches would be added later. The balcony was reserved for the press. The trial itself would take place onstage, which had been set as follows.

At the back center stage was the raised dais of the three-judge panel that would hear the case. Below the judges would sit their clerk and the official Hebrew translator. On the left was one long table for the defense, angled like a giant eyebrow, where attorneys Mark O'Connor, Yoram Sheftel, and John Gill would sit. Directly behind them was the dock in which Demjanjuk would sit with a Ukrainian translator at his side, flanked by two police officers.

There had been talk that Demjanjuk would sit in Adolf Eichmann's bulletproof glass booth, but security officials decided against that precaution. Behind Demjanjuk's two guards would sit another police officer, against the left wall, and, on the first day, John Demjanjuk Jr. During the course of the trial, the police officers and security guards would be rotated regularly. John Demjanjuk Jr.'s table would be moved back against the wall, and ultimately he would be asked to sit among the spectators.

On the right was the matching eyebrow, the two prosecution tables each seating four. At the front table sat Yonah Blatman, the state attorney; Michael Shaked, in effect the team's lead attorney; Michael Horovitz and Dennis Gouldman. The assistant attorneys sat at the second table. Behind the prosecution tables was a wall bearing a photographic blowup of a model of the Treblinka extermination camp. And next to the prosecution table was the witness box, from which the witness could face the accused and be scrutinized by the judges.

An Israeli flag stood on each side of the judge's bench; the seal of the State of Israel was affixed to the center of the back wall. This was no international tribunal. The proceedings were to be conducted in Hebrew, according to Israeli law and procedure.

Dispersed throughout the room were security guards in white shirts, police in blue uniforms, and military personnel in tan or green uniforms.

Shortly before 8:30 A.M., the prosecutors and defense attorneys, all in black robes, took their places, and began to shuffle the masses of documents piled high on their desks. The press had filled several rows downstairs, with television and radio reporters in the balcony. Their cameras, still and video, stood poised on tripods, like long-necked cranes peering over the edge.

Demjanjuk now entered, surrounded by four policemen. Wearing a brown suit, he had adopted Israeli custom and wore no tie, just an open shirt. He looked ruddy, overweight. Camera lights went on, as the whirring and clicking of press equipment began in earnest. Demjanjuk raised his arm in what some feared would be a salute but turned out to be a gentle wave of his hand. He shouted in his deep voice, *"Boker tov"*—Hebrew for "good morning"—and then, "Hello Cleveland," to the TV cameras. He shook attorney Mark O'Connor's hand, embraced his other American attorney, John Gill; and then hugged his son. Israeli codefense counsel Yoram Sheftel entered, sitting down between O'Connor and John Gill.

There was much arranging of Demjanjuk's seat.

The court clerk announced *"Beit Hamishpat!"* sharply. The room came to attention. All rose in anticipation, and the three judges entered from the right in black robes. Judge Zvi Tal, bearded and wearing a *kippah,* a skullcap, occupied the left chair. In the center was Presiding Justice Dov Levin and on his right Judge Dalia Dorner, who like her colleagues was wearing a black tie and white shirt.

"Good morning," Justice Levin said to the assembled crowd. "Please be seated."

The setting was dramatic: the stage, the call to attention, the public, the press. This was to be a public trial, but it would be no show trial. Judge Dov Levin was to make sure of that.

This was the first trial of a Nazi war criminal in Israel since Adolf Eichmann's in 1961. In every aspect, it showed how much Israel and the world had changed in twenty-five years. Eichmann had had to be kidnapped from Argentina to be brought to trial. This time Israel had applied for Demjanjuk's extradition from the United States, which upheld its treaty obligations and delivered him to Israeli authorities.

The trial of Eichmann was very much a trial conducted by the generation that had survived the Holocaust. The majority of Israel's population in 1961 was composed of survivors or their families. It was very much a trial to show the world that the Holocaust did occur and that a Jewish nation had risen from its ashes to sit in judgment.

The trial of Demjanjuk was to be the trial by the generation born since the Holocaust. The population of Israel was now made up, in its majority, of Sephardic Jews who had had no direct contact with the Holocaust and of a generation born since 1945. The presiding judge was Israel-born, and the other judges had been in Palestine during the Holocaust. The prosecutors and defense attorneys were almost all born after 1945.

For a generation removed from the crimes of the Holocaust, this was a more graphic trial than Eichmann's. Eichmann was tried as the master planner of the Jews' extermination, Demjanjuk was accused as their murderer.

Inside the courtroom, by the very nature of the legal process, facts emerged slowly; proof and evidence had to be found valid. Inside the courtroom, the process awaited a final judgment.

Outside the courtroom, reporters followed a daily story. A story needed headlines, developments, quotes. The judges and prosecutors, following the prohibition against discussing cases not finally adjudicated, were rarely available for comment. But defense supporters were more than available to speak and volunteered information freely to columnists and reporters. Misstatements between quotation marks were just quotes; they didn't need to be checked. The net effect was confusion, a vagueness outside the courtroom as to what had occurred at any given moment inside. It was no surprise that many were troubled by what they read of the case.

But inside the courtroom, the State of Israel was compelled by the criminal process to prove beyond any doubt the horrific allegations. This was no simple task, for the prosecution would have to break the conspiracy of silence the Nazis had wished to achieve by razing Treblinka in November 1943.

"Treblinka, with the terrible tragedy it embodies," the court would say in its verdict, "[was] the very end of a long, bitter, and tortuous road . . . meant to lead to a single goal, to exterminate the Jewish people and Jewish communities throughout Europe."

Hitler's Nazi philosophy and state policy of Aryan supremacy created racial laws that treated the Jews as subhumans, depriving them of their livelihoods and property, enclosing them in ghettos.

The monstrous German war machine needed constant feeding: raw materials, money, territories. The expansion of the German Reich meant, at the same time, the elimination of the Jewish population and the plunder of their property.

At the Wansee Conference in early 1942, plans were discussed for "the final solution of the Jewish question." The green light was given to the establishment of extermination camps, including Treblinka. The eastern half of German-occupied Poland—the "Gouvernment General," as it was referred to by the Nazis—held more than two million Jews at the time.

Dr. Josef Buehler, the State Secretary of the territory, stated in the conference protocol that "they will be happy if the final solution of this problem has its inception in the Gouvernment General. . . ." The solution was to build concentration camps where mass killings could occur without "arousing disquiet among the population."

Even before this, the Nazi regime had been considering "quicker and cleaner" methods of mass killing. The crippled, the infirm did not measure up to the Aryan superimage. Some eighty thousand to one hundred thousand "sick Germans"—mental cases, invalids, including children—were gassed by carbon monoxide. This was the "Euthanasia Operation," with headquarters in Berlin at 4 Tiergardenstrasse; its workers referred to the operation as "T4." The economic burden that these unfortunates posed to the State was ended by their murders, and the Nazis now looked to the economic relief of murdering Jews as well.

First there were mass shootings into ditches. But this was deemed too wasteful of ammunition, and too personally difficult for the soldiers. Next they tried "killing vans"—Jews were sealed in the backs of trucks; as the trucks drove, carbon monoxide was recirculated inside to asphyxiate the passengers. The trucks then arrived at giant ditches where the corpses were buried. But this, too, posed problems: Jews could be killed only in the tens, not the thousands or millions as they had planned; and it was too public—the driving around, the ditches in the forest.

On September 3, 1941, a gas prepared from acidic alcohol, "Zyklon B," was used at Auschwitz to kill Soviet prisoners. The Nazis were now encouraged: with a minimum of staff, mass killings could occur discreetly.

After the Wansee Conference in 1942, Reinhard Heydrich was named to head the extermination program and began planning the liquidation of the Jews of Eastern Europe. But Heydrich was killed by Czech underground fighters in May 1942, outside Prague. The extermination of Polish Jewry was then dubbed, in his honor, "Operation Reinhard." Odilo Globochnik, the former Gauletier of Vienna and Heinrich Himmler's personal friend, was put in charge, and a staff was formed to continue Heydrich's planning.

Jews were to be gassed at special concentration camps built in Eastern Poland. Plans divided the Gouvernment into districts, and directed the transports of Jews to one of three camps, each to be located near a railway system and designed to share equally in the murders.

Jews from the districts of Lwow and Cracow were to be sent to Belzec; the Lublin district Jews, for the great part, to Sobibor; and Jews from the Warsaw and Radom districts to Treblinka.

To find appropriate staff for the extermination camps, Operation Reinhard needed only to look to its recent past: the T4 workers were unusually well prepared, and were placed in key positions at the camps.

Christian Wirth was made chief extermination specialist, having proved himself at Chelmno in the operation of the killing vans. He was the first commander of the Belzec camp.

It was Wirth who decided that the camps would use carbon monoxide. And it was Wirth who, after experimenting with carbon-monoxide containers sent from Germany, decided that diesel engines should be installed adjacent to the gas chambers to produce the necessary poisonous fumes.

The camps were staffed by approximately twenty to thirty-five SS men. But this proved too small a force. A camp had to be guarded inside and out: soldiers had to ensure that the killings would take place with a minimum of disturbance. So this task was assigned to guard units of non-German collaborators, recruited for SS service at Soviet POW camps and trained at Trawniki near Lublin.

The commander of the SS training camp Trawniki, Karl Streibl, personally toured the Soviet prisoner-of-war camps to find suitable volunteers. The conditions in POW camps were inhumane. People were dying of starvation, malnutrition, and exposure. Though Streibl's orders were to recruit "Aryan"-looking soldiers, he selected the healthy, and those who had a skill, such as drivers.

Trawniki itself was staffed mostly with *Volksdeutsche*—ethnic Germans. Approximately thirty-five hundred guards were trained at Trawniki during its two-and-a-half years of operation. They were trained in weapons, and assigned to liquidate ghettos or guard extermination camps.

Guard units of ninety to one-hundred-twenty men were posted to each of these camps. They were called *Wachmanner,* but were also known as auxiliaries or *Hiwis;* they finally became known by Germans and inmates alike simply as the "Ukrainians," for almost all had been born in the Ukraine. They had volunteered for SS service while prisoners of war, captured or surrendered Red Army soldiers.

By the summer of 1942, Treblinka was set up at Malkinia, near the Bug River. Belzec and Sobibor were already in operation, but it was Treblinka that would become the "perfected" death camp. Its location, only forty miles from Warsaw, had been chosen carefully: an elongated wooded elevation, hidden from the surrounding highway and railroad line. In the forest, leafy trees made a shaded glade. One could hear birds singing.

There was a gravel quarry nearby. The SS brought some one thousand Polish and Jewish prisoners there to build what would be known as Treblinka AG, or the Treblinka labor camp. It would be used as a concentration camp for smugglers, but also as a camp to show others, should questions arise. The forced laborers as well as Jews from neighboring villages were part of the site-construction crew for the death camp. The laborers were eventually murdered.

The death camp was laid out as a rectangle, approximately six-hundred-sixty yards by four-hundred-forty yards (fewer than sixty acres), surrounded by a barbed-wire fence about twelve feet high, which was camouflaged by leaves and branches, and surrounded by tree saplings. Immediately behind this fence was a ditch about ten feet wide, behind which lay a bare strip of land some forty-five yards wide. This strip was marked off from the surrounding area by barbed wire and antitank obstacles (also called "spanish horses"). At all four corners of the camp were watchtowers, some with searchlights, all manned night and day by Ukrainian guards.

Inside the camp, there were three areas of equal dimension: the living quarters of the German and Ukrainian staff; the arrival area for the transports; and the actual extermination area. The living and reception camp was known by the Germans as the "Lower Camp" and by the inmates as "Camp One"; the extermination area as the "Upper Camp" or "Camp Two."

The staff living area had two long barracks for bedrooms, the kitchen, and mess hall. Facing the barracks was the commandant's house and the food warehouse (there was no shortage of delicacies confiscated from the Jews). There were also administration buildings, offices, workshops, stores, and an infirmary. A quarter-acre of this area was wired off: here were the Jewish laborers' living quarters, workshop, and square for holding roll call.

Behind the food warehouse was an area for the Jews from neighboring towns who had helped to build the camp. In recognition of their service they wore yellow stars and were allowed to live somewhat longer as the waiters of the Germans and Ukrainians, although in time these workers were murdered as well. Several women worked in the kitchens, and were among the only females allowed to live in Treblinka.

The camp was ready July 11, 1942. Eleven days later, the first transport from Warsaw left for Treblinka. The train would leave daily with no fewer than five-thousand Jews aboard. The transports would continue for the next thirteen months: eight-hundred-seventy thousand Jewish men, women, and children would pass through its gates. More, perhaps. Only fifty would survive.

The trains arrived at the reception area in the southwest section of the camp. Here was the Jews' first sight of Treblinka. They entered through a gate to a square. There they separated, men to the right, women and children to the left, never to see each other again. They were commanded to undress. Two barracks flanked the square: in one, the women and children undressed; in the other, the personal effects of the murdered were sorted and accumulated for shipment out of the camp.

The naked victims were then commanded to run up a fenced-in path. Past the gate, showers awaited them in the bath house. This path, called the *Schlauch*, the "tube," led to, the death camp. The Germans also called it the *Himmelfahrtstrasse*, or "road to heaven." The Jews were set upon by dogs and blows from the guards. They ran toward a gate and were forced into a building. Less than two hours after arrival, this was their end.

Except for minor industrial activity, the camp's only contribution to the German war effort was the confiscated property of the inmates. In a little more than a year, the camp shipped out about 25 carloads of hair packed in bales; 248 carloads of men's suits; 22 carloads of ready-made textile goods; carloads of medicines, medical equipment, and dentist's metal; 12 carloads of artisans' tools; 260 carloads of bedding, feathers, down quilts; 400 carloads of miscellaneous items. One inmate recalled spending six months sorting out fountain pens; another packing more than fourteen thousand carats in diamonds.

The Jews who survived the initial arrival did so because the Germans selected them to be forced laborers in Camp One.

Jews were forced laborers in the death camp as well. A small work group was selected occasionally from the lower sorting crew to walk the path to the death camp. The gate to the death camp and the fence surrounding it were camouflaged. Germans wanted to keep its activity secret not only to the outside world but also to each new transport of Jews.

Jewish workers who entered the death camp found a human mountain of corpses, among them the men and women of their own transports, of their communities, of their relatives. Under a hail of beatings, they were put to work immediately.

They were assigned various tasks: emptying the gas chambers, cleaning them before the next arrivals, carrying corpses to the pits, examining the corpses' mouths for fillings. In the ditches they found row upon row of dead bodies. Those who didn't work fast enough were shot and buried with the corpses.

Most of the buildings were made of wood, but the buildings in the death camp were made of brick. The gas-chamber building itself was hidden from the Lower Camp by a row of trees. The roof of the gas chamber was camouflaged with a green wire net whose edges extended slightly beyond the building's walls. Under the roof was a tangle of pipes. The walls were covered with concrete.

Within, the chambers looked like a regular shower room with all the accouterments of a public bathhouse. Its walls were covered with small white tiles. The floor was covered with terra-cotta tiles. Nickel-plated faucets were set into the ceiling. The work was finely detailed.

Standing next to the bathhouse was a large chest. A "dentist" would examine the mouth of each corpse as it was dragged out of the chamber and extract any gold, silver, or platinum caps he might find. More than one chestful of precious metal was accumulated each day.

Under a tree about forty meters from the bathhouse, a band of Jewish musicians performed for the Germans and Ukrainians. Concerts were held when new transports arrived, to cover the screams of the dying.

The inmates were marched up to the barracks, unaware of what awaited them. They went stony-faced, naked, pressed together. Fleeing the blows of the guards and the brutal cold of Polish winter, they rushed faster yet toward the chamber.

The machinery of the gas chamber was supervised by the Germans Arthur Matthes and Fritz Schmidt; but it was operated by two Ukrainians, Ivan and Nikolai. At a given signal they would admit the victims. Ivan and Nikolai, holding a heavy lead pipe or a bayonet, would force the Jews inside, beating them savagely as they moved into the chamber. Ivan often jabbed at them with his knife to hurry them along; amusing himself by slicing a breast or cutting an ear.

The screams of the women, the weeping of the children, the pleas for mercy, for God's deliverance, filled the air like the howling of wild animals. Between four-hundred-fifty and five-hundred people were crowded into a chamber measuring twenty-five square meters. The bedlam lasted only a short while, for soon the doors were slammed shut.

Ivan went then to the engine room at the side of the building and turned on the motor. It was a Russian diesel tank-engine, connected to the chamber's inflow pipes. The exhaust filled the chamber. Within a half hour, the victims lay dead, or were left standing dead, as there was often not an inch of space.

When the gassing was over, Ivan and Nikolai inspected the results. Occasionally the supervising German would put his ear to the door to comment *Alles shlaft* ("all asleep"). Ivan and Nikolai then moved to the other side of the building, where they heaved sliding doors that opened onto a ramp. There waited the Jewish laborers forced to carry corpses. When the doors opened, bluish smoke escaped.

At first the Jews carried the corpses to the ditches with their hands. Then a narrow-gauge track was built to drive the corpses to the ditches on a rolling platform. Finally, they used wooden stretchers.

The corpse-carriers worked two to a stretcher. Each stretcher held one adult, or two children. The workers ran and were allowed to pause only while the "dentists" fulfilled their task.

The corpses were tossed into the ditches, which were deeply carved pits. Once aligned in the ditch, a layer of sand was poured over them; then another layer of corpses; then sand, until the pit was filled. Occasionally the entire mound would heave and resettle. The pits would then be filled more and topped off. The corpse-carriers returned, running, forced at times to gallop like horses, to await the next gassing.

Soon it became clear that the capacity of the single gas house was not sufficient. Ten new chambers were built by the inmates in five weeks' time. Each chamber was twice the size of the old one. As many as twelve hundred persons could be gassed now at one time. Between ten and twelve thousand people were gassed each day, some days as many as fifteen thousand. The entrance to the new chamber bore a Star of David as well as a legend in Hebrew script: "This is the gate through which the righteous shall enter." When the construction was finished, the *Hauptsturmfuhrer,* the captain, said to his subordinates, "The Jew-town has been completed at last."

About two to three hundred Jewish forced-laborers lived and worked in the death camp. Many knew each other by sight. They were brothers. They had to work in tandem, carrying corpses on stretchers. The "dentist" could give them a moment to breathe. One could save a piece of bread for the other. One slept in the bunk above. One needed help to hang himself.

The Germans in charge, what couldn't they have at their will? For their amusement? In Treblinka the cruelty was so pervasive that fear had its gradations, sadism its own hierarchy. Survival was dependent on such knowledge. Kurt Franz, the assistant commander of the camp, was known as *Die Lalke,* "The Doll," due to his good looks. He held the roll calls. One survivor recalled that "the earth shook" when he approached. Franz would call to his attack dog, Barry, "Man bite the dog." To Lalke, Barry was the man, the Jews the dog.

About fourteen Germans worked in Camp Two; only two Ukrainians were permanently posted there. The work-Jews did not know the full names of their tormentors. They heard the names that the Germans and Ukrainians addressed each other by, and they had their own nicknames for them as well.

In Camp One, the Jewish workers had little contact with the guards; but in the death camp they worked closely by the two Ukrainians assigned there, Ivan and Nikolai. Among all the frightening figures in Treblinka, Ivan was the most feared.

His last name was not known to the Jews. He was a Ukrainian, and the Ukrainians and Germans called him Ivan. The Jews called him Ivan Grozny, "Ivan the Terrible."

Ivan was healthy, strong, and well built. He was in his early twenties. Most descriptions put his height at about six feet. He had several distinguishing features: he was already balding; both his ears stuck out from his round head; he had a short, thick neck, set in broad shoulders; and his eyes, which were close-set, shone with intensity. One survivor recalled they were normally grayish, but when he was drunk and killing they went white with anger. And he had ferocious energy for sadism. There was a *driven* quality to his brutality.

Ivan customarily stood at the entrance to the gas chambers and greeted those marked for death with beatings or cuts from his saber. He savored punishments to the workers as well. He liked to flog and to rape and to command others to perform sexual acts before him. He ordered one survivor to have sex with a corpse. Another recalled him ordering an inmate to copulate with a young girl crying out for her lost mother. Often he was drunk, and the alcohol fueled his cruelty, and the cruelty his drinking.

Even among the monsters of Treblinka, Ivan was more monstrous. As one survivor said: "What pleasure he took in his tasks!" One survivor recalled, "He would often pounce on us while we were working. . . . While he did this, his face showed sadistic satisfaction and he laughed and joked. He finished off his victims according to his mood at the moment." He worked with another Ukrainian named Nikolai, or "Kolka" for short. He also operated the gas chamber, he also pushed in inmates, he also beat them. But it is Ivan the survivors remember, it was his brutality that seared their memories.

The whole of the death camp area was 200 by 275 yards, so the actual space the Jewish inmates worked in, between the gas chambers and the pits, was small indeed. Here, they would see Ivan, often day in and day out, at close proximity, over a period of many months. It was as if, one survivor recalled, "they rubbed shoulders" with him. They watched him, they feared him, they knew him. How could they forget him?

During breaks or after gassings, Ivan could be found sitting with Nikolai, or roaming about other parts of the camp. He was free to do so. During the days of the heavy transports in the fall and winter of 1942, he would rush to greet arrivals at the train platform and then rush to greet them at the gas chambers. He was, on occasion, ordered to accompany details to cut trees for camouflage. He ate at the Ukrainian mess in the Lower Camp, and slept in the Ukrainian barracks.

Something else distinguished Ivan: he had a talent with engines, and not only the gas-chamber engine. Ivan had been a mechanic. He knew how to drive, which was unusual for a Ukrainian guard. He liked to visit the camp's repair shop, and often tinkered in the garage.

Ivan was well liked by the Germans, and held the other guards in disdain. On occasion, he was sent out of the camp; he was among the few permitted to leave regularly and venture into neighboring towns.

Beginning in January 1943, the pace of transports slackened. Early in the new year, Himmler visited the camp, and the corpses were ordered cremated rather than buried. No remains should exist. Jews were assigned to this task as well. They built a crematoria by placing railroad rails on concrete slabs to form a grill.

The corpses that had been buried in mass graves were exhumed by mechanical excavators. Some of the pits contained seventy thousand corpses. Up to three thousand gassed bodies could be incinerated at a time. After cremation, the ashes were checked for bone particles. The pits were then refilled, with layers of human ash, upon layers of sand, and finally topped off with soil. Seedlings were planted to conceal the evidence of mass killings.

As the gassings were fewer, the death camp became calmer. "And," recalled a worker, "Ivan became calmer, too." He was seen less, and the workers did not seek him out. The Jews of the death camp, no longer living in a state of perpetual fear, began to think of revolt.

There had been moments of resistance from the first days of Treblinka, but they were small instances, all unsuccessful, with huge consequences: one guard was murdered, and thirty inmates killed; a group escaped, but was caught and then hung and flayed to death; a tunnel was discovered, and workers were selected at random for death.

But now the time had come to act. The workers realized that as long as the Nazis needed them to carry and incinerate corpses they would be kept alive; but when their work was done, the Nazis would have no need for witnesses to their crimes.

During the months of June and July, the summer heat became increasingly unbearable. The leadership for the revolt was in Camp One. They tried to find a way to get arms. Time was running out. They devised a plan. After another postponement, the revolt was set for August 2. The Jews could not sleep beforehand. "The day of Judgment" was at hand.

August 2, 1943, was a sizzling-hot day. The inmates had a lucky break. Assistant Camp Commander Kurt Franz decided to take a group of Ukrainian guard units to go swimming in the nearby Bug River.

Inmates in both Camp One and Two were given preassigned tasks. The revolt was to start in Camp One; in Camp Two they were to cut the fences and ready the escape path. The excitement and tension were high all day. Each moment in the hot sun was an eternity.

The time for the revolt had been set at 5:00 P.M. A group from the nearby Treblinka labor camp was known to pass by the camp then. The plan was to liberate them to join in the revolt. But the nervousness among the inmates was so great, it was agreed they could not wait that long. Later in the day the time was changed to 4:30 P.M. The go-ahead was passed between Camp One and Two by a construction crew.

The prisoners in Camp One had managed to steal some weapons. One young man whose job was to spread disinfectant around the camp filled his canister instead with gasoline. Another young man, at the garage, sabotaged an SS armored car. Axes and wire cutters were stolen.

In Camp Two, because of the heat, the inmates worked at the incinerator from 4:00 A.M. until noon. But on that day, they needed a way to stay outside, near the camp's fences. That morning they worked at excavating corpses with special ardor. By noon there were still many exhumed corpses lying near the grills. The foreman of the Jewish incineration crew offered to keep the men working that afternoon in exchange for an extra bread ration. The SS man agreed.

The Jews prepared themselves for their escape. They would carry blankets to throw over the barbed-wire fences. They thought about the world outside: They would put on clothes under their coveralls. They collected gold and money from hiding places.

The signal was supposed to be an explosion, a grenade in Camp One. But a half hour earlier than expected, a shot rang out in the lower camp, and the revolt began. An SS man had stopped a young boy. Finding money on him, he arrested him and started to take him away. Afraid that the boy would confess to the revolt, another decided then and there to shoot the SS man, Kurt Kuttner, who was left on the ground bleeding.

Pandemonium broke out. The uprising plans were never put into effect. In the Upper Camp, one young man screamed out "Revolution in Berlin" to frighten the guards. The barracks of the Jewish workers were next to the camp's southernmost perimeter fence, where many now ran.

Flames shot up in the Lower Camp. Jews ran for the woods and swamps. The guards followed, shooting. The Jews armed with pick-axes and a few guns defended themselves as best they could and kept moving. Smoke and flame rose around the gas chambers.

The Germans called for reinforcements from the labor camp; Franz and the guards returned to camp. SS men in armored cars with machine guns and guards on horseback took to the woods to chase down the escaped inmates.

The revolt was no success. Of the eight-hundred-fifty inmates at both camps at that time, only three-hundred-fifty to four hundred were thought to have made it into the surrounding woods. Of those, two hundred were apprehended and summarily shot. Of those who escaped, perhaps only fifty survived the war's end.

The brick gas chambers had been set on fire but did not burn down. Though shots had been fired at many of the Germans and Ukrainians, there were few casualties.

After the revolt the camp was not rebuilt in its original form, but the gassings continued. During the month of August, several additional transports of Jews from Byalistock were killed in the gas chambers.

Treblinka Commander Franz Stangl was afraid he would be punished for the revolt at Treblinka. But because more than eight-hundred-seventy-thousand Jews had been killed there, the SS still considered the camp a success. Now the Russian front was advancing, and the camps needed to be dismantled, their "success" hidden. Stangl's talents were needed elsewhere. By the end of August, he had been reassigned to a combat position, leading an antipartisan force in Trieste. Several other Treblinka men would join him.

Kurt Franz became the camp's commander. By November 1943, every trace of the death camp was to be eliminated. One hundred Jewish prisoners remained to aid in this task.

The buildings were demolished. The Jewish workers were housed in railway cars. Thirty to fifty of them were sent to Sobibor for the dismantling work there. The rest were taken in groups of five to be shot. But before their death, they were given a final task: to cremate the group that had gone before them. The last group was burned by the Ukrainians. Then Franz and the remaining Ukrainian guards drove to Sobibor.

The landscape was leveled. All that remained as testament to what had occurred were sections of barbed wire, heaps of sand. A farmhouse was built with bricks from the gas chambers. A former Ukrainian guard brought his family and began farming the area. The fields were plowed and sown with lupine grass. Pine woods were planted. Treblinka was no more.

Toward the end of 1943, after Sobibor was dismantled, the guards of Treblinka were reassigned from Sobibor, some south to Trieste to help fight the Yugoslav partisans. Others were sent north to guard other small concentration camps.

*   *   *

Today, Treblinka is but a field of commemorative stones, unable to speak the truth of its history. And in Jerusalem sat a man about whom the mind strained at the question: Is it him?

To accept that Demjanjuk was Ivan the Terrible, the horrendous crimes recounted in court had to become real again. Then one had to accept that the man in the witness booth had committed them, and had long since been able to bury those crimes from family and friends. No doubt it was easier to believe he was innocent.

But in many ways, the Demjanjuk case was about the extraordinary becoming everyday and the mundane becoming extraordinary. The crimes of that "other planet," Treblinka, were tried in an Israeli court of law; and the accused "master sadist" of Treblinka sat in the dock in Jerusalem, very much a simple creature. The prosecutors were, for the most part, young, unknown, and untested. The defense was more heard from, than heard of. The judges were respected jurists, but of no international renown. Yet by the everyday process of law, the most extraordinary crimes of our time would be revealed.

CHAPTER 2

The Only Family He Had

On the night of August 2, 1943, a few of the inmates who had escaped Treblinka met in the forest outside the camp. As one survivor recalled years later, "Night fell and we could not get our fill of the intoxicating joy of freedom." They spent the evening exchanging accounts, boastfully telling tales. They were delirious with their success. By their account, the camp had been left in flames, their worst enemies had been vanquished. Every German or Ukrainian who had crossed their path had been killed. Kuttner had been shot; Matthes was dead. Nikolai had been stabbed, some said; yet others, that Ivan the Terrible was no more. Though he had not been seen the day of the uprising, some said Ivan had been killed in his sleep, one said he had been burned alive in the gas chamber, another said he had been hit over the head with a shovel and left for dead.

But this intoxication soon wore off. For those few Jews who managed to survive the escape found themselves in a world not eager for their return. They went their separate ways, forced to hide by day and travel by night. They feared the local population who often tried to turn them in for rewards. Even those who made their way to their hometowns in Poland found themselves suddenly alone. Their homes, their neighborhoods—all had disappeared. They were *alive*, though it seemed as though they had never lived.

A few survivors recorded their impressions of Treblinka then and there, or gave statements to an archivist. They had escaped Treblinka, but there was no assurance they would outlive the war. Their homes were no home, so they made their way elsewhere—to

17

Palestine, to Israel, Germany, South America, to begin anew. For if each night they returned to Treblinka, by day they did all they could to create a different life.

Among those deathcamp survivors who escaped Treblinka was Eliahu Rosenberg. He joined the partisans and later the Polish army, and was discharged in November 1946. He then served in the Bricha, the illegal immigration to Palestine, before arriving in Israel in 1948. It was a few years later, in the early 1950s, while Rosenberg walked along a street in Tel Aviv, that he first saw someone from the other world, Yankel Viernik. Originally from Warsaw, Viernik had been trained as a carpenter. At Treblinka, he headed the crew that built the larger gas chambers. As one of the few inmates who was allowed to go between Camp One and Camp Two, Viernik played a major role in the uprising. He had published his memoirs of Treblinka and then moved to Israel.

Viernik, along with survivors of the Warsaw Ghetto, had founded their own kibbutz, *Lohamei Haghetaot* ("the ghetto fighter's house"). Years later, he built from memory a model of Treblinka that sits today in the kibbutz's museum. Photographs of it would be used at the Demjanjuk trial as an approximate, if not exact, representation of Treblinka.

Now Rosenberg excitedly asked if Viernik knew of other Treblinka survivors in Israel. Viernik mentioned some names, inmates of Camp One whom Rosenberg did not know. What about the death camp? asked Rosenberg. Viernik mentioned that he knew one survivor, Sonia Lewkowicz, worked somewhere in Tel Aviv. Rosenberg remembered her—she had worked in the death camp's laundry. He couldn't believe she had survived. Where? he asked. Viernik knew only that the store she worked in was on Dizengoff, the city's main street.

Rosenberg spent all his free time trying to find Sonia. He was obsessed with the fact that she was still alive; it was as if his own sister had survived Treblinka. He walked Dizengoff from beginning to end, from eight in the morning until night. He went in one store after another. Finally, when he found her—at work in a hardware store—they wept in each other's arms.

Sonia told him about another woman, Bronka Sukno, whom they knew from the camp and who was also in Israel. She lived in a settlement, but Sonia did not know the exact address. Rosenberg searched from house to house until he found her.

Rosenberg had an Army friend named Yossef who told him he, too, knew someone from Treblinka, a man called Pinhas Epstein who lived in Petah Tikvah. Rosenberg didn't know the name, so he decided against making the trip to see him. But years later when they finally met, Rosenberg recognized him as Pavel, whom he indeed had known at Treblinka. They hadn't been good friends there, but in Israel their friendship grew.

Rosenberg continued the pursuit for his lost brothers and sisters. One day in the street in Tel Aviv, he ran into another death-camp survivor, Chaim Staier, who said he had seen Shlomo Hellman, also of the death camp. Rosenberg knew no Hellman, but he went to find him, and Rosenberg found the man he knew as Shlomo Becker. Hellman, in turn, had found another survivor, Avraham Lindvasser, with whom Rosenberg had worked at Treblinka. They now renewed their close friendship.

Eliahu Rosenberg had married and had two daughters. His wife knew he had been in a camp; she never asked about it and he rarely spoke about it. That was understood. On those few occasions when, with others, he did speak about Treblinka and Ivan, she saw the effect it had on him: he couldn't sleep or would have terrible nightmares. The sound of his cries during the night, the look on his face in the morning—she wanted to protect him from those harsh emotions. She came to realize that his friends from the death camp were really the only family he had.

Rosenberg later heard that the man who had slept in the bunk above him at Treblinka, a slightly older fellow, Yehiel Reichman, was alive and had emigrated to Montevideo, Uruguay. After Treblinka, Reichman, like Viernik, had made his way back to Warsaw only to participate in the Warsaw Ghetto uprising. In 1945, Reichman had been part of a Polish fact-finding commission that revisited Treblinka.

After the demolition of the camp in 1943, the grass grew green, covering the land where the killings had occurred. But in 1944, the Soviet Red Army overran the territory. The farmer fled; his farmhouse was demolished. Bombings pockmarked the ground.

When Reichman arrived, he found only fields of black earth. A gang of Gentile youths had taken over the area and were combing the earth for valuables: the Soviet bombings had first revealed the earth's true contents. The gang continued to plow for gold or jewelry. The youths left lying about those items that held no interest for them: whole collections of braided Sabbath candlesticks, women's marriage wigs. Bones, skulls, and piles of white ash heaped with soil stood where the incinerations had taken place. It was the valley of bones.

"We stood and we cried," Reichman recalled. "What can you say? Each remembered who they had left there."

Israel did not rush to commemorate the Holocaust. It was only in 1952 that the nation established a Holocaust Day. It would be seven more years before some form of public observance was set. Even then what was emphasized was not those who died but those who fought. As the Israeli daily *Davar* wrote on the first Holocaust Day, "The one suitable monument to the memory of European Jewry . . . is the State of Israel."

When the day was created to memorialize Holocaust victims, it was called "memorial for the Holocaust and Ghetto revolts." When Yad Vashem, Israel's Holocaust Memorial Museum, was formed in 1953, it was subtitled: "Memorial Authority for the Holocaust and Bravery."

In 1950, the Knesset passed the Nazi and Nazi Collaborators Law, the language for which came from United Nations declarations that granted universal jurisdiction to try war crimes and crimes against humanity. The UN declarations had been the basis of the laws under which the Nuremberg trials were held. In passing the Nazi and Nazi Collaborators Law, the Knesset affirmed both Israel's commitment to the prosecution of the perpetrators of the Holocaust and its moral authority to stand in judgment of them. But as there were no Nazi war criminals residing in Israel (nor were there likely to be any found), they first turned to trying their own. Between 1951 and 1954, Israel tried a number of *Kapos* and ghetto policemen who had entered the country with the wave of mass immigration. In 1954, capital punishment was abolished for the crime of murder under the penal law, but it remained enforceable for those tried under the Nazi and Nazi Collaborators Law.

In 1959, Yom Hashoah—Holocaust Remembrance Day—was officially set in the Israeli calendar the week before Independence Day, and on a day when the Warsaw Ghetto revolt was still in progress. The timing was meant to put the survivors forward as heroes rather than victims. And what better could show the strength of those who survived and their nation than what followed the next year: the kidnapping and trial of Adolf Eichmann.

Eichmann's trial ran for more than four months, from April to August 1961. The Jerusalem District Court issued its verdict on December 12, 1961. The Israel Supreme Court heard the appeal soon thereafter and issued its verdict on May 29, 1962, upholding both the verdict of the District Court and the sentence of death. After an unsuccessful appeal for mercy from the President of Israel, Eichmann was hanged in Ramla Prison on May 31, 1962.

Eliahu Rosenberg had been a witness at the Eichmann trial. It was not something he discussed with his family. He did not ask them to attend. His eldest daughter recalled that all he told her was that he was going to Jerusalem for the weekend.

In his testimony, he told of Treblinka and of Ivan and Nikolai. Watching his testimony, on film, I was struck by his boyish features. At Treblinka, he must have looked a child. How unmarked was this man, for he still looked a child. One expected to see some visual evidence of his suffering. But that would follow. For to compare Rosenberg in 1961 to Rosenberg today, was to see how his features had hardened. One could only assume that the lines finally etched in his face were pain not only from the telling, but from the retelling.

The Eichmann trial gave dignity to the survivors living in Israel; and allowed the Holocaust to find its place in Israeli history. The trial showcased Israel as a country living by the rule of law, and the Holocaust as a chapter of heroes, in which Israel could provide a heroic finale.

Soon after the Eichmann trial many Treblinka survivors were contacted about planned West German trials of former camp officers. The German investigations had been organized not by specific perpetrators but by the site of the crimes: Auschwitz, Maidenek, Treblinka.

A trial of former Treblinka SS men was held in Dusseldorf, West Germany, between October 1964 and August 1965. Ten men were tried. Among them was Kurt Franz, the infamous "Lalka"; Arthur Matthes, chief officer of Camp Two who supervised the gas chambers; as well as Gustav Munzberger, Franz Suchomel, and Kurt Kuttner, the chief officer of Camp One.

Though none of the *Wachmanner* were on trial, mention was made of the gas-chamber operators, Ukrainians named Ivan and Nikolai. Munzberger said that after the dismantling of Treblinka he had served in Trieste with Ivan. He had no idea what had become of him. There was a rumor he had been killed by the partisans.

West German law confined the trials to strictly personal guilt—individual excessive actions, above and beyond the Nazi framework. There was no guilt for complicity and conspiracy or even for "following orders" at Treblinka. Kurt Franz, who recalled Treblinka as "the best years of my life," was sentenced to life imprisonment with three other defendants. Five others were given lesser sentences of three to twelve years. One, Otto Horn, was acquitted.

A former male nurse in the euthanasia operation, Horn had been assigned to the death camp at Treblinka where he supervised the incinerations. Charged as an accessory to murder, there was no proof of "excessive actions" on his part such as voluntary stabbing or killing. Holocaust survivors spoke in his defense, but as one of them later recalled, "Let's just say that from among all of them, he was less evil."

Franz Stangl, the commander of Treblinka, was tried in Dusseldorf in 1970 and sentenced to life imprisonment. He died in prison, of a heart attack, a few months after the end of the trial.

Survivors were shocked at the Dusseldorf trials to learn that Germans whom they believed were killed in the revolt, such as Matthes and Kuttner, were in fact alive. The revolt had started when one of the inmates shot Kuttner, and there he was sitting in the dock. "When I saw him there in court," one witness said, "I had such a shock that they had to stop the court proceedings for a half-an-hour until I could regain my composure."

It was difficult for those who attended the trial in Dusseldorf to believe such creatures had been allowed to continue to walk the earth; that it had taken nearly two, almost three, decades to find them and bring them to justice. Kurtz Franz had lived undisturbed in his native city for fourteen years before he was arrested; Franz Stangl, though officially registered at the Austrian Consulate in São Paulo, Brazil, couldn't be "located" until 1967, twenty-two years after the end of World War II. How could that be?

CHAPTER 3

Treblinka? Surely, He Was Mistaken

Following World War II, many Holocaust survivors, determined to leave the past behind, emigrated to the United States. The few who spoke of their private hell did not find many who wanted to listen, and fewer still who believed them. The crimes of the Nazis were past. Hitler couldn't happen in America.

But others could not leave the past behind. It followed them everywhere, in their waking hours and in their sleep. When they read the newspapers, they clipped articles. They sought the few others who could understand where they had come from and what they had been through. They searched for lost relatives and friends. They hunted for news. They corresponded and met in European-style cafés to gossip. Who had lived? What had become of him or her? For the past, they had their own shorthand. A glimpse of numbers tattooed on a forearm told the story; others let it be known that they, too, had suffered, or in the particular one-upmanship of survivors, that they had suffered more.

Their primary interest, however, was not what they had been through, but how they were getting along. Who was a success? *Who wasn't?* Who had kids? *Who didn't?* The Old World nightmares had been their past; the American Dream was their future.

After the war, the Immigration and Naturalization Service (INS) began to receive allegations of Nazis living in America. Field agents were instructed to investigate each accusation. But there was no policy for prosecuting illegal Nazi aliens. The reports were treated like any case of fraud or misrepresentation, as if Nazis were no different than quislings or prostitutes who had falsely entered the country.

Cases involving Nazis were not easy to document or prosecute, much less win. Proper investigation required extensive historical background. Budgets were small. Hence the priority was low. Even the Eichmann trial, which attracted international coverage when it was held in Jerusalem in 1961, had virtually no impact on prosecutions in the United States.

By 1970, a poll taken by the Union of Hebrew American Congregations found that Jewish students had little interest in the Holocaust. It seemed ancient history at a time when Cambodia was being bombed daily.

All this would change, however, by the end of 1970s. Major universities would start Jewish history departments with oversubscribed offerings on the Holocaust. Congress would enact national days of remembrance for the Holocaust, and commemorative ceremonies would be held in many major cities. A national memorial to the Holocaust would be planned for the Mall in Washington, D.C., and Holocaust archives and memorials would be built across the country.

For the most part, the survivors themselves deserve credit for this turnaround. They realized time was running out. In the late 1970s, anti-Semitic incidents increased worldwide, as documented by the Anti-Defamation League. Simultaneously, revisionist historians claiming that the Holocaust had not occurred began to receive national media attention. Enraged, the survivors spoke up, and now found people ready to listen. They asked the world not to forget. Nazis were living in America. Why didn't the government do anything about it?

No one played a more pivotal role in advancing the prosecution of Nazi war criminals than Congresswoman Elizabeth Holtzman. In April 1974, Holtzman held a press conference and accused the government of failing to investigate and prosecute known Nazi war criminals living in the United States. From that moment on, she relentlessly goaded the government to action.

Before 1975, there was no systematic effort to investigate allegations of Nazi war criminals living in this country. The INS commissioner admitted that the government at the time had a list of fifty-three alleged Nazi war criminals, compiled primarily by the World Jewish Congress. Holtzman looked at the files: "It was appalling. It was no serious investigation. The most they ever did is to go interview the suspect or the person against whom the allegation was made and ask about their health. In some cases there would be leads given to them and they would never follow up."

In response to Holtzman's charges, the State Department agreed to help secure evidence outside the United States, where it was more likely to be found. This meant not only Israel, where many of the survivors lived, but also Germany, the Eastern European countries, and the Soviet Union. This had never been done.

Contacts with the Soviet Union were established in June 1975 when Representative Joshua Eilberg of Pennsylvania, and other members of the House Judiciary Committee, including Holtzman, visited Moscow to discuss Jewish immigration. They met with the Soviet Deputy Procurator General but the talks produced little more than rhetoric. But when asked whether they would cooperate with American requests for information on Nazi war criminals, the Soviet response was unequivocal: yes.

The Soviets had been interested in the prosecution of Nazi war criminals, or "Hitlerites," as the Soviets called them, since the end of World War II. The Soviet officials promised the American delegation that Justice Department lawyers would be put in contact with their counterparts in the Soviet Union. Though the Soviets had been aiding the West Germans in their prosecutions of war criminals since the 1960s, this marked the first time since the Nuremberg trials that there was any cooperation with the United States.

In 1973 the INS had set up a one-man office in New York to investigate Nazi war criminals; by 1977 it agreed to establish a special five-attorney litigation task force to prepare cases. Those cases involving U.S. citizens would still be filed and argued by the local U.S. Attorney.

The American public confronted the survivors' plight in another way during the 1978 NBC broadcast of the *Holocaust* miniseries on four consecutive nights. Although reviews were mixed, no one denied that the Holocaust had become a proper discussion subject for all Americans. The survivors found themselves heroes.

Still, not much progress had been made as to Nazi prosecutions; a few cases had been filed, with mixed results. In 1978, Representatives Holtzman and Eilberg ordered the General Accounting Office (GAO), the investigative arm of Congress, to inspect all records of the INS pertaining to alleged Nazi war criminals. Could a pattern be uncovered?

The GAO concluded that from 1946 to 1973 the INS had received allegations of possible former Nazi activity concerning fifty-seven people in the United States; charges were filed in only nine cases. Of these nine, three were lost at trial. Of the six that were won, the INS Board of Appeals reversed three. The GAO further found that in two out of three cases the INS investigators had not done an adequate job. There was, however, no evidence of a conspiracy. Rather, the INS failure was a matter of bureaucratic neglect.

The Holtzman–Eilberg investigations led to a political and public consensus for new action, no matter how late. Eilberg was defeated for reelection in 1978, but Elizabeth Holtzman kept her seat. As the new chair of the House subcommittee on immigration, she wanted the INS to have nothing further to do with the prosecution of Nazis. "It was impossible for a unit to function effectively within the Service because of the bureaucracy and the red tape and the general low morale within that agency." Specifically, she wanted the Justice Department to assume responsibility.

That wish was granted. On March 28, 1979, Representative Elizabeth Holtzman announced Attorney General Griffin Bell's decision to create within the Criminal Prosecution Division of the Justice Department the Office of Special Investigations (OSI), a unit specifically charged with investigating and prosecuting alleged Nazi criminals. The OSI annual budget was only 1 percent of the total Justice Department budget ($2.3 million); yet it was enough to fund an eclectic and committed staff of historians, researchers, and litigators.

A few years earlier, in 1975, the INS had received a list of possible Ukrainian Nazi collaborators at large in the U.S. Demjanjuk's name was among them, and he was listed as having been a guard at Sobibor, an extermination camp a hundred miles south of Treblinka. The list was compiled by Michael Hanusiak, an editor of the *Ukrainian Daily News,* a pro-Soviet newspaper published in New York.

Hanusiak, now in his seventies, was raised in the United States, the son of Ukrainian immigrants. But in 1969 the Ukrainian American League offered him a trip to revisit his parents' homeland. This proved an emotional experience for Hanusiak, and in the early 1970s, Hanusiak returned several times to the Ukraine. By now, he was working for the *Ukrainian Daily News,* a member of the Society for Cultural Exchange, a Soviet organization that promotes contact between the U.S. and the Ukraine, and it granted Mr. Hanusiak the access and contacts necessary to conduct research in the Soviet Union into Nazi collaborators at large in the United States. He combed through newspaper archives, met with Soviet journalists, Polish attorneys, and editors of the Soviet *News from Ukraine,* also a member of the Society. By the mid-1970s Hanusiak had compiled a list of seventy alleged Nazi collaborators living in the United States.

One of them, Ivan Demjanjuk, was described as currently living in Cleveland and as also being known as Demjanjuk, Ivan Nikolayevich (the son of Nikolai), born on April 3, 1920, in the Ukrainian village of Dub Macharenzi. Demjanjuk was sought for having allegedly:

Volunteered for the German SS troops and Security Police. Underwent training in the German training camp in town of Trawniki, Poland. In this camp those trained became masters in the art of hanging and torturing of civilians. From March 1943 served as a *Wachmann* with the SS unit in the town of Sobibor, Poland and later (from October 1943) served as a guardsman in the concentration camp in the town of Flossenburg, Germany. Personally participated in the mass executions of the Jewish population in the death camp Sobibor in Poland.

Also on the list was another Ukrainian, Fedor Fedorenko, living in Connecticut. He, too, was accused of being trained at Trawniki and serving as a high-ranking guard at Treblinka.

In October 1975, Hanusiak sent his list of alleged Nazi collaborators to Senator Jacob Javits of New York and Senator Abraham Ribicoff of Connecticut. Early in November, Senator Javits wrote that the list had been forwarded to the Immigration Service's newly created task force for the investigation of Nazi war criminals.

By November 1975, the investigation had begun in earnest. Before the end of the year, the INS set about locating and interviewing survivors of Sobibor; progress was slow. Investigators learned Demjanjuk's current address from the Cleveland telephone directory and verified that he lived with his wife and children in nearby Seven Hills. Without giving out any names, the Cleveland INS office began to contact Jewish organizations and survivor groups to locate potential witnesses. The New York office also contacted Jewish organizations they thought might be helpful.

But the INS thought it best not to confine its search for witnesses to the United States alone. Maurice F. Kiley, the New York INS District Director, wrote in mid-March to the Israel Police. The letter enclosed photos and information, asking assistance in the investigation of several alleged Ukrainian Nazi war collaborators, including Demjanjuk and Fedorenko.

The material was assigned to an investigator in the Special Unit of the Israel Police for the investigation of Nazi crimes, a seventy-year-old attorney, Miriam Radiwker. Mrs. Radiwker was soon to retire, but she was one of the unit's most adept investigators. Born in Poland, she had fled during the war to the Soviet Union, where she continued to practice law. In 1964, she arrived in Israel, where her legal background and ability to speak Polish, Russian, German, and Hebrew, helped her to obtain a position with the unit. More important was her sensibility: as a Polish Jew herself, Radiwker could understand the language of the camps, and of the survivors.

Radiwker reviewed the INS files. She had received nine names, seven of whom had been active only in the Ukraine. There was only a slight chance of obtaining information in Israel about their crimes. The other two, Fedorenko and Demjanjuk, had been active in Poland. Perhaps she could find survivors who could identify them.

First she placed a notice in the Jewish press: survivors with information about the activities of either Fedor Fedorenko of Treblinka or an Ivan Demjanjuk of Sobibor, two Ukrainian camp guards, were asked to come forward. She received no response.

She then decided to summon witnesses herself. She began her investigation with Fedorenko. She believed she was more likely to find persons who could identify a high-ranking Treblinka guard accused of mass murders. Demjanjuk was a lesser priority because there were fewer survivors of Sobibor, and Demjanjuk's role in the killings was not clear.

The Nazi war crimes unit maintained photo albums of suspects, called "photospreads," cataloged by nationality. The photospreads were an investigative tool, used like a police book of mugshots to locate witnesses. The photos sent by the INS, including Demjanjuk's 1951 visa photo and Fedorenko's 1949 visa photo, were pasted onto pages and placed in the album, labeled "Ukrainians." The photographs were all passport-type portraits, head-and-shoulders shots of men, more often than not, in coat and tie. Demjanjuk's and Fedorenko's photos were numbers sixteen and seventeen, respectively, and appeared among five others on page three of the album. Potential witnesses would be asked if they could identify anyone.

Radiwker, who had worked with two Treblinka survivors on another case, called them back in.

Eugen Turovsky came to her office on the morning of May 9. Radiwker asked him to recall his experiences at Treblinka. She asked if he recalled any Ukrainians. Then she showed him the photospread. "Please, sir," she said, "look at these, maybe you find anyone you know?"

Turovsky looked over the first page, and then the second, but when he came to the third, he became agitated. "That's Ivan!" He said, "That's Ivan of Treblinka."

Treblinka? Her information put Demjanjuk at Sobibor. Turovsky had made a mistake, surely. But Radiwker said nothing. Turovsky wanted to talk at length about this Ivan. She said he could return tomorrow to do so, but first he must calm down and see if he recognized anyone else. Turovsky then identified Fedorenko.

She summoned Avraham Goldfarb that afternoon. He had built the large gas chamber at Treblinka, and later carried corpses to the pits. He was now in his seventies. He found the photo of Demjanjuk familiar, even though he was in civilian clothes and older. It was, Goldfarb said, the Treblinka death camp guard who had "caused the gas to flow from the diesel engine into the gas chambers." The engine was located near the well at which Goldfarb worked: "I approached the well during the time that the same Ivan was pushing people into the gas chambers. He did this in the most cruel manner. We, the workers, nicknamed him Ivan Grozny, Ivan the Terrible."

Radiwker decided to confront Goldfarb about her information that put Demjanjuk at Trawniki and Sobibor. About Sobibor and Trawniki he could not say, but about Treblinka he was sure: "I can say that during 1942–43 he certainly was at Treblinka. But before the uprising in the summer of 1943, he already was not, as I recall, at Treblinka."

Goldfarb could not forget this man. "I saw clearly how he pushed the victims into the gas chambers with iron sticks and a bayonet. Even with his knife he cut the flesh off living people. I saw with my own eyes how, at the entrance to the gas chambers, he cut with his knife pieces of flesh from living people. I also saw that he cut the ears of those workers who were busy near the gas chambers at the times the bodies were removed." He had witnessed these events, he said, "from a distance of a few meters."

The next morning, Radiwker opened up a separate investigative file on Demjanjuk.

When Turovsky returned, she asked him if he knew the name Demjanjuk. "I am familiar with the name Demjanjuk," he said, "but even more so with the first name Ivan. I can well remember this Ukrainian. I knew him personally because he sometimes came into the shop to repair something."

He was shown the photos again. Again he pointed to Demjanjuk's photo. "That is Ivan," he declared. "Him, I recognize immediately and with perfect certainty." Turovsky gave a detailed physical description of the Ivan he knew: "Even then his hair looked the way it is here in the photograph, a high forehead starting to bald."

Turovsky had no access to the death camp, so could not, from personal observation, describe Ivan at work. But Turovsky said he saw Ivan when he passed through the workshop and near his living quarters. He also saw Ivan when he and other guards caught Jews, and dragged them from the woods into the camp.

Radiwker decided to call another Treblinka survivor, Eliahu Rosenberg, whose testimony she knew from the Eichmann trial. He told her he couldn't leave his job at the Ashdod Port. She offered to visit him.

The next day, in Rosenberg's office, Miriam Radiwker followed her usual procedure. When she showed the Ukrainian album to Rosenberg, asking him if he "recognized anybody," he singled out Demjanjuk. "That man looks very similar to the Ukrainian Ivan. I see great similarity with Ivan who was active in Camp Two and whom they call Ivan Grozny." Rosenberg was not willing to identify him with certainty—the man in the picture was older and in civilian dress. Ivan, at the time he knew him, was maybe twenty-two to twenty-three years old and always in uniform. But he was struck by the likeness. The distinctive facial construction was the same, the incipient balding at such a young age, the ears sticking out. Rosenberg believed that should he see Ivan, alive, before him now—he would recognize him.

Radiwker explained that her information placed the man he pointed to not at Treblinka, but at Sobibor. Rosenberg replied that although in the course of 1942 some Ukrainians were known to have been sent to Sobibor, he had seen Ivan until the last day at Treblinka. Radiwker asked if Ivan acted independently or on orders of higher officials.

"I can state with certainty," Rosenberg said, "that such cruelties and such sadistic murders as he perpetrated each and every day, were certainly not done by orders. . . . I saw from a distance of about four meters [thirteen feet] as he cut up people with his sword, mostly women on their naked bodies. This he certainly did on his own initiative. . . . [He] directly participated in the gassing. This I saw each and every day in the nearest proximity. I was not farther away than one or two meters from him. It was there I worked. I saw he shot a worker carrying corpses. . . . I personally received thirty whippings at a roll call [from him] because I had purloined a small piece of bread. There was a time when he ordered me to perform a sexual act with a dead woman who had been pulled out from the gas chambers. He was drunk at the time and I knew that it meant my death, because I was unable to commit such an act. The German *Scharfuhrer* [staff sergeant] Loeffler saved me from him."

The photo left Rosenberg in shock. To see Ivan alive, healthy—fat, well fed! He could see nothing else before him but Ivan, Ivan, Ivan. He did not identify anyone else at that time. Radiwker wrote up his statement. As the INS requested, she had been asking each survivor for the names of others who might have knowledge of Nazi collaborators. Rosenberg suggested Pinhas Epstein. Finally she warned Rosenberg that to talk about an investigation in process would jeopardize it. That presented no problem, as Rosenberg later explained succinctly: "I am good at keeping secrets."

Radiwker wrote up her report of the three interviews and on May 14, her superior, Major Gershon Lengsfelder, forwarded the surprising results to the INS.

The Demjanjuk case was under way.

CHAPTER 4

Dos Iz Ivan

John Demjanjuk has often said that he knew nothing of the allegations against him until the day the government filed its complaint on August 25, 1977. But they should have come as no surprise.

Early in May 1976, Vera Demjanjuk received a call from a man asking to speak to her husband. John Demjanjuk wasn't at home. The caller refused to reveal the purpose of his call, but said he would call again. He called twice more. Again Demjanjuk wasn't there; again the caller would not say why he was calling.

Within the week, however, he visited the Demjanjuks at home. As Vera told a reporter, he showed them his identification. He was Dirk Pauls, an official attached to the West German Consulate in Detroit. Repeatedly referring to the German telegram he held before him, Pauls said that John Demjanjuk was needed as a prosecution witness at a war crimes trial in Germany. The trial, he said, related to wartime activity at two locations in Poland: Sobibor and Trawniki.

Vera and her husband were startled, confounded, and somewhat frightened by the German's statement. John Demjanjuk refused to go to Germany. He knew nothing about Sobibor or Trawniki. Surely the German had made a mistake: the name on the telegram—John Nikolaiyevich Demjanjuk—was not his. His name, he said, was John *Mikolayevich* Demjanjuk. Little did it matter that the former was just the Russian language equivalent of the latter Ukrainian patronymic, and that Demjanjuk himself had stated on his visa application that Nikolai was his father's name. The Demjanjuks told the German to leave—he had found the wrong man, a case of mistaken identity.

By this time, the Cleveland INS office had begun its investigation of Demjanjuk. Agents were already interviewing survivors of Sobibor, but without success. Then when Miriam Radiwker's report on the identifications by Turovsky, Goldfarb, and Rosenberg was received by the INS in late May 1976, identifying Demjanjuk as having served at Treblinka, the INS refocused its investigation and began contacting Treblinka survivors.

The INS also contacted the witnesses on Demjanjuk's naturalization application, two friends from the displaced persons (DP) camps. Both lived in the Cleveland area. The INS contacted them in early June 1976, asking if they knew anything about Demjanjuk's wartime activities. Demjanjuk, they both said, had never spoken to them about the war. One couple said they thought John Demjanjuk was a very good man; that they would cry when they talked about how hard life had been in the Ukraine. Later they wondered to Demjanjuk why they had been questioned. He said he had no idea.

That INS agents were investigating alleged Nazi war criminals in the Cleveland area became the subject of radio programs and articles in the *Cleveland Jewish News*. Survivors of the camps with knowledge of atrocities were urged to come forward. A few responded, but none who personally knew Ivan the Terrible.

The INS also turned to Bessy Pupko, an indefatigable septuagenarian at the World Jewish Congress in New York. She provided a list of more than a dozen Treblinka survivors compiled from her own files. A few had since died; none of the others had been in the death camp. Of the thirteen interviewed, none could identify either Demjanjuk or Fedorenko.

The problem was that few prisoners from Camp One knew Ivan, and the majority of those who did from Camp Two saw him only once—as they entered the gas chambers.

Meanwhile, Miriam Radiwker continued her investigation in Israel. She was baffled by whether Demjanjuk had, in fact, been at Sobibor and she decided to summon some witnesses from that camp to see if they could provide some clue to the mystery. Dov Freiberg came in May 30. Demjanjuk's 1951 visa photo reminded him of someone, but he wasn't sure. Meir Weiss, another Sobibor survivor, recognized no one.

Undeterred, Radiwker shifted her focus back to Fedorenko, calling survivors from Treblinka's Camp One. On June 7, Shalom Cohen was shown Demjanjuk's photo and said it seemed familiar, but he couldn't identify him positively. He remembered that there had been a Ukrainian known as Ivan Grozny, but he was active only in

Camp Two. On July 4, she met with Shimon Greenspan, who recognized Fedorenko. But the next survivor, Arye Kudlik, didn't recognize anyone. Neither did Kalman Tideman, on August 17.

Then on September 21, Yossef Czarny came to her office. Czarny had survived Treblinka, and in 1945 ended up in Bergen–Belsen, where he met his future wife Frieda. In 1947 he obtained false documents to travel to Palestine clandestinely aboard the aptly named ship, *Providence.*

Neither Czarny, an accountant, nor his wife was comfortable talking about the war. It was, as Czarny later recalled, "a closed box." Yet he had opened that box for the Dusseldorf trial and he was ready to do it again. Czarny told Radiwker that he was born in Warsaw in 1926 and arrived at Treblinka having just turned sixteen. Czarny had been in Camp One where as a *Hofjuden*— "Court-Jew"—he had free access to the Germans' compound and the Ukrainians' kitchen. (The *Hofjuden* were Jewish workers used by the Germans to maintain the camp. They lived apart from and in better conditions than the other inmates.)

When Radiwker placed the photo album of Ukrainian suspects before him, Czarny immediately, at first glance, pointed to the photo of Demjanjuk *"Dos iz Ivan,"* he blurted out excitedly in Yiddish. "*Ivan Grozny von Treblinka.* My God! He lives!"

Later, he told Radiwker, "Thirty-three years have gone by, but I recognize him at first sight with full certainty. I think I would recognize him even by night. . . . It is the same facial build, the same nose, the same eyes, the same forehead. There can be no mistake."

Again Radiwker said that according to her information this man was not at Treblinka but at Sobibor. Czarny disagreed strongly: "This man is Ivan Grozny. He was in Treblinka until the last minute, until the uprising."

Czarny was confident: at the time he had been only four to five years younger than Ivan. He said Ivan was almost always drunk. And although Ivan worked at the gas chambers in the death camp, Czarny sometimes saw him at the transport reception.

She asked why he knew him with such certainty. Czarny answered: "He stood out and he distinguished himself. His terrible job was known. And his sadism was known. He was one of the most frightening images in the Treblinka camp, and, therefore, he will rest engraved in my memory forever and ever."

When he was over the shock of identifying Ivan, Radiwker asked Czarny if he recognized anyone else. He pointed to Fedorenko, saying that this man worked in Camp One but he did not recall his name. She took one statement regarding Fedorenko, and another about Demjanjuk.

On September 28, Radiwker interviewed Shlomo Hellman, who had been in Treblinka longer than anyone else she interviewed. Hellman, almost seventy, was retired. At Treblinka he had been part of the crew that built the large gas chamber and later carried corpses. He recalled Ivan Grozny as "a monster of a man."

Radiwker asked if he knew the name Demjanjuk. He responded "It means nothing to me." Asked to describe Ivan he could only say, "He was tall in height, and as far as I recall was about thirty years old. I don't remember that he had any rank or insignias." Radiwker showed him five photos. Among them was the 1951 photo of Demjanjuk. He did not identify him.

The defense would later argue that Hellman, of all people, should have recognized Ivan, if Demjanjuk truly was he. But the prosecution would counter that Hellman's vague description, with an inaccurate age estimate, merely reinforced the unfortunate truth: though he had not forgotten what had occurred, he could no longer recall sharply the features of Ivan or even recognize him. Fedorenko's photo struck him as familiar from Camp One, but, he said, "I can't tell you anything about him."

If Hellman's memory had failed him, Radiwker could have little hope that Gustav Boraks, already in his early seventies, would do much better. Nonetheless, on September 30, she traveled to Haifa to see Boraks, who had arrived in Treblinka on Yom Kippur 1942, with his wife, two sons, and virtually all of his relatives including his brother and sisters. Boraks had been a barber, a skill that saved him upon arrival. The rest of the transport, including his entire family, was sent immediately to the gas chambers. Boraks was put to work cutting the hair of the naked women on their way to the gas chambers.

Questioned by Radiwker, Boraks was familiar with the Ukrainian known as Ivan Grozny. When shown eight photographs from the police album, he pointed to the photo of Demjanjuk: "This is the photo of Ivan Grozny. I recognize him with one hundred percent certainty. I recognize him from his facial features. He was younger then, up to twenty-five years old. The face was not as full, but I have no doubt it is he."

Boraks had full opportunity to observe Ivan. "I saw him daily at the gas chambers as he brutally herded people into the gas chambers. . . . I was an eyewitness," Boraks said, "as Ivan Grozny shot some Jewish workers. It was not long before the uprising in the summer of 1943. There were few transports. We barbers did not have daily work and were taken several times a week to work in the woods. Ivan Grozny, together with a German SS man, went with us. We had to cut down trees. The branches were used for camouflage. The heavy tree trunks had to be carried into the camp. Ivan Grozny ordered us to run with the logs on our shoulders. If someone collapsed under the heavy burden, Ivan shot him on the spot. I saw a number of such cases from close up."

Radiwker's case was growing stronger and stronger. She had one more survivor to interview on October 3, Avraham Lindvasser. He had been a "dentist" in the camp and had worked daily near the gas chambers. Lindvasser, who was born in 1919 in Warsaw, left his hometown on August 28, 1942, on a large train bound for Treblinka. Of the thousands on the transport, Lindvasser told Radiwker, "Only two were separated to work. I, who claimed to be a dentist, and an electronics engineer." The rest were gassed to death.

Did he recall a Ukrainian at the camp by name of Ivan Demjanjuk? "I am not familiar with the name Demjanjuk," he said. "I remember a Ukrainian whose nickname was Ivan Grozny—the Terrible. He was active in Camp Two and I will never forget him." Radiwker showed him the eight photographs and Lindvasser had a strong immediate reaction to Demjanjuk's. "This is Ivan. I identify him with full confidence. That is his nose, his eyes, and his mouth."

Lindvasser said he had constantly worked near him: the dentist cell bordered "Ivan's actual work place"—the engine room. And he could not forget Ivan's "personal sadism." He told Radiwker, "He was not named Ivan the Terrible for nothing."

The three new identifications of Demjanjuk as Ivan Grozny of Treblinka—by Czarny, Boraks, and Lindvasser—were mailed to the INS. Miriam Radiwker retired soon thereafter.

The first known public accusation against Demjanjuk by name appeared not in the U.S. or in Israel but in the USSR—in Ukrainian on August 26, 1976, in an article, "At Different Poles," in the Soviet weekly, *Visti z Ukraini (News from Ukraine)*.

The article stated that: "Dem'yanyuk, [sic] who lives in the United States of America (3326 New Avenue, Parma, Ohio), does not like to talk about his past. But documents and witnesses talk about it."

Demjanjuk, the article claimed, surrendered to the Germans and ended up himself in a camp. "No, not the one where the Soviet prisoners were held, but where the Fascists trained men for punitive units." The accusations were supported by claims of documentary proof: "Certificate of Service Number 1393 issued by the Trawniki (Poland) training camp in the name of Demjanjuk Ivan Mikolayevych, born in 1920, which bears his photograph, has been preserved among captured German documents."

The document proved, the article contended, that its bearer

served from 22 September 1942 at "the Okshu scaffold" and from 27 March 1943 in the Sobibor death camp (Poland)."

Not only was there documentary proof but also the testimony of a "colleague," one Danylchenko, who was quoted as saying: "I first met and became acquainted with Demyanyuk [sic] Ivan in March 1943 in the Sobibor death camp (Poland), where he served in the SS secret forces as a *Wachmann* [guard]. . . ."

Danylchenko goes on to say that Demjanjuk wore an SS uniform, was armed, and participated in the mass murders of Jews at Sobibor, guarding and convoying them to the gas chambers. Danylchenko also stated that in the spring of 1944, he and Demjanjuk were sent to be guards at concentration camps in Flossenburg and Regensburg, Germany.

The article concluded: "Up to the last days of the war the Fascist toady served his masters faithfully; he went abroad after their total defeat. . . . Today the residents of Parma [a suburb of Cleveland] in the USA know Mr. Demjanjuk as an ordinary automobile inspector. And probably they do not know that in greeting him they are extending their hands to a murderer of innocent people who has escaped just punishment."

The article was puzzling in many respects: Like American-Ukrainian editor Michael Hanusiak's 1975 allegations, it only referred to Demjanjuk's wartime service at Trawniki and Sobibor and did not mention Treblinka. For the first time there was mention of documentary proof: a numbered Trawniki service certificate in Demjanjuk's name, bearing his photograph; and the testimony of a former guard, Danylchenko, who testified at an unexplained "preliminary investigation."

Hanusiak said later that Danylchenko was thought to have been tried for war crimes in Kiev in 1955 and that it was from Danylchenko's testimony that Demjanjuk's wartime activities became known to Soviet authorities. Trials of Soviet nationals who had served the Nazis in the death camps had been held in Russia as recently as the early 1960s. Was Danylchenko one of them? No one could confirm this; nor could anyone say whether Danylchenko was still alive—or, in fact, whether he actually existed.

Although the article was published in August 1976, it would not come to the attention of American authorities until months later. By the fall of 1976, INS investigations in Cleveland had received substantial attention in the local newspapers and on television. Though no names or biographical data had been revealed, it must have been obvious to John Demjanjuk that they were talking about him. Finally he was asked to appear at his local INS office to discuss allegations about his past with U.S. attorneys.

The meeting was scheduled for October 19, 1976. Demjanjuk appeared with his attorney, John Martin, a former Cuyahoga County prosecutor who had been recommended to the Demjanjuks by friends from work.

The man who was accused of being the fearsome Ivan the Terrible of Treblinka sat meekly outside the prosecutor's office. His head down, he appeared more like an overgrown child waiting to see the principal than a war criminal. Martin explained to the U.S. attorneys that Demjanjuk had come to him only that morning and therefore he was not prepared to represent him. A new date, a month later, was set. But the day before, Martin sought another delay.

In January 1977, Jay Bushinsky, the *Chicago Daily News*'s correspondent in Tel Aviv, interviewed several of the survivors who had identified Demjanjuk. He was most impressed by Lindvasser, who died only a few months after Bushinsky interviewed him.

Bushinsky's report was published in the *Chicago Daily News* in October 1977. Lindvasser was quoted as saying:

> I can still see "Ivan the Cruel" whipping out his sword and swinging at those poor defenseless people, slashing and shoving and screaming at them until all of them were forced inside the chamber. And then he would slam the door shut, check it once to make sure it was closed tight, and then walk calmly down the flight of steel stairs to the basement where the machinery of death was located.
>
> Once he got there, he would turn on the motors that manufactured the carbon-monoxide gas that went directly into the chambers. Within half an hour, all six hundred or seven hundred people in the three chambers would be dead.
>
> The basement below the three gas chambers was known as "Ivan's area." I saw this beast of a man turn on the motors so often that it pains me now—more than thirty years later—to even think about it. To do so is almost like killing me.

Lindvasser's work area as a "dentist" looked down upon Ivan's area. "People ask me now, how I could stand it—with all of those horrible things happening so near. With all of the terrible screaming and dying. I will tell you one thing we did. We worked with these little hammers, and every time they would put people in the chambers to die, we would start our hammering, all together, so that we would not be able to hear those terrible sounds of death. So people went out of this world hearing that strange hammering of ours in the background. . . . And this man, Ivan, now is living in your country of freedom. It is hard to believe, but it is true."

During 1977, the Demjanjuk matter moved along the legally required step-by-step procedure toward denaturalization. For months the necessary affidavits and approvals shuttled between Cleveland and Washington in Rube Goldberg-like fashion. To all who knew him, Demjanjuk gave no sign that he was even under investigation. Probably, he hoped the inquiries would disappear like the man from the German Consulate.

But on August 25, 1977, the U.S. Attorney for the Northern District of Ohio filed a six-page, six-count complaint that stated that Demjanjuk had not only lied on his immigration papers, but had the truth been known—that he was Ivan the Terrible of Treblinka—he surely would have been denied entry to the United States.

In bringing the case to court, the U.S. Attorney would seek to show not only that Demjanjuk lied on his application, but that his lies were incriminating. But first the government would have to show exactly where Demjanjuk had been during the war years.

Lawyers needed to figure out how Demjanjuk had gone from a small village in the Ukraine to service in death camp Treblinka and possibly Sobibor as well and why, when applying to enter the United States, had he filled out his forms as he had? On the latter, the INS would find information from a surprising source—Fedor Fedorenko himself.

Fedorenko was living in Waterbury, Connecticut, and was also being investigated by the INS. On May 25, 1976, Fedorenko appeared at the INS Hartford office, at its invitation, to discuss *his* visa entries for the war years.

Initially, Fedorenko had contended that the INS was investigating the wrong person. Now, he admitted that he had been at Treblinka, but he denied being a high-ranking guard or committing any atrocities. He had written on his immigration papers that he spent the war years in a town named Pelz. That was not entirely true. The clerk who had taken down the information on his application had misheard him. What he meant was Poelitz. And there was more.

Fedorenko said he had been born in Ukraine, had been drafted into the Russian army, and in July 1941, had been captured by the Germans. After being held at POW camp Rovno for two weeks, he was taken to the Chelm camp in Poland, where he stayed for two months. There the Germans picked him and some others as drivers and technicians and took them to Trawniki. Fedorenko said he spent some eight months there and at the end of 1942 was taken with others to Treblinka, where he was trained in weapons and made a camp guard. Although he knew that thousands of Jews had died there, Fedorenko denied any involvement in the killing. He insisted that the Ukrainian guards did not act of their own volition and were not allowed into the death camp. There were two exceptions—Ivan and Nikolai, who worked alongside the Germans.

Shortly after the uprising, in late 1943, Fedorenko claimed, he left Treblinka and was transferred to Danzig to be a concentration-camp guard; and from there to a smaller camp, Poelitz, a concentration camp for criminals. It was at Poelitz, he said, where he remained for a year, that he was a high-ranking guard.

Ultimately, Fedorenko would be shown to be lying about what he did at Treblinka, but not about the route he had taken. As to why he wrote Pelz on his immigration and naturalization forms, Fedorenko said that he wrote Pelz—and meant Poelitz—because Poelitz was not only the name of the camp, but the town nearby. If asked questions, he knew the town well. And *that,* was better than saying Treblinka.

Poelitz, Fedorenko reasoned, would be less known to investigators as a concentration-camp site; even if it were known, there would be only a slim chance that any survivor could identify him. Finally, even if he was found out to have served at the Poelitz concentration camp, his activities there were less damning than at Treblinka.

This would be of great interest to those trying to resolve why Demjanjuk had written on *his* application papers that he had spent part of his war years at a town named Sobibor.

CHAPTER 5

The Paper Trail

How could Nazis be living in America?

"The overwhelming majority of Nazi war criminals," said former OSI Director Allan Ryan, "came through the front door, with all their papers in order."

After the war, hundreds of thousands of war-torn people from Eastern Europe found themselves with little interest in returning home. If they were Jewish, their homeland held few pleasant memories; if they were non-Jews, their countries had been overrun by Communists. The refugees came to live in displaced persons camps; they were called DPs. The camps, which dotted Europe, were mostly located in Germany and Austria. Responsibility was divided among the Four Powers (the U.S., UK, France, and the USSR), and shared by the United Nations International Refugee Organization (IRO).

The DP camps became small cities of immigrants caught in a holding pattern between their past and their future. For some—the victims of the war—the DP camps were a refuge; for others—the perpetrators of those crimes—the camps were a haven, where they hoped to assimilate into the masses.

There were few, if any, records of Nazi collaborators. What records existed—such as at the Berlin Documentation Center, and those in the UN archives—were German SS confiscated records. No one was much interested in the collaborators.

At the DP camps, it was easy enough to hide your past; all you needed to claim was that your identity-papers had been destroyed or had disappeared in the war; the IRO would then issue an affidavit of lost papers and a new identity certificate.

Before one could apply for a visa to a foreign country, one had to be certified as a DP by the IRO. Its constitution specifically denied DP status to any war criminal, or person who voluntarily aided enemy forces.

The IRO screenings, however, were at best superficial: the investigators questioned; the applicants answered. Unless the applicant admitted complicity in crimes, or gave obviously false information, he became a DP. In the American zone of Germany, the U.S. Army administered the camps with the IRO. As the camps swelled in the immediate postwar years, it became apparent that the DP problem had to be dealt with.

Though the Soviet Union considered anyone born in a country now under its rule still a citizen, the U.S. would not allow forcible repatriation for anyone who did not wish to live under Communist rule. The United States slowly began to open its doors to increased amount of immigrants.

In 1948, Congress passed the Displaced Persons Act (the DP Act) that allowed hundreds of thousands of immigrants to arrive on American shores. But many felt that the DP act was written to provide relief to everyone *but* Hitler's victims—the Jews.

The DP Act was administered by three commissioners. Among them was Edward M. O'Connor, a thirty-nine-year-old New Yorker who had been very involved in Catholic relief in the U.S. and in Europe. He had lobbied strongly in favor of increased admission for Ukrainians and Balts. As commissioner, he approved the admission of members of the Waffen SS units and was criticized for favoring admission for Hitler's supporters over his victims. The Balts and Ukrainians were strongly anti-Communist—saving them from return to the Soviet Empire seemed a noble task. That some, as Red Army defectors, may have served on the side of the Germans, did not appear sufficient reason to deny them admission. But Commissioner Harry Rosenfield, who never saw eye-to-eye with O'Connor on this point, later said, "He felt they were given a bum steer; I felt a lot of them were bums." Edward O'Connor continued to be a vocal supporter of the "captive nations," as he called them, the rest of his life. Forty years later, his son, Mark, would be Demjanjuk's defense attorney.

To apply for a U.S. visa, the applicant was required to undergo a second screening by an American investigator. The DP Act and U.S. immigration law made it clear that citizenship would not be given to Nazis or Nazi collaborators. But the only security check was against counterintelligence (CIC) records and the records of the

Berlin Documentation Center. Anyone who passed the IRO screening could tell the same tale without fear of greater scrutiny. The overwhelming majority of applicants were approved. Visas in hand, they set out for their new lives.

In the years following World War II, among the hundreds of thousands who rightfully came to the U.S. were many Nazi collaborators. The exact number will never be known, though estimates range from several hundred to ten thousand. The same disdain for life under Communist rule that had led them to collaborate with the Fascists was their admission ticket to the U.S. And their anti-Communism would serve them in good stead in America in the 1950s; accusations of Nazi service would be brushed off as a "Communist plot," or a "KGB conspiracy." But it was not anti-Communism that made them Nazi war criminals; it was their murderous service and that they had to hide.

There were no documents to speak of their crimes. Who else would talk of them? Their SS superiors? Their fellow collaborators? Not likely. Their victims? So few had lived. Most never even knew their real names. Anyhow, who would believe them? It would just be one person's word against another's. And as the years passed, who would still care?

Nazi war criminals, Allan Ryan would say, "came here not by conniving with lawless government officials, but by the infinite easier method of simply deceiving the honest ones."

We go through life never thinking that we may have to prove we were here, or more to the point, that we were not *there*. But as we make our way we also unwittingly leave behind a paper trail—filling out forms for the present, with the answers of the moment—never thinking it will later come back to haunt us.

Investigators turned to what could be ascertained about John Demjanjuk without speaking to him, to the details of his immigration and naturalization forms.

Shortly after the war's end, in 1945, Demjanjuk entered a displaced persons camp in Landshut, Germany. He was still known as Ivan Demjanjuk. It was in the DP camp, two years later, that he met his future wife, Vera. She was a Ukrainian DP, five years his junior, who had been sent out of her native Ukraine as a forced laborer. She spent the war years working in Germany as a housecleaner.

Their courtship was brief. It would have been briefer still had Vera not already been married to another DP, Eugene Sakowski. As Sakowski would later relate, he and Vera had been married on May 1, 1947. A few months later, he was sent from the DP camp to work for three weeks in Belgium. Upon his return, he discovered that his wife was living with another man, Ivan Demjanjuk. They were divorced shortly thereafter.

On September 1, 1947, Ivan Demjanjuk was married to Vera Kowlowa. They moved to the Regensburg DP camp. He was about to begin a new life.

A few weeks later he signed up for a driving course, the prerequisite for a license. He passed with no problem. The license has a handsome photo; it bears his signature, no longer in Cyrillic script, but in Latin characters.

License in hand, he found a job driving trucks for the Americans and working in the motor pool. The Americans found him to be a skilled driver; he drove the truck long distances, crisscrossing Germany; sometimes traveling alone. He drove eight hundred miles in a day, he would brag later.

In early 1948, Demjanjuk began to fill out forms. First he told the camp police he had lost his personal papers. They issued him a certificate attesting to that; then a few days later he received an ID card from the IRO.

Demjanjuk then applied for assistance and certification from the IRO, the first step in the screening procedures that would lead to a visa out of the DP camps. His form is dated March 3, 1948. The four pages listed twenty-one questions. The form was to remain in IRO custody and be periodically updated. It was an important document. Demjanjuk filled it out for himself and his new wife.

Demjanjuk said he was born in Kiev, USSR. The form requested a listing of the towns, provinces, and countries in which he had spent the last twelve years; and how, by whom, and at what wages he had been employed during that time.

Demjanjuk, who had been born in 1920, stated that from 1935 until April 1937, he was a student, earning no wage, and living with his parents in Koziatyn [also known as Kazatin], USSR. But he also noted that his only schooling was attending grammar school in Koziatyn (Kiev) from 1927–30. Next he was a driver for the Firma Auto (an auto company), earning forty zlotys (Polish currency) in "Sobibor–Chelm–Poland"; and in January 1943 was deported to Germany.

From January 1943, until October 1944, Demjanjuk said he lived in Pilau, Germany, and worked at the Port for twenty Deutschmarks; after which he was transferred to Munich, Germany, where he worked at a warehouse and was paid in food only.

From May 1945 until July 1947, he was at Landshut—the DP camp—where he said he worked as a driver for UNWRA–IRO at the wage of one hundred Reichmarks. Since then he had lived at the

Regensburg camp, where he was earning the same wage as a driver for truck company 1049 at the American military post.

He told the officer that his first choice was Argentina; Canada, his second. He didn't want to return to the Soviet Union because of "political and religious reasons." Demjanjuk was sure that as a skilled driver he could find work, as he put it, "in his profession."

The inspecting officer saw nothing in Demjanjuk's personal history to give pause. His story seemed straightforward. The IRO officer summarized: "In the year 1937 he fled from Koziatyn USSR to Poland. In Poland he was living till 1943. In the year 1943, deported to Germany. All the time worked in Germany to end of war. He wants to emigrate with his family to Argentina or Canada."

Only in retrospect can the form be scrutinized, and seen as suspicious, even incriminating. Only someone who knew a great deal about Holocaust history, and who knew Demjanjuk's personal history and later alibis in great detail, would have been able to question his entries.

Consider the dates: Why mark the time with the months and years of April 1937, January 1943, October 1944, and May 1945?

Was it a coincidence that April 1937 was when Demjanjuk first began to work with tractor engines in the Soviet Union—eventually becoming a tractor driver and mechanic; that January 1943 was when the gassings took on a lesser pace at Treblinka; that by October 1944, the extermination camps were dismantled; and that May 1945 was when the war ended?

Why list Sobibor, Chelm, and Pilau? Sobibor was the site of a death camp; Chelm, the POW transit camp from which Soviet prisoners were recruited for SS service, and which Demjanjuk would later claim as his alibi. And Pilau? Investigators would later learn that Pilau was a town near the Danzig port, where a small concentration camp existed, and where executions took place. Pilau was part of the Stutthoff complex of concentration camps, of which Poelitz (Fedorenko's alibi) had also been part.

Demjanjuk was listed on the form as a "skilled driver." Years later, Demjanjuk would deny he could operate a car until 1947. This, too, could be seen as incriminating. For throughout the form, he lists his employment as a driver—particularly during the time he was accused of being the mechanic for the gas chamber's diesel engine at Treblinka. The form says Demjanjuk worked after the war as a driver for the IRO itself. Wouldn't the IRO be able to verify this? Why lie? Why was he afraid to admit to being a "skilled driver"?

To emigrate to the United States, there had to be at least a sponsor or job waiting. The Demjanjuk family had grown with the birth

of daughter Lydia in 1950. They waited with the hope that someone would request their help. In December 1951 they received word
that a farmer in Decatur, Indiana, Donald Coulter, had applied that
he would employ refugee aid on his farm.

Demjanjuk went to the American consulate in Stuttgart, on December 27, 1951, to fill out a visa application to the United States.

On this form he was again asked to give his residence since age
fourteen. He changed the dates slightly, listing himself at Sobibor,
Poland, from 1934 to 1943; at "Pilau, Danzig" from 1943 to September 1944; from then until the end of the war in Munich. After
that he listed with precision all the DP camps he lived in, even if
only for a few months—Landshut, Regensburg, Ulm, Ellwagen,
Ulm (again), Bad Reichenall, and Feldafing.

He listed his occupation as driver, his nationality as Polish. He
stated that he was able to speak, read, and write Ukrainian, German, and Polish. Asked to list his education, the form said, "total: 5
years" (on the IRO form he had put 1927 to 1930). The address of
his parents Nikolai and Olga, he said, was not known. He gave his
mother's maiden name as Martschenko. This would later prove of
interest when Polish residents near Treblinka would recall Ivan the
Terrible's name as having been Marshenko.

When asked if he had any identifying scars, Demjanjuk answered
"scar on left hand." Actually, the scar was on the inside of his left
arm—halfway between his elbow and his armpit—from having had
removed a blood group tattoo only a few years before. He also had
a large scar several inches long, on his lower back near his spine,
that he failed to reveal. He had been wounded while serving as a
Red Army soldier. Some of the shrapnel was removed in 1941; the
rest, in 1948.

A photo was required. Demjanjuk submitted a passport-sized
photo of himself in jacket and tie. He looks smug, happy, confident.
His face is full. His dark hair is close-cropped but there is a small
tuft atop his head; his hairline recedes around it. His ears stick out.

It was this picture—taken eight years after the Treblinka uprising—that the survivors would see in the late 1970s; in which they
would recognize the shape of the forehead, the face, recall the eyes,
the neck, the shoulders, the build, the hairline of a person they once
knew; upon which they would comment that he looked older, fatter. It was this picture that would make them gasp and say, "This is
Ivan."

John, Vera, and Lydia Demjanjuk arrived in the United States in
February 1952 aboard a troop ship, the *W. G. Haan*. The week-

long voyage was rough and crowded; they had to share a cabin with another family, a woman and her four children. But in later years Vera Demjanjuk would recall that when the ship entered New York harbor, and she saw the Statue of Liberty, she cried.

The Demjanjuks, speaking no English, carrying all their possessions in two boxes, traveled by train from New York to Decatur, Indiana. At the Coulter farm, home was a small, cold room of the farmhouse. John tended to a few pigs and sheep. There was not enough work on the farm to employ them full time. In letters to friends from the DP camps, living in nearby Cleveland, Vera told of the cold winter, and the odd jobs they did to make ends meet.

"They had a roof over their heads," Anne Lishuk would later recall, "but not much else. They barely survived. I remember Vera hardly had enough milk to feed the baby. When I wrote Vera that winter, I always put in a little money, because I know how bad it was for them."

Through new friends, the Underwoods, John Demjanjuk soon found a job as a mechanic in an auto-repair shop. But by summer, they were desperate to move. Their friends the Lishuks were living on the west side of Cleveland, among many fellow Ukrainians. William Lishuk had found a job at the Ford Motor Company plant on Brookpark Road, and heard it was expanding. The Demjanjuks decided to give Cleveland a try.

The Lishuks invited them to stay in their home until they got settled. William Lishuk even drove them from Decatur to Cleveland.

It was Vera who found work first, as a scrublady with the Federal Reserve Bank in downtown Cleveland. Soon after Lishuk took Demjanjuk to the Ford employment office and within the month, Demjanjuk was working as a mechanic in the engine hot-test department.

Before long, Demjanjuk rose to the position of "motor balancer." As a member of United Auto Workers of America local 1250, he had a steady job with high union pay, full benefits; he was entitled to overtime as well, which he frequently collected.

"He was always so good with his hands," recalled Gerald Kravchuk, another friend from the DP camps who had settled in Cleveland. "He was willing to work hard and there was a need for good mechanics. He got a pretty good job right away."

Vera also worked hard. She found work as a "coiler" in the General Electric plant.

That fall, the Demjanjuks were able to move into a two-room apartment at Seventh and College Avenue, in a Ukrainian neighborhood on the south side of the city. They went regularly to nearby St. Vladimir's Orthodox Church, built in 1924 by Ukrainians who had left Russia after the Communist Revolution. The church was the center of Ukrainian community life.

In August 1958, after having been in the United States for more than six years, Demjanjuk applied to become a naturalized U.S. citizen. He scrupulously entered the addresses of every home they had ever had in Cleveland, their employment history, all the personal details of their lives—even Vera's brief first marriage.

As to visible distinctive marks, the typed words "operation scar on back" had been crossed out, at his request; "scar on left wrist" was written instead. As one of the judges in Israel would remark, a suspicious person might think he had something to hide.

On November 14, Demjanjuk received his naturalization certificate. At that time Ivan Demjanjuk legally changed his name to John Demjanjuk. He was an American citizen. "It was the happiest day of our lives," Vera later told a reporter.

The next twenty years passed quietly, like a good night's sleep. At Demjanjuk's U.S. denaturalization hearing, almost forty people would offer to testify to his good character. They knew him from work, from church; some had known him since his first days in the United States.

A second daughter, Irene, was born in 1960; son, John Jr., in 1965. They were, in many ways, the picture-perfect immigrant family. John could be seen in his light blue Pinto, driving to work, like any other commuter. Often he worked the night shift; in the day he played with the kids. Other parents envied his ability to fix children's bikes. On the weekends, John mowed the lawn or gardened in his Bermuda shorts. On Sunday, the family went to St. Vladmir's Church.

The children grew up. They were good kids. The girls had their first Communion. John Jr. was an altar boy. Their future seemed bright. They grew up surrounded by community and friends. In 1976, Lydia was married at their church; more than two hundred well-wishers celebrated in St. Vladimir's new banquet room.

The Demjanjuks worked hard; they saved their money to live a better life. They moved many times, each time to a better neighborhood. By the mid-1970s, they had settled in the Seven Hills suburb. Like others on the block, their home was a ranch-style house on a half-acre lot. Two tall, leafy pines stood at the edge of the lawn, sheltering the Demjanjuks from the street. They bought another acre behind the house, "for the future." The inside was filled with Ukrainian handicrafts; group pictures of the three children hung above the fireplace.

* * *

The allegations shocked Demjanjuk's friends, one of whom described him as "one of the nicest men you'd ever want to meet. He's the kind of guy who would stop to help you fix a flat on the road, even if he didn't know you. Just a real sweet guy."

Father Stephen Hankevich of St. Vladimir's Ukrainian Orthodox Church told a reporter, "They are good, hard-working people."

"They have had a hard life," said Anne Lishuk. "They come to this country same as us—deaf and dumb. But they learn the language, and they work hard, and now their life should be good. It isn't fair. . . . For as many years as we've known Johnny, he never once said anything about all this. Even when we are sitting around with the vodka and telling stories, he never says anything about the war years. I don't believe it. It isn't fair."

Yet from the moment of the first accusations, others would rethink every fact of Demjanjuk's life in the United States. Why was it that someone who was a naturalized citizen never traveled? In all his years in the U.S. he went once to New York, once to Canada. His wife, though, visited the Soviet Union twice. Did he have something to hide? Something to fear? Why was it, in all the drinking and toasts, he never revealed anything of his wartime activities? When he became maudlin, he would talk about how he and his parents had suffered during the famine in Ukraine. But never once did he complain about the hard life as a POW during the war years. Why?

Even his churchgoing was now puzzling. Demjanjuk was raised in a Communist, atheist home in the Soviet Union. He never had any religious education, never showed any signs of religious conviction until after the war.

His had become a life of few risks, little danger. Does a man trying to conceal his past hide in a life of perfect behavior? How could a person commit such acts of sadism and then live for thirty years as the perfect family man and community member? Wouldn't there be evidence of his cruelty and rage—bar fights, child abuse, wife beating, kicking a dog? There was none.

On the surface, John Demjanjuk's life in America offered no clues as to his past. But it could be said that he did nothing to call attention to himself, that he sought, above all, not to be noticed.

CHAPTER 6

Conversation by Documents

On the morning of August 25, 1977, John Demjanjuk was working at the factory as usual. At home the phones started ringing, and they would continue to ring all day. The children were the first to pick up, and were stunned to hear reporters tell them that the U.S. attorneys wanted to strip their father of his citizenship for having been Ivan the Terrible of Treblinka, a Nazi war criminal, a brutal murderer of men, women, and children. Vera kept reporters at bay, but by the time Demjanjuk got home, photographers were waiting in the driveway.

The next day, newspapers published Demjanjuk's name for the first time. The Demjanjuk home was besieged by journalists from radio and TV. The Demjanjuks consented to one interview that afternoon with a reporter from a local television station, Bob Franken of WJKW-TV. His report was aired that night on Channel 8. "The family wanted a chance to deny the allegations," Franken later told a reporter.

Demjanjuk sat on the family couch with his wife. He was wearing an open-neck short-sleeve shirt, and had on thick, black-rimmed glasses. Vera Demjanjuk wore a simple checked dress that belied her distraught look. The tension and stress upon both was apparent. They looked, in one reporter's words, "depressed, haggard, and close to hysteria."

From off-camera, Franken asked if the allegations were true. "No, no," answered Mrs. Demjanjuk. John Demjanjuk said in his thick accent, "I don't know nothing about it. I was no anyplace what they are writing now. I was German prisoner. I don't know nothing about it because . . . nobody was here, just call me one time."

"Is not true! Is not true! Is not true!" Vera blurted out, then slumped against her husband's right shoulder. In the film frames, one can see that it took a few seconds before Demjanjuk realized she had fainted. Only when he lifted his right arm, intending to put it around her, did he realize she was unconscious. He immediately jumped to his feet, clasped his hands together at his chest, as if in pain himself, turned to look directly at the camera and began crying. Franken called an ambulance and Vera was taken to a hospital. Her blood pressure was abnormal. The next day John Demjanjuk removed the adhesive backed letters spelling his name on the mailbox and ordered an unlisted phone number.

Three-and-a-half years passed before the trial began in February 1981. The delay was caused by the fencing match that is the trial discovery process: the prosecution attempting to get information from the accused, to bolster its case with additional evidence; the defense finding out what the prosecution knew and trying to counter it.

The filing of charges received international attention. But perhaps no article was read with as much interest, or would come to play as great a role in the case, as the September 1977 English language edition of *News from Ukraine*. It contained a quarter-page article on page three entitled, "Punishment Will Come."

The article began, "According to American press, the Department of Justice of the United States brought a criminal charge against war criminal Ivan Demyaniuk [sic] who after the war found refuge in the city of Cleveland and avoided just punishment for his murderous services which he obligingly offered to the Nazis" [the charges were actually civil in nature].

Written by the same journalist as the earlier Ukrainian article about Demjanjuk, it used many of the same phrases. But the source of the subsequent shock waves was not the article's contents but rather the illustration that accompanied it. The earlier piece had mentioned a Trawniki certificate number 1393 that had been issued to Ivan Demjanjuk. But this time the certificate itself was reproduced. In two separate photographs were the cover and inside leafs of what would come to be known as "the Trawniki card." The card itself was one piece of green cardboard, printed front and back, and folded across the middle to form a pocket-sized identity document. The cover, two inside leafs, and back cover, all carried important information.

The card bore, on its inside right side, the picture of a young soldier with a striking resemblance to John Demjanjuk. It placed one Ivan Demjanjuk—one with the same nationality, birth date, place of birth, and father's name as John Demjanjuk—in 1942 at an SS camp, Trawniki, where Soviet war prisoners were recruited and trained for service at the extermination camps. The card said Ivan Demjanjuk had an identifying mark—a scar on his back. And it listed his assignment in March 1943 to death camp Sobibor.

Though the INS had been trying to interview John Demjanjuk since 1976, he had been able to postpone any actual discussion of his war years until April 1978. Accompanied by his attorney, John Martin, Demjanjuk then met with assistant U.S. Attorney Joseph Cippolone in his Cleveland office.

Demjanjuk claimed to be unable to remember anything thirty-five years ago; but his memory was quite sharp on certain things, such as the series of hospitals he went to after he received his back wound in the battle of Kerch. He was a tractor driver before the war, he said, and a truck driver after.

As to his alibi for the time in question, he said that he was in two camps, Rovno, and another whose name he could not remember. He said he spent the time there building barracks.

Cippolone wanted him to acknowledge either that he had been a Communist Party member because he had served in the Red Army; or that he was a Nazi collaborator who had served at Sobibor or Treblinka. Demjanjuk repeatedly answered the charges with a curt "No."

Meanwhile, the INS had asked the Israeli authorities to conduct more interviews. As Miriam Radiwker had already retired, the request was turned over to another investigator, Martin Kollar.

Kollar was also well suited to the task. A native of Czechoslovakia, he had served after the war as part of the Czech legation to the Nuremberg trials. He moved to Israel in 1965 and soon found work with the police's war crimes unit. By 1978, he was an experienced member of the staff.

The INS wanted two other Treblinka survivors interviewed, Sonia Lewkowicz and Yakov Shmulewitz. Sonia Lewkowicz, who was born in 1922 in Poland and now lived in Tel Aviv, came to the Yaffo Police station on March 15, 1978. Lewkowicz told Kollar she had worked in the death camp's kitchen and its laundry. She recalled the Ukrainian Ivan who operated the gas-chamber engine: "Ivan was about twenty-five years old. I especially remember his stare, which was frightening. His behavior was the behavior of a man in a trance. He shouted very loudly. He never walked with empty hands. Sometimes with a riding whip, sometimes with a stick, another time with a metal pipe. He always beat on the inmates with everything he had in his fist. I saw this several times. I often hung the laundry on lines that were put up near the gas chambers and took it down after it dried. . . ."

The INS had sent eight loose photographs, each numbered, to be shown one by one to the survivors, to see if they could be identified. The photographs were all of men in civilian dress of the same age. Lewkowicz recognized the visa photo of John Demjanjuk as Ivan, based on the curvature of his forehead. Fedorenko she recognized but could not name.

Kollar reread Radiwker's files and noticed that Rosenberg had recommended she talk to Pinhas Epstein, another survivor. Kollar called Epstein to his office two weeks later.

Epstein spoke so fast and with such passion that Kollar found he couldn't take verbatim notes, but when Epstein looked at the photos, Kollar took down his remarks word for word. Epstein examined them closely. When he got to Demjanjuk's picture, he stopped to concentrate. He said the picture was not sharp but it reminded him greatly of Ivan. He was struck by the shape of the face, the high arching forehead. Even the short neck on broad shoulders—this was exactly the way Ivan looked, he said. Then he turned to the photo of Fedorenko and identified it as a true likeness.

The Israel Police were also able to locate Georg Rajgrodski, a death-camp survivor living in Germany, and he, too, identified Demjanjuk as Ivan.

Meanwhile, in the U.S., Demjanjuk continued to deny that he was ever at Treblinka, and the prosecution and defense continued to delay his trial. But in Fedorenko's case the INS and the U.S. Attorney were ready to proceed with his denaturalization before the District Court in Ft. Lauderdale, Florida, where Fedorenko had retired to.

Fedorenko admitted to having been at Treblinka, but only as a perimeter guard. He said he was "forced" to serve the Germans and was innocent of the atrocities attributed to him. Fedorenko claimed that although he joined his fellow guards in shooting at inmates during the Treblinka uprising, he merely "shot over their heads."

The witnesses were many of the same who had identified Demjanjuk: Turovsky, Epstein, Czarny, Lewkowicz. Israel Police investigators Miriam Radiwker and Martin Kollar also testified.

The witnesses, for the most part, did not speak English. The prosecutors did not speak Hebrew, German, or Yiddish, and were not familiar with the historical background of Treblinka or the background of the witnesses. Little was presented on the role of guards at Treblinka. The defense attorney and even the judge doubted much of what the survivors said about Fedorenko's activities at the camp. This questioning of the very facts of their experience at Treblinka carried over to doubts about the Israel Police investigators and the procedures they had undertaken, and the identifications they had conducted.

The net effect made Fedorenko's claims more credible than they would have been. The question of his crimes at Treblinka somehow became, in the view of Judge Norman Roettger, the litmus test; and his claim that he acted under coercive orders, his defense. Further the judge was willing to take into account, as a mitigating factor, Fedorenko's many years in the United States as a good citizen.

But Fedorenko was on trial for concealing his Nazi service from the U.S. Immigration authorities. *The question was:* Was he at Treblinka as a guard? To that even he admitted.

Judge Roettger, however, decided *for* Fedor Fedorenko. He rejected the government's evidence that Fedorenko had committed war crimes and found that the lies on his application were not material misrepresentations great enough to strip him of his citizenship—moreover, even if the misrepresentations *were* material, equitable considerations—such as his advanced age and good citizenship—served as alternative grounds for finding in his favor.

After the decision, Sonia Lewkowicz told *The Jerusalem Post:* "They treated us like we were on trial. In Germany [at the Dusseldorf trials], they would never do such a thing. In Germany, they were very correct. But in Florida, they heard our testimony and they laughed at us."

The Fedorenko appeal was argued by Allan A. Ryan, Jr., then an Assistant U.S. Solicitor General. In his early thirties, Ryan was a graduate of Dartmouth and the University of Minnesota Law School, and had been a law clerk to Justice Byron White of the U.S. Supreme Court. He was tall, thin, with a well-trimmed beard. A former Marine, he brought to his cases a look of authority, efficiency, and integrity.

The Fedorenko case had come to him by routine assignment. His first inclination, based on the judge's decision, was not to appeal. But INS attorney Martin Mendelsohn asked to him read the transcript of the trial. He did, and became convinced that he could win. After all, Fedorenko had admitted he was at Treblinka.

The United States Court of Appeals, Fifth Circuit, agreed. It reversed Judge Roettger's decision, and Fedorenko was stripped of his citizenship.

To Allan Ryan, the fact that Nazis were living in safety in America was incredible. It was criminal. But what struck Ryan most, after arguing the Fedorenko appeal, was that he could do something about it. He sent a copy of the decision to the Justice Department's criminal division, which oversaw the Nazi prosecution unit, the Office of Special Investigations (OSI). Ryan asked if he might help with similar cases.

The OSI had been formed in the spring of 1979 and was just getting under way. Walter Rockler was its first director and Martin Mendelsohn, originally head of the INS task force, was made deputy director.

A former member of the prosecutorial staff at Nuremberg and a senior partner in the Washington, D.C., firm of Arnold & Porter, Rockler had agreed to take a six-month leave to set up the office, hire staff, and make some headway on the backlog of cases, accusations, files, and investigations.

The OSI had inherited several hundred cases from the INS, the Demjanjuk case among them. But responsibility for it fell between the two prosecutorial regimes: though investigated by the INS, the case had been filed by the U.S. Attorney in Cleveland two years ago. It still hadn't gone to trial. Two years had gone by, and the case wasn't ready for trial yet. OSI wasn't happy about that; they wanted to take command. But the assistant U.S. Attorney felt his office was handling matters just fine. The question was, who would be in charge? The OSI or the U.S. Attorney?

The OSI felt that many INS cases had been lost without cause by local prosecutors who had not sufficiently prepared their cases and had not been sufficiently informed of the background of the crimes and witnesses. They did not want to repeat the mistakes of the Fedorenko trial.

After Fedorenko, many of the Israeli witnesses were reluctant to testify again in the U.S.; they felt they had been abused not only by the defense but by the court and the prosecutors as well. Mendelsohn had to assure the Israel Police that OSI attorneys would be fully involved in any future prosecutions.

By 1979, John Horrigan was directing the Demjanjuk case from the U.S. Attorney's office. Mendelsohn would have liked to wrest it away from him, but he found Horrigan a tough, able senior prosecutor who wanted the case. They agreed Horrigan would argue it *in partnership* with the OSI.

Mendelsohn assigned a young attorney from OSI, Norman Moskowitz, to assist Horrigan. Moskowitz, thin, compact, and with a mustache that accentuated his intensity, was born in New York in 1946. He had been a graduate student in Russian studies at Princeton, and was a 1977 Harvard Law School graduate. Before joining OSI he had worked at the National Labor Relations Board for two years. Today he is the top litigator in the U.S. Attorney's office for the Southern District of Florida.

Mendelsohn assigned Moskowitz because he spoke Russian and Hebrew. It was a lucky choice, because although Mendelsohn and Horrigan didn't get along, Moskowitz and Horrigan did and remain friends to this day. They worked well together and quickly understood each other.

While Horrigan prepared the evidence already gathered, Moskowitz coordinated the gathering of foreign evidence. During the summer of 1979, the question before him was how to establish Demjanjuk's wartime whereabouts. Demjanjuk had been born in the Ukraine and claimed to have been a POW in western Poland during the time he was alleged to have been trained as an SS guard and assigned to Treblinka. Eli Rosenbaum, then a Harvard law student working at OSI as a summer clerk, remembered seeing in the files a photocopy of the *News from Ukraine* article with the Trawniki ID card. He was dispatched to the Library of Congress to obtain an original issue of the paper. He then took that to the FBI lab· to reproduce the card. But when enlarged the card became a fuzzy series of dots.

Moskowitz decided to cable the American Embassy in Moscow: would the Soviets offer information about the original Trawniki card? Would they consider sending it or even a copy? Were there other records of a man named Ivan Demjanjuk?

Moskowitz had reason to hope so. At war's end, as Russian armies pushed the Germans westward across Poland, they seized many war documents, including the administrative files of the German SS in Lublin, the capital of the district responsible for the Trawniki camp. The Soviets had maintained extensive war records and statistics. Further, more than twenty-six million Soviet citizens had died during World War II, leaving a deep wound in the Russian political consciousness. The Soviets had participated in the Nuremberg prosecutions and had even held their own trials of "Hitlerites" that the Soviet media covered extensively.

In the pages of Soviet propaganda, they vaunted their assiduous prosecution of Nazi war criminals and often criticized the United States for its inaction. In 1976, the INS had formally requested the Russians' cooperation in American trials of former Soviet citizens who had committed Nazi atrocities on what was now Soviet soil. And in several instances, including the Fedorenko appeal, the Soviets had sent documents or depositions to the INS, most of which had remained in file cabinets throughout the years of INS inaction.

Horrigan and Moskowitz were determined that even without the original card, they would confirm its contents and existence.

In the fall of 1979, Moskowitz and OSI criminal investigator Bernard Dougherty traveled to West Germany. They visited the Berlin

Documentation Center and the Ludwigsberg archives, and met with West German prosecutors to study past prosecutions relating to Treblinka and Trawniki. Accompanying them as translator was OSI's George Garand, who had been a translator at the Nuremberg trials.

On the morning of November 14, OSI investigators went to the home of Otto Horn, a male nurse, who had worked at T4 (the Euthanasia Institute) and had been assigned to Treblinka. Tried and acquitted at the Dusseldorf trials, Horn was later interviewed by Gitta Sereny for her book on Treblinka commander Franz Stangl, *Into That Darkness*. The OSI had contacted her, and she had informed them Horn was alive and residing in Berlin.

Otto Horn was shown a site plan of Treblinka. He appeared familiar with the camp in general and the death-camp area in particular. Ivan of the gas chambers, he recalled, was stocky, had black hair, cut short, and a full rounded face with no distinguishing marks. Horn remarked that Ivan had enough technical ability to repair and maintain the gas-chamber engine, and that he was known to be able to drive an automobile, which, Horn said, was rare among the Ukrainian guards. During the evenings, Ivan and some of the others would travel into nearby Polish towns and become drunk and boisterous. Horn stated that he had never seen Ivan abusing prisoners.

Horn was then shown two sets of eight loose photographs. The first, of men in civilian clothes, had among them Demjanjuk's visa photograph; the other, of young men in uniform, included a photograph of the soldier on the Trawniki card. Horn studied them at length. He picked out the visa photo, then the Trawniki photo. They were, he said, photos of the same person.

They resembled, he said, Ivan of the death camp.

After a few more moments, Horn was willing to positively identify the photos as being of the Ivan he knew. He said he would be willing to do so again in a more formal setting—as long as there was no press or publicity.

Later that same day, Moskowitz and Dougherty visited Dr. Wolfgang Sheffler, an acknowledged expert on Nazi history. They were full of questions concerning the Trawniki card. Sheffler had never seen such a document before. It was a *Dienstausweis*, a service pass. Sheffler explained that such documents were issued to guards, *Wachmanner*, who were, at Trawniki, mostly Soviets. The Trawniki trials had been of Germans; most documents he had seen from the camp pertained to Germans. He would check to see if such a document did, in fact, exist; and whether this one was historically accurate.

Were documents from Soviet archives reliable? In twenty-five years of research, Sheffler said, he had never encountered evidence of tampering. If the Soviets were sincere in their desire to see Nazi war criminals prosecuted, fabricating documents was not in their interest—one forged document would destroy their credibility forever.

Moskowitz pointed out that the card had one weak area: there was no indication of Demjanjuk's assignment to Treblinka. The card showed him transferred only to Sobibor. Moskowitz suggested it was possible that Demjanjuk may have been transferred back and forth between the two camps, with no official record. Sheffler agreed to look into it. He also was prepared to testify as an expert witness, but only on certain conditions: he wished to be completely neutral—his name had to be provided to the defense, so it, too, could utilize his expertise.

In late November, Moskowitz called Martin Kollar at the Israel Police. His call was followed by a letter a few weeks later asking him to notify Rosenberg, Epstein, and Lewkowicz that they were to appear as witnesses in the case of *U.S.* v. *Demjanjuk*. Moskowitz told Kollar that as the main investigator on the case, he, too, would be called as a witness. Moskowitz predicted that the trial would begin in March 1980. But there was more. Included in the letter were eight loose head shots of young men—all in similar uniforms, all of similar age and ethnic background. Among them was the man from the Trawniki card, enlarged and cropped to the same size as the others, which the OSI said represented Demjanjuk in the years 1942–43.

The OSI asked that the pack of photographs be shown to the three persons mentioned above. Moskowitz wrote "It is most important that the photospread be shown under conditions that are above any suspicion of suggestiveness."

The Trawniki photo, placed among the loose photographs, was shown to Epstein, Rosenberg, and Lewkowicz in a series of separate interviews. Each immediately recognized the photo as Ivan, and as looking closer in age and weight to Ivan at Treblinka than the visa photo. Rosenberg even remarked: "This very much reminds me of [Ivan], but I think that it is a photograph from a period before Treblinka. I saw him with a fuller face, perhaps by then he managed to eat better."

Rosenberg was right about the time sequence. And it made sense that Demjanjuk would be thinner arriving from the POW camps than at Treblinka.

*   *   *

In late 1979, Rockler and Mendelsohn decided they could not work together. Mendelsohn was allowed to assume another post in the criminal division of the Justice Department, but he soon entered private practice in Washington, D.C. Today he is, inter alia, counsel to the Simon Wiesenthal Center.

Allan Ryan, who had sent the Fedorenko appeal to OSI with a note saying he would like to help in other such cases, was now asked if he wanted to be its next director. But, he replied, he was no expert. Having won one case, Rockler said, made him more expert than anyone else at OSI.

Rockler explained that he had only taken the position temporarily and offered that Ryan could come on as his deputy for the next three months if he would assume the directorship afterward. He accepted.

In January 1980, shortly before Ryan assumed the directorship, he and Rockler took a trip to the Soviet Union. They were there from January 26 through 31. They met with General Roman A. Rudenko, the Procurator General of the Soviet Union, and his associates. General Rudenko, who was in his seventies, had been the Soviet Union's prosecutor at the Nuremberg trials. He was of the Stalin era, and was a fearsome and feared personage. Nonetheless, Rockler and Ryan received a pledge of cooperation in trying Nazi war criminals issued by Aleksandr M. Rekunkov, the First Deputy Prosecutor who would replace General Rudenko after his death several months later.

"Soviet prosecutors have expressed willingness to permit Soviet witnesses to testify in American courts against former Nazi collaborators, providing they are healthy enough to travel and are willing to go," Rockler and Ryan told The New York Times, a few days after their meeting. They said the Russians had also agreed to allow lawyers to take testimony and cross-examine witnesses in the Soviet Union and to videotape the proceedings for use in denaturalization trials. The Soviets would respond to requests from the prosecution as well as the defense.

In return, the Soviet Union asked whether citizens deported from the U.S. could be sent to the Soviet Union to stand trial. Ryan gave the Soviets no guarantees.

From the Soviet Union, their next stop was Israel. "The general purpose was to introduce ourselves, meet with all the people, to tell them what we were doing and to convey our seriousness," Ryan said later.

Upon his return to the United States, he followed up the meeting

in Moscow with a long diplomatic cable. The pledges of cooperation, Ryan said, "were very vague." The Demjanjuk case had been
mentioned in Moscow. As for the card, "My approach was to say
to the Soviets that we need the material direct from the source."

Several months down the road, in the spring of 1980, Ryan said,
"we received a photostat of the Trawniki card and a general assurance that the original would be made available at trial."

Meanwhile, pretrial discovery was still under way. Between the filing of the complaint in 1977 and the actual trial, attorneys for each
side conducted a conversation of documents. In "written interrogatories" and "supplemental answers," one side asked, the other
told. One side told; the other asked for more information. No one
gave away more than was necessary; but each let the other side
know enough to conduct its own further inquiries, should it feel so
inclined.

In December 1979, Demjanjuk visited his attorney's office in
Cleveland to reply to a questionnaire the prosecution had sent. It
had been over two years since the initial complaint against him was
filed, and over a year-and-half since he'd been deposed at the U.S.
attorney's office. Asked, among the questions, to cite the places he
had been a POW and the type of work he had done there, he replied, "Russia—laying of railroad tracks. Poland—(Chelm) building huts." This was the first time Chelm was named as part of his
alibi. He also said that before the war's end he had been taken to
Graz, Heuberg, and Bishophofen. This too, was new.

John Horrigan wanted to ask Demjanjuk a few questions—in
person. Courts tend not to favor the "redeposition" of witnesses,
but Horrigan asked for the right to do so, based on new evidence
uncovered since the 1978 deposition—the Trawniki card and other
new witness statements.

On February 26, 1980, Horrigan questioned Demjanjuk, in the
presence of his attorney, and he repeated that he had been a POW
during the war years. Horrigan confronted Demjanjuk with his own
signature in Cyrillic on a copy of the Trawniki card. Demjanjuk
would not say it was his.

But could he say, without a doubt, that it wasn't like the way he
wrote his name in 1942?

Demjanjuk replied, "It is like I wrote my name."

The prosecution informed the defense of the names and addresses
of new witnesses; when they were interviewed and who interviewed
them. The documents revealed who among those contacted identified Demjanjuk's visa picture as Ivan, who did not; who recognized

the Trawniki picture as Ivan, who did not. Survivors had been contacted from both Camp One and Camp Two; from Sobibor, and even from Flossenburg. There was even a notation that the OSI had received protocols from witnesses in the Soviet Union, including one from the mysterious Danylchenko, which they never used. Prosecutors accounted for every lead, whether it proved useful or not.

On March 14, the government filed a supplemental answer in which they again listed the names of persons contacted. Among those was a new name, never listed before: Yehiel Reichman of Montevideo, Uruguay.

Reichman, whose family in Lodz, Poland, had been in the textile business for more than three generations, had spent the last thirty years as a leader of the Uruguyan textile industry. But he had not forgotten, for one moment, why he lived in South America rather than his native Lodz. Before the war he had five brothers and sisters. One brother had been sent to the Soviet Union; the others accompanied him to Treblinka and were murdered shortly after arrival. He survived because he volunteered as a barber and later as a dentist.

Reichman had been a witness at the Treblinka trial in Dusseldorf, and this was how U.S. investigators learned of his existence. In 1980 they called him, asking if they could question him about atrocities at Treblinka. He responded that he would travel anywhere, at his own expense, to give his testimony. Reichman occasionally went to New York on business and said he would call before his next trip to arrange a meeting.

On March 12, Yehiel Reichman met with OSI attorneys Moskowitz and George Parker at the New York Statler Hilton. Also present was Helen Meyerowitz to translate for Reichman, who spoke in Yiddish. Reichman was shown a stack of loose photographs, and asked if there was among them a person familiar to him from Treblinka. He studied them for a long time, examining each one carefully.

As Reichman later explained, he is not a person to make rash decisions. He examined the pictures over and over, but finally, he singled out Demjanjuk's 1951 visa photograph, saying he believed it was a photograph of Ivan from Treblinka. He was asked to sign the back of the photograph.

Demjanjuk's trial did not begin until February 1981. On January 31, 1981, Kollar received a telegram, asking him to call again upon Gustav Boraks. Kollar asked Boraks, who lived in Haifa, to meet him at the police station there on February 3. Boraks was helped to the station by his son Yoram because of his age and because Boraks was illiterate and spoke only Yiddish.

Kollar held in his hand Boraks's 1976 deposition. But he need not have worried. Boraks recalled every detail of his experience in Treblinka. Kollar was so impressed that years later he would recall how Boraks, when shown the photos, pointed immediately to the Trawniki photo and slapped down his finger on it, saying, "Ivan."

In December 1979, Norman Moskowitz had predicted that the trial of *U.S.* v. *Demjanjuk* would commence in March 1980. He was too optimistic by only a year.

CHAPTER 7

That's America?

When Jerome A. Brentar, a sixty-four-year-old Cleveland travel agent, heard in 1980 that Soviet-supplied evidence was being used against Demjanjuk, he took it upon himself to support the defense financially. Brentar is a deeply religious man of Croatian upbringing and anti-Communist sentiment. A former officer of the International Refugee Organization (IRO) in Europe, Brentar saw the Trawniki card as another example of how far the Russians will go to spread fear among Eastern European immigrants in the United States.

"The Soviets are dead afraid of the Ukrainians," Brentar has said. "They want to show that they can use the Justice Department of this country to do their dirty work."

Brentar feared Demjanjuk's extradition would lead to other extraditions based on equally false Soviet-supplied evidence. His belief in Demjanjuk's innocence was absolute: "You get a sense when you talk to someone whether they're telling the truth," Brentar said. "I would put my hand in the fire for him."

But Brentar had other interests as well. He was associated with Holocaust revisionist groups. Was it just coincidence that he was the Ohio representative of the St. Raphael Society, whose motto was "aid for the traveler in need" and that it was a St. Raphael Society in Italy that aided one "traveler in need," Adolf Eichmann, to escape to Argentina in 1947?

Others saw Demjanjuk in a different light. Charles Nicodemus of the *Chicago Sun-Times* recalled meeting him in 1977:

He was a muscular, thickset six-footer and his eyes blazed with anger as his moon-shaped face darkened in what seemed like a blush of hate. "Get off of my property," he growled, stepping from behind his power mower and picking up a bamboo rake. "Go. Go. No questions. I answer nothing. Go," he repeated, brandishing the rake like a baseball bat. Coming face-to-face with the man raised a chill along the back of my neck and a sickness in the gut. . . . When Demjanjuk brandished that rake it was easy to picture "Ivan the Terrible" [wielding his six-foot pipe]. . . .

Which was the real Demjanjuk?

United States of America, plaintiff v. *John Demjanjuk,* defendant, began on February 10, 1981, in Federal District Court in Cleveland before Chief Judge Frank Battisti. Denaturalization cases are civil; there was no jury present for the six-week trial.

A few days before it opened, about four hundred and fifty Ukrainians attended a rally at St. Vladimir's Church to raise funds for Demjanjuk's defense. On the day of the trial, a group of supporters gathered in downtown Cleveland to burn a Soviet flag and picket the courthouse. Protests and counterprotests continued outside the courtroom throughout the trial. Among the placards were many signs questioning the use of Soviet evidence, such as, "Get USSR out of U.S. Courts." Others had different agendas—"Six Million Lies," one read.

Twenty federal marshals stood ready inside the courthouse to keep the peace. Judge Battisti had reserved the largest courtroom in the building, the ceremonial courtroom, the room in which new citizens were sworn in, so that all who wished might be able to attend the trial. Vera and the three Demjanjuk children sat in the front row every day. The empty jury box was reserved for journalists and sketch artists.

The prosecution began by presenting an expert witness, Professor Earl Ziemke, of the University of Georgia, to explain the military history behind the capture and recruitment of Red Army soldiers by the Germans. Next, Professor Dr. Wolfgang Sheffler explained the "Final Solution" and the role of the Trawniki camp. Dr. Sheffler testified that although he had never seen a card identical to the Trawniki card, all the information on the card—the issuing authority, the chain of command, the ranks of the signatories, the equipment issued, the oath given, the seals used, the typeface, printing, and type of paper—was historically accurate. There was no reason to suspect it was a forgery.

The testimony of Dr. Sheffler was corroborated by Heinrich

Schaeffer, a former Trawniki paymaster for Ukrainian guards. When showed the ID card, Schaeffer recognized it as the official ID card issued to all persons training at Trawniki, adding that he himself had been issued such a card. Schaeffer said photographs were taken of everyone at Trawniki in the summer of 1942.

The first "eyewitness," Otto Horn, the former Treblinka SS man, did not actually appear in court. He appeared on videotape. Horn spoke dispassionately of the events at Treblinka as though he were a bank clerk talking about a bad check. Horn recalled seeing Ivan at the gas chamber, directing the prisoners inside.

"This is Ivan probably," Horn said, pointing to Demjanjuk's 1951 visa photo; when shown the Trawniki photo, he said, "As far as I can recall, Ivan looked like this."

Horn's testimony was followed by the testimony of five Holocaust survivors. They brought forth the full power of their memories to recreate the unimaginable, the unbelievable. Their words took on heightened intensity amid the formality of the ceremonial courtroom with its high ceiling and gold-leafed frieze.

The survivors testified: again and again, the victims arrived in cattle cars; once more they undressed and walked passed the barracks and the rag-sorters. They made their way through Camp One, the work camp, and up the path to Camp Two, the Upper Camp, the death camp. In the hushed courtroom, the witnesses seemed once again to hear the engine, the cries of the murdered. There, once again, they saw Ivan, ablaze with anger, drunk with viciousness. Ivan, in his early twenties, balding, with his ears sticking out . . . tall, strong, his thick neck, his broad shoulders, his high forehead . . . Ivan the Terrible.

They recalled in detail meeting with Israel Police officers, and looking at the 1951 photo. It was Ivan—older, fatter, but the same man. And the Trawniki photo—it looked even more as he was *then.*

Yehiel Reichman, then sixty-six, testified first because the prosecutors felt he was the most personally impressive of the witnesses. As a "dentist," Reichman had seen Ivan at the gas chambers day in and day out. He had identified the 1951 photograph in New York, the year before. He had no problem doing so again.

But Demjanjuk's attorney, John Martin, asked him, in cross-examination, if he hadn't been shown another folder of several photos in New York, from which he'd failed to identify anyone? Reichman denied this. He recalled only one stack of photos each of which he had examined carefully, one after another, for a long time. Martin asked that Reichman now be given the folder of photos he was speaking of. But before Martin could pose another question, Reichman immediately pointed to one of the photos.

Judge Battisti intervened: What was he pointing to? Reichman answered that among the photos there was one that looked even more like Ivan looked at Treblinka than the visa photo. It was the photo from the Trawniki card. Martin would argue that Reichman had been shown the photo in New York and had had no reaction to it. But Reichman would maintain that he saw only one pack of photos in New York, and that today on the stand he saw the face of Ivan.

Reichman was followed to the stand by Pinhas Epstein. He, too, identified the visa photo of the Cleveland auto worker and the Trawniki photo as the Ivan he knew. Next was Eliahu Rosenberg, whose testimony would place Demjanjuk at the gas chambers.

When Rosenberg had first arrived in Cleveland for the trial, he was in a terrible state of tension. His wife feared the hostility of the local Ukrainian community, but Rosenberg was anxious about seeing Ivan again.

The day of Rosenberg's testimony, Demjanjuk was already seated at the defense table. Cleveland in February is still very cold. Demjanjuk had on an overcoat and a hat and was wearing his glasses. The prosecution and defense tables stood next to each other, so even though Rosenberg tried, he could not look Demjanjuk straight in the face. "He was sitting near me but he didn't look at me," Rosenberg recalled. But at the end of the session, Demjanjuk got up. He started to leave. Rosenberg was struck. Now John Demjanjuk stood before him. "That's him!" Rosenberg said to his wife.

At first Rosenberg felt relief—his identification from a photo had been confirmed by seeing the man in person. But it soon turned to anger. Ivan arrived unescorted by police, and left surrounded by friends and family—a totally free man! It threw Rosenberg into a total outrage.

Rosenberg said to prosecuting attorney Norman Moskowitz, "That's America? That a criminal like this can go about completely free?" Moskowitz assured him this was not the end of the story, only the beginning of the process.

Georg Rajgrodski, a seventy-one-year-old architect who lived in Germany, had been assigned at Treblinka to carry corpses from the chambers to the burning pits. Sometimes he had to remove corpses from the gas chambers. From his work at the chambers he knew Ivan well.

Ivan had once given him twenty lashes for being late to a roll call. "I exerted all the effort I could to keep from crying out, and that's why I'm here today." Rajgrodski explained that if someone cried out while Ivan was whipping him, he continued to beat them until they were quiet, "and then he would shoot them in the back of the neck."

In November 1942, Rajgrodski testified, a violin was found among the possessions of the dead. The inmates of the death camp were asked if anyone could play the instrument. Rajgrodski said he could. Afterward, a *Kapo* (Jewish foreman) named Singer recruited him to work in the kitchen. Singer wanted him to play Viennese songs for him.

Rajgrodski recalled that in the summer of 1943, he played in a trio with a clarinetist and a harmonica player. The guards, Ivan among them, he testified, often came to hear them play. That sweet music played in the death camp seemed shocking; but stranger still, was that the music affected the murderers. Rajgrodski related that one time Ivan "turned around and wiped tears from his eyes."

Rajgrodski had no trouble identifying Ivan from either the visa photograph or the Trawniki card.

Sonia Lewkowicz, then fifty-nine, testified that upon arrival at Treblinka she said she was a laundress. This saved her life. During her testimony, Lewkowicz tried as best she could to look Demjanjuk in the eyes. Horrigan asked her: "What do you remember about this Ivan?"

"Terrible fear," she responded. "He was always busy. He screamed and he ran about. He adopted the style of the Germans. He beat very much and he always threw fear on everybody. We were all terribly afraid of him. He beat the Jewish prisoners." She was asked to describe him. "He was a young man. I don't know his exact age. He was young. He was light; he had light eyes and he had protruding ears."

The prosecutors were troubled by Demjanjuk's total complacency during the recitation of his atrocities. "The look in his eyes," Moskowitz told *The Miami Review* in 1987. "I'll never forget the look or the man: there was no remorse on his part."

The U.S. government had made many requests to the Soviet Embassy, all to no avail, for the original of the Trawniki card. But, in the second week of the trial, the OSI received a phone call from the Soviet Embassy: the Trawniki card was there. The examination could be conducted at the Embassy, but the Soviets would not even be present. Each side could call its own expert, who could use his own instruments in an unhampered fashion. The card could be presented to Judge Battisti for inspection, after which it must be returned to the Soviets.

Gideon Epstein of the INS, a forensic expert on disputed documents, inspected the Trawniki card for the prosecution. He tested the paper and the ink, and made photographic blowups of the document so he could check for signs of tampering. The Trawniki card, he concluded, had not been altered. He found the signatures by Trawniki SS officials authentic. He could not verify the signature of Demjanjuk, however, because there were no other examples of Demjanjuk's signature in the Russian alphabet.

The prosecution's final witnesses were immigration officials. Harold Henrikson, the vice-consul who processed Demjanjuk's visa application, testified that if he knew an applicant had served in a camp such as Trawniki, or been an extermination-camp guard, he denied him a visa. The prosecution rested.

If the defense could cast even a shadow of reasonable doubt, Demjanjuk would be acquitted. Demjanjuk offered, in his defense, a written statement from Fedor Fedorenko. Fedorenko had been shown copies of both the Trawniki card and the visa photograph. He denied ever seeing a card like that or ever having seen either the person on it or the person on the visa photo at Treblinka.

But Judge Battisti did not find Fedorenko's testimony credible. At his own trial, Fedorenko had testified that a Ukrainian named Ivan operated the motors of the gas chambers. But for the Demjanjuk trial, he claimed that he didn't know such an Ivan or remember his appearance.

John Demjanjuk took the stand. In his blue three-piece suit, thick black glasses, he looked fit and rested, more like a member of the legal staff than the accused. He spoke in Ukrainian, his deep voice resonant in the courtroom. Demjanjuk showed no emotion as he answered his attorney's questions. He told the judge that he had never been at Treblinka; he had been a prisoner of the Germans, he insisted, briefly at Rovno and then at another camp, Chelm. His entire tale took less than a half-hour.

John Martin then asked for and received a five-day recess; he wanted to consult his documents expert. Later, Martin would swear that he never had the opportunity to examine the Trawniki card to his satisfaction; that both experts he contacted could not test the card except in their own laboratories; that the Soviet Embassy had refused to release the card to the United States, nor would it release a paper sample; that the documents expert he ultimately engaged to examine photographs of the card, Joseph Tholl, never rendered an opinion.

When the trial reconvened the next week, Martin announced he would call no expert to challenge the authenticity of the card. He had no further evidence to present.

Three months later, on June 23, 1981, *United States of America*, plaintiff v. *John Demjanjuk*, defendant, was decided. In a forty-four-page decision, Judge Battisti found that Demjanjuk had illegally procured his naturalization by concealing his service as a German SS guard at Trawniki and Treblinka and by his subsequent willful misrepresentations. He was Ivan the Terrible of Treblinka; he should have never been allowed to enter the United States. His citizenship was immediately revoked.

Demjanjuk remained free, pending his appeal. Appeals could, and would, take years. He had received news of the verdict at work. He would continue at the Ford plant. He would continue to worship at St. Vladimir's. He had home, work, church, and friends. All still clung to his attorneys' claims that the case was a trumped-up affair based on false, forged, Soviet-supplied documents. All prayed that on appeal he would be vindicated.

CHAPTER 8

Next Stop, Tel Aviv

After the Eichmann trial, many wondered why no other Nazi war criminals were brought to trial in Israel. Some said that *any* trial after Eichmann would be anticlimactic, others that the young Israeli state had no desire to set up a perpetual gallows in Jerusalem, trying one Nazi after another.

Demjanjuk's Israeli defense attorney would argue that Israel had renounced prosecuting Nazis after Eichmann because of the reparations agreement with West Germany and now was prosecuting Demjanjuk only because he was a Ukrainian collaborator, not a German.

But the answer was far simpler. Eichmann had been kidnapped and this was not a precedent that the Israel Police sought to follow. They were interested in upholding the law, not breaking it. That meant extraditions. And extraditions did not seem a likely, or even a viable option. Israel had few treaty agreements with other countries. The few it had were not always practicable. For example, under German law no German citizen can be extradited to another country.

To understand how Demjanjuk came to be the first person tried as a Nazi war criminal since Eichmann, one first has to understand the role the Israel Police played in the process.

To investigate Eichmann's crimes in preparation for his trial, the Israel Police created the "06 Bureau" in 1960 (so named because there were five police bureaus already in existence). After the trial the department came to be known as the Unit for the Investigation of Nazi War Crimes.

The unit did not initiate cases. True, there were no war criminals in Israel, but there were witnesses—the Holocaust survivors. So even though the unit could not prosecute, it could aid other countries in gathering evidence for their cases. And elsewhere in the world Nazi war crimes prosecutions increased dramatically after the Eichmann trial.

According to Israel Police statistics, as of the end of 1984, investigations had been undertaken against 4,500 suspects. Eight-hundred files, grouped by ghettos, towns, and concentration camps had been opened. Forty thousand depositions had been taken. The great majority of these trials had taken place in Germany. Of the verdicts received, there had been 105 life sentences, and 200 lesser prison terms. Fifty-two committed suicide. The secretary of the unit estimated that as of April 1988, there were 900 files, and there had been 10 percent more verdicts in each category.

In the 1970s, the unit began to hear from the United States, which was commencing several denaturalization proceedings. The Israelis were still focused on police assistance, rather than on war crimes prosecutions taking place in Israel.

"Extradition . . . was not something that the Israelis were interested in," said Martin Mendelsohn. "Quite the contrary. The Israelis resented the notion that they should, in effect, become the dust bin again and sweep up all of the world's debris, and have to put them on trial in Israel. The Minister of Justice was against extradition. He wanted prosecutions. But he wanted prosecutions in France, in Germany and Austria. He felt that Israel should not be burdened with putting these cases on. The crimes were committed in Poland, Germany, and France; that's where the trials should be."

Marvin Henkin and Dennis Gouldman were the two attorneys for the Justice Ministry's International Division. They extradited criminals who had committed fraud, robbery, murder, or who were involved in drug dealing or embezzlement. They had never made a request for a Nazi war criminal.

Yet by 1979, Nazis were being uncovered across the world. The Ministry of Justice began to question: How should it react? And for the first time, its lawyers wondered if they could, or even should, use extradition for Nazis. They decided to try.

In 1979, Franz Wagner, the deputy commander of Sobibor, was found in Brazil, and Peter Menten, who was accused of murder as well as the looting of Jewish art treasures, was uncovered in Holland. In both cases, Israel filed for extradition. In both instances, the application was denied.

In June 1981, Allan Ryan, then OSI director, visited Jerusalem for the first World Gathering of Jewish Holocaust Survivors. Ryan held a press conference. "I went over there to locate witnesses," he later recalled, "to let the survivors know who we were and what we were doing."

During his trip he met with attorneys from the Ministry of Justice and Foreign Ministry and suggested they take a more aggressive stance toward extradition. The Israelis agreed only to consider such action. "It was a conservative response," Ryan said. "They [Gouldman and Henkin] are careful, analytic attorneys. They proceeded cautiously."

But they did proceed. Some attribute the seeming change of philosophy to the newly elected Begin government. But Gouldman later said it was more a question of evolution: "The question started to arise, well, suppose you complete your denaturalization cases and you get somebody deported. What happens then? We began to ask ourselves is it sufficient just for somebody to be deported, or leave to another country? Is there no way they can be tried for what they did?"

Most people in Israel, as well as in the United States, believed that the U.S. forced Israel to accept the Demjanjuk case. The truth is different. The wheels of Demjanjuk's Israeli prosecution were set in motion during an hour-long informal meeting between Israeli and U.S. Justice officials at the Justice Ministry offices in Jerusalem on Sunday morning, January 24, 1982. Attending were OSI attorneys Neal Sher, Rodney Smith, and Eli Rosenbaum, who were in Israel on other matters; and Israelis Dennis Gouldman, Marvin Henkin, and Colonel Menachem Russek, who had commanded the Nazi war-crimes unit since 1977.

Gouldman was concerned about what would happen to those proven to be Nazis and denaturalized as U.S. citizens. Sher explained the procedures for deportation. From the Israeli point of view, Gouldman said, deportation to a country that would prosecute them would be "satisfactory." He did not want Nazis sent to countries that refused to put them on trial.

Under U.S. law, Sher said, deportees usually can choose the country to which they will be deported. But the Attorney General can set aside that first choice, if doing so is in the "national interest."

Israel would consider making an extradition request itself, Gouldman said, but two considerations were paramount: 1) possible legal obstacles to extradition and 2) selection of the "right case" for the first extradition attempt. Sher believed that strong legal arguments could be made for an Israeli extradition request, but he could not guarantee success. He agreed that finding the right case was important.

The first case must be a murder case, said the Israelis, emphatically. Sher told them that several of the U.S. cases involved murderers, but proof of the crimes was not always the basis for denaturalization. For example, in Fedorenko's case, it was enough that he admitted being a former Treblinka guard.

But Gouldman pressed Sher: Was he prepared to suggest a candidate for Israel's first extradition request?

Sher said he wasn't in a position to do so, nor did he think it appropriate for him to volunteer a name.

Gouldman turned to Colonel Russek, head of the Israeli war-crimes unit. Russek had been listening to the careful conversation and did not want the meeting to end so abstractly. A Polish Holocaust survivor himself, Russek was a small but forceful man of military bearing. White-haired, his gaze was direct; his manner, courteous. He was not so much intense as intent.

Gouldman asked if Russek could suggest a suitable subject for an Israeli extradition request.

Russek didn't hesitate. He had a name in mind.

John Demjanjuk, he said.

Demjanjuk was a "proper" first case. He was a mass murderer who had killed with his own hands; his crimes at Treblinka were well known, his American citizenship had already been revoked, based on the testimony of Israeli witnesses. To let him go unpunished was unthinkable to Russek.

And Russek wanted a trial in Israel. It was he who had to deal with the Americans before there even was an OSI; he had watched them approach each case as new. He had stood by the sidelines while the U.S. had lost certain cases or withdrawn in others or won still others only to see the deported criminal spend his remaining days residing comfortably in a Mediterranean beach town. He had listened to the survivors complain about the way the foreign courts had treated them. He, too, was a survivor. He, too, was an Israeli. He felt their anger. He, too, wanted justice. And he wanted it in a courtroom in Jerusalem.

When John Demjanjuk's citizenship was revoked, it never occurred to him, his family, or his supporters that Israel would request his extradition. If they worried about anything—because the accusations had been a KGB plot—it was his being deported to the Soviet Union.

The denaturalization decision was appealed, to no avail. As a first step to deportation, Demjanjuk received an order to appear in court in July 1982. When, on his lawyer's advice, he didn't show up, he was arrested. A special set of handcuffs had to be used; the normal ones didn't fit his strong wrists.

To protest, he went on a hunger strike. On July 21, the three Demjanjuk children and a friend did the same, sleeping outside the Cleveland Justice Center. Their hunger strike lasted eleven days, until Demjanjuk was released; he later said he didn't appear in court because he was still appealing the denaturalization decision.

It was after that incident that the Demjanjuk family decided to find a new attorney. They turned to their supporter Jerome Brentar for advice. Brentar turned to his friend Edward M. O'Connor, whom he'd first met in Germany in the early 1950s. One of the three original DP commissioners, O'Connor had long been a friend of the ethnic communities. He had even, at Brentar's suggestion, testified as a defense witness at Demjanjuk's denaturalization trial.

O'Connor's recommendation? His son, Mark. Though Mark O'Connor had no immigration expertise, limited appellate background, and not much major trial experience, Ed O'Connor told Brentar not to worry. He promised he'd stay involved.

Later Mark O'Connor would tell a radio audience that he'd agreed to take the case after Demjanjuk's daughter Lydia called him up in tears. "Whenever I get a lady on the phone who's crying and begging me to help her father, who was about to be deported to the Soviet Union, I at least take a look at it. Too emotional. That's one of my main problems in my practice. I get too involved with my clients. And as a result of this phone call I went to Cleveland. I sat and talked with this lady—Lydia—and after talking to her and talking to the man himself and looking at his other children and his animals and his garden and so forth and the evidence for about three or four months, I got involved."

Demjanjuk's deportation hearing opened, after several delays, on April 11, 1983. During the course of the case, O'Connor brought in a Cleveland attorney, John Gill, as his documents expert.

On October 31, 1983, the State of Israel requested the extradition of John Demjanjuk and asked that a warrant for his arrest be issued on the charge of murder. Demjanjuk, however, remained free after posting a $50,000 bond, secured by the deed to his home.

The extradition proceeding did not begin immediately. First the U.S. had to finish the deportation hearing begun the previous April.

Mark O'Connor became a familiar figure to the Cleveland press. In his mid-thirties, with red hair, bright blue eyes, and a square jaw, he was a handsome, charismatic figure. He spoke at rallies for Demjanjuk's defense. He gave interviews, he wrote letters to the papers. He was dramatic. He was verbose and argumentative. He was fervent.

O'Connor told the press, for example, that only a Nuremberg-style military tribunal could have jurisdiction over alleged Nazi war criminals.

But in court, his arguments, his evidence, his witnesses, often lacked any legal relevance.

During the course of the hearing, Demjanjuk would not address the substance of the allegations. Mark O'Connor would neither admit nor deny the charges; neither admit nor deny the facts. Demjanjuk was given the opportunity to choose the country to which, if unsuccessful in his case, he would be deported. He would not name a country. The Soviet Union, being his country of birth, was selected by the court. Demjanjuk requested political asylum: to be deported to the USSR, O'Connor argued, was cruel and inhuman punishment. But still he refused any other possible destination.

During the course of the hearing, the government resubmitted, in effect, the evidence of the denaturalization hearing. Demjanjuk testified again in his defense. He continued to say that he had lied on his immigration papers to avoid repatriation to the Soviet Union. Demjanjuk now added that he'd had to hide not only that he had been a POW but also his service in the Vlassov army (an anti-Soviet fighting unit under the German aegis that Demjanjuk claimed to have been recruited into after his POW service).

"Do you think," OSI attorney Bruce Einhorn asked, "Ukrainians who operated gas chambers in death camps should be citizens of the United States?"

"It depends on the conditions," Demjanjuk answered. "If they were forced to do so, or did this voluntarily."

Demjanjuk was uninvolved during most of the case. It was hard for observers to imagine this man holding the fate of so many in his hands. He seemed awkward, far too simple to be "Ivan the Terrible."

Demjanjuk "is a very passive personality," O'Connor would later say. "I observed him in his home in Seven Hills, Ohio. His wife would tell him when to mow the lawn. His wife would tell him when to take out the dog."

But his composure broke when his son took the stand. John Jr. stated that if his father were deported to the Soviet Union, he would have no choice but to go with him, which would be a terrible hardship for him, being an anti-Communist. As soon as John Jr. began to testify, Demjanjuk started to cry. Vera, seated in the front row, wept hysterically.

As part of Demjanjuk's defense, O'Connor chose some unlikely experts. He called Jerome Brentar to testify about IRO screening procedures. Brentar had not been a screening officer at Demjanjuk's DP camp. He testified that IRO screenings were scrupulously conducted. But if Brentar was right, it made no sense that Demjanjuk would write Sobibor and Pilau if, as he claimed, he'd never been there.

O'Connor also called Rudolf Reiss, a former Trawniki man. He claimed to be a documents expert but was found to be no such thing. The defense also called Nicholas Nazarenko, who appeared in full Cossack military dress with saber and bandoliers. These three would be found by the court to have no information pertinent to the proceeding. But later, all three would be found to have ties to Holocaust revisionists (see Notes).

During the course of the trial, O'Connor wrote letters to the courts, to judges, to the press. Typical was his charge that "fraud" had been committed on the Trawniki card and that the Soviets had admitted it.

One day, in April 1984, O'Connor appeared unannounced at the Soviet Embassy in Washington. Shown to a Soviet consul familiar with the Demjanjuk case, O'Connor brought up the Trawniki card. The card bears a Russian translation from 1948, in purple ink. In the photostat of the card that the Soviets first provided, the translator's name had been blocked out. The consul explained this had been done to protect the translator. But the name was clearly to be found on the original. In the United States, the original had been photographed in its entirety, without restriction, and the photos had been submitted in court.

But the "blocking" on the photostat was, to O'Connor, an "alteration." The "altered" evidence was proof of "fraud," and evidence of forgery in the case. He would, even in Jerusalem, still cite this as the central evidence of fraud. It was not an argument that won much consideration in court. If this was his "central evidence," Demjanjuk and his family had no reason to be surprised by what followed.

On May 23, 1984, Judge Adolph F. Angelilli found Demjanjuk deportable on all seven counts. The court denied defense motions to terminate deportation, to grant asylum, or to suspend deportation. But the judge did grant Demjanjuk the opportunity to leave voluntarily within thirty days to the country of his choice. If he didn't leave, the deportation order would take immediate effect, and Demjanjuk would be deported to the USSR.

Demjanjuk did not leave the country. He appealed, again to no avail. And on February 14, 1985, when the INS Board of Appeals upheld the previous ruling, it found that Demjanjuk should not have been granted the privilege of voluntary departure. That was unavailable, as a matter of law, to someone who had participated in Nazi persecution.

Up until that moment, Demjanjuk could have left for any country that would have accepted him—Argentina, Canada, only an hour's drive from Cleveland. Even Germany. But now it was too late. Demjanjuk was placed in the Cleveland County Jail in April 1985. Shortly thereafter, he was transferred to the federal prison in Missouri. His attorneys continued to petition a variety of courts to overturn the denaturalization and deportation orders with no success. The deportation issue resolved, the extradition proceeded. During the end of 1985, Demjanjuk was found extraditable. Demjanjuk's defense submitted a grab bag of motions, all to one purpose: keeping Demjanjuk in the United States.

An appeal was made to the Supreme Court, which declined to hear the case. All legal remedies had been exhausted, but O'Connor continued to promise his family that Demjanjuk would never be allowed to leave the country. It was unimaginable, he said, that Demjanjuk would be extradited based on "Soviet evidence." The media were notified; senators and other politicians were called. Nonetheless, in February 1986, Demjanjuk was moved to the Metropolitan Correctional Center on Park Row in New York City and prepared for departure.

A last-minute appeal was made to the Attorney General on February 27, 1986. It was rejected. On that same day, Demjanjuk's extradition was authorized by U.S. Secretary of State George Schultz.

That same evening, Demjanjuk was led aboard a regularly scheduled El Al 747 and seated in the business-class section. He was handcuffed and accompanied by two U.S. marshals. The flight left John F. Kennedy International Airport around six in the evening.

Next stop: Tel Aviv.

CHAPTER 9

Operation Justice

In 1985, as Demjanjuk appealed his order of extradition in the United States, Dennis Gouldman, in Israel, pressed the Israeli Ministry of Justice to assemble a prosecution staff. But the ministry was cautious. It waited. When the U.S. Court of Appeals for the Sixth Circuit affirmed the order of extradition on October 31, 1985, only then did the whole matter, suddenly, become real.

Usually in a criminal case, a crime is discovered, the police department conducts an investigation, an arrest is made, an indictment is drawn up by the state attorney. But here, the first three stages were compressed into one. Although the crimes were forty years old, the investigation would begin with the suspect, Demjanjuk, already in Israeli custody. The Ministry of Justice decided that the investigation had to be coordinated by both the State Attorney and the Israel Police. The joint team was dubbed "Operation Justice."

On the police side, Assistant Commander Alexander Ish Shalom was put in charge. Dog-faced, with a permanent five-o'clock shadow, Ish Shalom looked like a police officer. He had a certain notoriety for extracting testimony from suspects in the "Jewish Underground" (a group of extremist Jewish terrorists) case. For his staff, Ish Shalom recruited Colonel Menachem Russek, police officers Chief Superintendent Zvi Ariel (who spoke German fluently and had worked on other international criminal matters), Sergeant-Major Zvi Shalom Tamari, Superintendent Arye Kaplan (who spoke

Russian), Inspector Izia Sobelman (who spoke Ukrainian), and investigator Etty Hai.

State Attorney Yonah Blatman assembled his staff. Dennis Gouldman was assigned to prepare the legal issues relating to Demjanjuk's detention during investigation, and to research answers to any possible legal challenges to Israel's right to try him.

Michael Horovitz, an attorney in the Tel Aviv prosecutor's office, applied to be part of the prosecution team. Fluent in English, German, and Dutch, Horovitz had been born in New York, raised in Holland, and was a child of Holocaust survivors. A tall, thin, nervous man with a quick mind and a dark sense of humor, Horovitz once said "you could say I was raised in the lap of the Holocaust." He had come to Israel as a volunteer during the Yom Kippur War, and a year later settled in Tel Aviv. A former police fraud investigator, he had worked on large criminal conspiracy and drug cases as an attorney in Tel Aviv's State Attorney's office.

Blatman also recruited three lawyers in their early twenties and thirties, Eli Gabai, Eli Avraham, and Gabriel Finder, who would work long hours to provide a backbone of research. They would track down obscure articles, contact foreign experts, work out every possible cross-examination question. All were familiar with the American legal system, (two of the three, in fact, were graduates of American law schools). And among them they were familiar with German, Hebrew, Yiddish, and Russian, languages that would be necessary in their research. As children of Holocaust survivors, Finder and Avraham were committed to the case not only professionally, but emotionally as well. Dafna Bainvol, a senior litigator in the Jerusalem District Attorney's office, would later join the team.

Blatman quickly realized that preparing the Demjanjuk case was a full-time job. But as State Attorney he had other responsibilities. He needed to find someone whom he could trust to lead the team, to coordinate with the police, to delegate and oversee the prosecution. He turned to a young man in the Jerusalem District Attorney's office, Michael Shaked.

Shaked was born in Jerusalem in 1945 to a Polish father and German mother, both of whom had left Europe before the war. German was spoken in the home. A graduate of Hebrew University's law school, at the District Attorney's office he had worked on a series of complex criminal litigations, some political in nature. His success in these cases had earned him the respect of the Jerusalem District Attorney, and brought him to Blatman's attention.

Shaked was a serious man with a polite, forthright manner. He was modest, and it was with some difficulty that one learned that he had been decorated in the Yom Kippur War, or that he had served his country in intelligence and diplomatic posts. But Shaked was not without ambition, although his aspirations were more personal than material. He had spent most of his legal career in the Jerusalem District Attorney's office and did not seek out the Demjanjuk case. He was aware, however, of its importance.

Gideon Hausner, Israel's Attorney General, had argued the Eichmann case. Shaked was only a senior attorney in the State Attorney's office. He was aware that in the eyes of the Israeli public and the legal community, there were other, more likely, candidates for the job. But offered the task, he readily accepted.

The first course of action for the attorneys was to review the material from all the U.S. proceedings, not only the verdicts, but the thousands of pages of transcripts, depositions, and exhibits. Then there were the materials from cases that might relate only tangentially to Demjanjuk. They would have to comb archives in Israel, Poland, and Germany.

Many in Israel had assumed the U.S. had delivered to Israel an open-and-shut case. Yet Shaked found a far more difficult case than he or anyone had imagined. Of the ten survivors who had positively identified Demjanjuk over the years, four had since died. Turovsky, Goldfarb, and Lindvasser had died in the late 1970s; Rajgrodski, just weeks after testifying at Demjanjuk's denaturalization trial.

Then there was the problem of the Trawniki card. The Americans had received the card from the Soviet Embassy during the trial. But the Soviet Union had broken off diplomatic relations with Israel after the 1967 Six Day War. There was no reason to believe that the Soviets would cooperate with Israeli prosecutors. They asked whether the U.S. might approach the USSR about acting as custodian for the card during the trial, but there was little hope that the Soviets would agree.

The prosecutors had their work cut out for them.

On the morning of February 28, 1986, El Al Flight 004 cut through the bright winter sky, landing at Tel Aviv's Ben-Gurion Airport. The plane taxied to an out-of-the-way runway, and came to a halt. A staircase was rushed to the plane's front door.

Within moments, Demjanjuk appeared. He was in a brown suit, shirt open at the neck, no tie; his hands were cuffed in front. Standing between two burly U.S. marshals, he looked pale, pudgy, overweight. As they descended the steps, a trio of Israeli Police officials, with Alex Ish Shalom in the lead, walked up. They met halfway.

The marshals uncuffed Demjanjuk, and Ish Shalom instructed Israel Police officers to place their set of cuffs on him.

Ish Shalom, his comments translated into Ukrainian, identified himself as a police officer, then told Demjanjuk he was being arrested under an Israeli statute for bringing Nazis to justice; that he had the right to remain silent; and that anything he said would be used against him. The marshals then handed over his U.S. prison medical files.

Walking between the Israel Police officers, Demjanjuk proceeded down the stairs. With only a few steps to go, he stopped and turned, and pointed emphatically to the ground, despite his handcuffs. Demjanjuk asked if he could "kiss the ground of the Holy Land." Officer Izia Sobelman conveyed the request to Ish Shalom. No, he said, dismissing the idea with a flip of his hands, keep moving. A gaggle of reporters was waiting on the tarmac, shouting questions at Demjanjuk as he was led straight into a police van and taken to nearby Ayalon Prison.

Israel's ambivalence about the upcoming trial was evident in that day's editorial in *The Jerusalem Post:*

> Truth to tell, there can be little satisfaction for Israelis in the coming trial here of Ivan Demjanjuk. . . . The trial will not be much of an educational experience: since Eichmann, awareness of the Holocaust by the Israeli post-Holocaust generation needs no such boost, while people abroad who still deny the Holocaust will keep denying it even after the verdict is rendered. Thus the verdict will have no deterrent effect.
>
> What, then, is the point of the coming trial? The point, very simply, is that Israel had no other choice.

At Ayalon Prison, where Eichmann had also been held, Demjanjuk was housed in a newly built wing. Officials originally had said Eichmann's same cell would be used, but it was not suitable for modern security and surveillance.

Demjanjuk's cell was installed in a large yellow room divided into two parts: one, the cell itself; the other, for warders who would watch Demjanjuk twenty-four hours a day. The windowless cell contained a single bed, closet, table, and chair. Lying on the bed was his new wardrobe: two orange jumpsuits, a pair of blue pajamas, socks, rubber slippers, and underwear. For his court appearances, Demjanjuk would be allowed to dress in his own clothes.

The cell was examined to ensure that Demjanjuk could not harm either himself or his guards. Wooden boxes were placed over pipes and protruding edges; all eating utensils were made of plastic. The wing had its own cement exercise yard where Demjanjuk would have a one-hour exercise period twice a day.

The marshals had reported to Ish Shalom that during the flight from New York, Demjanjuk had looked out at the window and said, "They don't understand. It was wartime. . . ." Ish Shalom asked Demjanjuk about this. Demjanjuk answered, "If I had been at Treblinka, and there was a war on, then I would merely be fulfilling orders."

On Monday, after a weekend in prison, Demjanjuk traveled under heavy guard from Ayalon Prison to the Jerusalem police headquarters for his first detention hearing—a procedure to determine whether a suspect against whom charges have not yet been filed should continue to be held in prison.

The officer's lounge had been converted into a courtroom for the hearing. Demjanjuk's handcuffs were removed. Judge Aaron Simcha, a Jerusalem magistrate court judge, reviewed a file the police had prepared. Its aim was to show that Demjanjuk should be kept in prison because there was sufficient evidence to show he was Ivan the Terrible of Treblinka. Testimony was given by Ish Shalom. As he spoke, Demjanjuk looked down and shook his head, "No, no, no."

Judge Simcha asked Demjanjuk if he had anything to say to the court. Demjanjuk stood up and, ignoring his interpreter, spoke directly to the judge in English. "I was never in the place you call Treblinka, and I never served the Nazis. I was myself a prisoner of war. How you can transform a prisoner of war into a gas-chamber operator is beyond me."

"It seems to me," Demjanjuk said, "that you've already determined my guilt and that my punishment is certain to be death." Simcha assured him that he would be tried fairly under the Nazi and Nazi Collaborators Law but if proven guilty, he was likely to be punished by death.

Back at Ayalon, Demjanjuk underwent his first interrogation. As with the many others that would follow, Demjanjuk began by saying he refused to cooperate. The police officers questioned him anyhow. And Demjanjuk would always answer the questions posed.

Usually, three investigators sat a table, asking questions in English. When Demjanjuk insisted on having words translated into Ukrainian, Officer Sobelman did so. At the end of each session, a report of the interrogation was drawn up. Demjanjuk refused to sign it.

Izia Sobelman told *The Jerusalem Post* that Demjanjuk appeared calm, "but I feel that, behind his civilized facade, he's actually quite afraid of what lies ahead of him."

Ish Shalom would later recount that his questioning followed the pattern of: "You say you were there. Convince me. Where were you? You say you were in a POW camp. Who was there with you? You say you slept in bunk beds. Who was in the upper bunk? It stands to reason that you would know these people."

"He was not able," Ish Shalom would say later, "to give so much as one name. He couldn't. He didn't remember or he didn't want to."

The police team found Demjanjuk's answer, when cornered, was always the same: "We couldn't act differently, there were pressures. We were prisoners of war." He would immediately insist, "I wasn't in Treblinka; but even the Ukrainians who were in Treblinka, they really had absolutely no choice at all."

Demjanjuk claimed that the investigators had no right to question him, that they shouted at him. But Demjanjuk did not, could not, keep his mouth shut. He had a need to explain himself.

Asked how he had spent the war years, Demjanjuk would invariably add new inconsistencies and incongruous facts to his previous accounts. For example, he continued to deny that he had been recruited to the Trawniki training camp from a POW camp and from there to Treblinka; or seen others recruited. He insisted that he couldn't have been taken to Treblinka from Chelm (the POW camp he claimed he remained at), because he was "skin and bones." But this implied that he knew that the healthy were recruited, as the prosecution would argue later. Why, if he was so weak, would he have been recruited as a soldier for the Vlassov Russian Liberation Army?

If he was a POW at Chelm, for so many months, why didn't the Germans ever take down his name? For the first time, Demjanjuk said they had. Asked how old he was when the German ID card was issued, he said: "I was twenty-one or twenty-one-and-a-half. I don't know what they wrote on the card." That was about the age on the Trawniki card. Demjanjuk must have realized this, for after a moment's reflection, he changed his mind and said, "I've never seen such a thing."

Demjanjuk also mentioned that his group at the POW camp—he used the German word *Gruppe*—had a Jewish *Kapo*. Prosecutors and historians would show that Jews were not allowed to remain alive as German POWs at Chelm. *Kapo* was a term, they insisted, Demjanjuk had learned elsewhere.

As to what he did at Chelm, Demjanjuk now said, for the first time, that he dug peat. That he had put Sobibor on his visa applications, and had admitted to lying on the forms, was, to Demjanjuk, of little consequence. "Everyone lied and Jews lied, too," he said.

Demjanjuk did not feel that his case was worth so much trouble. He asked investigators: "Why are you making a big deal out of me? Eichmann was big and Ivan was small. Besides, I'm not Ivan. There's a mistaken identification."

One of the most important and damning exchanges occurred on April 4, 1986. Russek asked a seemingly casual question: Had Demjanjuk ever visited the Polish villages of Kosow or Miedzyrec Podlaski? It was not an innocent question. The first town is near Treblinka; the second is a larger city almost halfway on the road between Treblinka and Sobibor. Demjanjuk's reaction was strange. He said nothing, and looked away. Russek repeated the question and asked for an answer. Demjanjuk said, "No comment."

Ish Shalom expressed surprise and asked, "Why no comment?"

Said Demjanjuk: "You are pushing me to Treblinka."

But as Russek would later observe, *they had not mentioned Treblinka.*

Despite his denials, Demjanjuk still felt some need to explain. At a subsequent interrogation in April, he said, "Can you imagine . . . the Germans come up to you and tell you, you must come with us. Who can refuse? This, they don't understand. So, what trials? To try, for what? . . . When the Germans would offer to collaborate, who could have refused? Isn't that clear? There was a war. Germans who were in the SS. Why aren't they asking them? Why aren't they tried? [Why] only the Ukrainians?"

Though Demjanjuk would claim he was being persecuted and harassed, he did not complain about prison life. He spent much of his time reading *The Jerusalem Post,* writing letters, and compiling a Ukrainian-Hebrew phrase book. He decorated his cell with letters from well-wishers and pictures from his family. He sang Ukrainian songs. He exercised regularly.

Demjanjuk had taken to doing push-ups in his cell. He could do sixty at a time. Once he reportedly challenged his guards to a contest. But young and healthy as they were, they were no match for Demjanjuk.

He was friendly with his warders. He practiced his Hebrew. With one guard, who spoke Russian, he often conversed at length, telling about life in the Ukraine, and wondering why he was being held in prison. But Demjanjuk was not always so calm and easygoing. One day, a few weeks before the trial was to begin, Ish Shalom went to Demjanjuk's cell. Demjanjuk demanded that he leave and started to push him, his large hands grabbing the policeman. Ish Shalom knocked Demjanjuk's hands off him and shouted: "This is Israel and you should not push me. This is not your private cell. This is not Treblinka."

He explained that they had come to show him some pictures. Then he noticed that Demjanjuk's cell was decorated with letters and he saw hanging there a picture of his wife, Vera, holding a photo of the two of them from the time of their wedding. Ish Shalom said "Look, I have the same picture"; he had a photostat that he gave to Demjanjuk. He kissed the photo, then returned it, refusing to keep it.

During his incarceration, Demjanjuk was visited by a group from the Israeli parliament, the Knesset, that inquired about his treatment. He had no complaints. But one day, when former Soviet dissident Natan Sharansky, touring the prison, was shown Demjanjuk's quarters, he started shouting that he was innocent.

Sharansky, who was born in the Ukraine, told him in their native tongue: "I don't know. But I met people like you in prison. And all I can say is that here [in Israel] you will have a fair trial, and there [in the Soviet Union], you know you would not. So you are better off here than there."

Demjanjuk's first detention hearing had occurred in Jerusalem. The second took place at Ayalon Prison. Because of security precautions, it was easier to transport the judge to the prisoner than the prisoner to the judge. A makeshift courtroom was set up in the warder's lounge.

In mid-March, Mark O'Connor arrived in Israel. The next day he met with Demjanjuk for an hour. The day after, he met with ministry officials, who outlined the trial procedure. Demjanjuk had the right to appoint his own counsel; if he could find no suitable attorney, one would be appointed for him. Generally speaking, Demjanjuk's attorney would have to be admitted to the Israel Bar. But in 1961 an amendment was passed to permit Eichmann's attorney, Dr. Robert Servatius, to appear with permission from the President of the Israel Supreme Court and the Justice Minister.

The Chamber of Advocates recommended that O'Connor be accepted as Demjanjuk's attorney but criticized him for talking to the press so often. In his last official act as Justice Minister, Moshe Nissim approved O'Connor's request for permission to represent Demjanjuk.

O'Connor asked the State to pay his fees, claiming that Dr. Servatius had been paid 10,000 German Marks ($5,000) per month while representing Eichmann. This was not true. A sum equal to approximately $30,000 was set aside for translation services. The same arrangement was made for the defense in the Demjanjuk case.

O'Connor did not attend the April 15 detention hearing. He was out of the country searching for witnesses. But over the next few months, O'Connor began to outline his defense, scattershot, in the pages of the Israeli dailies. That Ivan of Treblinka was dead, he said, was confirmed by statements given by Eliahu Rosenberg in 1947 and Avraham Goldfarb in 1961. About the Trawniki card, he said: "Valery Kubanov of the Soviet Embassy and Judge Frank Battisti told me they knew of the forgeries, yet proceeded with Demjanjuk's deportation in light of OSI and KGB pressure." There were mistakes in the angle of the photo on the card; the uniform was the wrong one.

O'Connor promised that for each witness who identified Demjanjuk, he would present another who would swear this was a case of mistaken identity. Two of the witnesses in the denaturalization case had already recanted, he said. Three of the eyewitnesses had been declared unfit and were suspected of having coordinated their evidence at the Fedorenko trial. Finally, O'Connor claimed to have uncovered three witnesses in Poland who knew the real Ivan the Terrible and would verify that Demjanjuk was not the man who manned the gas chambers.

In the meantime, Demjanjuk remained in prison. No indictment had been filed. Israel's Attorney General, Yitzhak Zamir, asked the Supreme Court in June for a ninety-day extension of Demjanjuk's detention. Supreme Court Judge Yacov Maltz granted the request but said he hoped the prosecution would submit its indictment at the end of the extended period.

In early July, the Demjanjuk family, Vera, Irene, her husband, Ed Nishnic, and their baby, Eddie Jr., flew to Israel. They went directly from the airport to Ayalon Prison. Appearing unannounced, they asked to be let in and were refused. Vera burst into tears, "We've come all this way. Why won't they let us see him?" she asked. They were informed that prison has visiting days and hours. They would be allowed inside two days later, on Friday, and although prison regulations allowed only for a thirty-minute visit once a week, they would be allowed two-hour visits twice a week.

The family's reunion took place with O'Connor and James McDonald, who came as O'Connor's assistant. They were escorted to Demjanjuk's cell and they found a suntanned, robust, and trimmer John Demjanjuk waiting to greet his family. He rushed to his wife and showered her with kisses, then turned to his grandson, whom he had seen only once previously. The family was surprised to find him so fit and in such good spirits. The conditions were better than they had been in the U.S., and Demjanjuk reportedly offered this critique of prison fare: "They put too much vinegar in the salad but the outstanding bread makes up for this inconvenience."

There was no talk of the upcoming trial. Demjanjuk asked about family finances and about his son. He was concerned that they watch over their own lives.

Meanwhile, the prosecution staff began to visit the survivors and their families. Rosenberg recalled one evening when he talked late into the night with Michael "Mickey" Shaked. They ended up in tears; in each other's arms. Shaked also visited Boraks in Haifa and was struck by the sharpness of the memory of this man in his eighties.

Meanwhile, Israel Police received a phone call from Yehiel Reichman, who was visiting Israel with his grandchildren. Reichman said he would travel there at any time to testify at his own expense. Horovitz ultimately spent many hours with him on the telephone in Montevideo and they would form a kinship, a friendship.

There was still the problem of the Trawniki card. Prosecutors made a formal request for it, and an informal one, too, through the special interest section of the Netherlands Embassy in Moscow. The Soviet Union did not reply. Appeals also were made by private individuals, such as Allan Ryan, and by organizations, such as the World Jewish Congress. Still, no answer.

There was, however, one more trump card to play. In August 1986, the Prime Minister of Israel, Shimon Peres, wrote to "My Dear Armand"—Dr. Armand Hammer—and asked that in his upcoming conversations with Soviet leaders, he request the Trawniki card and other documents that might be relevant. As a P.S., Peres suggested that it would help if the Soviets would allow Israeli prosecutors to come to the Soviet Union to work with their Soviet counterparts.

Peres attached a brief "Note concerning Ivan Demjanjuk" written expressly for the Soviets. Demjanjuk was described as having "betrayed his homeland by volunteering to serve with the German SS forces," which sounded like Soviet agitprop. Even more telling was that in all the description of Demjanjuk's activities at Treblinka and the atrocities committed there, the word "Jew" did not appear; instead the word "victims" was used.

Horovitz was dispatched now to Germany, where he spent long hours in the archives, searching for documents and depositions to buttress their case. Gabriel Finder traveled to the United States to review materials and meet with experts. The pieces were falling into place.

But all the while concern was growing among the Israeli public that no indictment had been filed. Demjanjuk himself addressed this at his hearing on August 23, reading a prepared statement in Ukrainian: "Nine years ago, the Americans started to investigate suspicions against me. In Israel they knew this. What have they done so far? On what grounds have they brought me here and on what basis did they ask for my extradition? They brought me here—they had nothing against me and now they have only started to search. Six months is a long time and yet they have not pressed charges. Looking for false witnesses would take them many years, because I did not do anything they accuse me of."

For the prosecution, the problem was not lack of evidence but the overwhelming amount of it. Shaked and his staff had put in ninety-hour weeks trying to come to terms with the sea of documents and information. They had spent long hours with survivors and their families. Every step in their attempt to unravel the mystery of Ivan had been arduous. The staff often seemed numb, dazed by its knowledge. Prosecutors didn't know if their evidence would succeed in court; they didn't know how their witnesses would hold up; they didn't know how the court would view their presentations or what the defense might attempt. But the more time they spent with the evidence, the more they became convinced of one thing: John Demjanjuk was indeed Ivan the Terrible of Treblinka.

The prosecution promised to file an indictment by October 1. Nonetheless, the feeling grew that an indictment *must* be filed soon. On September 16, 1986, Barbara Amouyal wrote in an editorial for *The Jerusalem Post,* "John Demjanjuk is no Adolf Eichmann, nor will his sentencing arouse feelings of sweet revenge and pride in Israeli law so widely felt by the community at large and the world's Holocaust survivors during the Eichmann trial. . . . The Demjanjuk trial has also become a trial for the Israeli justice system."

On September 29, two days earlier than the self-imposed deadline, Attorney General Yosef Harish released the indictment. The prosecution staff sent one of their youngest members, Eli Gabai, to deliver the indictment to the clerk of the Jerusalem District Court. This was to send a message—that as far as the State Attorney was concerned, the Demjanjuk case was a routine criminal prosecution.

The suspect was charged under the Nazi and Nazi Collaborators Law with crimes against humanity, war crimes, and crimes against the Jewish people, and with murder under the penal code of the State of Israel. The indictment ran seventeen pages in Hebrew, twenty-six in English. The statement of facts was divided into thirteen sections, followed by a list of fifty-three witnesses, of which twenty-five were from Israel, three from Poland, eleven from Germany, one from Belgium, and thirteen from the U.S. There was the added notation that the depositions of deceased survivors Goldfarb,

Turovsky, Lindvasser, and Rajgrodski would be introduced. The charges were followed by a request to keep Demjanjuk in jail until the end of the trial.

Ernie Meyer wrote in *The Jerusalem Post*, "The indictment makes hair-raising reading even to those well acquainted with the facts of the Holocaust."

On October 1, Chief Justice Meir Shamgar appointed the panel to hear the Demjanjuk case. Justice Dov Levin would preside; District Court Judges Zvi Tal and Dalia Dorner would also serve.

As a judge, Dov Levin was thought to be easygoing during the proceedings and stern in the verdict and sentencing. Eschewing neither a purely liberal nor conservative stance, Levin's decisions could be characterized only as a "case-by-case" approach. His clerks said he was able to dictate quickly a cogent opinion that was elegantly phrased. He was said to have been chosen for the case because of his reputation for "managing" a trial and because, being a recent appointment to the Supreme Court, trial experience was not so distant in his memory.

Judge Tal, an orthodox Jew, was known as a strong supporter of defendants' rights; Judge Dorner, a former military judge, was thought to be tough on prosecutors and defense counsels alike. All in all, the three judges, one religious, one a woman, none a Holocaust survivor, was deemed a good team by the Israeli legal community.

Under Israeli law, the defense has sixty days after the indictment to prepare its case. O'Connor began by taking the offensive. He described the detention hearings at the prison as a "star chamber process." "We will prove on an almost day-to-day basis the whereabouts of John Demjanjuk," O'Connor told the Associated Press (AP) when the indictment was filed. He claimed it was an injustice to learn the charges and evidence seven months after Demjanjuk had been incarcerated. But, of course, he knew full well the charges and much of the survivor testimony. What he was not prepared for was the quantity of foreign documents the prosecution had assembled from archives in Germany and Poland. They provided indexes and summaries, and O'Connor was overwhelmed. Still, he was not one to let it show.

O'Connor talked to the press regularly. Once, he demanded police protection because of death threats made against the Demjanjuk family in Cleveland and his own family in Buffalo. He also lamented frequently that he could not find local counsel. The Israeli Bar Association provided a list of attorneys.

On October 15 *The Jerusalem Post* published a report about defense efforts in Poland. Jacek Wilczur, chief specialist at the Central Commission for the Investigation of Nazi War Crimes in Poland, said that several U.S. citizens and their Polish assistants had been trying for years to find "false witnesses" to help prove John Demjanjuk was not Ivan the Terrible.

Jerome Brentar reportedly visited Poland in 1984 and received from one Tadeus Bernarczyk a false description of Ivan the Terrible. James McDonald visited Poland at the end of September 1986. Residents near Treblinka reported McDonald's visits to authorities, saying he had told them exactly what evidence he sought. The Polish "witnesses" were promised trips to the U.S. and financial rewards that would be considered generous by Polish standards. Such promises had been made in the past, Wilczur said, and the central commission, which is part of the Polish judicial system, knew that McDonald, too, had employed this technique.

Frank Walus also made several trips to Poland on behalf of the defense, at Brentar's expense, to locate evidence. But there was no evidence that linked him to the effort to locate "false" witnesses.

The prosecution also had their doubts about the value of this testimony. They had listed Bernarczyk as a witness. This was meant to signal to the defense that the prosecution had information that, as one young prosecutor said, paraphrasing Shakespeare's Hamlet, "Something's rotten in Poland."

O'Connor's response, that "Wilczur's wild, unsupported claims smack of a typical KGB-style smear campaign, using Communist Party organs to discredit potential defense witnesses," failed to address the substance of the charges. But the fact that the prosecution seemed ready to call Bernarczyk gave a certain weight to the story— that and the fact that the defense never did call the Polish witnesses.

On October 19, O'Connor appealed the order to keep Demjanjuk in prison until the trial's outcome. O'Connor argued that because he wasn't allowed enough time to review the evidence against Demjanjuk, he couldn't offer a proper defense. On November 10, an Israeli Supreme Court Judge rejected the appeal. O'Connor was not present, nor had he arranged for anyone to appear for him.

O'Connor later explained that he had telephoned from Frankfurt and was surprised that a postponement could not be phoned in. "I begin to wonder," he told the press, "whether the Demjanjuk trial is becoming hallmarked by departures from the very principles of universal justice and human rights that the trial seeks to vindicate."

On November 18, O'Connor asked the court for a six-month delay; the three-judge panel instead scheduled the trial for January

19, 1987. O'Connor said he still had not found an Israeli lawyer to his liking. He was given a list of six available attorneys.

In the following weeks, former Justice Chaim Cohn said he was willing to join the defense and Tel Aviv attorney Gershon Orion said he had accepted a Bar Association proposal to assist O'Connor. But O'Connor engaged neither.

The next snag occurred when the court realized that it had set the trial date too late. Under Israeli law, a trial must begin sixty days after the indictment is issued; a postponement may be granted, but only if the defense agrees to it. O'Connor refused to make *any* agreement with the prosecution—even if it would grant him the delay he requested. Therefore, the trial had to begin by the end of November. At the same time, the defense learned that the court had rejected its appeal of Demjanjuk's remand to prison. Still, O'Connor would not agree to an extension. The judges decided to open the trial officially on November 26. At that time, they could recess until January.

John Demjanjuk was brought by police convoy to the Jerusalem District Court in East Jerusalem. The small courtroom was filled with Justice Ministry officials and the media. During the forty-minute hearing, Judge Levin asked whether Demjamjuk understood the charges against him. O'Connor replied that the defendant would waive further explanations. But Judge Levin insisted on hearing from the accused himself. Demjanjuk shouted in Ukrainian, "I am not Ivan the Terrible! I am innocent! They want to hang me!" The judge asked him to respond instead to the question, as posed. Demjanjuk said he understood the indictment; but was not the person to whom it referred.

Levin then asked O'Connor to respond to the indictment. O'Connor said he was not yet prepared to do so. But he did say: "The accused is not the man to whom the [indictment] refers." He complained that he had been able to review only 5 or 6 percent of the case documents. O'Connor asked "to reserve my plea till the beginning of the full trial." Levin replied that at this stage, that amounted to a plea of not guilty. The judge announced that the trial's next session would be in January. He hoped that by that time O'Connor would be more familiar with the prosecution material and would have an Israeli attorney to assist him.

The delay proved fortunate for the prosecution as well. In mid-December, Prime Minister Shimon Peres received a surprise phone call from Armand Hammer. The Soviets had granted him temporary custody of the Trawniki card. If the Prime Minister might dispatch someone to London . . . Peres did so immediately.

The envoy returned with a letter from Hammer. Enclosed was a small green cardboard document—the Trawniki card. It was the original. The Israelis could examine it as they liked. The Soviets requested only that the document be returned by Hammer when the Israelis were done with it. Also enclosed was a letter from S. Chetverikov, deputy head of the Department of the USA and Canada, Ministry of Foreign Affairs of the USSR, stating that "no other documents on Demjanjuk's case have been found." The card was taken directly to the Israel Police.

On December 30, Yoram Sheftel, a thirty-eight-year-old Israeli attorney, appeared in court for O'Connor. He announced that he was acting as O'Connor's assistant, and had come to seek a further delay in the case.

Sheftel, or "Sheffie" as he liked to be called, was not an unknown in Israel. He had more than ten years experience in criminal law. He was flamboyant, and he had taken several cases that had attracted tabloid attention.

Sheftel told the court that O'Connor, who had just returned to Israel on December 22, had to leave again suddenly. O'Connor had hastily summoned him to a 5:00 A.M. meeting at Ben-Gurion Airport to ask him to substitute for him at the hearing.

"We are very unhappy about the way in which Mr. O'Connor conducts himself," said Judge Levin. "We have granted him several delays: we, too, have schedules and we're treating him with kid gloves." But the court agreed to a one-month postponement until February 16, at the suggestion of the prosecution (which welcomed the additional month to prepare its case).

Sheftel later revealed he first met O'Connor in late November at Ayalon Prison. O'Connor had seen him there, meeting with clients, and watched as he was deferred to by guards and prisoners. It was clear he knew his way around. Sheftel said he knew immediately who O'Connor was and who his client was. They met, they talked, they came to terms: O'Connor was to be "lead counsel," Sheftel was to be defense adviser on Israeli criminal law and procedure. His expertise would be in Israeli police and identification procedures. At his own insistence, Sheftel would not cross-examine Holocaust survivors about their memory or Treblinka, only about police procedures and photo identifications.

But why would an Israeli defend Demjanjuk?

This was, Sheftel would say, the sort of case a lawyer dreams about, that comes once in a lifetime. It appealed to Sheftel's politics, which can best be described as anti-establishment. He leans to the right in matters of Israeli politics, and to the left on personal freedoms. Sheftel was strongly anti-Communist and suspicious of the

Soviet Union—the KGB was capable of any sort of treachery. More importantly, Sheftel was a militant Zionist. He resented the Israeli establishment for accepting the case: he believed the U.S. had forced this case upon them. He was angered that Israel wanted to use Demjanjuk, a "common Ukrainian peasant," as a scapegoat for having shirked its duty to prosecute Nazis for the last twenty-five years.

Sheftel's anti-establishment views were also reflected in his life-style. Slight in stature and build, he wore a closely trimmed beard and when not in his lawyer's robes, he was often seen in a Japanese T-shirt, love beads, and a key chain with the Playboy "bunny" logo attached to his pants buckle. He drove a white Porsche, one of the few in Israel.

With O'Connor as lead counsel, John Gill the documents expert, and Sheftel, local expert on police procedure and criminal law, the defense team was complete. But were they ready?

What distinguished this trial from routine cases was how well the broad outlines of the case were known to both sides beforehand. Like a symphony that has been performed by many orchestras, the testimonies of the survivors, and the Trawniki card, were not new to the players.

Eichmann's trial in Israel twenty-five years ago marked his first appearance in court. The testimony was unexpected. Here, many of the same witnesses had already testified in the United States. Demjanjuk himself had testified. In spite of this, or perhaps because of it, there was a certain drama awaiting.

Demjanjuk and his supporters had been given a decade to de-claim his innocence. The Israeli prosecutors had spent a year con-ducting extensive and exhaustive preparations. The burden was so much greater for the prosecution; the stakes, so much higher for the defense. Now, in Jerusalem, the symphony was to be given its final performance. All that preceded it was rehearsal.

CHAPTER 10

A Different Planet

Demjanjuk's trial began in earnest promptly at 8:30 A.M. on February 16, 1987.

"Good morning," Justice Levin told the assembled crowd of three hundred spectators and journalists. "Please be seated." He then turned to Demjanjuk's attorney: "Mr. O'Connor, please make preliminary arguments."

The first five rows of the courtroom had been cordoned off for dignitaries. Attending that day were Knesset members Dov Shilansky and Sheva Weiss, as well as official observers from the Polish Nazi War Crimes Commission, the Ukrainian Church Metropolitan from New York, and the children and grandchildren of the Holocaust survivors who were to testify.

The windowless hall could barely contain the tension.

O'Connor, now in his early forties, with close-cropped reddish hair and deep blue eyes, bespoke a certain intensity. Before formally addressing the court, he fiddled with his translation radio and adjusted his headphones. Levin suggested that rather than trouble with translation, he might try to learn Hebrew before the end of the trial. Everyone laughed; it was the last light moment that day.

O'Connor spent two-and-a-half hours arguing that even though Israel had the right to try Demjanjuk by virtue of universal jurisdiction, it should nonetheless return him to the United States because his identification was based on suspect Soviet-supplied evidence.

O'Connor was a theatrical performer. His black robe flowed as he strode across the stage, he waved his hands for emphasis or

94

clasped them in front like a country preacher. His face would tighten like a fist raised in anger; a moment later, his brows would smooth and widen to show his good cheer. His rhetoric was flavored with colorful phrases—some more colorful than relevant:

"If this is only the second time in history, with regard to the State of Israel, the young State of Israel, that the sword of St. Michael has been taken out in the use of long-arm jurisdiction to bring back into the House of Zion an international criminal, a criminal whose crimes offend all mankind, if, in fact, the second time around we have a situation where there is not the proper rationale, there is not the proper underpinnings in this case, and we do not get acquittal, what then does the world do with the precedent that's been set down by this tribunal, by this legal Sanhedrin?

"Even more heinous, Justice Honor, is the concept of a killer state determining that an individual, perhaps an Israeli citizen, is an enemy of all mankind. . . ."

Levin counseled O'Connor to remain focused on the legal aspects of jurisdiction.

"A lot of the prosecutors and the defense counsel came to this country shackled with the chains of legal obfuscation," O'Connor said. "In the power of this tribunal we will be able, unlike in the forum of the United States, to disperse the fog that surrounded it dialectically and rhetorically before it came to Israel."

Judge Levin was confused: "Should we, in fact, have the hearing in order to disperse the fog—and to find there is no evidence against the accused—or should we not deal with the case all together because we don't have the jurisdiction? What is your exact argument?"

Levin suggested they begin the hearing; O'Connor could save his arguments for the defense's opening address. But O'Connor begged the court's indulgence: once the witnesses appeared, the moment would be lost forever. "History is a fickle bride, Your Honor. She must be treated properly, because unfortunately, in this situation, if we were to pass over, at the critical stage, the jurisdictional issues that are involved, and lay them in concrete so that there is no question of what must be decided at the appellate level, if necessary, I fear that in the heat of the adversary environments, which we will have before us today, to forge justice, that it will be lost forever. We will no longer have the respect of the bride, which is all so important."

Did O'Connor believe that the State of Israel had jurisdiction over Ivan the Terrible? Judge Dalia Dorner asked. O'Connor said he would show there was not one "scintilla of evidence that this human animal had the first name of Ivan or the last name of

Grozny." Nor was there any evidence, he said, that Ivan of Treblinka's last name was Demjanjuk. "I have a solemn responsibility to defend the life of my client against Ivan Grozny, the archetypal figure."

Levin reminded him, "To prove something you need evidence, but we are at the stage where no evidence has been produced."

O'Connor turned to his next argument: speciality. Under Israeli law, the rule of speciality holds that one can be tried only for the crimes on which the extradition is based. As the U.S. order was based on charges of murder, Demjanjuk could not be tried under the Nazi and Nazi Collaborators Law. The naming of specific acts of murder in the extradition order, he argued, reduced the charge to common-law murder.

Defense counsel Sheftel, called upon to elucidate, said he believed in the innocence of the accused, but felt compelled to comment on the defects of the extradition. If the indictment and extradition do not match, he argued, they fail.

Prosecutor Gouldman said the facts at issue *were* the same—the murder of Jews in the gas chambers and the murder of Jewish forced-laborers in the camp. The United States was aware that Demjanjuk would be tried in Israel under the Nazi and Nazi Collaborators Law. Gouldman argued, "The issue is to decide the nature of the crime and not the technical interpretation of the term in one or another country. . . ." Demjanjuk was on trial for the exact same offense that had brought him to court in the U.S. and that had been at the very heart of the extradition request.

The morning's pace had been slow and the arguments tedious; by 11:30, the first break was welcome. After the recess, O'Connor reiterated his argument, this time insisting that the court, in effect, was being asked to denigrate the Eichmann case. "It's been asked to fit common-law murder into genocide." The only course left open, O'Connor said, was to return Demjanjuk to the U.S. for proper trial.

Conversely, Sheftel argued that Israeli law made a clear distinction between murder and the crimes of the Nazi and Nazi Collaborators Law. If Demjanjuk was extradited to be tried for murder, then he could be punished only in accordance with the charge of murder. It was no small difference: in Israel, murder carries a maximum penalty of life imprisonment, as opposed to the Nazi and Nazi Collaborators Law, which allows for the death penalty. Because of the confusion, Sheftel argued, the court should seek an opinion from the U.S. Secretary of State.

Levin promised to rule later. He asked O'Connor to state formally whether there was an alibi in the case. O'Connor seemed unprepared to proceed, and asked for a break. But Levin countered: "We have time to listen to it here and now for as long as necessary."

After a few verbal clarifications, O'Connor explained that there was nothing incriminating about the accused's first name: "The man sitting behind me and in front of his son, Johnny, is John Demjanjuk. When living in Ukraine in the Vinitza region, he was Ivan Demjanjuk as Mr. Sharansky was Anatoly and now he is Natan." Demjanjuk, O'Connor said, had been caught up in a whirlwind of three great powers—the United States, the USSR, and Israel, each proceeding in this case with different political objectives.

"John Demjanjuk has never been in any death camp in any capacity." O'Connor admitted that he wasn't prepared to formally present Demjanjuk's alibi, but he could bring forth some of its details from memory (the alibi was later submitted in writing): Demjanjuk was transferred to Chelm, O'Connor said, and kept there in inhumane conditions for eighteen months, beyond the period in question; at no time did he operate the gas chamber at Flossenburg, Regensburg, or Sobibor.

The next break was at 1:00 P.M. The judges left; Demjanjuk was led out. Suddenly an elderly man stood up and began to shout. He identified himself as a Holocaust survivor. Mordechai Fuchs was his name. He started to scream at the accused. The police led him out. Then another survivor, Yisrael Yehezekeli, started to shout. He knew the Ukrainians, he said. He had lost his whole family to them. "They're lying," he said, motioning to the empty defense area. The TV crews rushed back in. The security guards thought it better to let him calm down rather than remove him forcibly. He was crying: "All my family was killed . . . why did the judges let this man speak and they don't let me speak? I have to get it off my chest . . . why do they let them tell such lies? I knew the Red Army." After a few moments, he was led outside.

John Demjanjuk Jr., a tall, soft-spoken man of twenty-one, had arrived in Israel a few days earlier. A church member had donated the cost of his travel. Now he, too, left the courtroom. His eyes were small and dark with jet lag. He had visited his father in jail and found him in good spirits and spiritually well with a Ukrainian prayer book in his cell. His father had gained a few pounds since he last saw him, but as the son said, "He's had nothing to do but write letters."

Levin began the afternoon session by ruling that Israel did have jurisdiction to try Demjanjuk under the Nazi and Nazi Collaborators Law.

Sheftel said the defense was willing to admit all facts stated in the indictment up to Demjanjuk's POW internment; and it would even admit that there was a monster named Ivan Grozny. But the defense categorically denied that this monster's surname was Demjanjuk, "simply because not a single survivor ever said so in testimony." In fact, said Sheftel, many had spoken of the death of Ivan Grozny.

Sheftel asked that the prosecution, in its opening remarks, speak only of Demjanjuk and not of the Holocaust or Treblinka. "After forty years of research and study of the Holocaust, every person with a reasonable amount of education anywhere in the world, unless he declares himself to be anti-Semitic, knows full well the main facts," he said.

But Judge Levin disagreed: "A great many people in the world and in Israel, too, and even in this hall, do not know all the facts in full detail." Levin said it was possible that the evidence should be narrowed, but one just couldn't take it for granted that every person in Israel, or even in the courtroom, knew all the facts of the "Final Solution."

"Does this court feel," Judge Levin said, "that all the facts referring to what happened in the camps, which the indictment refers to, are or have been brought to our knowledge? They have not. And it is as simple as that."

Yonah Blatman, the State Attorney, rose to present his case. "Before us stands an accused by the name of John Demjanjuk. He is the Demjanjuk who has been known as 'Ivan the Terrible' and he stands before you accused of the most terrible crimes ever committed in the course of history. . . .

"Until the Second World War nobody considered that millions of men, women, and children, naked, could be driven with the help of whips and iron rods into the gas chambers, where they were gassed and were taken out dead."

Thus began Blatman, his gray hair a mop, his salt-and-pepper mustache adding a professorial air to his comments. He stood slightly hunched, his glasses sliding low on his nose, as he read from his notes. He seemed to list to his right as he spoke.

Demjanjuk and his son listened impassively. Demjanjuk leaned his face against his right wrist.

Blatman stopped occasionally to gulp water. Pointing to a map of Poland that stood on an easel behind him, Blatman identified the areas where the majority of Polish Jewry had once lived. And he showed the remote areas where the three camps were established, Belzec in March 1942, Sobibor in May 1942, Treblinka in July 1943. "They were active for a year-and-a-half and in them one-million-eight-hundred-thousand Jews were exterminated." Blatman also pointed out the Trawniki camp near Lublin, which served as a training camp for Ukrainian guards—"among them John Demjanjuk," he said.

Blatman told of the freight trains that brought Jews to the extermination camps and returned only with their possessions. Without the trains, said Blatman, "it would have been impossible to carry out this diabolic plan." He promised to introduce records of the transports as evidence.

Only a handful of Treblinka's Jewish laborers managed to escape in the August 1943 revolt. "The rumor was circulated that Ivan had been killed at the time of the revolt," he said. "This court is going to show how false this rumor was."

The extermination camps were shrouded in a veil of secrecy, Blatman said. German documents referred to them only in euphemisms. Secrecy oaths were taken, and relevant documents destroyed. Even today, a visitor to Treblinka finds no trace of the actual camp; it was all hidden, he said, destroyed so the world would never know, never believe. It would seem, Blatman suggested, that the murderers who took their lives had also sought to deprive them of their deaths. "The more Jews they slaughtered, the fewer witnesses remained to testify to the atrocities." But the Nazis didn't succeed, he said, in eradicating the facts from the annals of history: "The survivors who lived through the most horrendous deeds in the history of mankind have not forgotten the Nazis and cannot forget what the Nazis perpetrated against them."

Blatman now set the individual acts back into the larger context: "How could it happen that precisely when human culture arrived at such a pinnacle of success, the concept of mass annihilation was invented? . . . How is it possible that a people that gave rights to some of the finest minds, philosophies, and ethics also conceived of the concept of genocide? . . . How can it be [that] precisely the same people who were considered to be the inferior races were willing to cooperate in perpetrating this horrendous deed?"

Blatman highlighted the landmarks in the rise of Nazism. In Nazi ideology, the supremacy of the Aryan race was unquestioned, as was the inferiority of the Jewish race. The doctrine of Hitler, as the Nazis rose to power, and Nazi policies toward the Jews, were intertwined. The government allowed and encouraged the looting of Jewish property and the burning of synagogues, as long as there was no threat to *German* life. In 1935, the Nuremberg laws were enacted, stripping Jews of German citizenship. Harassment increased, culminating in the infamous *Kristallnacht* ("night of the broken glass"), on November 10, 1938.

As Germany extended beyond its own borders, so did its policies of hatred toward Jews. "The German occupiers saw fit in all cases to find those who would collaborate with them in the countries occupied. . . . We will prove that Ivan Demjanjuk is one of those taken prisoner who collaborated with Germans."

Fault lay not with the Ukrainian nation or all of its people, said Blatman. Though the testimonies of survivors are rife with tales of persecution by Ukrainian nationals in the ghettos and in the camps, this was not the case with all Ukrainians: "Everywhere there were some who did not agree with what was going on. That was their moment of glory. There were some individuals who risked their own lives to save Jews. . . ." "But," Blatman continued, "this was but a drop in the sea of hatred toward Jews."

In part because his face had been partially paralyzed (the result of a stroke), in part because of his professorial manner, there were no dramatics in Blatman's presentation. His comments were delivered straightforwardly. There was no art to his oratory. Yet the courtroom spectators strained to hear every word.

"As the Nazis perpetrated their plans, their attitude toward human life became more and more nonchalant," Blatman explained. They began by murdering their own mentally ill. In 1939, the euthanasia program was established. Dozens were employed to help kill the mentally ill by pumping carbon monoxide into "sick" rooms. In July 1941, the wholesale killing of Jews and Communists began; they were gathered and shot as the Germans conquered new territories.

In September 1941, Nazis at Auschwitz began experimenting with a gas known as Zyklon B. At about the same time, thousands of Jews were put to death in mobile gassing trucks driven to, and from, the Chelmno camp. Not long after, many of the officials in the euthanasia program were assigned to supervise the use of mobile gas chambers, which were attached to a high-power gas pipe. This was the beginning of Operation Reinhard. But for the Nazis, killing Jews was not enough—there had to be an economic benefit as well—so the death camps were born: Jewish possessions could be plundered before deportation, and after, healthy Jews could be put to work. But when they had fulfilled their usefullness to their tormentors, *then* they would be murdered.

Demjanjuk looked alternately interested and bored; sometimes he yawned. There were school girls in the audience, and the defendant's seeming indifference caused many of them to shudder. If he was guilty wouldn't he . . . wouldn't he commit suicide? How could he be such a good father, grandfather, husband?

Blatman read from a presentation Heinrich Himmler made to SS officers on October 4, 1943:

I want, in all sincerity, to present to you a very difficult chapter, and we must discuss this most frankly. Nonetheless, we will never talk about it in public. I am now referring to the evacuation of the Jews, to the annihilation of the Jewish people. This belongs to those matters that can be uttered easily. The Jewish people will be destroyed, says every party member. It says clearly in our platform that the Jewish people must be destroyed, and we are carrying this out. But how can one stand up to all this? There is a certain amount of frailty involved sometimes. . . . We have been forced to carry out this most difficult task. It is a glorious page in our history, but it is one that has never been recorded, and never will be. We have taken their wealth. . . . All in all, we are entitled to say that at this point, that out of a love of our people, we have fulfilled this difficult task, and this has not caused any damage to our soul, to our spirit, and to our character.

"The question therefore arises," Blatman continued, "should one judge a person for acts committed forty-five years ago—and is indeed Israel the proper place to do so?" He reviewed the line of legal decisions and declarations beginning with the Allied Declaration on January 13, 1942, followed by the laws of the international court of Nuremberg concerning war crimes and the crimes against humanity that were recognized by the United Nations' General Assembly in December 1946. The UN further affirmed that genocide was a crime punishable by international law. Nazi war crimes, each and every one, were recognized as subject to international jurisdiction. The charter of the Nuremberg trial, which was emended and ratified by the UN General Assembly, was adopted by the Israeli Parliament, the Knesset, in its complete text, as part of the Nazi and Nazi Collaborators Law of 1950.

"That the Jewish people, who were the object of such crimes, became the subject to try the criminal is a great historic right," Blatman said. The right of Israel to enact such a law, even though it was established after the Holocaust, and to try criminals under this law, was challenged and upheld at the time of the Eichmann trial by the Supreme Court of Israel as being in accordance with the law of nations and international law. And the arguments put forward to halt Demjanjuk's extradition were rejected by the U.S. courts.

There were some who said Demjanjuk was no Eichmann. "While

Eichmann was a bureaucrat and a planner of these atrocities, a bureaucrat who even was taken aback and frightened when he witnessed these atrocities," Blatman said, "Demjanjuk had an actual hand in perpetrating these acts. In our view, he actually had a hand in pushing and shoving hundreds of thousands of victims of Eichmann and, in fact, committed atrocities on them before they went into the gas chamber."

Blatman continued: "Some forty years have passed since then, but in no way does this diminish the ability or the responsibility to identify Demjanjuk. . . . We will leave no doubt about the identity of Ivan the Terrible."

John Jr. slid down in his seat.

Michael Shaked, the lead prosecutor, rose to outline the evidence. One hand on the table, one on his waist, Shaked related the broad outlines of how the case came to Israel's attention through the investigation of police officer Miriam Radiwker; how in the course of the U.S. investigation, the Trawniki card came to light.

The first witness, Yitzhak Arad, who was chairman of the Holocaust Memorial institution, Yad Vashem, would provide the historical background. This was necessary, Shaked said, because the testimonies of survivors "seem to be taken from a different planet."

"However," he said, "we would be escaping reality were we to attribute these deeds to some distant planet. It is true they took place in the very cradle of European civilization and it is, of course, very difficult for us as human beings to comprehend a single moment of what took place at Treblinka. In fact, it is inconceivable for us to either understand or believe that such a phenomenon as the transportation of human beings in cattle cars, six thousand or eight thousand human beings in cattle cars, to a train station, actually took place. To believe that two hours later, this entire human cargo disappeared in the gas chamber as though it had never existed, and the train was to return with the clothing, with the teeth in well-sorted packages for recycling. This is something that, when recounted here, simply can not be grasped. Human nature seeks to escape these descriptions. Human nature, I believe, can not fully take in, can not comprehend the phenomenon of what happened at Treblinka."

The weight of the description of Treblinka seemed to deaden the judges' faces; Demjanjuk lazily scratched at his.

Shaked continued: Survivors who came to Israel and began recounting what they had seen, were thought mad. Dr. Arad's testimony would make understanding the Holocaust no easier, but Shaked felt it vital to present the historical chronology, "so that those nightmares can be anchored in the documents, in the testimony, in the contemporary history of the Third Reich." He also promised to provide experts who would confirm the historical background of the Trawniki card and authenticate the photograph as John Demjanjuk's.

Returning to the testimony of survivors, Shaked said that the prosecution would call to the witness stand only those survivors who had worked in the death-camp area and were in close daily proximity to the accused and had looked into his eyes. Many years had gone by, Shaked acknowledged; at Treblinka, the witnesses were in their late teens or early twenties, today they are in their sixties. "Of course, there are questions of repression, suppression, of forgetting, and there are, on the other hand, those of memory, which accompany them for the rest of their lives." It is the recognition of Demjanjuk that guarantees that those who pointed at Demjanjuk's picture, Shaked said, were, in fact, pointing at the Demjanjuk who was at Treblinka, the man they knew at the camp.

Over the years, Demjanjuk had often contradicted himself. Shaked promised to clear up those contradictions by using Demjanjuk's own previous statements and the testimony of expert witnesses. Shaked paused. "There can be no doubt," he said, "this may be one of the last trials where it is possible to bring to the stand witnesses who can say, 'We were there, we saw what happened with our own eyes. We can testify as to what happened.'"

The school girls sat quietly, tears in their eyes.

"The subject sooner or later will have to step down from the witness stand and become a part of history."

CHAPTER 11

The Biggest Cemetery

As Holocaust historian Dr. Yitzhak Arad took the stand, defense counsel Sheftel objected. The defense did not, Sheftel said, dispute the Holocaust or dispute the existence of Ivan Grozny. There would be no need even to cross-examine Dr. Arad on historical context, even on a single point. But, Sheftel said, "if the prosecution insists on calling Dr. Arad—we submit that this is not for the sake of this hearing, but for the sake of the sixteen television cameras in the hall . . . to turn this into a show trial for the sake of the mass media. The most outstanding example in history of this are the Moscow trials. . . ."

Levin fumed with anger: "This remark should not have been sounded in an Israeli courtroom. The court is interested in factual and historical background. . . . [Dr. Arad's] testimony seems to us to be of importance."

As Dr. Arad stood at the witness stand, dressed in jacket and striped tie, he could have passed easily for a university professor. He was short and sprightly. His glasses framed a broad, cheerful face topped by curly dark hair. He spoke into the microphone in a clear, strong voice. Born in Lithuania in 1926, he was in Warsaw when the war broke out. He managed to return to his Soviet home-town, but not all his family was so lucky. Other members died in the Holocaust, some in Treblinka. Since 1972 he had been chairman of Yad Vashem, Israel's Holocaust Memorial Authority. He was the author of a book about the Operation Reinhard camps—

Belzec, Sobibor, and Treblinka—that had been published in 1987 in the United States.

Dr. Arad described Treblinka as "the biggest cemetery of Polish Jewry." Treblinka, he said, was not a mere haphazard event, but the outcome of human deeds, fueled by a history of anti-Semitism, that began in the early 1930s with Hitler's speeches, followed by sanctioned persecution of Jews. "Ghetto-ization" was merely the next phase in the overall plan for the annihilation of the Jews.

He described at length the work of T4, the institute at 4 Tiergardenstrasse near Berlin, that promoted euthanasia for the mentally deficient and handicapped. Arad told how the T4 personnel trained in the techniques of death later became involved in the death camps.

After the German army invaded the Soviet Union in June 1941, orders were given to four SS *Einsatzgruppen* to destroy the Jews in conquered Soviet regions. Pogroms against the Jews were encouraged by the local populations, Dr. Arad testified, and Jewish POW camps were selected for "special treatment"—death.

Documents were introduced to show that on July 31, 1941, Reichmarshall Goering wrote of going ahead with the necessary preparation for the *Gesamtlosung*—the "comprehensive solution" of the Jewish problem. Official acts by Hitler, Himmler, and Heydrich led to the "Final Solution" at the Wansee Conference on January 21, 1942.

Arad described how the T4 program begat the killing vans of Chelmno and how Odilo Globochnik, the SS and police commander of the General Gouvernement in Lublin, received the order from Himmler to establish the three extermination camps of Operation Reinhard—Belzec, Sobibor, and Treblinka.

Dr. Irmfried Eberl, who had directed Operation Euthanasia, was Treblinka's first commander. He was replaced by Franz Stangl, who previously was commander at Sobibor. Stangl's deputy commander at Treblinka was Kurt Franz, who had been an SS officer at Belsec. In the last days of Treblinka, Franz would be its third and final commander.

Possessions taken from the Jews at Treblinka were valued at 178 million Reichmarks—$445 million dollars.

Dr. Arad explained that only about thirty-five German SS men were assigned to each camp, but that they were assisted by some one hundred and ten auxiliaries, most of whom were Soviet citizens recruited from German POW camps. They were trained at the Trawniki camp, not far from Treblinka and Sobibor.

The auxiliaries were given military drilling and dressed in dark brown or black uniforms. They were organized into units, and sent either to the ghettos, where they were involved in roundups, acts of brutality, and liquidations of the ghetto, or to the extermination camps.

Dr. Arad turned to the large photographs mounted on the wall behind him. He explained that they were photographs of a model of Treblinka constructed by Yankel Viernik, a survivor of the camp. The model was inexact in some respects, but accurately represented the landmarks of the camp. As Dr. Arad described the model, Demjanjuk peered to get a better look.

Arad told of life at Treblinka, speaking matter-of-factly, yet in fast, sometimes indignant bursts. He detailed the daily routines, the discipline of the camp, the division of labor, the different assignments. As he talked, he seemed to be staring Demjanjuk in the eye.

He told of Ivan and Nikolai and how, in his historical research, their names had turned up in the deposition of Stangl at the first Dusseldorf trial, and in the trials of the Treblinka men in Dusseldorf, Germany, in 1964 and 1970.

When Arad described the uprising, he estimated there were seven hundred Jews in the entire camp that day; one hundred and fifty were able to escape. Of those, Arad said, "only fifty or sixty actually lived to the day of liberation."

Levin asked, as if he had heard wrong, "Do we take it that from all those who went through the Treblinka camp, only some fifty or sixty survived?"

"Yes, only fifty."

Arad further testified that one German was wounded and two or three Ukrainians were killed in the uprising.

There were rumors of Ivan's death, he said, but no one actually saw him dead. Arad had interviewed Avraham Goldfarb, one of the survivors who had recounted Ivan's death. "I asked him whether he had actually seen Ivan the Terrible being killed. His answer was, 'No, I did not see it.' He had merely heard of it."

Dr. Arad had scoured all available research and had never found anyone who admitted to killing Ivan or to seeing him dead. Because there were no transports on that day or the preceding ones, Arad believed that Ivan and Nikolai had nothing to do in the death camp at the time of the revolt. And SS officer Gustav Munzberger had testified at his trial at Dusseldorf that Ivan had fought with him among the partisans in Italy after the closing of the camp.

Finally, the prosecution had compiled a painstakingly comprehensive record of train transports from Jewish communities to Treblinka that Blatman wished to submit as corroboration of the more than eight-hundred-seventy-thousand murders. Prosecutors felt the impact of the statistics would remain vivid in the judges' memory long after Arad had left the stand. It had taken months to assemble this information. But Levin would not allow its admission. The records of the train transports, he said, were not facts the defense disputed.

Sheftel had said Dr. Arad would not be cross-examined by the defense, yet O'Connor now rose to do so. He spent the next day-and-a-half reviewing the geographical details of Treblinka. Finally, Arad told him in exasperation, "I wasn't there."

But O'Connor's intent was clear. After Dr. Arad had difficulty identifying a certain place on the photo-model, O'Connor said, "[If Dr. Arad] can't from the representation decide what one of the critical elements of the government's case, in terms of evidence, is, how can any of the other things be clearly defined when the eyewitnesses, who are not experts, come and turn to that map?" Levin admonished him that such remarks were best saved for summation.

Another set of O'Connor's questions sought to determine who could see what from where: if the *Schlauch* ("the tube" or path between Camp One and Camp Two) extended to a certain point; if the embankment was a certain height; if those in the Lower Camp knew what was occurring in the Upper Camp.

During the afternoon session, the room became so crowded that eighty people were left outside. Despite all press predictions to the contrary, word of mouth was transforming the trial into an event. The crowd was a mixture of young and old, Sephardic and Ashkenazic, students and soldiers, the observant and the nonpracticing.

Indeed it was becoming a place at which an appearance *had* to be made. In the afternoon, Justice Minister Abraham Sharir put in a fifteen-minute appearance. A week later, Prime Minister Yitzhak Shamir would also stop by. The court office was busy scheduling visits for schools and Army units throughout the country.

A great many Hasidim attended, which was surprising, given so secular an event. Shalmi Balmor, the education director of Yad Vashem, speculated: "They are obsessed with the Holocaust, each in a personal fashion because they never discuss it at their Yeshiva. They can not deal theologically with the question: If there is a God, why did He let the murder of the six million occur?" But an Israel government press adviser had a different view: "It's free, they don't have jobs they have to be at. They can't go to movies or theater so this is an acceptable performance."

O'Connor tried to get Dr. Arad to admit that it was unlikely that Demjanjuk could have been Ivan Grozny of Treblinka. Was it possible that a twenty-two-year-old Ukrainian Red Army soldier and POW could murder repeatedly, and do so with sadistic glee? Demjanjuk was never part of the T4 euthanasia staff; only its members, he argued, were psychologically inured to killing. O'Connor repeated the phrase "T4" in his questions as if, mantralike, the judges would be convinced that only T4 staff could have operated the gas chambers. O'Connor also implied that the Germans would have recruited only tall blond Aryans—not a dark-haired Ukrainian such as Demjanjuk. But Dr. Arad found no factual basis for O'Connor's conjectures.

O'Connor also suggested that not every member of the "Ukrainian units" was Ukrainian. Dr. Arad confirmed that the Soviet POWs included other nationalities, and even some ethnic Germans born on Soviet territory, but there was no question that the "Ukrainian" staff of Treblinka included many Ukrainians. Then O'Connor wondered whether a lowly Ukrainian—as opposed to a commanding German—would be entrusted with operating the gas chambers. Arad answered that the gas chambers at Treblinka were supervised by the Germans Matthes and Schmidt, but they were known to be operated by two Ukrainians—Ivan and Nikolai.

O'Connor attempted to show that Jewish workers had no face-to-face contact with Ivan. Arad, however, testified, "I have no doubt that the people who were involved in this terrible work for weeks and even months had an opportunity to look in the faces of the Germans and Ukrainians who made them do this work." Questioned further, Arad said there was direct *contact:* "They stood one facing the other."

Now O'Connor pressed further: Would those who thought themselves the highest form of life speak to the lowest? And would the work-Jews dare speak to the SS face-to-face? By way of explanation, Arad told of the Jewish musicians who performed for the Germans and Ukrainians. He said, one survivor, Rajgrodski, recalled in testimony to Yad Vashem that Ivan and Nikolai "liked these songs and were very impressed by our playing." Arad said there were many opportunities for the workers to observe the Germans and Ukrainians.

Next Sheftel took up the cross-examination. He tried to confront Dr. Arad with the testimony of survivors who claimed that Ivan had been killed.

Sheftel quoted the late Shlomo Hellman, a survivor who told Yad Vashem in 1961 that during the uprising, the Jewish inmates "overpowered the Germans, and Ivan the Terrible was overpowered and was pushed into the furnace. At the first camp there was heavy battle, and I set the gas chambers on fire together with others and began to escape. . . ."

Arad said he was familiar with the testimony but doubted its veracity: "The description of this whole passage, which is very heroic—the overpowering of the Germans, even of Ivan, the heavy fighting, setting the gas chambers on fire—I took this to be a heroic description. . . ." Arad pointed out that Hellman also spoke of the killing of Matthes; but Matthes lived and was convicted at the Dusseldorf trial. Kuttner was the only German wounded during the uprising, he said once again.

As for Rosenberg, Dr. Arad said, "It is not as though Rosenberg had seen this. It seems to be more wishful thinking than what actually happened. Ivan the Terrible was such a hated figure that his killing became a symbol of the revolt's success." But might it not be "wishful thinking," Sheftel asked, that motivated the identifications by the survivors? Levin disallowed the inquiry: "That is a question for a psychologist, not a historian."

At the end of his testimony, Dr. Arad asked if he could make a short statement. Levin said no. But after Dr. Arad left the courtroom, the reporters were waiting. He told them he wanted to stress that not all Ukrainians were like Ivan the Terrible. "This is important to stress," he said. "Hundreds of thousands of Ukrainians fought loyally in the Red Army to defeat Nazism and many gave their lives. Even in the camps there were other sorts of Ukrainians. I feel I have to say this."

No one could know beforehand what it would feel like to hear of the murders at Treblinka in a courtroom in Jerusalem in 1987. So far, it had not been so painful, or so incredible. When Arad spoke of the open pits and the more than eight-hundred-seventy-thousand dead, no one gasped. Treblinka was largely hidden in the mountain of minutiae presented on the stand. Ivan and his crimes were still far away—on that "other planet" of which Shaked had spoken. Yet the crowds that grew each day signaled that the trial was taking hold in a way no one in Israel had imagined possible. The French use the word *procès* for trial; that seemed appropriate. A process was under way. The fact of Treblinka was again in the air.

A Jerusalem cab driver, Max, described the first days of the trial to one reporter as "calm." He was right: there was the genteel manner of Yonah Blatman; the politeness of O'Connor; Judge Levin's touches of irony, the silence of Judges Tal and Dorner. Even Demjanjuk looked calm.

For all of Israel, the sport of Demjanjuk-watching had begun. Whether on television or in person, Demjanjuk—his big, round head, his large hands—was mesmerizing. His face was not intelligent but neither was it troubled. His glasses gave him a contemplative look. He often sat with his mouth half open. There was an idiot-savant look to him. Was he truly so simple? Or something far worse? To look at him, was to see passivity; yet it was not hard to sense anger brewing within. It was not impossible to imagine a younger, leaner, angrier man.

O'Connor's questions meandered, but his flamboyant court manner, his exaggerated courteousness, held the promise of a hidden agenda. O'Connor was zealous in his defense, red-flagging the record with his comments. Israelis were not used to such courtroom theatrics, and so his behavior created suspense and drama in the trial. What was he getting at? How would this affect the case? Was there a kind of chess game at work, where a question and answer now, like a crafty opening, would have ramifications later? By the end of the trial's first week, O'Connor had captured the interest of the Israeli public. Many said that he was trying to make points for some imaginary jury. But for O'Connor, the public *was* the jury.

Each night after the trial, the prosecuting attorneys would retreat to their offices to continue working. The press would wait. After the public had cleared the hall, Demjanjuk was led through the courtroom and into a police van. On the night that ended the first week of testimony, as he passed by the officers he laughed merrily and said, *Leila Tov* ("Good evening" in Hebrew). They laughed, too, and shrugged.

Somewhat later the defense attorneys left the convention center. They got into a small white rented Subaru. John Jr. drove O'Connor and Gill to the American Colony Hotel, where they were staying. A few minutes later, Sheftel got into his white Porsche.

The American Colony Hotel in East Jerusalem is a former pasha's residence. The staff is mostly Arab; the food, nonkosher; the decoration, Moorish. The bar is a well-known hangout for foreign journalists. Each night after court, members of the defense team, as well as Demjanjuk family members, were willing to talk to the press about the trial. At first, they spoke with confidence about their performance, the innocence of their client, and their inevitable vindication.

On the Sunday evening after the first week of the trial, the mood at the American Colony was upbeat. The first Holocaust survivor was to testify the next day, and the defense was sure that discrepancies would be brought out to prove that the wrong man had been accused. But none could deny the strain. And John Jr., not yet hardened by the trial, broke down in tears in front of a Cleveland journalist, expressing his frustration that it was *his father* at whom everyone had been staring. And it was his father whom the first survivor would accuse tomorrow.

CHAPTER 12

The Survivors' Tale

The question was: Did the survivors remember what they could not forget? Did they really know this Ivan? What was the nature, duration, and quality of their contact with him? Under what circumstances were their observations made? What did they observe him doing? How often did they see him? And why, after forty years, would they remember *him*?

This was critical: When they looked at the photospread in 1976, or 1978 or 1980, why did they pick Demjanjuk? On what was their identification based? How definite was it? Was it assured? Was it immediate? Was it spontaneous? Were there reservations, and if so, what were they?

The answers to these questions would not turn on subjective feelings but on the facts of the evidence. The police reports, with their identifications, would be corroborated by the survivors as well as the investigators themselves. Was there any reason not to take them as fact? The answer would be found in the courtroom, and on this, in effect, the whole case rested.

"My name is Epstein, Pinhas. Son of Dov and Sara. I was born in Czestochowa in 1925 on the third of March. I lived together with my parents and the other members of our family in Czestochowa until the day we were removed from there and we were taken to the place where we were taken." With these words began the testimony of the first survivor to appear in the case, Pinhas Epstein.

To the listener today—after a half-century of Holocaust accounts—each survivor's tale can sound remarkably similar; the hor-

111

ror becomes routine. Whether a story takes place in Warsaw, or Czestochowa; at Treblinka, or another camp—it is one tale of ghettos, roundups, boxcar trains, brutal arrivals. Even the commandants seem alike—imperious, arbitrary, cruel in surprising ways. Stories of dogs trained to bite genitals: even that, is heard more than once.

Yet for each survivor, his or her individual experiences were unlike another's. Words fail to communicate the humiliations, and degradations. To be at a camp, one survivor has said, was like receiving a hard slap on the face, from which one reeled, surprised, stunned, dazed, hurt. And then another; and then another . . .

Because, or in spite, of this, the testimony of the survivors in Jerusalem was never less than compelling. As they took the stand, the entire country seemed to come to a standstill. The trial was broadcast live on television and radio. It was broadcast everywhere: on public buses, in every shop, in people's offices and their homes. Drivers on the way to work would pull their cars over to pay closer attention to the radio.

For a nation that had heard enough of the Holocaust, for a generation that had learned it all in school—well, they *knew*, but they *didn't know*. No one had anticipated the pull of the truth, the power of the survivors' tale. No one had realized that while all slaps may feel alike, each hurt is unique.

No survivor had seen everything, or had known everything. And in court, no survivor could tell everything they had seen or known of Treblinka. But what they did tell painted a nightmare world. Dr. Arad had given the context of events, but he could not speak for the survivors. A generation needed to be reminded in a courtroom in Jerusalem that no account of the Holocaust, no testimony of Treblinka, could speak for the survivors themselves.

Epstein, who was sixty-two, had retired from his job as a heavy-machinery operator with Solel Boneh, an Israeli construction company. A tall, sturdy man with wavy reddish hair and gold-rimmed glasses, he had the look of a scientist. He wore a brown sports jacket, but radiated a certain formality. He spoke with conviction and the entire room fell silent for his testimony.

Pinhas Epstein was fifteen in 1940, when the Czestochowa ghetto was established. For the next two years, he was idle: Jews could neither go to school or work. He recalled that on the evening following Yom Kippur, the doorbell rang at each and every house in the ghetto. Jews were ordered out and taken to the railroad station. There they were forced to board boxcars. He was separated from his family.

Soon after arriving at Treblinka, Epstein was ordered to accompany an old woman to the "lazarette." As far as he knew, a lazarette was an infirmary. But not at Treblinka. When he arrived at the so-called lazarette, he found a pit. In it were two live babies. "And then an SS man told us to go up to this woman and put her into the pit," he testified, "and once she was in the pit, he shot her, and the woman fell out of our hands. In the pit there was a fire— not a flame, it was a sort of . . . how shall I describe it? . . . this smoldering fire, and these babies were on top of this fire. The weeping, the crying of these babies, is ringing in my ears to this day."

Epstein tried to describe Treblinka as he saw it then: "The air was impregnated with death. . . . I was seventeen years old, Your Honor, I had never seen a corpse up till that moment. . . . I was absolutely paralyzed. And this continued for three days. There was murder, there were beatings, there were stabbings. It was quite indescribable."

They were commanded to sit on the ground. Epstein recalled they saw a bathtub of water. This was a trap. Whoever took a drink had his head whacked by a German rifle butt.

An SS man pointed at Epstein and said, "You—you go this way," motioning him out of the group. "I moved over to the side, then my younger brother, David, spotted me, and he got up and approached me. An SS man saw him doing so. He turned to him and with the butt of his gun, cracked open his skull. I became dizzy for a moment and [when I looked] this young boy had disappeared. I never saw him again."

Epstein spent three days in the Lower Camp before being chosen to work in the death camp. He would remain there for almost eleven months, until the uprising. He carried corpses. He testified that while waiting, "We heard cries, screams—unbelievable—I sat down in a place where I could see the entrance of the gas chambers. This was the so-called *Machinehaus,* the engine house. I saw someone go into this engine room, and later I was told this was Ivan, Ivan the Terrible.

"After the people had been introduced into the gas chambers and after the screams and when all this had died down, the gas engine was activated, the engine that introduced the gas into the chambers. I saw this man—a big, thickset man who activated and operated the engine. He pressed a button and disactivated the engine. And then we would wait about twenty minutes or half-an-hour and then we were told to open the doors—very wide doors—and remove the corpses."

Most of the SS men, Epstein testified, seemed indifferent to the atrocities; yet one officer, new to the camp, was horrified by what he saw. To get away from the corpses, he ordered Epstein and another inmate to rake the *Schlauch* under his supervision. Though no longer standing directly at the chambers, Epstein now witnessed the naked prisoners running toward the chambers.

He recounted how assistant camp commander Kurt Franz, having heard that an escape was being planned, gathered the inmates. Franz got hold of a boy named Kamera, a foreman of the corpse-carriers. He had been a neighbor of Epstein in Czestochowa. Kamera was asked to point out who was going to escape. He was beaten savagely.

"This young man had no control left at all. You could not recognize any face, his face was just a bloody mess." Kamera pointed indiscriminately to some twenty-odd people. They were told to leave the line and lie down on the ground facedown to await punishment.

"And this is how the massacre began. Ivan, with his iron pipe, Nikolai with his sword, the SS people with their whips. And the massacre began, blood began, blood was flowing freely." Epstein's face flushed with anger; his revulsion was obvious.

On another occasion, he recounted, a group managed to escape the camp's perimeter. But the first snow had just fallen, so the prisoners were tracked down easily and returned to camp. They were beaten for the entire day. Epstein recalled that Ivan was among those tormentors who broke the prisoners' arms, hands, and legs. The escapees were then hanged.

"Your Honor, I remember one other instance, and I have nightmares about this to this very day," he testified. "One day a living little girl managed to get out of the gas chambers. She was alive. She was speaking. A girl of about twelve or fourteen. People who took the corpses out of the gas chambers made her sit down on the side, and this little girl, her words ring in my ears still. She said, 'I want my mother.'" Epstein paused, to wipe away tears from his eyes. "After all of these corpses were taken out and placed on the side, we were commanded to sit down as always. Ivan took one young man from among us, whose name was Jubas. He struck him brutally with his whip, he lashed at him, he ordered him—'Take off your pants.' I am ashamed before this court to repeat the words that Ivan used. If I may . . . it would be outright blasphemy for me to repeat this. This is also vulgar language."

Levin reassured him: "If you feel this is important, then say it. If it's not too disturbing for you . . ."

"He struck Jubas," Epstein said, "and he ordered him—'take off your pants, and *davay ye batch.* . . .'"

"What does that mean?" Levin asked.

"'Come fuck' . . . And Jubas leaned over this little girl, and this act, as I understand it, did not actually take place. He leaned over this child—it was an act of obscenity against this child. . . ."

Jubas eventually died in the typhus epidemic. As for the little girl: "Later [she] was taken wherever all of the corpses were taken—near the pit—and there she was shot. I didn't see who shot her. Ivan was one of the—I find it difficult to compare him to anyone—not even to an animal. Because I know that animals, when they are satisfied, they do not attack. I once saw on television an animal researcher who studied animals in the jungle, and she explained that when a herd of animals is hungry, they prey upon other animals and they tear the other animal, the prey, to shreds. But once they are satisfied, they lie beneath a tree. Gazelles may pass by, and the predators do not attack them. Even if this is a predatory animal, Ivan was never satisfied. He would prey upon his victims every day, every minute so that I cannot even compare him to an animal, to a beast. He was never satisfied."

Epstein brushed away tears. He testified that he had watched Ivan at work from yet another vantage point. One day, Epstein testified, an SS man named Karol promised to assign him to the kitchen detail: "He said to me . . . with eyes like that, with hair like that, with the way I looked then . . . I was made to go into a kitchen to work. And there I worked for a brief period, maybe a week. And from that kitchen, when I went to bring water to the kitchen, or when I went to bring firewood, I saw all of the most terrible spectacles of what Ivan would do, day in and day out, each and every hour of the day."

Epstein found it difficult to describe the conditions under which they labored in the death camp. He said, "I should also like to add that there wasn't a single night when there weren't people who took their own lives, people who cracked up, people who broke down spiritually, mentally, physically. People who had found among the corpses a sister, a relative, a neighbor, a friend. These were spectacles that I cannot find words in the human language to describe. And no matter how much I try to explain and to describe this—it cannot be described. There is no beginning and no end . . . you need years to describe it and to try and understand it. I think that the human brain cannot conceive, cannot grasp—I'm not talking about seeing it, but yet you can't grasp it when it's being retold. It's inconceivable to understand what took place in this abattoir, in this slaughterhouse, what was done to human beings. . . . Ivan would be especially bestial toward people whom he discovered to be religious. I can't describe it. I can't explain it. I don't know how to go about explaining things logically." Epstein put his head down on the lectern.

Levin asked him to regain his composure. This was a court of law, he said, and Epstein would have to restrain himself from emotional outbursts.

With Shaked gently leading, Epstein completed his narrative of Treblinka, concluding with, as Shaked put it, the one happy moment, the uprising. From the death camp Epstein had escaped into the forest. "I kept going," he testified, "I went as far as I could. I didn't know really where I was going . . . I went wherever my eyes led me. I didn't have a specific place to go to. I didn't know whom to go to. I didn't have a name of anyone, I didn't have an identity— I didn't exist. I hadn't been born. I didn't belong to anyone. No one belonged to me."

Epstein made his way back to his hometown of Czestochowa: "On the first night I slept in the cemetery, the Polish cemetery of the non-Jews. . . . On the following day I entered the city. I went into a courtyard where I had lived, myself, and I looked around. There was complete chaos. I looked through the windows and I clung to the ground. I couldn't move—I knew that this is the place where this person lived and where that person lived and all of my neighbors. After all, I had grown up there, and all this no longer exists. All of it has disappeared. And where am I to go? Whom am I to turn to? And the world was going on as if nothing had changed.

"I used to go out and sleep in different ruins of houses that had been demolished by the Germans in the ghettos. I would go out in the morning. I'd see children going to school, people going to work—the world went on with business as usual, as if nothing had changed. . . . What helped me at the time was to see how the world was going on. This is what drove me on. And I kept wandering, it was worse than being a dog. Because if you are a dog, at least no one pays any attention to you. But if anyone had caught me, if anyone had noticed me, if anyone had found out that I'd escaped from Treblinka, it's difficult to describe the torture I would have had to endure. Finally, with the help of one Pole who was the only . . . good-natured, good-hearted woman in this ocean of hatred— there was this one spark of humanity, and there were so very few such sparks—this person helped me, this angel, helped me to forge documents." The papers enabled Epstein to get to Germany, where he spent the rest of the war working with a group of laborers.

Shaked led Epstein to his safe arrival in Israel in 1948, and life thereafter. "I have children," Epstein said. "I have five grandchildren. And I have rehabilitated myself and this nightmare called Treblinka, which is called Ivan, which is called Nikolai, which is called Gustav; and all of those names pursue me to this very day.

"A few days ago," he continued, "we celebrated a holiday in Israel—*Tu B'shvat* [Arbor Day], the day dedicated to the trees, and I was watching the little children of the kindergartens, small children, marching out to plant trees. And I observed them, and I saw these children, these small children, who did not know that after marching a few steps in Treblinka their lives would be severed. Innocent children."

Intently watching this exchange was an aristocratic-looking woman who had been attending the trial for several days with her children. Asked then why she had brought her children, she had answered, "It's so important. They must know." But there was another reason. She was Epstein's eldest daughter.

Levin, clearly uncomfortable, turned to the prosecutor. "Mr. Shaked, any other questions?" Shaked put the Israel Police's album of Ukrainian photographs before Epstein; it had been almost nine years since he had identified Demjanjuk. Now he recalled full well his identification and the physical characteristics upon which it was based: "The brow, the round face, the very short neck, the wide, well-set shoulders and slightly protruding ears—this is Ivan as I remembered him. . . . When I met him in Treblinka, he must have been between twenty-two and twenty-five."

Epstein pointed spontaneously at Demjanjuk, and said, "Yes, he's sitting *there. There he is!*"

A gasp came from the audience. A few persons applauded.

Judge Levin immediately called the room to order, admonishing the public not to interfere with the proceeding.

Epstein also remembered his identification of the Trawniki card photo in 1979. "I said this is Ivan as I remembered him from Treblinka. . . ."

Michael Shaked had a final question: When he had just then pointed at Demjanjuk and said, "There he is," how could he be sure it was Ivan after so many years?

"If it please the court, when I was brought to Treblinka, I was a boy of seventeen. Ivan was twenty-five. We, 'together' were at a certain place for eleven months, together in very close quarters. He carried out deeds so atrocious that no words can describe them, deeds that have become so indelibly imbedded in my memory. A man of that age has not changed to this day to the point where he would become unrecognizable. There are certain features that after so many years are marked in one's memory and cannot be erased."

With increasing agitation, he testified, "I see Ivan every night. My poor wife, I dream about Ivan every night. I envision him every night, he is imprinted in my memory. I cannot free myself of these impressions."

Epstein began to describe how he had recognized Ivan when he saw him on TV, stepping off the plane in Israel, but Levin said what he had seen on television was not of interest to the court right now.

"Well, then," said Epstein angrily, "I see Ivan the way I remember him, the way he is in my mind's eye. There he is," he pointed at Demjanjuk, "just the way he is!" Epstein, his face taut with frustration, angrily hammered the witness stand, *"There he is! There he is! There he is!"*

Judge Levin told Epstein to restrain himself: "I realize that it is difficult to contain your excitement," he said, "but, please, we are in the process of a trial here and things must be conducted in a calmer manner."

"I apologize," Epstein said, "but still . . ."

Levin: "Yes, we understood you, sir, but please understand us, too."

"This is the man, the man sitting over there."

"Yes, we heard you," the judge replied.

"Age has, of course, changed matters, but not to the point where he would become unrecognizable. I see him, I see him, I see him. . . ." Epstein sobbed.

Levin again turned to the prosecutor: "Mr. Shaked?" he asked.

"I have finished, no more questions," Shaked said.

Judge Levin explained to Epstein that he would be questioned now by Mr. O'Connor, who had the right to defend his client to the best of his ability. And it was Epstein's duty to answer questions, no matter how difficult, as calmly as possible.

"*Mar Epstein, tzohoraim tovim* [Mr. Epstein, good afternoon]. *Shalom, Baruch Hashem* [Hello, praise God]," Mark O'Connor began in his American-accented Hebrew. He quickly switched to English. O'Connor started by questioning Epstein's assertion that he had recognized Demjanjuk as Ivan when he saw him on television. O'Connor's goal was to examine the detrimental effect of media coverage on the trial, but the strategy backfired: Epstein explained that Demjanjuk's "way of walking was the one I remember at Treblinka." O'Connor would ask him later to demonstrate the walk. That, too, proved a miscalculation. Epstein stood, and with small steps and arms swinging, walked a few steps. It was a striking identification: Epstein had accurately portrayed Demjanjuk's distinctive gait. Demjanjuk watched with great interest, and everyone else watched Demjanjuk.

O'Connor attempted to test Epstein's memory with a barrage of questions, yet each was posed as a challenge: "Can you tell us, *if you remember.* . . . Did you testify *and is it true that.* . . . Did you say *and is it fact that.* . . . *You'll correct me if I'm wrong.* . . ." O'Connor read from a yellow legal pad, his heels together, his toes pointing out, knees slightly bent. His method was to question "the mind of the seventeen-year-old boy from Czestochowa," as separate from the aging witness now accusing his client.

O'Connor's questions probed at matters that bore little, if any, relevance to the trial: he explored minute details, as if any lapse in Epstein's knowledge or memory would invalidate his identification of Ivan. O'Connor asked whether a certain SS man, Munzberger, could have been born on the Volga. Epstein, annoyed, replied, "How could I know?" Later O'Connor asked why the typhus victims were taken to the hospital and not killed in the pit like other sick people. Epstein shrugged angrily, and said, "Believe me, I do not know."

"What month did the epidemic take place?"

"When it comes to the time of the month and the date and the week, I can't tell you. As soon as I was put into Treblinka, time stopped. . . . People who were ill did not receive medical treatment. Do you think this was a sanatorium?"

It was impossible to know whether O'Connor's questions, delivered so courteously, were meant to unhinge him—as when he asked Epstein to point out on the Treblinka model the exact spot where his brother had been murdered—or to mock him, as when he asked him what color his hair had been then.

At the lunch recess, Epstein's wife, his son, and two daughters and his five grandchildren, rushed to the stage. The policemen did not stop them. The family embraced in one hug, tears flowing. Epstein's son had never heard the particulars of his experience; his daughters knew even less. "You're too young," he used to tell them, even after they were grown with their own children.

When the court reconvened, O'Connor questioned Epstein's contacts with other Treblinka survivors. The implication was that the witnesses had colluded, yet O'Connor never asked him directly and had no evidence to support such a claim. Epstein confirmed that although he had known only inmates of the death camp, in the years since the uprising he had met with other Treblinka survivors, and had testified with them at trials in Dusseldorf, Ft. Lauderdale, and Cleveland.

O'Connor asked Epstein whether he and the other survivors had attended a ceremony at Yad Vashem on the fortieth anniversary of the uprising. They had. Epstein testified the survivors also used to gather on August 2, at a Tel Aviv cemetery, Nahalat Yitzhak, where a memorial stands to the survivors of Treblinka. "That is a day and an hour when we remember all that we had to go through." He said he met often with Eliahu Rosenberg at weddings, social occasions, and funerals as well. O'Connor asked if they ever discussed their experiences of Treblinka.

"Sir, we are comrades, we are more than comrades, we are brothers, because we were born on the same date, on the second of August, 1943. I have two birthdates." But though Epstein said he would recall with others what they had been through "to the end of our days"—there was no evidence that they had ever discussed the Demjanjuk case, or any other, among them, or had coordinated their identifications or their testimony.

As a concluding question, O'Connor wondered about Epstein's in-court identification. "After you saw the pictures," he said, "and after you looked him straight in the face you said, 'That is the man.'"

Epstein remained firm. "I am convinced," he testified, "convinced that opposite me is sitting the man Ivan the Terrible, the Horrible, who was at Treblinka."

Judge Dorner had a question: "Tell me, Mr. Epstein, how often did you see Ivan?"

"Your Honor, I saw Ivan every day, at all hours. I rubbed shoulders with him, if I can so put it. . . ."

"How is that possible?" asked Judge Dorner.

"Well, he was passing by me. It was such a very small area. Everything took place in this very limited area. He was active near the gas chambers, and I would come to the gas chambers in order to pick up the corpses, and he was there all the time. After the corpses were taken out of the gas chambers, he would stand there and he would look at the results of what he had done to them, this gouging of eyes, the cutting-off of parts of a girl's breast. He was standing there enjoying his handiwork; he would hit the prisoners with his iron rod and enjoy seeing the cracked skull. This was just a few inches away from me. It was such a very, very narrow piece of ground on which we were; and he was looking at it with such enjoyment—the cracked skulls, the crushed faces, babies still tied to their mothers by the navel—looking at it as if he had done a tremendously good job; and, of course, he would brutalize the victims, brutalize the prisoners. I cannot find a word in the human language, in a cultured language, what to compare him to. It was a creature not from this planet, Your Honor.

"One says 'murderer,' 'assassin,' or writes 'murder,' but then once he has done the deed and he sees the results, there is usually a feeling of regret, but Ivan never, ever in the eleven months I was in Treblinka, never, ever showed the slightest regret. It is inconceivable, incomprehensible, how a person could act like that. Women who were pregnant with stab wounds in the abdomen. I have no words. I cannot, Your Honor, really, not describe this. A man's healthy brain cannot take in, cannot grasp what went on in Treblinka. It is not on this planet. Almost one million people were massacred, assassinated: women, children, old people. Why? I ask. Why? Because they were Jews. It was Ivan. . . . How this horror who is not from this planet . . . I just cannot grasp it . . . if I were to tell the tale to the end of my days, every day, and each day. Treblinka has no beginning and no end. And whoever was in Treblinka will never get out of it; and whoever was not in Treblinka will not go into Treblinka. It was the sort of horror that did not take place on this planet."

Epstein was distraught. Watching him, his two daughters were in tears, as were others in the audience. Levin asked him to signal when he had regained his composure and could continue.

Defense counsel Yoram Sheftel wanted Epstein to acknowledge that at Treblinka, he never heard Ivan called Demjanjuk and that he had no way of knowing Ivan Grozny's real first or last name. Epstein answered: "I knew that Ivan was his first name. I heard everybody calling him Ivan. Nikolai called him Ivan. The SS men called him Ivan, and from this I know that this was his name . . . but no, I did not [hear] mention the name Demjanjuk."

Epstein had one more request: "If the bench permits me to say one sentence to the accused."

Levin was adamant: "No, no, no. No, by no means."

Outside the courtroom, the reporters gathered around Epstein. "What was the comment you wanted to make?" one asked.

"If the judge wouldn't let me make it to him, do you think I'll tell you?" Epstein said gruffly as he headed out to meet his family.

But after the trial had ended, Epstein revealed what he had wanted to say to Demjanjuk: "You, who were so powerful at Treblinka, who held the lives of people in your hands, and you who did with them whatever you wanted; you, who were so brave, be brave now. Tell the court who you are and what you did."

CHAPTER 13

Those Eyes, Those Murderous Eyes

Eliahu Rosenberg gripped the witness stand firmly. Long retired from his job as a warehouse manager at the Ashdod port, Rosenberg worked part-time at a bank. He stood barely five feet tall, yet he was a powerful, intimidating presence. Dark curly hair with silver waves complemented his deeply furrowed face; he wore thick glasses with purplish frames, and his eyes were dark and intense. As he stood in court, barrel-chested, refusing to sit, he seemed like a small bull, ready to charge.

Rosenberg was born in Warsaw, and grew up in an orthodox home. He lived with his parents and sisters, attending private school, until the outbreak of the war. His father, who ran a mirror factory, was murdered by Germans one winter night in 1941, while out to buy milk. Rosenberg, nineteen at the time, became the family's breadwinner, scavenging the streets of the Warsaw Ghetto for food.

He last saw his mother on the train to Treblinka. She just had time to hand him something, a ring, and they agreed to contact each other if they escaped, through a certain Christian acquaintance. Rosenberg never saw his mother again. He later traded the ring for a piece of bread.

Now he was asked to identify the camp from the blowup behind him. His memory was sharp. As he pointed, he made some corrections: "This was here . . . this was later moved." Where he had been, he could describe; what he had seen was before him again.

Rosenberg stood at the lectern, his fists clenched, his face tensed with rage, as he described the Jews running up the *Schlauch* and into the gas chambers, to their deaths. His fists shook in the air, as he recalled their last cries. Winter, he said, was worse than summer: "Polish winter is . . . very, very cold, twenty or thirty degrees below [centigrade]. You must understand that these children were naked. A hundred or eighty meters away from me, and they came from the direction of Camp One, in that cold winter. . . . You can't imagine the kind of screams that human beings can emit . . . like dogs. The children wailed in a manner that filled the entire space around us. In the beginning, I, too, was very affected by this, but I later became numb. It was so difficult. No one asked me to look at them. I could see them for myself. And then when people ran into the gas chambers, they ran, they just wanted to get out of the cold. They saw something in front of them and they ran."

Rosenberg had worked first as a corpse-carrier. This exhausted him, but to save his own life he had to find ways to conserve his strength: "I managed to make a friend of one of the *Dentisten,* by name of Lindvasser, who has since died. Now when I came to Lindvasser, this *Dentisten,* he, too, was scared to death. I said, Avraham, be a little slower in looking for the gold teeth, because that was the one second where I could rest. Somehow I rested the stretcher on my knees, because I was crouching, as it were. For me, this one second made all the difference. It did give me this tiny bit of respite. . . ."

Rosenberg later managed to get assigned to details that lessened his chance of being beaten. He became one of the *Bademeisters,* the "shower cleaners," who washed the chambers and cleaned the ramp between gassings. Sitting there on the ramp, he saw Ivan and Nikolai perform their tasks and heard death come to those inside the chamber.

Levin asked if he saw Ivan and Nikolai operate the engine.

"Yes," he answered. "I didn't see his finger pressing, I didn't see him moving a handle." Rosenberg said he always saw them in the engine room, though not always together; sometimes one was inside, one of them was outside.

"And you saw them?" asked Judge Levin.

"With my very own eyes," he said. Rosenberg wanted to tell the court what he heard inside the chambers as he sat outside. "It's a very agitating and very shocking thing—I'll try and tell it slowly," he said. "When the victims were inside, the first ones did not know where they were going, it was so very well decoyed and camouflaged. . . . But by the time the chambers had filled up, I would start hearing at the other end a most ghastly scream, crying, weeping, '*Mame,*' '*Tate,*' 'Aba,' 'Ima,' the names of children. It was dark inside. No light. Even the openings in the roof did not let any light in . . . the screams, the shouts were terrible. '*Mame*,' '*Tate*,'—Mother, Father—'Hear O God of Israel—*Shma Yisrael*.' I listened to this for fifteen-twenty minutes. Then these screams died down. And then I heard moaning, groans, and that, too, subsided until it became quiet. Often I saw inside strong young people—it is inconceivable, it is incomprehensible, how they were fighting and trying to get their heads above the others in order to get a tiny bit of air.''

Finally, Rosenberg agreed to sit down. He went on to testify that he at one time had worked on the incineration crew, which also put him in a position to observe Ivan. Next to Ivan's work area were barrels of fuel, and Rosenberg was given permission to retrieve a bucket of diesel fuel to pour on the corpses.

Shaked now tread lightly: "Mr. Rosenberg . . . a general question. You spent eleven months at Treblinka. How did you endure that?"

"To receive beatings was an everyday matter over there," Rosenberg answered, "but I was careful not to be beaten in a murderous fashion, in a brutal fashion. Why do I say murderous? Because if any of us was beaten on an exposed part of our body, he was a candidate, so to speak, to be killed. Again, we weren't afraid of being killed. I wanted to be killed, but with a bullet in the head . . . there was no other hope there anyhow. If I tell you that if I had any hope, there was a sort of dream; but hope to get out of there, there was no hope. So my only hope, my only aspiration, was to get a bullet in the head and to finish with it all.

"How did I survive, however, how was it possible for me to spend eleven months or more in that place? There were two reasons. First, I mentioned earlier that I worked for several months in the gas chambers. The murderers did not enter the gas chambers themselves . . . except for one who would count the corpses together with me. . . . When I was there, I was far from the actual field of bloodshed . . . so I had a sort of breathing time, to catch a friend of mine and we told one another that if we want to live at all—however absurd that may seem—we must not work too hard and we must think up something.

"Whenever we would carry a corpse . . . or whenever we would walk from the pit to the incinerator, we both had to agree to throw this stretcher down and hide. You couldn't do it by yourself, because if one did it, they would ask where is the other one? So we always had to act together. And then we would hide, it was a little bit later on, in the time of the incinerators, we would hide under the incinerators. . . . We hid in the smoke, which is why to this day I have a bad eye and a bad throat. We could hide in the smoke, as long as an hour or two and rest from this hard labor and the beatings. This was one period.

"At a different period, when I took the corpses out of the gas chambers, and there were big piles there, I had to join and help carry. I could not sit down and rest. So I walked with this friend of mine again. We always walked together. So we went together to relieve ourselves, and we couldn't go one by one. We would throw the stretcher down. No one would notice a stretcher lying on the side. And thus I could hide out for an hour or an hour-and-a-half, until a German spotted us or one of the people in black spotted us. And they could not see us more than once, because if they'd seen us even once, I'd wind up being a candidate for death. And thus I managed. Somehow I was quicker than others, or I don't know what, and I survived. I'm not claiming to be a hero or anything."

Shaked asked, "What did you see Ivan inflict on the victims, things that you saw with your own eyes?"

"In the earlier months, I would stand on the *Rampe* [the platform and ramp outside the gas chamber's exterior doors—by which the corpses were removed], I would see him holding a sort of sword in his hand . . . and sometimes he would cut off a piece of nose, a piece of ear, stab, you just cannot comprehend why, why. . . . After all, there was no very good reason why he should go up to a person and cut off a part of his ear. He was not a human being. He was not being a rational human being at all, and he was a young man, to boot. He had some sort of education. He came from a certain country . . . to get blows, to beat—all right, yes, we'd seen where people beat you. But this sort of torture—this brutalizing—this torturing people by cutting off parts of their ears? Nobody had ordered him to do so. He did it of his own accord. I never heard a German tell him to do so. . . . A little later, a German, in fact, told him to keep off doing such things."

Rosenberg told of one incident in which three escapees were apprehended. He saw Ivan coming out of his cabin with a new instrument of torture, a large nail. But a German officer by the name of Loeffler saw what Ivan was about to do and shouted at him: "*Los! Los!* [Get off, get away!]" and ordered him back to his cabin.

Strangely enough, this one German officer, whom Rosenberg recalled as puny, seemed the only person Ivan feared at Treblinka. But Loeffler was no humanitarian. It was he who ordered Rosenberg and others to escort the captured to the gas chambers and lock them up. Later Lalke held a roll call—the three men were hanged on a tree.

"I understand," Shaked said, "that this Loeffler also saved your life on one occasion."

Rosenberg nodded yes: "This was at an earlier time—much before the incident that I have just described. It was in late summer. We had cleared the corpses from the gas chambers. As soon as I got to the ramp, Ivan came out of his *cabina*. . . . I stood there and he beckoned me. He told me to take off my trousers, and lie down on them [to have intercourse with one of the corpses there]. I had no choice. I saw this, and within a minute I understood, this is it. I have had it. [I would be killed] Either [by] his iron pipe or else some other way.

"Loeffler, he was looking there. I ran toward him. I said to him, *Herr Scharfuhrer* [Sergeant, sir], Ivan tells me to have sexual intercourse with a dead woman. So Loeffler approached Ivan, screamed at him. And Ivan turned to me and said, 'You will pay for this.'"

Rosenberg had no way of knowing if Ivan had remembered his threat; but some months later Ivan did punish him. While removing garbage from the kitchen, Rosenberg stole some bread and shared it with others. A young boy was found with the stolen bread and when asked where he had got it, he blamed Rosenberg.

Rosenberg's punishment was thirty lashes of the whip. "Ivan got out from his cabin with his *Peicher*—a whip. There was another one, Gustav. He did not do it alone. I had to count, Your Honor. In the end, I said *"spaciba"* ["thank you" in Russian]. I immediately pulled up my trousers and put on my clothes and ran back to the barracks. I couldn't move for a couple of hours, but I got over it."

Rosenberg also recalled that in 1942, he was on the *Rampe* when he saw Ivan leading an elderly Jew toward the fence. Religious Jews appeared to provide Ivan with a special provocation.

"I saw that he was accompanied by an elderly Jew with sidelocks, did not have any hair on his head, a long beard, and Ivan went up to the fence pulled the fence apart and this Jew was pushed by him, either by his feet or his trunk, into this barbed-wire fence, and Ivan started beating him with his iron pipe. This Jew was writhing in pain and screamed until he stopped screaming and crying."

On the day of the uprising, Rosenberg testified, his job was to put a blanket over the barbed-wire fence so others could climb over. When the revolt broke out, earlier than expected, he ran to the fence with the blanket, but he didn't have to throw it on the fence because others had already broken out, and there was an opening. He ran and climbed over the antitank obstacles. "I still don't know to this day how I managed to climb over it," he said. "I jumped . . . it must have been about three meters."

Shaked now addressed Rosenberg's 1947 statement that Ivan had been killed. Rosenberg explained that he was in Vienna in 1947 for the Bricha (the Underground to Palestine). When people heard that he had survived Treblinka, they urged him to speak to Tadik Friedman, a Polish Jew who worked at the Jewish Agency and tried to track Nazis. Rosenberg agreed. The conversations occurred at two sessions. Rosenberg spoke in Yiddish, and Friedman translated his comments into German as a typist recorded the interview.

Rosenberg's 1947 account is detailed and intimate. The document does, however, give his birthdate as May 10, 1924, (Rosenberg was born in 1921) and the date of his arrival at Treblinka as August 20 (Rosenberg arrived in September). Those discrepancies would be brought out in the cross-examination; but he told Friedman that his first night in Treblinka was the eve of a Jewish Holiday and some religious Jews prayed in the barracks (the Jewish Holidays in 1942 were, in fact, in September).

As for Ivan, Rosenberg did not describe his physique, but his function at the gas chambers and that he was "feared because of his especial bestial brutality." Rosenberg described instances of his brutality. He also noted that "Ivan was the only Ukrainian who was allowed without any special permit to go to the nearby village, where he got himself whiskey and food." Rosenberg described the revolt, and said "some prisoners stormed the barracks of the Ukrainians, where Ivan slept, and beat them to death with shovels."

Shaked placed the original crumbling, yellowing typescript before the court. Rosenberg explained that he'd found out later that what his friends had told him in the forest was, "a story—fiction—a mere boast . . . even those who had told the tale hadn't seen it for themselves." It had been wishful thinking.

If Ivan hadn't been killed, what had become of him? Rosenberg said he first found out in 1976. Shaked asked him to recall Israel Police investigator Miriam Radiwker's 1976 visit. When Rosenberg saw the 1951 visa picture, he said that the man looked familiar from Treblinka. But Mrs. Radiwker said he wasn't at Treblinka. "She said he was at Sobibor. I said, I know this man. Ivan. Ivan Grozny. Madame, I said, he was different, a little younger, a little leaner." Rosenberg recalled that at Treblinka, Ivan was twenty-two to twenty-three years old, tall, with light-colored eyes, a receding hairline, dark, close-cropped hair, a strong man." Later he also told how in 1979 he had identified the Trawniki photo for Inspector Kollar.

Shaked showed Rosenberg the police photo album from which he had identified Demjanjuk, then asked: "You told Mrs. Radiwker if you saw Ivan alive today you would recognize him?"

"*Nahon* [true]," Rosenberg replied.

Sheftel realized what was coming and jumped up to object. He insisted that an in-court identification was irrelevant, misleading, and of little probative weight. The court overruled him.

Shaked said: "I should ask you to look at the accused."

Rosenberg, looking straight at Demjanjuk, had a request: "Will you ask the accused to take off his glasses." Before the translation, Demjanjuk removed his glasses; but as O'Connor rose, he quickly put them back on. Judge Levin asked, "Mr. O'Connor what is your position?" After some hesitation, O'Connor said, "My client has nothing to hide."

Demjanjuk stood and removed his glasses. He leaned over to O'Connor: "I want that he come close to me—right here." Demjanjuk pointed to the edge of his booth. "Shh," said O'Connor, but honored the request. With a flip of his hand, O'Connor ordered, "Mar Rosenberg, come over."

Rosenberg stared straight at Demjanjuk. He stepped away from the witness stand, their eyes still locked, and took off his glasses. As he walked across the room there was complete silence and time stopped.

Demjanjuk stood, awaiting him, smiling. O'Connor had a demonic grin. Rosenberg walked quickly. He stopped at the edge of the booth, no more than a foot from Demjanjuk. They stared at each other for a second. It seemed like an hour.

"*Posmotree!* [Look at me!]" Rosenberg barked at him angrily.

Demjanjuk suddenly stuck out his hand, and said, "*Shalom*" with childish glee.

Rosenberg recoiled in shock and disgust; he stumbled backward. He cried out "Murderer! Bandit! How dare you put out your hand to me!" Rosenberg never heard the cry that rose from the spectators as his wife, Adina, sitting in the third row, fainted; their daughter, Rivka, caught her in her arms. The police promptly carried her out of the courtroom.

What had been Demjanjuk's intention? To show that forty years later, they were equals; that bygones were bygones? To show that he was not a monster, but just a man? Or was Demjanjuk mocking him, challenging him now, even as he had then?

Rosenberg returned to the witness stand and rested his head on the lectern. A few moments passed. Judge Levin called the room to order and turned to the witness and said, "You were asked to come close. You stopped and looked. What is your answer?"

Rosenberg stood again. He said, "This is Ivan. I say so unhesitatingly and without the slightest doubt. Ivan from Treblinka—from the gas chambers. The man I am looking at now. I saw those eyes, those murderous eyes."

Could O'Connor convince the court otherwise?

"*Shalom Mar Rosenberg, Baruch Hashem* [Hello Mr. Rosenberg, praise God]," O'Connor began.

"*Shalom,* to you, too," Rosenberg replied.

O'Connor asked Rosenberg about the differing dates for his arrival at Treblinka. Rosenberg maintained that he had always told investigators he arrived before the Jewish New Year and he had left it to them to supply a date consistent with the Gregorian calendar. O'Connor came back to this several times. Finally, Rosenberg said, "I repeat again and even if he asks me a million times that I arrived in Treblinka before the Jewish New Year."

The interaction between O'Connor and Rosenberg had a certain edge: each sought to outsmart the other—yet each respected the other's right to try and do so. At one point, O'Connor asked him to look at a map; but Rosenberg explained that he was nearsighted. O'Connor reacted as if he had suddenly stumbled across a major exonerating fact. "You weren't shortsighted yesterday," he said referring to Rosenberg's confident in-court identification. O'Connor then launched into a battery of questions about the witness' eyesight. But Rosenberg answered them all.

O'Connor asked Rosenberg if he had ever written down his experiences of Treblinka. To everyone's great surprise, Rosenberg revealed that before the war was over, he had written something in Yiddish. He had given the document to a representative of the Polish government; he had not seen or heard of it since. Sheftel took note of this. Later the defense would locate this document and ask Rosenberg to be recalled so he could be cross-examined about it. In it, as in the 1947 Friedman document, he recounted the death of Ivan.

O'Connor returned to the Friedman document. Rosenberg replied that he had initialed each page without actually reading the German. "Perhaps I was naive," he said. "I never thought it would come to court. We spoke to each other in Yiddish."

But O'Connor had a more provocative line to pursue. Earlier, he had made Rosenberg detail all the tasks he was made to perform *while* others died. Now he asked him about the Jews from Grodno. O'Connor's strategy was not yet clear. But Rosenberg retold the incident: a transport of Jews from Grodno had dared to try to escape while running up the *Schlauch.* They had pushed aside the branch-covered wire fence and scattered.

Rosenberg and other death-camp workers were immediately ordered into their barracks enclosure. From there Rosenberg watched the fate of the escapees. The greater part were shot trying to flee. Approximately thirty men were caught alive, and were led to the small gas chamber and locked inside.

O'Connor asked whether it was Rosenberg's "option" in the death camp to stay outside or to go into the safety of the barracks.

"I don't understand what you ask about options," Rosenberg responded angrily. "They did whatever they wanted. . . . They weren't afraid of us, for heaven's sake: It was a slaughterhouse. The Germans weren't afraid of us; because a second later I could have been [murdered] instead of one of the victims."

An especially gruesome death was inflicted upon the captured who were locked in the gas chamber, Rosenberg recalled. Rather than turning on the diesel engine, the Germans poured chlorine through a window above the chamber. The victims were left overnight to decompose and die.

In the morning, Rosenberg was assigned to pull them out. "They were not even bodies anymore," he testified. "We had to grab them by the heads and pull them out, because their skin was red. They were bloated. And when we touched such a victim, the skin came off."

O'Connor now asked, "Mr. Rosenberg, was it ever in your heart the time you were watching this happen—to try and do something to help those men that were running outside naked?"

So this was O'Connor's interest in "options." Rosenberg was anguished: "How could I have done so? How could I have helped them? I had no contact with living human beings there. If I saw what I saw, all I saw was people who were getting into the gas chambers. I had no contact with them. I could see them in front of me, five meters [sixteen feet] away from me. They didn't even have a chance to look up at me. . . ."

Shaked objected, saying the question had a provocative element and O'Connor could argue what he wished in summation. But Judge Levin told Rosenberg he must answer.

Rosenberg responded, calmly at first: "In what manner could I help these people? How? With what? With screaming?" With increasing anger, he said: "Should I have screamed at them: 'Don't get into those gas chambers?' They didn't want to get into the gas chambers. And if, God forbid, any of us would have screamed, shouted toward them—I don't wish you, Mr. O'Connor, to even look at what would have happened to such a person. They would have shoved him straight alive into a pit full of blood. So don't ask me questions of that manner, Mr. O'Connor. I implore you. You weren't there. I was there—*ask him*," Rosenberg pointed to Demjanjuk in the dock. "Ask him," he began to shout. "Let him tell you. Let him tell you what he would have done to me." Rosenberg was overwrought.

"Mr. Rosenberg, Mr. Rosenberg . . ." Judge Levin told him that his shouting was out of place.

"I was never asked such a painful question in my life," Rosenberg said. "Even the worst anti-Semite never asked me a question of this type. Whether I could have helped such an unfortunate. Who could have helped me then? You want me to tell you what went on there?"

"Mr. Rosenberg," said Levin sternly, "that completes your answer to this question."

Judge Levin, though, had a question for O'Connor. During Rosenberg's reply, Demjanjuk, his face deeply flushed, had shouted something at Rosenberg, which O'Connor had not heard because of his translation headset.

O'Connor conferred with Demjanjuk for a second, then announced that he wished *Demjanjuk* to repeat his comment. He asked that the comment be seen "in the proper context of a man who has been in a jail cell for almost a year in solitary confinement, sitting, listening patiently—suffering in his own way; holding it all in, trying to maintain his spirituality—he did say something, Your Honor. It shows he's human. And he said it in Hebrew."

Levin told O'Connor he had local counsel for this purpose. But rather than let Sheftel speak, O'Connor said Sheftel had told him, "Two words he heard were: '*Atah shakran* [You are a liar].'"

Judge Dorner had a question. She wanted to know from Rosenberg, as she had from Epstein, why he was certain that this was Ivan and not someone who looked like him.

When he saw the picture of Ivan for the first time in 1976, Rosenberg said, he recognized the face, although it was fatter and older. Still, he was hesitant about making a positive identification. But at Demjanjuk's denaturalization trial in Cleveland in 1981, he had sat across from the defendant and been unable to take his eyes off him. Although Ivan kept trying not to look at him, Rosenberg managed nonetheless to get his glance. And when he saw his face, he had no doubt. And finally now, now that he had walked up to Demjanjuk and looked into his eyes, "I have no shadow of a doubt, Your Honor. This is him."

Always curious about psychological dynamic, O'Connor asked, "How was it possible that John Demjanjuk would cower and not look him in the eye in Cleveland, his hometown, but would do so in Israel?"

"Maybe he was ashamed in front of his family and friends," Rosenberg replied.

Sheftel took over the questioning. Rosenberg had been shown the same photospread twice, once in 1976 by Radiwker, and then again by Kollar in 1978. In 1976, he identified Demjanjuk from the spread; in 1978, Fedorenko. Why, Sheftel asked, didn't he mention Ivan again in 1978? Rosenberg insisted he did. But then why didn't he identify Fedorenko in 1976, when he was first shown the photospread? "In 1976, when I found out he [Ivan] was alive," Rosenberg said, "I was in shock."

Wasn't the real reason, Sheftel surmised, that Rosenberg asked to approach Demjanjuk here in court, that he couldn't be sure from the witness stand that he was Ivan? Judge Levin interrupted the defense counsel to remind him that it was O'Connor who had asked Rosenberg to come closer. Levin assured Sheftel he would remember that moment full well until the end of the trial. Sheftel rephrased his question accordingly: did Rosenberg respond to the request to come closer in order to better identify him?

"No, sir," said Rosenberg. "The truth is entirely different. . . . The intention was for him to look at me and perhaps to remember me. . . . Every day I was next to him . . . I was beaten by him. I saw what he did. Refresh his memory full well, he'll remember me."

It was now past six-thirty, the normal time for ending the session. Judge Levin asked the prosecutors whether they had any redirect (questions in light of the cross-examination). Rosenberg had been on the stand for three days, delivering what would amount to more than five-hundred pages of trial transcript. He was an important witness, and the success of his testimony would be crucial to the prosecution. The success of his cross-examination, which had lasted more than fifteen hours, would, therefore, be all the more important to the defense. And the redirect would be a barometer of what damage the cross-examination had done.

So it was not without significance when Mickey Shaked rose, turned to the court, and said, "No, we do not have any redirect."

CHAPTER 14

Simple Men

As Rosenberg testified, an American journalist named Nancie Katz interviewed citizens outside the courtroom about the phenomenon occurring inside.

"Other things will be forgotten," said Ira Hammerman, one of several hundred people who waited in the forty-degree weather for a chance to get inside the courtroom. "But this is of historical significance. By being present, I feel like I'm taking part in history."

"I have to be here," said gray-haired Shusta River, a Russian native who moved to Israel in 1949. "I am a survivor. I wasn't in Treblinka, but I was in another place."

"I have to see what the witnesses are saying," said twelve-year-old Alan Helmreich, who'd skipped school to watch. "It should never be forgotten what happened." But a waitress at a Hungarian café in downtown Jerusalem was of another mind. She whipped up her sleeve to flash the number tattooed on her arm and exclaimed to Katz, "I don't listen to it and I don't play it here. I was in four concentration camps! I was there. I had enough!"

The survivors' testimony received coverage the world over. Britain's tabloids gave great play to the gruesome details. Newspapers in the Netherlands and Germany ran daily accounts. In the United States, only Cleveland's *The Plain Dealer* carried daily reports. Most major newspapers reported the more dramatic moments of survivor testimony. But the coverage of testimony gave way quickly to coverage of "the trial phenomenon."

The courtroom was jammed to capacity; an annex had to be built so the trial could be broadcast over closed-circuit video on a large screen.

On the trial's tenth day, a small man, somewhat disheveled, took the stand and identified himself as "Yossef Czarny, son of Abraham, born on the twenty-seventh of July 1926 in Warsaw." If Epstein radiated dignity, and Rosenberg animal instinct, then Czarny was the simple man, a poor soul whose misfortune it was to have been sent to Treblinka.

When war broke out, Czarny had just had his bar mitzvah. His mother, a diabetic, died as the ghetto was starting. "But at least she was buried in an honorable way," he testified.

Food was scarce. Czarny, with great emotion, recalled how he and a friend had to scavenge the ghetto to eat. "I humiliated myself. We were begging. We had no choice." Police were posted on every corner. Threats were carried out routinely. Czarny lived with his father, a Hasidic businessman, and his three younger sisters.

"The greatest shock that I remember," Czarny told the court, "was when my father of blessed memory came home before curfew . . . I thought I didn't see right. I said, '*Tate*, is that you?' The policeman had cut off his beard and his sidelocks. I was brokenhearted. He was brokenhearted."

As conditions in the ghetto worsened, there was less and less food. Czarny's father was so weak with hunger he could no longer speak; his sisters did not have the strength to leave their beds and wait in food lines. His father died, and was taken out to the gates of the ghetto in a wheelbarrow. Czarny ran after it to cover his father's face with a piece of paper.

In Warsaw, a notice was posted a few days before Rosh Hashanah, promising bread and jam to anyone who went to the train station. "It is difficult to describe," Czarny testified, "what that meant. This word *bread*. Whoever has not lived through this and felt [what it was like] not to have bread . . . the jewel in the British Crown was not as valuable as a piece of bread."

They were told that they were being sent east, to work in the fields of Russia. "But to say we did not know that this was our end—we did know," Czarny said. Remembering the thirst of the people inside the boxcars, Czarny brought his fingers to his lips. "I remember people were going stark raving mad. They began drinking urine. *A bisele pishi.* They actually did that." He began to sob. He apologized. Levin suggested he have a drink of water and calm down before continuing.

But Czarny could not restrain himself. "Excuse me," he said in Yiddish between sobs, "my daughter is listening to me. Why does she have to hear this. Why?" His eyes searched out his daughter from among the spectators, "*Zippele, dos iz vos iz gevorn, fun dayn tatn* [That is what became of your father]."

He recalled in such great detail his arrival and first day at Treblinka that he had to remind the judges, "Everything that I am telling the court took not hours, but seconds."

Czarny wanted to explain how it was that he had survived to tell his tale. At the end of the woman's shed, he said, at the very entrance that led to the gas chambers, a Ukrainian guard crooked his finger and motioned to him to step out of the line of newly arrived Jews.

Czarny joined a group who were led into a shed and locked in while the gassings occurred. Inside, he could hear the Jews from the transports meeting their fate. "I could hear the same spectacle . . . the same '*Sh'ma Yisroel*' . . . the same heartrending cries and the shouts of the Germans, too, in German, '*Schneller, schneller,*' and the same murderous blows. And the bodies left lying in the courtyard. The same thing happened again. But later we heard, perhaps it was an hour or so later, and by then I could pick up more of what was happening around me, there was pastoral peace, pastoral calm. Everyone was already dead. You could hear the birds singing, since the camp was in a forest clearing, surrounded by woods."

In between the gassings of the arriving transports, the Jews in the shed were let out to pick up the victims' clothing from the courtyard and sort it. Czarny estimated there were six transports that day. In the late afternoon, he hid among the clothing. The others in his group were murdered. He was discovered by Jewish forced-laborers who gave him clothes—"there was no lack of clothing"—and food and water. The next morning, he went out with the workers and met the *Kapo,* named Krakowsky. "He asked me: 'How are you doing?'" Czarny said. "'How are things in Warsaw?'—as though I knew what things were like in Warsaw. He said, 'Don't be afraid, you're new here.' But I was afraid to say, to ask, 'Why am I new?' I understood that something was strange. He said, '*Yo, Yo mayn kind*—yes, yes, my child. Don't be afraid.'" Czarny was assigned to sort the clothing.

Czarny had arrived there after the High Holidays. "There was already frost," he recalled, "ground frost. This was already autumn in Poland. And I was employed in this sorting job until about May, until after Passover. And then I was transferred to the *Hofjuden* [court-Jews] detail, that was the cleaning of the yard and the square."

Czarny was asked how he came to be transferred to the *Hofjuden*. "One day, Lalke—Kurt Franz [deputy commander of Treblinka]—called me. It is very, very difficult to describe to the court what this meant when Lalke called you. I simply have no words to describe it. I remember he beckoned to me from afar, he said: 'Come on, come on—you—little one. Come here.'

"And I said to myself, well, that's it. This is the end. . . . I stood to attention and he asked me, 'How old are you?' And I answered him in Yiddish, 'I'm eighteen years old.' So Lalke says to me, 'No that's not true.' And I said to him: '*Yavol, Herr Scharfuher, Sturmfuhrer*—[Yes, Sergeant, Lieutenant]'—I don't quite remember what we called him—and he slapped my face. He had gloves, which had been lined with pieces of metal. And he slapped me on the right ear. I fainted. I fell to the ground.

"Somehow I was lifted from the ground, probably some of the forced-laborers whom he had called lifted me from the ground. And I remember blood trickling down from my ear."

Czarny was told he was to report to Franz's living quarters the next day.

"What should I do? Lalke means death. That's it. I so wanted to live. I so wanted to live, I did not want to die. But I had no choice."

After the morning roll call, Czarny reported to Lalke at his quarters in the German compound. "He was sitting there in an armchair, and I remember it—as if it were today. And he said: 'Take off the boots.' Instead of pulling back, instead of letting me do so, he pushed his boot into my face. He must have been—he was drunk. I don't know how I managed to get the boots off his legs.

"After I had taken his boots off, he said to me: you are going to be a *Hofjuden*. I didn't know what a *Hofjuden* meant, Your Honor. And once again, he slapped me and he said, 'Polish.' He said to me, 'If it isn't going to be as bright as a mirror, you know what is in store for you—you know what you will get.' I think for two days, a day-and-a-half, I don't quite remember, I polished his boots. Not all the time, of course."

Czarny was taken to the chicken coop. "Altogether what didn't they have? They had a pigsty. They had stables with horses. They had a chicken coop so that they would have fresh eggs. And then I was employed on jobs in the chicken coop."

"Is there even a historian," Czarny asked, "who can understand that sort of thing, and if there is such a person, where is he?" Now he was sobbing.

"My daughter, Zippele," Czarny asked, "where is she? *Ikh hob kayn breyre nisht* [I have no choice but to tell]."

Judge Levin asked him to regain his composure; Shaked offered him a glass of water. But Czarny could not calm down. With his long, fleshy face and gray hair standing on end, he looked the part of the sad clown. He asked, "Why should I have come to such a path? I am humiliating myself. . . ." Czarny's face folded in on itself as tears streamed down his cheeks.

"Nobody knew about it. What can I do? They ruled our lives. Then he broke into Yiddish, again begging: "Children, don't forget us, don't forget us." His sobs erupted from deep inside him.

Czarny had been a *Hofjuden* from Passover until the day of the uprising. The *Hofjuden* had to wear a yellow cloth triangle on their clothes. He was free to move about the chicken-coop area and also had free access to the German compound where he cleaned stoves in the kitchen. Occasionally, he went to the Ukrainians' kitchen after their meals to gather leftovers for the pigsty and chicken coop.

Czarny testified that when the revolt broke out, he ran from the camp. Once outside its boundaries, he kept running. "There was a force within me that drove me to save myself. . . . I wanted so desperately to live. I did not want to die. Why? I have no answer. I don't know." Czarny managed to swim across the river, even though he did not know how to swim. Finally in the forest, Czarny fell to the ground. He cried out to his dead parents to ask why he had been allowed to live.

He broke into sobs. The audience was hushed except for the clicking and whirring of cameras.

"Please calm down," Levin said.

"I am trying, Your Honor, I am trying, but I am reliving Treblinka. Your Honor, I am in Treblinka right now. Right now I am sitting in Treblinka, and in Jerusalem, too . . . we have been praying for Jerusalem. Yes, that's right. I am in Jerusalem."

Later Shaked asked him to recall those occasions when he saw Ivan Grozny. Czarny responded that when the transports arrived, the SS would stand there to issue commands and on several occasions Ivan Grozny was among them, "standing together as a peer, as an equal of the masters with them." Ivan was known to be brutal, and Czarny feared him.

Judge Dorner asked if Czarny knew him and came across him.

"Did I come across him? Yes, madame; yes, Your Honor. Not only once. Ivan Grozny I saw more frequently because I had more opportunities, because I was a *Hofjuden*."

Czarny said he also saw Ivan Grozny because the chicken run where he worked was on the path leading from the death camp to the German quarters. "Throughout all of these transports, as I said, from time to time I saw him. I saw when a transport would arrive. People were not only beaten, they were sometimes shot. On one of these transports, I saw how Ivan Grozny was pointing his pistol and shooting in the direction of the fence, the fence that is in front of a track, the outer fence. And I saw a young girl, who apparently had succeeded—you know, when transports arrived everyone knew what was waiting for them—in spite of everything. So each person sought some way of saving his life . . . and I could see him pointing his pistol in this direction. But since the fence is green, apparently the reflection of a human being was not so obvious on that background. I could see her climbing up the fence, but he pulled out his pistol and shot at her. In those moments I saw him shooting her, and I still had a chance to see, I just had a chance to catch the look of this girl as she fell down."

Czarny said he also saw Ivan as he walked around or went to get food or when he went to the Germans' living quarters. Czarny said he often saw Ivan Grozny coming along the path from the death camp. "Even if I didn't want to, I always wound up seeing him. I wanted to keep away, but I did see him often—often when I was going to pick up food from the Ukrainian kitchen, too." Czarny testified that Ivan was four, five, or six years older than him at the time.

When Miriam Radiwker put the album of photographs before him in 1976, "I opened it up," he now testified, "and saw a number of pictures. I came to one, and I said immediately, Your Honor, *immediately, Dos iz Ivan—Ivan Grozny von Treblinka.* I recognized him from the first look, immediately, without a shadow of a doubt."

Czarny said he had become quite agitated because the picture was of a man older than the one he knew at Treblinka; the man in the photo was in civilian clothes and his face was fuller. "Well, I saw this, my God, he's alive, he's alive."

"You are saying this with a certain amount of agitation," Levin said, "and forgive the expression, rather dramatically, but how was it at the time?"

"It was the same dramatic expression as I am using here. This dramatic touch will accompany me for whatever is left of my life."

Czarny testified that after he identified Ivan as having been at Treblinka, Radiwker said he had been at Sobibor. "I said, that's impossible, he was in Treblinka, he was not in Sobibor. Ivan Grozny was in Treblinka."

Cross-examination was comparatively short—only three hours long. Czarny had been in Camp One, not the death camp, and O'Connor wanted to ascertain how Czarny could know Ivan, or know what he did. Czarny answered that Ivan's normal place of assignment was in the death camp and his duty was to introduce gas into the gas chambers. Said Czarny, matter-of-factly, "He was a sort of mechanic."

Judge Dorner asked, "How did you know this?"

"It was no secret. Of course, we were living on borrowed time, but we knew what was going on. There was some sort of contact. There were no secrets."

There were moments, particularly before the break, when the witness grew tired and Czarny was unapologetic. Often he said, "I just can't remember." Yet his willingness to define those matters he recalled and those he didn't lent his testimony even greater credibility.

Sheftel focused on the identification reports. He argued that because Radiwker wrote out two reports on Czarny, one concerning Fedorenko, the second concerning Demjanjuk, there must have been two separate identification sessions. And as the Fedorenko report was written up first, Czarny could not have pointed immediately at Demjanjuk's picture. Sheftel tried to bully him: "Ivan, you did not point to at all. Not under any circumstance. You did not mention his name. You did not point to him. You did not say, 'Here is Ivan of Treblinka.' You did not say anything that has to do with Ivan. You pointed to . . . Fedorenko."

"My first reflex was Ivan," said Czarny firmly. As to why Radiwker did not mention this in the Fedorenko report, Czarny's curt reply was that Radiwker could be asked that when *she* testified. Czarny's testimony was unshakable. But the experience of testifying left Czarny shaken.

Czarny had been afraid that testifying would be too emotionally stressful. He had even asked the prosecution if he might be excused from it. But the prosecutors had said, "If not you, who?" "What could I answer them?" he said later. "So I agreed."

Testifying in Jerusalem proved both easier and harder than it had been in Dusseldorf or Ft. Lauderdale. A court is a court, he said, wherever it is, but the difference is the public. "I feel at home in Jerusalem"—which made it easier. But to relive the experiences of Treblinka there, was more difficult. Recounting his testimony, Czarny's eyes started to tear: "I never believed that I would stand in Jerusalem and speak in Hebrew and give testimony about what happened to us there. . . . Even though I was in Jerusalem, I felt that day that I was exactly in Treblinka. I didn't know anything, just that I was in Treblinka. . . . The hardest part was seeing my children upset. The whole time I was talking and feeling as though I was in Treblinka, I was still thinking, 'I don't want to upset my children.'"

Professor Dina Porat, a historian of the Holocaust, had interviewed Czarny on videotape for Tel Aviv's Beth Hatfutsot (Museum of the Diaspora). She offered Czarny a copy of the tape for his family, but although his wife was also a survivor, he would not accept. Until that day in court, he had never brought himself to tell them of his experiences. He reacted the way he did, Porat said, because of the public disclosure, or exposure, which weighed heavily upon him. She believed he felt humiliated, "because he is among those survivors, who almost apologize for surviving."

After testifying, Czarny said that when his children were young they would ask his wife about the number on her arm. His wife was more open in talking about the Holocaust than he was; but even she became upset when Holocaust programs were broadcast on television. Their children learned to turn the programs off. Once they became older, Czarny said, there became an "agreement of silence." "The children did not want to distress us by asking, and we did not want to distress them by telling." Czarny's wife could not come to court, but the children did. . . . "And the children, they were themselves in hell while hearing what happened."

Nevertheless, he said that he felt after the testimony, "as though a huge weight has been lifted from me, even though this weight has accompanied me my whole life, every day. Something has gone from me." He smiled.

"There are two things the Germans could not take away from me, my memory and my spirituality."

In contrast to Demjanjuk's ruddy good health, the next witness, Gustav Boraks, was the frailest thus far. His wife helped him to the podium; she was led to a seat in the front row.

Seated, Gustav Boraks could barely see above the podium. He had a full head of white hair and a face as brown as a paper bag. He wore a white turtleneck and tan jacket. Boraks was forty-one years old when he arrived at Treblinka. His wife and two children were killed there. In Israel, Boraks started a new family and was now a grandfather.

Shaked stood close to Boraks as he testified in Yiddish. Born in 1901, in Vienun, Poland, a small town near Lodz, he had been a barber and had had his own barbershop. He was married with two children, "Pinhas,"—he gave a pause that must have struck the prosecution with fear for his memory—"and Yossef."

Boraks's barbershop was confiscated. He was taken to a prison and transferred to Cracow. There he was arrested for not wearing an armband. The Gestapo beat him mercilessly and amused themselves by throwing him down four flights of stairs. His wife was able to save him by trading her fur coat for his life. From Cracow, Boraks and his family were transferred to the Czestochowa ghetto.

As Boraks testified, Shaked tried to put him at ease. It was not easy. Four months earlier, when Shaked had visited Boraks in

Haifa, his mind was clear and his answers poured forth. Eighty-six years old now, under the glare of the klieg lights, his age had caught up with him. Shaked asked questions to which Boraks offered no answer. So Shaked asked more precise questions to which Boraks needed reply only "yes" or "no."

After testimony by the intense Epstein, the energetic Rosenberg, and the emotional Czarny, Boraks's very frailty seemed itself a statement about the future of Nazi war-crimes prosecution. The witnesses were a limited precious resource. A matter of a few months could make a great difference.

Boraks was like a cranky child. Upon hearing Judge Tal's deep Yiddish, he said he preferred Tal as an interpreter to the court's. "Him, I understand," said the witness. Judge Tal agreed to oblige him. Many in the audience smiled.

With Tal as translator, Boraks became more animated. As he focused on Treblinka, his memory seemed to flow again. He told how upon arrival at Treblinka he was thrown from the boxcars to the ground. He didn't know what was happening. They asked for barbers, but Boraks didn't reply, "My wife and children were going to be killed, I wasn't going to raise my hand." Later when they found out he was a barber, he was beaten about the head for not having volunteered.

At first the barbershop was in the Lower Camp in a shed where fifteen benches were arranged for fifteen or sixteen barbers. He was to cut the women's hair. He recalled that "They didn't want to come in, but Ivan would take his bayonet and with his bayonet he would force them into the barbershop. . . . The women were wounded and pieces of flesh, whole pieces of flesh were hanging behind them, the blood was dripping."

Every time a transport arrived, there was a signal—a whistle—and the barbers were to show up to cut hair. When there was no transport, he sorted clothes, putting them into bundles to be loaded back onto the trains and taken away. If a Jew did not do his job well, if he didn't remove the Jewish patch from the clothing, he was shot. He remembered Lalke riding his horse and shooting into the latrines when the Jews were in the toilets.

Boraks also worked on a camouflage detail. Workers would collect branches. "Two people would carry a tree, and I was walking with a young man of seventeen or eighteen. I was strong enough to carry the tree, but the young boy didn't have the strength, and he fell down. So Ivan walked over to him, when he fell, and shot him."

Shaked shortened his usual questions and jumped forward to the critical moment—Boraks's meeting with Radiwker. Shaked asked what he had said after looking at the photo album of Ukrainians. "I said to her," Boraks testified, "I know Ivan and the other one—what's his name." Never mind, Shaked said. But a few moments later, Boraks said excitedly, "Fedorenko is the other one. I just remembered his name was Fedorenko." This, too, elicited smiles.

Shaked handed him the album. He opened it. Turning over the first page slowly, he immediately pointed to a face on the next leaf. "That is Fedorenko," he said, "and this is Ivan." He pointed with assurance to Demjanjuk's photo.

Shaked asked why he recognized him. "He had a full face, a high forehead, and small eyes."

"Why do you remember Ivan?" Shaked asked again. "Because he was all the time at the place where the hair was being cut," Boraks said. A bit exasperated, Shaked said, "But why did he stick in your memory?" "Why? Because he was tall. . . ," Boraks said, "he had an elongated face and a peaked cap."

Shaked decided to try a different tact. He showed Boraks his deposition from 1976. Boraks recalled it and said Radiwker's arm was in a sling, so she had brought along someone else. Boraks said that at the time of Treblinka, Ivan must have been twenty-two or twenty-three.

He said Ivan's uniform was green. But the auxiliary uniforms were usually black, as Boraks had told Radiwker in 1976. Shaked asked if he would like his memory to be refreshed by his earlier deposition. Sheftel objected, and it was sustained. Shaked tried another tact, asking Boraks whether the court should rely on his statement in 1976 or his testimony in court.

The earlier statement, Boraks said sincerely. Shaked left it at that.

Boraks recalled Kollar's visit in 1981. Shaked asked if he had found anything in the photographs. "Fedorenko and Ivan," he testified. Shaked began to follow this up, but Sheftel objected that if the answer Boraks gave did not suit the prosecution, they nonetheless had to accept it.

"I think the witness may remember better than we do," Shaked said. In fact, Kollar had shown Boraks two stacks of photographs that day, one with Ivan and the other with Fedorenko. Shaked set about putting the same photographs before him. They had since been glued to a cardboard sheet.

Boraks pointed at the Trawniki card photo, saying: "Ivan. Ivan Grozny." Boraks repeated that he recalled him because, "He used to roam around the area where we would cut the women's hair."

Levin asked how much hair he cut off. "It wasn't a haircut," Boraks said. "We would grab the hair and cut it all off." Under further questioning, Boraks said the hair was sorted and put in an oven where it was cleaned. He said children were also brought to him, but a few minutes later he said their hair wasn't cut. At first, he couldn't remember whether the women were dressed or naked, but then he recalled they were ordered to undress. He said Fedorenko once shot a woman who refused.

Gustav Boraks looked out at the audience, his small, dark eyes set in a pug face. At the recess, he pulled a small sandwich from his pocket and munched on it peacefully.

"Mar Boraks," O'Connor began the cross-examination, "can you indicate what color my gown is?" Was O'Connor mocking Borak's reply that Ivan wore a green uniform? His next question also went straight for the jugular: he asked Boraks if he could name his children. Boraks replied, without difficulty, that he had two sons, Pinhas and Yossef, who were killed with his first wife in Treblinka; and one from his second wife, named Yoram.

But Boraks was tired, and the long day now began to wear on him. At moments he became confused. O'Connor asked him about Fedorenko: "Do you remember testifying against Fedorenko in the United States?"

"Yes."

"Do you remember the year?"

"No."

"Do you remember how you traveled from Israel to Florida so that you could speak to the court in that trial?"

"Yes. We went by train." But O'Connor continued, asking where he stayed in Florida. Boraks answered, "In a hotel."

O'Connor discussed the Fedorenko case. Boraks said he had traveled with Sonia Lewkowicz but had not spoken with her in a great many years.

There was the possibility that Boraks would say something damaging to the prosecution case. Yet for all his weaknesses, he yielded nothing. Boraks said that the survivors had sat together in the courtroom and had had dinner together. But when asked, "Did you talk about Treblinka?" The answer was emphatic: "No, we didn't speak about that."

O'Connor asked Boraks if he remembered the number for his barracks. "One hundred," he answered. This was wrong but, on reexamination, Boraks instinctively pointed to his coat lapel, to show that one hundred was *his* number at Treblinka, not the number of his barracks.

O'Connor asked about an SS man named Suchomel. Boraks surprised the spectators by replying, "Suchomel wasn't a bad man. He was OK." Boraks said Suchomel oversaw the *Goldjuden* (literally "Gold Jews"—Jewish workers whose job it was to sort the gold, currency, and other valuables which were to be sent to Germany).

O'Connor asked if Suchomel had ever come to his aid before Commander Stangl. Boraks told how, one day, as he was performing his duties as a barber, his sister-in-law and her children came before him. She knew her husband was dead, and that she was about to die. But she begged him to save her children. She wept and fell all over him. Boraks was powerless.

For this, that his sister-in-law wept in his arms, Lalke ordered Boraks to undress and enter the gas chamber. But Suchomel intervened on his behalf. He said Boraks was a good barber and that he should be saved. Boraks was allowed to live, but his sister-in-law and the children went to the gas chamber.

Suchomel, he testified, would come in and say hello to him every other day or so. Boraks saw him up to the day of the uprising and even on the day itself. Boraks said Suchomel had hidden in a barracks because he was afraid the Jews would kill him.

"Did you kill him?" O'Connor asked.

"No-ohhh," said Boraks. "If not for him I would not be alive."

Levin asked if he knew whether Suchomel was killed in the uprising. He said he didn't. Judge Dorner asked, "Did you kill anyone?" Said Boraks, "Heaven forbid, no, I couldn't so much as kill a fly!"

O'Connor asked why the prisoners called him Ivan Grozny. "Because he was a *groyser bandit* [a great criminal]—he killed children," said Boraks. He admitted he had seen Ivan only in Camp One.

Boraks had left Haifa at 5:00 A.M. that morning. As the afternoon wore on, it became obvious that Boraks's mind was weakening under the strain. The more tired he became, the less he could remember or wanted to remember. After a short while, the defense rested.

Yet the prosecution forged ahead with its redirect. It seemed heartless to continue, yet it would have been worse to ask Boraks to return the next day. Shaked felt there were a few points that needed clarification. He brought out that Boraks had testified at Dusseldorf against Suchomel. Boraks nonetheless maintained that Suchomel was "the best of all of them." The prosecution rested at 5:55 P.M.

Still Judge Levin had two questions. First, he asked Boraks to repeat the story about Suchomel saving his life. He did, with precision. Levin asked his second question: "You said you went to Florida by train. What train stop did you get on at?"

"I was wrong," Boraks said, "I made a mistake. I flew." Levin smiled. "From where to where did you fly?"

"From Katowice," he replied. This was a city in Poland. Some in the audience giggled in embarrassment.

"From where did you depart?"

"From Poland. From Poland I went to America."

Judge Dorner tried to change the subject and asked, "Have you heard of Demjanjuk in Treblinka?"

"Yes," Boraks said.

"Who was he?" Dorner asked.

"He's sitting over there," Boraks said, nodding his head in Demjanjuk's direction.

Levin thanked the witness, and said in heartfelt tones, "We wish you a long life, and we hope you never have to think back to those experiences publicly again."

"Amen," Boraks said.

CHAPTER 15

A Police Matter

That the Demjanjuk case was a police matter was something you forgot while listening to the survivors' testimonies. But Alexander Ish Shalom, the officer who directed Demjanjuk's prison interrogations, returned the case from Treblinka to police routine: suspect, arrest, imprisonment, interrogation.

Ish Shalom was called to the stand to introduce police reports of the interrogations as well as numerous documents with which Demjanjuk was confronted during the questionings. As each form or report was introduced, O'Connor asked to examine it, an action that considerably lengthened the process. O'Connor would take an exaggerated look at each paper, then offer it to Demjanjuk for his own inspection.

Demjanjuk would pore over each document, then confer with O'Connor in animated whispers. The defendant could be overheard, speaking in thick English, challenging each piece of evidence. This was strange. The documents had been acknowledged, and unquestioned: Demjanjuk's 1947 driver's license, his visa application, his IRO application, his naturalization certificate. Over the years he had seen these documents often and he had never challenged them before. Why now say, as he did to O'Connor, "I do not recognize the picture. It is forged." or that the picture on his naturalization certificate "is a fake."

When among the documents the Trawniki card was submitted, O'Connor asked to see it; he admired it as though it were a work of art. Smiling, he turned it over, handed it to Sheftel and Gill, and then gave it to Demjanjuk. As Demjanjuk peered at it, O'Connor grinned. Leaning over to Sheftel, he motioned to the anxious prosecution team, "Look at their faces. . . ."

The prosecution sent their law clerk, Eric Bukhatman, across the courtroom stage to retrieve the document. Before handing it back, O'Connor made, as a joke, a slight feint with the card.

Rather than challenge the interrogation reports, O'Connor used this as an opportunity to decry Demjanjuk's prison conditions and deride the circumstances under which the interrogation had been conducted. But O'Connor never argued that Demjanjuk's statements were coerced and he had never filed any complaint on conditions with the prison authorities or the courts.

Ish Shalom had been Sheftel's law school professor on police procedure. So it was, therefore, with a certain relish that Sheftel cross-examined him. Sheftel disputed the prosecution's contention that Demjanjuk was identified by people who knew him; not unknowns who needed to pick him out of a lineup. He set out to show that the identifications, if held to Israeli legal standards for a lineup, would fail.

As Ish Shalom had not been operating under Sheftel's assumption—that a lineup was necessary—Sheftel's questions seemed to come out of left field. Ish Shalom could not really answer them, except to say that he did not see fit to conduct the procedures Sheftel argued were necessary. Sheftel was in his element. This is what he did best, grilling police officers; and what he enjoyed best, attacking authority figures.

Ish Shalom revealed during his testimony that there had been a sixth—and secret—police member of Operation Justice. One of Demjanjuk's prison guards had been a police "plant," assigned to befriend him and pry information out of him.

His name was Arye Kaplan. Born in Vilna, Lithuania, he had served in the Red Army for two years, he told the court, before coming to Israel in 1973. His recent cover, he said, was not ideal; he'd told Demjanjuk that he was the son of a Lithuanian father and a Jewish mother, and was a private in the Red Army, that he had emigrated to Israel but that he didn't like it there, and hoped to emigrate soon to the United States.

He spoke Russian, so he and Demjanjuk had conversed a great deal. Kaplan was never sure he had Demjanjuk's complete confidence. He offered to help Demjanjuk avoid the prison censor by sending and receiving the mail at his home. Demjanjuk agreed.

When the Demjanjuk family visited, Kaplan was introduced as a friend.

When they talked, Kaplan testified, often Demjanjuk volunteered information. But when Kaplan pressed beyond a certain point, Demjanjuk would end the conversation. A certain leitmotif ran through their conversation: Demjanjuk was not at Treblinka, but Kaplan, as a soldier, could understand that a war was on and one should not try those who were only following orders. Describing his suffering at the POW camp, Demjanjuk said he would have killed for a loaf of bread.

On one occasion, Demjanjuk said, "At Ford plant working with me were Germans who were in the SS. Why didn't anyone question them? They're only after Ukrainians. Isn't that clear? There was at work Germans who were in the SS. Any witness who speaks against me will be from the SS. We had to collaborate." He made it seem as though anyone who had burned a corpse of a Jew was a collaborator. Jews had also been collaborators, according to him, and he mentioned the *Judenrat* (Jewish council). He was also interested in Kurt Waldheim, about whom he had read.

Demjanjuk was interested and involved in his defense, Kaplan testified. He was cheered when newspapers reported accounts saying Ivan had died in the uprising, and the fact that a man in Spain, Garcia de Ribes, had said he was at Treblinka, that he knew Ivan the Terrible and Demjanjuk was not he. (Garcia de Ribes, who spent only a day in Treblinka's Lower Camp, was visited by the Demjanjuk defense. But they did not find his evidence credible enough to call him as a witness.)

Kaplan reported that Demjanjuk was almost obsessed by the report of an eighty-five-year-old in Trieste who said he knew the family name of Ivan Grozny. Demjanjuk said, "To this day the family name of Ivan Grozny is not known." (This man was visited by the prosecution. And though the Italian government would later announce that they were investigating Demjanjuk's activities in Trieste in 1943–44, the prosecution did not think the evidence strong enough to stand up in court.)

Kaplan asked Demjanjuk about how Ukrainian Church members and other Ukrainians in the United States viewed his case. Demjanjuk said they well understood that a person who became a German prisoner of war had to carry out orders, as the Germans would otherwise have punished him. But, he said, it was unjustifiable if the person, performing his duty, exceeded orders and acted on his own initiative. Such a person should be punished. Demjanjuk agreed that Eichmann should have been punished because he gave orders, "but those who didn't give orders, the smaller ones, performed them as they were told, and the question is whether they added on [acts] on their own."

A few weeks later, Demjanjuk told Kaplan that "the conditions in the prisoner-of-war camps were inhuman, that when a German would appear, a *Kapo* would immediately order [the prisoners] to remove hats and the people stood and were afraid to move. If the German didn't like something about someone, he would shoot him on the spot." Demjanjuk again made it clear that he wasn't talking about himself. But, he said, "if we assume that we are speaking of himself, although this isn't so, then it is also clear that there is nothing to try [him] for." The prosecution found this incriminating: There were no *Kapos* in POW camps; *Kapo* was a term used in the concentration camps.

Demjanjuk insisted that he could not operate an engine before the end of the war. He would have had to have been a driver; to be a driver in the Soviet Union, he said, you need seven years of education—and he had only four.

Demjanjuk blamed the Ukrainian famine, Kaplan testified, on a Soviet official named Kaganovich, who was, Demjanjuk said, a *zhid*—the derogatory term for Jew.

On cross-examination O'Connor argued that *zhid* is the normal term for Jew in Western Poland. Kaplan answered that he would say *yehudi* and that to a Russian, *zhid* is a derogatory term. "Ask your client," said Kaplan, "but to me it's derogatory." In fact, there was a period in the Soviet Union when it was a criminal offense to use this term.

At the day's end, Demjanjuk rose from his seat, heaved a sigh of dismissal, and made a downward dismissive motion with his hands, to show his disgust and frustration; then he hugged his son.

CHAPTER 16

An Intimation of Hell

In the courtroom in Jerusalem, the mind fled the words and searched for other details. Sitting there, one was divorced from the outside world, the press accounts of the trial, Israel's domestic and international problems—but one was also distracted from the crimes at issue. The very setting—a stage, cordoned off by police officers—created a certain distance.

Unlike the Eichmann trial, which was steeped in formality, the Demjanjuk trial was collegial; the opposing lawyers shook hands, chatted; the journalists, attorneys, translators, and court and government press office officials knew and greeted each other. The security officers throughout the room, so young—the visiting soldiers and students, the third generation—Demjanjuk's reactions—all these were distractions.

When the final survivor was called to the stand, it was easy to be distracted by the dignity of his appearance, the eloquence with which he spoke of the unspeakable, but months later, his account of Treblinka would haunt many as the one that brought them closest to an intimation of hell.

Yehiel Meir Reichman spoke in Yiddish in a tired but lilting voice. As he was the fifth witness to tell his tale, the territory was familiar. Reichman's descriptions, however, were particularly concrete.

He began, "Your Honor, I will tell you everything on behalf of those who can no longer tell the story, my sister and the others." At

150

seventy-two, he was an impressive figure. But as he talked of Treblinka, the weight of the subject bore down on him, dulling the usual sparkle in his eyes.

When Reichman arrived at Treblinka, he knew their journey, as well as their lives, had come to an end. He told his sister to leave their suitcases: "We will not be needing them here." Because Reichman had thought they were embarking on a short trip, he had advised his sister not to eat before. She went to the gas chambers hungry. He would never forgive himself for that.

Shortly after his arrival, Reichman, like the others who had survived, was chosen to sort clothing. As he ran to gather clothes, he saw a naked woman holding her son in her arms. "At that moment," Reichman testified, "one of the blaggards came and tore the child out of his mother's arms, grabbed him by the feet and smashed his skull before his mother's eyes." The whole room gasped.

Reichman spoke directly to the judges, his heavy face turned toward them. He told the court he volunteered to be a barber. "What did I have to lose?" he said. The next morning, Reichman heard the cry, "Barbers out." He went with a friend who had told him to prepare scissors, and they were led toward the gas chambers. "This was the most horrifying job, even though I spent only three days there. There they brought in running naked women, and we were made to cut off their hair in five cuts, five snips of the scissors."

The barbering took place between the gas chambers. "There was one chamber that was open on both sides, and there they arranged benches where they put the victims—the victims who, a few minutes later, would no longer be alive. There were moments, terrible moments there, and you saw the reaction of the people there. . . . For example, a woman sat down in front of me and said, 'Do me a favor. I'm here with my daughter, but she is still in line behind. Don't cut my hair so quickly. I want to go to my death with her.' But I could not even fulfill this last request because I was being whipped."

Blatman asked if he remembered anything else from that place. Reichman recalled a woman who said: " 'Tell me the truth, I see that I am about to die. But young people, are they allowed to live? Will my son survive? Will he be allowed to live and take revenge?' A young girl came in, and when she saw everyone crying, she broke into hysterical laughter and cried out: 'You should be ashamed of yourselves. Who are you crying for? Let us not show our enemies that we are about to die frightened.' "

The barbers had to pack the hair very painstakingly into bags. There was a rumor, Reichman testified, that the hair was used to reinforce metal for ammunition. The Ukrainian guards and a German supervised the barbers, who were forced to sort clothes when they were not cutting hair. When a transport arrived, they would hear the call for barbers.

Reichman wore a gray three-piece suit. His expressive face grew red under the lights, but remained soft, set off by his silver-white hair and creamy complexion, wrinkled only at the eyes. The memories were like a weight, forcing his chin down on his chest.

"When you were working at the sorting area," Blatman asked, "did you find anything personal?"

"Among the clothes, I found my sister's frock. I tore off the cloth and kept a piece. I had it in my pocket for many months."

Once in the death camp, Reichman became friends with Dr. Zimmerman, a *Kapo* of the dentists. Zimmerman knew the Germans and the Ukrainians because he held the key to a box near the workshops where valuables, taken from the corpses, were stored. When the Ukrainians and Germans went on leave, they would come to him and pick up valuables for which he would get a loaf of bread. The bread was often wrapped in a newspaper; in this way the prisoners learned what was going on in the outside world.

Reichman asked Zimmerman to give him cyanide because he didn't have the courage to hang himself. Zimmerman didn't have any but told Reichman to hold on—he would try and get him assigned to the dentist's crew. Zimmerman told Matthes, the German in charge of the death camp, that more dentists were needed. So the order was issued: anyone who was a dentist, step forward.

Reichman, with no true training, marched out of line and thus became one of the dentists. "The work was as follows," he testified: "Every time a transport arrived with people who within a few minutes would be dead, we were called. We would go down. There were many bowls, one on top of the other. We were arranged in a group of six . . . six of us for each lane. The first person would have a bowl in front of him with water in it [the bowls and water were for cleaning the extracted teeth]. He had to check the stretcher-bearers and to see whether the corpse on the stretcher had any teeth, any false teeth. . . . If it did, he would pull the stretcher-bearer out of line . . . and pull out those teeth. . . ." Each dentist carried out a similar function and that way all of the corpses were checked.

"When there were no transports, we were in our shed. There we were supposed to separate the teeth in different types, to separate the natural, the real teeth from the false. Sometimes inside the crowns, there were valuables like diamonds. In addition, we were supposed to clean thoroughly the gold teeth so that they would be absolutely spotless. Each week we turned over a suitcase of teeth that we estimated at ten kilograms [twenty-two pounds]."

The teeth were washed in a well that was located, in Reichman's estimation, some three to four meters from the gas chambers.

"I would like to tell the court what happened near the well to *mein Haver* [my friend], Finkelstein. While I was washing teeth there together with Finkelstein, next to this well, this demon Ivan"—Reichman pointed spontaneously at Demjanjuk—"came with a drill . . . he turned it into the buttocks of Finkelstein, telling him: 'If you yell, I shall shoot you.' Finkelstein was seriously wounded. Blood was streaming from him. He was suffering unutterable pain but he could not yell because he was given this order that if he dared to yell, he would be shot. Ivan threatened him." Finkelstein kept his silence, and survived the drilling.

Throughout this account, Demjanjuk was slowly shaking his head "no."

"Ivan was the superdemon of Treblinka," Reichman testified. After Treblinka, while still in a bunker in Warsaw in 1944, Reichman began to think of giving evidence, and he thought of Ivan. "He is engraved in my memory, night and day, and I've never had any peace."

Reichman was asked to describe Ivan's job at Treblinka. He answered, as Czarny had: "He was a mechanic. . . . It was his job to start the gas in order to kill the people in the gas chambers. In Treblinka, there were two buildings of gas chambers. The first had three chambers. Next to it stood a separate entrance, and there stood a machine rather like a car engine. It was here that Ivan had his seat . . . he had the *honor* of turning on the gas."

"With what loyalty he fulfilled his task." Reichman sighed. His large, expressive hands were held out in front of him, his arms moved like a bellows, in and out, as he exhaled.

"One day, when I was sitting at this bowl to do with the false teeth, Ivan drove past with a horse and cart carrying products to Camp Two. As he passed by, one could hear screams from the gas chambers; when he heard those screams, it meant that people were being shepherded into the gas chambers. He left the horse and cart, and ran to his quarters to take a long iron bar, a round bar, took it on his shoulders, and ran over to the gas chamber so that he would get there in time to beat up the people being shepherded into the *Schlauch*. . . . That was his pleasure. That was what he lived for and was his greatest pleasure in life. . . . The sadism of this demon has no equal anywhere. It was his pleasure to take a knife, to go up to an ordinary worker, to cut off his ears. When [the worker] came back, he would tell him to strip and then shoot him to death. . . .

At that particular moment, he didn't have any obligation to do that. But when he heard the screams and the cries, he was so enthusiastic that he abandoned his horse and cart . . . to give his last *presents* to the victims as they were going to the chamber."

Levin's face clouded. The judge asked where the iron bar was located. Within the building of the small gas chambers, Reichman explained, there was a small room that housed the machine. "He was the mechanic who turned on the gas, and it was there that he kept all his tools, the drill, the knives, and the iron bar that he used to hurt people."

Blatman wanted to stress how much contact Reichman had with Ivan. "He was my neighbor," Reichman testified. "I saw him on every occasion. From the well, it was very close to the engine room." Reichman enumerated the opportunities he had to see Ivan. He saw him outside working hours, from the yard of their barracks. He often saw him sitting with his friend Nikolai on a bench outside the engine room. The two men, Reichman said, would spend "companionable hours together." When Reichman carried corpses, he frequently saw Ivan because the carriers would have to wait the half-hour while victims were gassed.

"And we had to sing for them," he testified. Judge Dorner asked for an explanation. "This was between one group of the dead and the next," Reichman said. "We would have to carry corpses away as quickly as possible, because they shouted at us that 'these pieces of shit' had to be disposed of as fast as possible. But while we were waiting for the next set of victims to be gassed, we were told to sit down and then we were told to sing songs that they liked."

When working as a dentist, Reichman saw Ivan several times a day. The dentists, as he had testified earlier, worked in a group of six in a line. When he was among the first in line, closer to the gas chambers, he would almost always see Ivan.

In 1945, when hiding in a bunker in Warsaw, Reichman wrote his memoir of Treblinka, recalling his eleven months there. He remembered a few of the criminals' names, but he remembered Ivan the most.

Judge Dorner asked why.

"This devil I carried within me," Reichman testified. "I saw him every step. I saw him at night, I saw him during the day. I saw his murderous sadism. I saw him everywhere I turned. I saw him in everything I did, with his heinous deeds."

Reichman testified that the American Embassy in Montevideo contacted him in 1980. He was asked if he would take part in trials relating to Treblinka. Reichman said that whenever called, he would "speak in the name of those who can no longer speak for themselves." He told the court that he made arrangements so that the next time he was in New York, he met with officials from the OSI. Four persons were waiting for him, with a recording machine. Sheftel objected, saying the defense had never received a transcript and didn't know one to exist. The prosecution said it, too, knew nothing of a recording of the session. Reichman continued, saying, he was shown a stack of photographs. He examined them at length, looking at each picture several times. "I, by nature, do not easily say 'yes' or 'no' off the cuff, so it took me awhile. I concentrated until I said what I said. . . . I said, my opinion is that this is Ivan of Treblinka." It was the only photograph he selected.

Afterward, he returned to Montevideo until summoned to Cleveland for Demjanjuk's denaturalization trial. At that trial, he singled out the photo he had identified previously. But he was also shown another set of photos. "There I recognized a picture that was even more similar than the other one, because in court they showed me a picture that was just the right weight, even more similar to the way he looked in Treblinka." It was the Trawniki photo.

Shown the set again, he quickly pointed to the Trawniki photo, saying, "This is Ivan."

Gill led the cross-examination. He stressed that Reichman would not have looked at Ivan because the prisoner worked at a run and feared him so, and was afraid of being *"gestampelt"* (marked). Gill had read Allan Ryan's book, in which Ryan had written, "At Treblinka, eye contact was forbidden." Ryan also had written that at the denaturalization trial, Reichman would not look Demjanjuk in the eye. But Reichman tried to make it clear to Gill that though he did work at a run and under a hail of beatings, there was still great opportunity to look around and observe.

Gill also stressed that the *Kapos* provided a layer of insulation between forced-laborers and Ukrainians, so that Reichman would have had no contact with Ivan. There was no historical support for this theory, and it showed a lack of understanding of Treblinka.

Reichman was not ashamed to speak of *Kapos*. His own *Kapo*, Zimmerman, had saved his life. Gill asked if *Kapos* could punish fellow Jews. Reichman said that he was never the subject of such punitive measures, nor did he ever see them carried out. He could only speak of what he knew.

Gill's focus continued to be on the misdeeds of the Jews. He asked questions such as, "People like yourself, sorting clothes, were all of them taking money, or was it just your friend that suggested it to you?"

But Gill was not alone in questioning the survivors. At one point, asked if he could see into the *Schlauch*, Reichman answered that he was not in the *Schlauch,* and couldn't see it, "otherwise I wouldn't be here today." A wire-service reporter commented, "The others said they did. Maybe he's the first one to tell the truth." This same reporter said she felt sorry for Demjanjuk; this was a show trial, she said, "because this is Israel," and the verdict and sentence were foregone conclusions.

Gill spent hours following this line of questioning, which had little if no bearing on the case. The judges were patient, but clearly exasperated.

Gill challenged Reichman's descriptions of landmarks on the diagram of the camp, again without any seeming bearing on Reichman's ability to observe Ivan. Gill asked, "You indicated earlier that this was the women's section, is that correct?" Reichman looked at the diagram. There was one building in the women's area. Reichman recalled two structures there. But Gill's question was not that.

"My question, Herr Reichman was: Do you know where the laundry was hung up to dry after it was done by the women that were forced to do this task?"

Judge Levin interrupted: "Mr. Gill, I have a question. . . . Of everything of the camp at Treblinka, where people—more than eight hundred fifty thousand were murdered and thrown into pits—and you do not deny this—is it important for us to know where they hung the laundry?" Levin continued angrily, unable to restrain himself, "Aren't you exaggerating in these questions? Did he hang up the laundry? Why do we have to waste the time of the court on points that are so marginal. . . ? Are we going to decide whether a person has committed so terrible an offense or not on the basis of where the laundry was hung to dry?"

Gill continued to ask about money taken by Reichman or other Jews from the dead. Gill asked whether some work groups had easier access to valuables. Reichman answered that, of course, the *Dentisten* had an easier chance than the others. But what was Gill getting at?

He asked whether Reichman knew of Ukrainians being granted furloughs or being transferred from Treblinka only to return after several months. Reichman said that he could not confirm this, but it was the opinion of Jewish inmates that the Ukrainians were given permission occasionally to leave the camp. Reichman wiped his brow with his blue handkerchief.

Gill was so tall, his robe fell only to his knees, and as he went through his questions he made checks on a legal pad. He was nearing the end of the pad when he asked whether the survivors of Treblinka met on a yearly basis. Reichman testified that he did not meet with them on a yearly basis, only when he came to Israel. Gill asked whether they talked about Treblinka. "We talk about everything," Reichman answered. He was always especially happy to meet old friends from that tragedy. But his regret, he said, his voice sharp, was meeting so few of them; and that each time, there was one less.

Gill brought out the fact that Reichman's 1944 memoir described Ivan only sketchily, as a "healthy powerful horse." Reichman gave this reason for the memoir's brief description and his more detailed one in court: "I never thought that I would have an opportunity, a moment in my life, when I would have to blame, or cast accusations at, this devil. First, because I was not sure that I would ever be reunited with those who lost everyone they had there. He was a devil like all the other devils, but the more I concentrate, the more I think back on it, the more I recall things vividly. Because when it comes to Treblinka, I cannot free myself of Treblinka. Sometimes I do not sleep, I wake up screaming. Believe me, it is impossible to remember everything. They didn't succeed in breaking us totally. We managed to clutch with our very last shreds of strength. What else do they want from us?"

Sheftel had questions about the photo identification in New York. No report had been made after the session, but in 1986, one of the participants, OSI investigator Tom Fusi, submitted his version of events. There were certain discrepancies between his and Reichman's version. Sheftel focused on these.

Fusi claimed the interview had been conducted in English. This was a mistake, Reichman said, as he does not speak English. He said there was a woman who translated from Yiddish. In fact, the translator, Helen Meyerowitz, who had retired in Israel, was a spectator at the trial.

Sheftel moved to the more serious: Fusi claimed Reichman looked at two different sets of pictures. Reichman recalled only one set. He said the meeting took a long time, several hours, and he was handed a packet of pictures, each of which he examined for a long time. "One of the pictures, so I said, was in my opinion, of Ivan." At the Cleveland trial, however, he identified a second picture of Ivan, the Trawniki card photo. It was easy to identify, Reichman said, because he was in uniform.

But according to the report, Sheftel said, he was shown that picture in New York and failed to identify it.

Why would Reichman identify the visa photo and not the Trawniki photo, which was, by Reichman's own reckoning, in uniform and closer in age to Ivan at Treblinka? If he did not recognize it in New York, why would he do so in Cleveland? It did not make sense. But Reichman could offer no explanation other than that he did not recall being shown the photo in New York.

Next O'Connor took up the questioning. He promised to take only a few minutes, but returned to a detailed examination of life at Treblinka and the uprising. O'Connor asked how he would have felt to be recaptured after the revolt. "Terrible," Reichman said. "We would do anything, to kill ourselves rather than go back, because we knew what was awaiting us. We would have been hung by our feet . . . we might have been subjected to all sorts of torture before we saw death, for death itself was not all that much of a problem."

O'Connor: "The fear of the return to the clutches of Ivan was even greater than the fear of death, sir. Is that true?"

Without the slightest doubt, answered Reichman.

Surely the death of Ivan, O'Connor asked, was in the minds of those who took part in the revolt?

Blatman objected to the question as hypothetical and good only for summing up. But Levin allowed it, gently chiding Blatman: "I think that is very cruel, Mr. Blatman. He is now coming to the punch question, as it were, and you want to stop defense counsel."

Reichman prefaced his comments by saying, "I want to make it clear that in Treblinka there were a great many Ivans. He was not the only one in Treblinka. There were a great many Ivans. There were many murderers." But, as to Ivan the Terrible, he said, had they been able to kill him, they would have done so. On redirect, Reichman reaffirmed that on the day of the uprising, as there were no transports, Ivan was not at work. Reichman didn't remember whether he saw Ivan on that day.

O'Connor concluded the cross, thanking him and wishing him "in the true sense of Moses . . . *biz hundert un tsvantsik* [may you live until one hundred and twenty]." Reichman replied: "Well, it is a little too much, but it can't do any harm." Reichman then thanked, "from the bottom of my heart . . . the court of Israel, which has taken upon itself the task of bringing to trial one of the most terrible of devils." He also thanked the State of Israel for its effort and prayed "that every decent person in the world will remember what happened in the various Treblinkas." Reichman's mike was removed. He stood up and walked slowly out of the courtroom.

One more survivor, Sonia Lewkowicz, was supposed to testify. She had testified at Dusseldorf, in Ft. Lauderdale against Fedorenko, and against Demjanjuk in Cleveland. But she was never called as a witness in Jerusalem. She could not overcome her anxiety and fear of being on the stand, reliving those experiences for direct examination, then enduring the cross-examination. The prosecutors hoped she would change her mind before they rested their case. But she did not.

The prosecution, in essence, had now put forward its most important evidence against John Demjanjuk, their eyewitness testimony. Was it enough? Reporters were equally divided. They had witnessed five old men on the stand, and they didn't know whether this was strong enough. The witnesses had not persuaded them entirely. They still had doubts.

But were they reasonable doubts? It was one thing not to be convinced, another to have a reasonable basis to doubt the veracity of the witnesses. Was there any objective evidence on which to doubt the survivors' proximity and contact with Ivan? Any basis for doubting the Israel Police identifications? To answer that, the investigators themselves would testify.

CHAPTER 17

The Investigators

Miriam Radiwker was petite with short, frosted hair. She looked twenty years younger than her actual eighty-one years. In her stylish black-and-white knit dress, she looked more like a fussy Polish wife at a ladies' luncheon than a veteran police officer on the witness stand.

Radiwker's testimony retraced the steps of her investigation. She identified the photos she had shown and described the witnesses interviewed, their reactions, including those who had identified Fedorenko and those who had failed to identify Demjanjuk. All this was told in a forthright and detailed manner, leaving an impression of thorough police work.

Three of the survivors Radiwker interviewed, Turovsky, Goldfarb, and Lindvasser, had since died. Normally their statements would be inadmissable, as the judges couldn't gain an impression of their credibility. But the Nazi and Nazi Collaborators Law had provided for just this situation, allowing evidence to be introduced in Nazi cases that might not otherwise be admitted. This provision, known as Section 15, was used more than a hundred times in the Eichmann trial. As Judge Levin explained, Section 15 does not dictate how the court should regard the evidence, it only allows its consideration.

Shaked argued that some of the identifications—Lindvasser's, in particular—were unequivocal.

Proving himself a keen observer of human behavior, Levin said, "'Unequivocal' depends on the vocabulary and the nature of a person. A person who never admits to being one hundred percent sure of something, when he is, that is unequivocal, but the person who is only ninety-seven percent sure when they always say one hundred percent, is not so sure. That is why it is important for the court to observe the demeanor of the witnesses." The court said the weight of the statements would be decided, after summation, in the verdict.

On this day, as in the past, O'Connor became, as one of Judge Levin's clerks observed, something of a *nudnick*—a nuisance. Throughout the direct examination, he objected, and often commented in the form of an objection.

In 1976, at the start of the Demjanjuk investigation, Radiwker was seventy. At first, one wondered at the wisdom of having so aged an investigator in charge of a case that would, no doubt, take years to come to judgment. But in the course of O'Connor's cross-examination—his "test of memory"—Radiwker showed herself a formidable personage with a vital and precise memory.

O'Connor spent the better part of a day dwelling on her auto-biography, the towns, schools, and details of her early life. But if his purpose was to trip her or tire her, to diminish the impression she made on the court, the effect was the opposite. O'Connor tried to get her to testify as to the treachery of Soviet law, under which she practiced during the war, but Radiwker said she had managed as best as she could for her clients. And she made it clear, "I'm no friend of the Soviet legal system."

When answering questions, Radiwker tended to turn her shoulders away from the defense counsel and answer directly to the court. But O'Connor was not to be dismissed so easily.

As far as he was concerned, Radiwker was as much an identifying witness as the survivors, because the testimonies of the deceased survivors were submitted through her. In effect, he said, it was as if *she* were pointing at Demjanjuk, and saying, "That's Ivan." No question, therefore, was too personal. A man's life turned on her testimony and her memory. She had "a responsibility *before God* and a responsibility under the system of natural justice in Israel to sit there and be able to respond effectively."

Levin informed O'Connor that he misunderstood both Section 15 and the court's position on the testimonies of the deceased survivors, and that by no means did Radiwker "point to the accused and say this is Ivan."

Just before leaving Poland, Radiwker told the court, she took her husband and daughter to Auschwitz. What she saw there moved her to vow that "I would do anything to bring these people to justice." Once in Israel, she learned the police were recruiting. Despite her age, she was hired by the war-crimes unit after impressing its director with her legal background and language abilities.

O'Connor probed as to the source of the original allegations against Demjanjuk. Radiwker said she knew only that they came from the U.S. As far as she knew from the information, he was charged with having been at Sobibor. She didn't have a chance to look into his having been at Flossenburg. As to Trawniki, she did speak to one survivor, a Mrs. Engelman, but she had been there during a completely different period. And as to Sobibor, "I did everything in my power to find out whether he had, in fact, been in Sobibor or not."

Radiwker said she had called witnesses from Sobibor. She had even asked the witnesses from Treblinka about whether Demjanjuk might not have been in Sobibor instead; but when she did, "I really ended in an argument with them. . . . Goldfarb's answer, for example was no—and yes. But before the uprising, he was no longer there. Rosenberg said that he was there until the last day. Czarny, I remember . . . I said to him, 'Listen, on the basis of the information that we have, he was in Sobibor and not in Treblinka,' so Czarny told me: 'Madame, that is not true. That is not the truth. He was in Treblinka up to the last day, he was there.'

"What else could I do? I really did my very best to carry out the investigation as fairly and as objectively as possible. I asked Czarny, and I did everything in this case beyond the call of duty. I asked Czarny, 'Why Ivan? Why do you remember Ivan more than anyone else? Why not Fedorenko?' So Czarny said in simple words: 'He stood out. He was extremely good in this horrible task. He was the most brutal among them, and that is why I remember him, and I will remember him to the end of my days.' So what else could I do? If he did not know Fedorenko, well, he did not know Fedorenko. And if there was the tiniest little nuance, any shades of meaning, it was put down in the protocol."

O'Connor asked how she traveled to the Fedorenko trial.

"I got there with my husband a few days before, and there was Don Glucksam with us."

Levin: "The question was, what means of transportation did you use?"

"Not by train," she said, provoking giggles in the audience.

O'Connor turned angry. Witnesses in a trial are not, before their own testimony, supposed to listen to other testimony, or to read the press accounts. O'Connor tried to make something of this, but Radiwker admitted that if on the news there was something about the trial, "some small fragment, I didn't pay too much attention, and I tried not to get involved in it. I am a jurist."

As to the trial in Florida, Radiwker maintained her conduct was above reproach: she came by separate flight, stayed in the same motel but not the same room, ate in the motel dining room but not at the same table as the witnesses. She had no contact with them except at one festive meal given by a woman from Miami for the witnesses and prosecutors. All in all, she complied with arrangements made by the U.S. Justice Department.

She did remark how rudely, poorly, and roughly the judge treated the witnesses in the Fedorenko case. "It was harsh, it was unpleasant, ostensibly every witness was a liar, a deceitful person, I cannot imagine, I cannot describe for you the kind of treatment they received."

O'Connor asked, "Was it not true that there was some indication by this judge that, in fact, the witnesses that you had examined were coached?"

"My witnesses don't need coaching," Radiwker said angrily. "I didn't hear this type of criticism, but I felt the atmosphere."

Radiwker was cross-examined the next day by Sheftel. He found much at fault with the testimonies and identifications she had conducted. If Turovsky, the first survivor who came to her office, reacted "at first glance" to the picture of John Demjanjuk, why didn't the report of May 9 reflect that? He questioned every nuance of language and treated every report in the most literal sense. If a witness said it *might* be Ivan, why was that an identification? If she filed two reports, then were there not two separate sessions?

Her current testimony was at odds, in certain respects, Sheftel said, with her testimony at the Fedorenko trial. At that trial, Radiwker explained, she was not allowed to check her notes, so she may have spoken inaccurately.

What was the *purpose,* Sheftel asked, of showing the survivors the photospread. Her answer crystallized the identification issue in the trial: "Well, to test his powers of memory, his impressions, but there is a difference according to my own experience, whether the witness was for a considerable length of time in the proximity of this criminal, and then you accept things in a different way when he identifies a person. It's a different sort of identification from what the judge did in a hall full of the public. Maybe I am wrong, and you need fewer photos. Some people can identify someone from only a few photos, and another person, if you put thirty photos to him, unless he had been in the proximity of the person involved, would not recognize him."

Sheftel wanted to know why she didn't arrange the photos differently, why Demjanjuk was the only almost-bald head on the page.

"I simply put before them what I had received. I am really not responsible for Demjanjuk's bald pate."

People in the audience began to laugh, and Demjanjuk himself doubled over in laughter at this, his whole head turning red as he slapped his knees.

Sheftel wanted to know why she attached no importance to the fact that certain Treblinka survivors didn't identify anyone. Or why she didn't confront survivors with previous testimony that Ivan had died in the revolt.

Radiwker was aghast: it would have been inappropriate to confront the witnesses. What they said, or didn't say, she took down, as they said it. That was all. Anything else was forbidden and would have been improper. She was, after all, she said, an investigator.

On the morning of Monday, March 23, 1987, the clerk shouted *"Beit Hamishpat"* at 8:30 A.M. as usual. This was the signal for the court to begin. Investigator Martin Kollar was ready to take the stand, but instead Sheftel rose.

He had a motion to present that moment: he was calling upon the court to disqualify itself because of its hostility and bias toward the defense. Sheftel spoke for thirty-five minutes, citing instances that he felt evidenced the court's "attitude of incredible hostility." He detailed the number of times judges had criticized the defense, interrupted their cross, or overruled their objections. All these, Sheftel said, were objective proof of their bias.

That the defense would make such a claim came as little surprise, but the motion came earlier than anyone had predicted. And having Sheftel, the Israeli attorney, be the one to criticize the court was also noteworthy—O'Connor was always sensitive to public perception. Sheftel played the bad cop; O'Connor, the good cop.

The court deliberated for a full two hours before returning a decision. "It is our unequivocal opinion that there is no grounds for Mr. Sheftel's case." The court said it had overruled questions by either side. "In the system of adversary trials, the court need not be passive. As the trial proceeds, it must conduct the proceedings by being on the alert to make certain that the deliberations in the case in no way deviate from proper procedure." The court said it had acted "with unusual leeway," noting that "precisely because of the gravity of the case that looms over the accused, we have been unusually patient in the course of this trial and have gone far beyond the usual proceedings. We have allowed far more than what is relevant and customary and permissible in trials that take place in the Israeli court system, even in the gravest among them."

Sheftel appealed to the Supreme Court while the case proceeded, to no avail. The Supreme Court, reaching a verdict within a week, found that the judges' frequent intervention was always pertinent and helped to clarify the long and complex questions of the defense counsel. The court had acted toward the defense, the Supreme Court said, with tolerance and greater patience than was at times required.

Finally, Kollar took the stand. Born in Czechoslovakia in 1920, he was held in forced-labor camps during World War II. His family—and all his relatives—were exterminated. "I swore that if I got out alive, I would bring my family's murderers to justice," he testified. In the course of his nineteen years with the police, Kollar had worked at the behest of the governments of Germany, Austria, Canada, the Netherlands, and the United States.

Kollar testified he met with survivors Epstein, Rosenberg, and Lewkowicz, beginning in 1978. He also met in January 1980 with Boraks and his son at the Haifa police station. Kollar had in his hand the statement Boraks had given Radiwker in 1976. "This was one of the surprises of my life. With what accuracy, and with what clarity, he described his life in Treblinka. . . . His memory was astounding. . . !"

O'Connor's cross in the afternoon retraced Kollar's own history. He asked the officer if he had had any contact with the Treblinka investigations before 1978. "To my great regret," he answered, "Eastern Europe was full of such places and this particular one I had not had any contact with."

At the Fedorenko trial, O'Connor asked, had he testified that when Epstein spoke in his office, he needed to, "direct this witness, or give this witness direction?"

"When Epstein began speaking," Kollar answered, "he spoke freely without interruption. He gave me a vast and very plastic description and a very vivid one. Within a few minutes, I had the feeling I was with him, there." But soon Kollar saw that Epstein could continue at great length on aspects of the camp not relevant to his investigation. "At certain points, I said: 'Would you please get back to the subject. . . .'"

Next Sheftel cut straight to the heart of the matter: Did he remember when he interviewed Rosenberg about Fedorenko on April 13, 1978, whether Rosenberg at that time also identified Ivan? "I don't rule this out," Kollar said.

But Shaked later introduced transcripts of the Fedorenko trial to make it clear that Rosenberg *did* talk about Ivan when Kollar summoned him to speak about Fedorenko. The defense had failed to extract any major challenges to the veracity of the survivors' identifications.

CHAPTER 18

The Card

Was the Trawniki card authentic? That was the next hurdle for the prosecution. During the course of the Demjanjuk trial, more than eight thousand pages of trial transcript, one-hundred-ninety-nine hours of trial testimony, and fifty days in court would be expended to confirm that a simple four-by-six-inch green cardboard identification document once belonged, as the prosecutors said it did, to Ivan Demjanjuk. The card would be subjected to the most rigorous analysis imaginable; its many colored inks, stamps and seals, its photograph of a young soldier, all would be scrutinized inch for inch, word for word.

Most forged documents, fake IDs, driver's licenses, passports, transcripts, and false papers are meant to be shown to an official, not a forensic, documents examiner. Occasionally, they are looked at by dealers, historians. But it is rare that any document is held up to the scrutiny of officials, historians, *and* forensic documents examiners.

Even in the most famous cases of "successful forgeries," such as the Hitler diaries or the Hofmann Mormon letters forgeries, the falsifications were uncovered quickly when forensic documents experts conducted thorough, systematic analyses.

Most observers assumed it was the prosecution's job to prove the card authentic. In fact, just the opposite was true. Legally, a government-issued document, more than twenty years old, was presumed authentic, unless shown otherwise by the defense. In a sense, the card was "innocent until proven guilty," authentic until shown to be a forgery.

Nevertheless, the prosecution was not one to leave things to chance. It sought to answer each and every question that the defense had raised over the years.

The prosecution presentation followed a certain architecture: the historical authenticity of the card; the forensic examination— the signatures, the stamps and seals; the paper and ink; and finally, the photo.

Prosecutors called two experts to speak of the card's authenticity in relation to other known documents and materials about Trawniki. The first, Helge Grabitz, Hamburg state attorney for the prosecution of Nazi war crimes, had been the chief prosecutor at the trial of Trawniki commander Karl Streibl, who had been acquitted under the strict German definition of criminal liability. Nevertheless, Grabitz's case files had come to constitute the greatest source of knowledge on the Trawniki camp. She was followed by Dr. Wolfgang Sheffler, the West German professor and Operation Reinhard expert who had testified at Demjanjuk's denaturalization trial.

The Trawniki camp, as they explained, played an important role in the Final Solution. The camp was under the authority of the SS as well as the German police. Its purpose was "instruction" of auxiliary forces—the training of Soviet prisoners recruited from POW camps to participate in each step in the Jews' extermination: to serve as ghetto policemen, to liquidate ghettos, to round up Jews, to load them into trains, to accompany the transports, and finally, to serve in the death camps. "The Trawnikis," said Helge Grabitz, "did the dirty work."

Arriving at Trawniki, she said, the former POWs underwent enlistment procedures: a personnel file sheet was made for each; before a recruitment was posted, a service ID was issued, which also listed the equipment he had been issued.

The Trawniki card, Sheffler said, was a *Dienstausweis,* a service pass—not a file document. It was meant to be carried by the bearer as an identity card.

Because the service passes were issued to the non-German guards, the cards played no part in postwar German trials of Nazis; nor did they surface in historical archives.

The Trawniki card was said by the defense to be a one-of-a-kind document. No one had ever heard of or seen another one. But the prosecution could now put this claim to rest. They had uncovered German archival documents—correspondence by camp commander

Streibl complaining about problems with the passes; and several letters about a *Wachmann* named Susslov who had lost his Trawniki card and needed a replacement.

Grabitz and Sheffler were able to confirm the signatures of Streibl by their familiarity with his handwriting and by introducing several other documents Streibl had confirmed at his own trial. The card also bore the signature of a man named Ernst Teufel, the supply master for whom they introduced other acknowledged original documents bearing his signature. The witnesses testified the signatures were the same.

The Trawniki card said on its face that it was issued to an Ivan Demjanjuk. It listed his birthdate, birthplace, name of his father, and other personal information about the color of his eyes, hair, and height. For the most part, the personal information was shown to be the same as *John* Demjanjunk's.

But there were several important errors and omissions: the card contained spelling errors; there was no date of issue; the height was incorrect; and the card, although it listed a posting to Sobibor in March 1943, listed no posting to Treblinka. This did not jibe with the German reputation for meticulous record keeping.

But both Sheffler and Grabitz testified that Streibl himself had complained to his superiors about chaos in the Trawniki records. They said the documents were full of errors—the prosecution submitted examples of other Trawniki documents with similar errors—because they were filled in by *Volksdeutsche* (ethnic Germans) whose proficiency in spelling and German were not great. The documents were all the more subject to errors, the experts testified, because they were printed locally (as opposed to Lublin police documents, which were printed in the Reich).

Sheffler told the court the mistakes *added* to the document's credibility. "The essential elements of this *Dienstausweis* tally with historical knowledge as we have it, and the individual building blocks fit into each other," he testified.

One of the card's "suspicious" entries was the equipment listing, where a "2" had been entered over a "1," next to "*Unterhosen* [underwear]." The prosecution introduced the 1942 German order requiring Trawniki men to be issued two pairs of underpants instead of one.

As to the date of issue: Sheffler and Grabitz dated the document by Streibl's and Teufel's ranks. Streibl had received a promotion earlier that year; Teufel was promoted on July 19, 1942, when Himmler inspected the camp. The card has Streibl's new rank but not Teufel's, which meant, the prosecution said, that Demjanjuk arrived at Trawniki sometime before July 19.

Demjanjuk had admitted he was captured in the battle of Kerch, which took place in May. He had admitted he was at the Rovno POW camp for a few weeks—and even if he did go to Chelm, and was recruited there—he could have arrived at Trawniki by July 19. The training at the camp took three to six weeks—which meant that by early September he would have had to have been posted elsewhere. This scenario, according to the prosecution, fit with the survivors' testimony that Ivan was already in the death camp in September, when they arrived there.

Still, that the card listed the bearer's height as 175cm (5′8¼″), remained a major discrepancy. Now 180cm (5′10¼″) tall, Demjanjuk had estimated that in 1941 he was 185cm (6′1″). How could the card belong to Demjanjuk with such a mistake? Was this a sign of forgery?

Grabitz testified that, to the best of her knowledge, there was no machine at Trawniki that measured a new recruit's height during induction. Most likely, recruits were asked to state their height to the enlisting officer in the same manner that one does now for a driver's license. This did not explain why the discrepancy occurred in Demjanjuk's case, just that such discrepancies occurred regularly at Trawniki. The mistake in height was no evidence, the prosecution was saying, in and of itself, of forgery. Further, mistakes of height were common. Demjanjuk's various American documents, which he had acknowledged filling out himself, showed his height to range between 5′11″ and 6′1″. Still, none of these was so great a discrepancy as appears on the Trawniki card.

So the prosecution played its trump card: it introduced two documents belonging to defense witness Rudolf Reiss, one of which listed his height at 1m 70cm (5′6⅓″), the other as 1m 90cm (6′2″)—a greater discrepancy even than that on the Trawniki card.

Its introduction was a sweet moment for the staff, which had long tried to find ways to show that such mistakes were common. Sweeter still because Gabriel Finder, one of the young prosecutors, had uncovered the discrepancy in the Reiss documents only late the previous night.

A far greater problem for the prosecution was that the Trawniki card listed no assignment to Treblinka, only to two other places: a work farm, "L.G. Okzow," on September 22, 1942; and to death camp Sobibor on March 27, 1943.

"The postings were not always faithfully entered," Sheffler testified. The prosecution produced other Trawniki personnel cards and paybooks of persons who were known to have been at Treblinka and other camps, but whose Treblinka posting was not listed.

"Essentially, the card is correct," Sheffler concluded. "If someone wanted to use Trawniki documents to manipulate them to forge them, he would have to possess supernatural abilities in order to create the sort of situation where a variety of aspects must be borne in mind. And he would have to be familiar with each and every one in order to do a good forgery.

"I can not stress this enough—in the past twenty or twenty-five years," he continued, "we have not come across a single document that comes from Nazi sources or Nazi files and that has played a part in the different Nazi trials, or that has come from the East Bloc countries, that would have been forged. Not a single one."

"It would be nothing short of a sensation if this *Dienstausweis* were not authentic. I can only speak as a historian, but this is a genuine *Dienstausweis* of someone who was at Trawniki."

But what about the document itself; even if the information on it was accurate, could it be a forgery?

Israel Police Chief Superintendent Amnon Bezalelli, the head of the police laboratory for criminal identification, traveled to Germany to examine other original documents bearing the same stamps and signatures. He found each element of the Trawniki card consistent with them, even under microscopic analysis.

The photo belonged on the document; and he found it had been placed on the card prior to being stamped. The fact that the upper seals covering the photo and the document did not now match perfectly was explained by the fact that the photo had fallen off and been reglued, he said. The purple translation ink (dated 1948) was absorbed into the document at a *later* date than the others (dated 1941).

There was no evidence whatsoever, Bezalelli said, in examining the inks, paper, and stamps, to date the card later than 1941; what's more, the card bore convincing signs of aging consistent with other Trawniki documents; and there was no evidence of alterations, erasures, or corrections. The document gave no indications in any way of being a forgery.

The Trawniki document had three signatures: Streibl's, Teufel's, and one that, reputedly, was Demjanjuk's. Streibl had signed in German script; Teufel in German gothic; Demjanjuk had been written in Cyrillic (Russian alphabet) script. Known and acknowledged signatures of the three had been collected. But only contemporaneous signatures of Streibl and Teufel were available for comparison.

Bezalelli shared with the court the actual process of his examination of the signatures. Using blowups of the signatures, he walked the court through his critique of the individual components of the signatures—the formation of the letters, the stop and starts of the pen.

What was most important, Bezalelli said, was that the signature is flowing, and consistent with other known signatures, rather than so precise and mannered as to suggest it had been copied.

Streibl's signature was carried out with such confidence in all of its elements that Bezalelli found it convincing beyond a doubt. It was "inconceivable," he said, that such a signature was a forgery. Teufel's signature also gave no indication of forgery.

The two signatures were convincing, he said, "with the highest degree of certainty." So much so that he was willing to judge the document authentic based on the two signatures alone.

No Cyrillic Demjanjuk signature was found from the 1940s. The first acknowledged signature of Demjanjuk was in 1947 in German-Latin characters. But Bezalelli had prepared a detailed letter-by-letter examination of Demjanjuk's signature. As with the other signatures on the card, he walked the court through the landscape of curves, arches, lines, and depressions, to reveal what features were characteristic of the writer.

Demjanjuk's signature in Cyrillic script contained several unique letters with no equivalent in the Latin alphabet, such as the letter [Я] ("Yah"); and certain letters that are different even when that letter appears in both alphabets (the Cyrillic "M" looks more like a Latin "u"). Bezalelli did have some Cyrillic signatures to look at— ones Demjanjuk had been asked to make in 1986 while in Israeli custody. The problem with these, as Bezalelli saw it, was that Demjanjuk had been influenced by forty years of writing in Latin script. "He has not gone back to the handwriting he used in the 1940s."

Nonetheless, Bezalelli had marked forty-one points on the Trawniki signature that he compared to the twelve Latin signatures and fifteen Cyrillic ones—all originals—that he had gathered. He found a number of identical characteristics. He was impressed "by the inner authenticity of the signature" and had seen no signs to indicate a forgery. But because of the lack of contemporaneous signatures, he felt compelled to qualify his opinion as "between high degree of reason and somewhat lower degree of reason."

Bezalelli's conclusion, though, was certain: "On the basis of all the examinations I conducted, the document is authentic. I have no doubt of this. . . . I can determine this with certainty."

Gideon Epstein, the senior forensic documents analyst of the INS, also testified about the signatures. Epstein, who is certified by the American Board of Forensic Documents Examiners (the only certifying body for forensic documents analysts in the United States), had examined the card and the earlier photostat of it several times in the U.S. He first saw the photostat on December 18, 1980, for the OSI; he photographed and examined the original with his own portable laboratory at the Soviet Embassy in Washington on February 27, 1981.

A few weeks later, during Epstein's testimony at Demjanjuk's denaturalization, a clerk from the Soviet Embassy appeared with the original and allowed the court and Epstein to inspect it there. The original was replaced for the record with Epstein's photographs.

Epstein traveled to Germany for the trial in Jerusalem and examined the originals of the Streibl and Teufel signatures. And he examined the card again in Israel.

Like Bezalelli, Epstein testified that in comparing handwritings, he looked for "the unconscious habitual characteristics" of a signature. He, too, found the signatures of Streibl and Teufel natural, fluent—in short, authentic beyond a doubt.

Epstein was prepared to testify about the Demjanjuk signature, but Sheftel objected. Nothing in Epstein's expert opinion suggested that he would testify about the Demjanjuk signature. Accordingly, the court sustained Sheftel's objection, and Epstein was prohibited from testifying about it.

Nonetheless, Epstein said, based on all his examinations of the document past and present, "my conclusion to the overall document is that it is a genuine document, that it does not bear any evidence of being in any way fraudulently prepared. . . . The document is genuine."

This opinion was supported by Dr. Anthony Cantu of the U.S. Treasury Bureau, an expert in the chemical analysis of documents. Cantu used a hypodermic-needle probe to take samples from the Trawniki card and its photo and compared them with samples from known Trawniki documents.

Dr. Cantu tested the inks by "thin layer chromatography" (TLC), which examines long and short ultrawaves in the infra-red zone, and by laser. He found them, in all cases, consistent with the other Trawniki documents, available in 1941, and containing no materials from a later date.

The same was true for the paper, made of unbleached pulp and ground wood. It contained no glass or synthetic fibers, or agents that help retain the paper when wet, or optical brighteners (the Hitler diaries forgeries were discovered because of the presence of optical brighteners in the paper).

The prosecution had one more detail to confirm: the photo.

Bezalelli had made a complete examination of the photo, comparing it to other Trawniki identity photos. He found them similar in every way, including the thickness of the photographic paper and the fact that the same improvised frame was used when printing them.

In the card's photo, there is a white rectangle on the bearer's left breast pocket. The number on it is not completely discernible to the naked eye. But by enlarging the photo and printing it on paper of differing contrasts, Bezalelli revealed the number to be 1393—the same as the document's.

Demjanjuk would not admit the photo was of him. So the prosecution set out to *prove* it. Comparisons between photos and living persons were not done regularly by Israeli police. Courts had seen closed-circuit photos of bank robbers and traffic violators, and hidden photos of drug dealers at work. Police regularly attempted to match up photos to skeletal remains. But in Israel no one had ever tried to match a person with a forty-five-year-old picture for identification purposes; nor had identifications based on them been introduced in Israeli courts.

In West Germany, however, there was one person qualified to appear in court as an expert on the identification of a person based on photographs. His name was Reinhardt Altmann, from the *Bundeskriminalamt* (BKA), the West German police's central criminal-identification department.

Altmann testified that because of the physical uniqueness of each person, individual characteristics could be used for identification, much as fingerprints are.

Altmann described in particular how the "lip mucosa"—the grooves on the lip—could be used to identify a person, as could the lines on a forehead, or the shape of the ear. Altmann said that often in burglary cases, where no fingerprints could be found, the police uncovered good ear prints on the door.

In analyzing the Trawniki photo he had found twenty-four different facial characteristics that were identifiable and comparable. Using other acknowledged photos of Demjanjuk, he attempted to compare each one to the Trawniki card photo. First the two photos being compared were displayed on separate TV screens. Then, using a video-mixer, the photos were halved, and combined, making one image.

Using his own scale of measurement, Altmann compared the landmarks. He concluded that there was "a very high degree of probability" that the person in the Trawniki photo was the same as in the other acknowledged photos.

To the naked eye, the results were visually striking.

Altmann's scale was not statistically correlated to probability of error, but only distinguished among levels of certainty. Nonetheless, Altmann said, "For me, there is not the slightest doubt that these photographs are of one and the same person." Still, the court was distressed by the lack of actual scientific underpinning for Altmann's comparison technique.

Altmann's photo-comparison technique, accepted in the West German courts, was nonetheless a good foundation for the prosecution's next expert, whom they hoped *would* be accepted by the court.

Dr. Patricia Smith, born in England, held a degree in dentistry as well as a master's and Ph.D. in anthropology from the University of Chicago in the United States. Her studies had been in physical anthropology, of how the body and bones grow; all her graduate and later work had been in morphology, the study of facial features. She was one of the most impressive expert witnesses who appeared at the trial.

Professor Smith had stopped practicing dentistry full time in 1963; after she emigrated to Israel in 1969, she continued to practice part-time to support herself, as well as during her army service and on an emergency basis in the Yom Kippur War. The author of more than seventy-five publications, she was now a professor in the Department of Anatomy and Embryology at Hebrew University.

The task before her was to set criteria—scientific criteria—for comparing the Trawniki photo to others. Smith approached the problem by returning to the basics of genetics and morphology.

Scientifically, each individual is unique. In terms of human growth, individual facial characteristics—morphological features—can be identified, measured, and compared. No two persons are identical, and like fingerprints, there is a point beyond which similar characteristics mean that they can only belong to one and the same person.

The two individuals who genetically are most alike are identical twins. A colleague of Smith at the University of Adelaide in Australia had for years been conducting a study of identical twins, in which, under very controlled circumstances, the twins were photographed. Smith requested and received several sets of twins photos.

She had identified eleven individual features on the human face that were also easily identifiable landmarks on a photo. Again following scientific procedure, Smith established a baseline from which measurements could be carried out.

Smith then took measurements of the eleven morphological landmarks on the sets of twins photographs. The measurements were repeated five to seven times over an extended period of time. By correlating the figures for each set, Smith established the degree of variation found between two persons who are the least different, genetically, that two different individuals can be.

She then took two photographs that Demjanjuk had acknowledged and the Trawniki photo, and measured these by the same method. She was able to carry out measurements for all eleven landmarks, using exactly the same measuring device. Each photograph was measured five times over a period of two weeks; then summed up and averaged, to obtain both an average measurement and also to estimate the error involved.

A table was drawn up comparing the twins sets and the Demjanjuk/Trawniki set. The mean difference between the Trawniki photo and an acknowledged photo of Demjanjuk was substantially smaller than even that of the closest set of twins.

Demjanjuk and the man in the Trawniki photo were less different than the identical twins—they could not be different persons, she testified. John Demjanjuk and the Trawniki man were one and the same.

When trying to identify skeletons, a photo transparency of a missing person is often superimposed over a photo of the skull, to see if they match. Smith performed this comparison as well.

The photos were enlarged so that the distance between the left eye and the mouth was the same. Smith tested the procedure with a set of twins to show that there was no matchup, even with identical twins.

The Trawniki photo was printed on a transparent sheet, and then placed over the acknowledged Demjanjuk photo.

There was a complete concordance between the two.

"There can be no shadow of a doubt," Smith said, "that we are dealing with the same individual."

But lest anyone have any doubts, Smith had one more demonstration. She had videotaped Demjanjuk in prison a few months earlier and had superimpositions performed between a still frame and the Trawniki photo.

O'Connor objected. In what was certainly one of the trial's most bizarre moments, O'Connor made his most detailed presentation. It was one of the rare occasions where he cited precedent. The references he cited, however, were not legal, but biblical; his arguments, he claimed, were Talmudic.

O'Connor wanted the court to review the video in chambers, "before this slander is allowed to go not only to the bench but to perhaps hundreds of millions of people. . . ." He invoked the biblical books of Genesis and Exodus, by which Miriam became leprous, and the tale in which God punished Joseph for bearing false reports to his father. O'Connor's speech was filled with biblical citations from Genesis, Exodus, Psalms, and the book of Proverbs.

"Our position," he said, "quite simply stated is this: every human being has a right to his good name and reputation. In essence, to his face. And this is probably the most carefully documented human right in all of biblical and Talmudic law. . . . With regard to the loss of face, we can see throughout the ages that the loss of face was akin in fact to a bloodletting. Because indeed to have a loss of face is to have the blood drained from the face of the individual that is being slandered. And that, in effect, was a bloodletting and one of the greatest crimes that could be committed as far as biblical law and later Talmudic law was concerned. . . ."

To cover the smiling face of John, "whose goodness radiates," O'Connor said, with the photo "of the *golem* . . . of Ivan Grozny—the 1942 [Trawniki] picture—we see this as grossly slanderous. . . . We might just as well have had the witness make a Purim mask and put the Purim mask on the defendant and walk him around the stage as proof, in fact, that the Purim mask of the 1942 photograph was the same individual."

There was more. The slander, O'Connor said, was upon the one who made it, the ones who hear it, and the worst punishment was for those who allowed it to be heard. It was not *he* who was threatening the judges, O'Connor said. The consequence of their actions was their own (implying that it was God Himself who would punish them).

Judge Zvi Tal, an orthodox Jew who gives a well-attended Talmud class every Sabbath, explained first that matters uttered in court are not slanderous or libelous. Levin said that throughout O'Connor's long and detailed argument, the court had not heard a single legal point. The video was allowed.

It was played on three monitors: one to the court, one to the defense, and one to the spectators. The entire room sat silent, entranced, during the seven-minute film.

Demjanjuk is first seen in his orange prison garb, standing in the Ayalon Prison yard. He is smiling, and squinting at the light in his eyes. The camera freezes and the superimposition begins: half his face now, half the Trawniki photo.

Like a magic wand waving away the years, one face slowly faded into the other as each detail—from the tip of the ear through the crease of the nose, the indent in the chin—matched up.

The screen then performed selective impositions: just the eyes . . . just the mouth. The 1942 photo had more hair; Demjanjuk's face was now fatter, and the skin sagged, he had little neck—but still one saw the complete similarity between the two.

"Continuing down the face, you can see the exact superimposition," Smith said, "the exact continuation of the position and line of the earlobes. And on the face itself the position, shape, direction, inclination, every detail on the nose and upper lip, are identical. . . .

"In other words," Smith said, "the identity of morphological features, the identity of the distance between the morphological features, is identical. . . . I was asked what was the statistical probability of two individuals having identical morphological features. . . . [It is] one in several hundred billion. . . . [Based on] all the examinations that I have carried out, my conclusion is that the 1942 photograph was, in fact, taken of the individual John Demjanjuk seen in the other photographs and seen in the video today."

Although legally, the impact of Smith's comparison would not be great, to the viewer, the impact was enormous. The frame, with half of the Trawniki man's face, and half Demjanjuk's face now, was a powerful image. The past joined with the present—it told in one image what, in great part, the prosecution was attempting to accomplish.

CHAPTER 19

Defense Techniques and Tensions

In April 1987, as the prosecution began presenting evidence on the Trawniki card, the courtroom days lengthened—the trial had been in session for two months already, and there was no quick end in sight. The court had given great leeway for O'Connor's idiosyncratic notions of courtroom behavior and procedure. Sheftel's abrasive manner, however, angered the judges, and they were less successful keeping themselves in check with him. They had been more tolerant than they would have been in an ordinary case, but their patience was wearing thin.

In the previous November, the prosecution had given the defense documents and summaries of documents and an index to the documents. Each defense lawyer, in time, would blame the other, but they often seemed unfamiliar with the foreign material and needed time to further prepare. This did not reflect well on any of them.

The defense tried to stall by making motions to the Supreme Court that failed. Judge Levin canceled sessions, at the defense lawyers' request, to give them more time to prepare. Cross-examination was dragged out all the more.

Sheftel continued to infuriate the court by making references to a show trial, and Levin warned that if Sheftel did not show respect, he would find himself outside the courtroom. Sheftel apologized, but it did little to shake his bad-boy image. He took great delight in all of the attention. He received journalists in his Japanese T-shirts and love beads. He asked everyone to call him "Sheffie." Most reporters found him charming in person. "Good value" is the way

Treblinka Model: A wood model of the Treblinka death camp built by survivor
Yankel Viernik. The original sits in the museum of Kibbutz Lohamei Hagethot in
Israel. The fenced-off area in the upper left-hand corner of the model is the
extermination area. *(AP/Wide World Photos)*

Demjanjuk as a Red Army soldier *(Reuters/Bettmann Newsphotos)*

The 1942 Trawniki photo *(Reuters/Bettmann Newsphotos)*

1981: Demjanjuk at his daughter's wedding *(Reuters/Bettmann Newsphotos)*

The 1951 visa photo that survivors first identified as Ivan *(Reuters/Bettmann Newsphotos)*

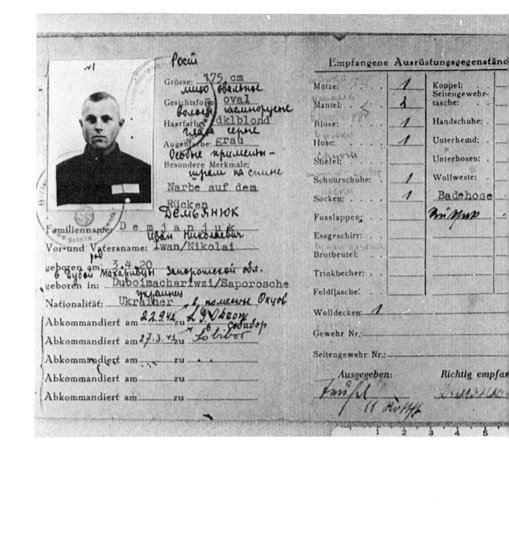

Росіи

Grösse: 175 cm

лицо овальное

Gesichtsform: oval

волосы темнорусые

Haarfarbe: dklblond

глаза серые

Augenfarbe: grau

Особые примени-

Besondere Merkmale:

шрам на спине

Narbe auf dem

Rücken

Демянюк

Familienname: D e m j a n j u k

Иван Николаевич

Vor- und Vatersname: Iwan/Nikolai

geboren am: 3.4.20 _запорожской обл._

geboren in: Duboimachariwzi/Saporosche

Украины

Nationalität: Ukrainer _в каменне Окуов_

Abkommandiert am 22.9.42 zu _Сободор_

Abkommandiert am 27.3.43 zu _Sobibor_

Abkommandiert am _____ zu _____

Abkommandiert am _____ zu _____

Abkommandiert am _____ zu _____

Empfangene Ausrüstungsgegenständ

Mütze:	1	Koppel; Seitengewehr-tasche:	
Mantel:	1	Handschuhe:	
Bluse:	1	Unterhemd;	
Hose:	1	Unterhosen:	
Stiefel:		Wollweste:	
Schnurschuhe:	1	Badehose	
Socken:	1		
Fusslappen;			
Essgeschirr:			
Brotbeutel:			
Trinkbecher:			
Feldflasche:			
Wolldecken:	1		
Gewehr Nr.			
Seitengewehr Nr.:			

Ausgegeben: Richtig empfa

The Trawniki Card: The 1942 service pass issued to Ivan Demjanjuk at the Trawniki training camp for SS guards. The pass was folded in the center and carried by the bearer. The handwritten notations are a 1948 Russian translation. (Allan A. Ryan, Jr.)

From left to right are Demjanjuk's daughter, Irene Nishnic, his wife, Vera, and his son, John, Jr., listening to closing arguments in Jerusalem, 1988. *(AP/Wide World Photos)*

Jerome Brentar, Demjanjuk defense supporter whose ties to revisionist organizations would taint the defense. *(Zoom 77)*

February 28, 1986. Demjanjuk arrives at Tel Aviv's Ben Gurion Airport. Behind him to the left are the American marshals who escorted him from New York. To the right are Israeli police officials. *(Reuters/Bettmann Newsphotos)*

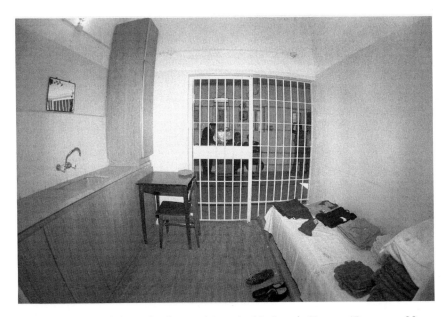

Demjanjuk entered this jail cell upon his arrival in Israel. *(Reuters/Bettmann Newsphotos)*

The courtroom in Jerusalem, constructed on the stage of the small hall of Jerusalem's convention center, February 16, 1987. American defense attorney Mark O'Connor (standing left) delivers his opening statement. *(Reuters/Bettmann Newsphotos)*

The judges: Zvi Tal, Dov Levin, Dalia Dorner *(Zoom 77)*

Defense attorneys: Paul Chumak, Yoram Sheftel, John Gill *(Zoom 77)*

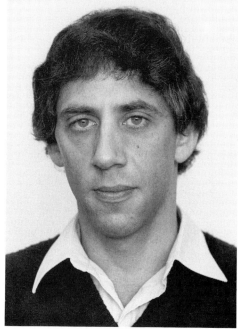

Prosecutors (counterclockwise from top): Yonah Blatman, Michael Shaked, Michael Horovitz *(Zoom 77)*

The surviving witnesses

"There he is! There he is," Pinhas Epstein shouts. As a seventeen-year-old corpse carrier in Treblinka's death camp, he "practically rubbed shoulders" with Ivan. *(Reuters/Bettmann Newsphotos)*

Yossef Czarny weeps while giving testimony. He was a "court-Jew," serving the German and Ukrainian staff, and often saw Ivan on the path from the death camp and in the guards' mess hall. *(Reuters/Bettmann Newsphotos)*

Gustav Boraks looks at the album from which, in 1976, he identified Demjanjuk's 1951 photo as Ivan, while prosecutor Michael Shaked looks on. Boraks was barber in Treblinka where he cut the women's hair before they were forced into the gas chamber. *(Reuters/Bettmann Newsphotos)*

Yehiel Reichman. As a "dentist" in the death camp, extracting teeth from the mouths of corpses, he worked a few meters away from Ivan, whom he called "the super-demon of Treblinka." *(Reuters/Bettmann Newsphotos)*

A dramatic confrontation: Treblinka survivor Eliahu Rosenberg angrily spurns Demjanjuk's offered hand as Mark O'Connor looks on. *(Y. Zaken/Media)*

The three new Trawniki cards delivered by Armand Hammer. (Reuters/ Bettmann Newsphotos)

Demjanjuk being carried into court to hear the verdict in his war-crimes trial. (AP/Wide World Photos)

A handcuffed John Demjanjuk shouts that he is innocent after being convicted by the Israeli District Court of being Ivan the Terrible. *(AP/Wide World Photos)*

one American novelist assessed Sheftel after dinner at the American Colony Hotel. Throughout the trial, Sheftel made deliberately provocative statements to the media: "I have a girlfriend I don't intend to marry." . . . "Demjanjuk told me that if he'd had a Jewish lawyer from the beginning he wouldn't be in the mess he's in now."

Though his posturing made good copy for the media, the Israeli public often found him offensive. He was called "the most hated man in Israel." His Hebrew was said to be lower-class. He was the sort of lawyer, one attorney said, who represented pimps, prostitutes, and drug dealers. He seemed always to be spitting as he talked, a court regular said. For many, his lack of decorum represented the "bad Israeli"—rude, obnoxious, devious.

In court, it was clear he tried the patience of the judges. Michele Lesie wrote in Cleveland's *The Plain Dealer:*

> Those who watch the proceedings closely know that when chief Judge Levin is annoyed, he jerks his head sharply to the right and holds it there eaglelike, revealing a rigid angular profile. . . . With his white hair and black robe and with the seal of the State of Israel hanging on the wall directly behind him, Levin in these moments looks as though he should be embossed on the back of a coin. . . . The judge has been doing this more and more lately. . . . There are three things Levin will not stand for: unclear, rambling questions whether relevant or not; improper courtroom behavior; and any reference whatsoever to the proceedings as a "show trial." O'Connor and Sheftel managed to be called on the carpet for all three last week.

But when Sheftel was heckled, it was Levin who silenced the protesters. "He is carrying out a very important role here," Levin said. And when derogatory posters of Sheftel were displayed outside the courtroom, Levin ordered them taken down, and asked police to investigate the persons behind them for possible prosecution.

Still, as the trial dragged on, the momentum slowed, and tension grew. It seemed to affect the very room itself: one morning there was a series of blackouts. It was eerie, seeing the guards form an immediate protective phalanx around Demjanjuk before leading him out of the room.

On another day, Demjanjuk didn't want to attend court because he wasn't feeling well. Prison doctors found nothing wrong with him. He was brought to court, but allowed to remain on the cot in his holding cell to listen to the day's proceedings on closed-circuit transmission.

To have the dock empty was strange. Attendance dropped immediately. It highlighted what many were aware of: that people wanted to stare at Demjanjuk, to see if evil might have marked his face. But the truth of the matter was that what made Demjanjuk all the more compelling was that he was a blank, a cipher.

In his effort to suppress any information as to his past or his reactions, he became a screen upon which each viewer projected his or her own interpretation. And for this reason, one stared all the harder, all the longer, looking for a clue, a trace, a flicker.

O'Connor remained tense. His family arrived in Israel. Now, he was constantly on show with his picture-perfect family. They ate each night in the American Colony Hotel dining room, like a tableau vivant from Norman Rockwell. The children came to court each day. His wife, Joyce, sat in the first row, furiously taking notes. O'Connor talked to the press of his love of Israel, of the Israeli people, of how he was thinking about enrolling his children in school there and opening a law practice. The children smiled, as if on cue.

The O'Connors wanted the press to know that in taking on this case, they, too, had come to understand the survivors. "I've lived with the Holocaust for the last five years," Joyce O'Connor told one reporter. "I've lived in Treblinka for five years," Mark O'Connor told another.

It was difficult to size up O'Connor: reporters often left interviews with him, shaking their heads in puzzlement. He was always so "on," it was hard to tell when he was being sincere. And though he seemed to treat actual legal procedure cavalierly, he took every nuance of the proceedings—each comment of the judges, each objection of the prosecution, almost each answer of the witnesses—seriously and personally.

O'Connor was in the habit of striding across the stage, and walking up close to a witness to establish a certain personal dynamic. But when he did so with Hamburg State Attorney Grabitz, the English from his translation interfered with the German coming into her headset. She asked that O'Connor step back. He acted as if it was his physical presence that had upset her, and later he made a show of standing back "a comfortable distance," saying with a hint of sarcasm, "We always want a witness to be comfortable."

But normal Israeli practice would have him speaking from his desk, Judge Levin explained. O'Connor motioned as if he could not hear. Shaked pointed to the defense table. *That,* to O'Connor, was a personal offense. He was furious. Even hours later, he fumed about this perceived "insult."

At times, O'Connor seemed in a trance. He would repeat words, mantralike, in cross-examination. His anger would erupt and subside. Asked about this, he explained that his main interest was in psychology. That if he had not become a lawyer, he would have wanted to be a Jungian psychologist.

"What you're doing is projecting results," O'Connor said. "At every stage, you're projecting results as if they had happened. There's alterations of that or there's perturbance involved with that; there appears the reaction that takes place and sometimes appears to be anger—but it's pretty well contained. . . ." But O'Connor's rambling cross-examinations and theatrical gestures made him more like a magician: his questions were often exercises in misdirection. Some court observers had yet another explanation for O'Connor's performance: the Demjanjuk family was in the audience.

In April, Demjanjuk's two daughters, Lydia Maday and Irene Nishnic, and Nishnic's infant son, Eddie Jr., attended the trial. They were upset by the judges, who seemed to overrule the defense at each turn. They had their doubts about whether the trial was fair. But they were even more troubled by O'Connor.

They found him long-winded and not particularly effective. When they sought to discuss aspects of the case with him, he was dismissive and, at times, downright rude. They also wondered at the sight of O'Connor, dining with his family each night at the American Colony, like a local celebrity, at a time when he constantly told the family there was not enough money.

They sent Demjanjuk's son-in-law, Ed Nishnic, president and administrator of the John Demjanjuk Defense Fund, to observe. Just a few years before, Nishnic had worked at an Ohio employment agency, where he met his wife, Irene, then a secretary there. He was familiar with the case before he met Irene, but not active in the Demjanjuk defense. That soon changed.

At first, Lydia, the eldest child, had been the family spokesperson. When she stopped doing so, John Jr. took over; but in no time the Demjanjuk defense became Ed Nishnic's full-time occupation. He believed himself to be slick and media-savvy. As chief fundraiser, he toured the U.S., Canada, and Australia.

He arrived in the Jerusalem courtroom in a blue pinstripe suit, monogrammed shirt, and black, wing-tipped shoes, buffed to a high polish. In his early thirties, he'd recently grown a beard.

But as Ed Nishnic was on his way to Israel, O'Connor decided to travel home and to Cleveland. Upon his arrival in the States, he telephoned the Demjanjuk family. Hearing that Nishnic had gone to Israel, O'Connor began to berate the entire family, saying they had walked into the lion's lair. O'Connor claimed, as he had many times before, that John Demjanjuk's life was in his hands. Without him, "John would hang." Vera and Irene were frightened.

O'Connor returned immediately to Israel. He found Nishnic at the American Colony Hotel. Nishnic had spoken to Gill and Sheftel. He now conferred with O'Connor, who reiterated that John's life hung in the balance. O'Connor portrayed Sheftel as a Mossad (Israeli Secret Service) plant, Gill as brainwashed by Sheftel. By listening to them, O'Connor warned, Nishnic was just playing into the hands of the Israelis.

John Demjanjuk's trust in O'Connor was great. But his family felt that Demjanjuk was not entirely in touch with his case. His daughters complained that when they visited him, he avoided discussing any important issues, preferring to show them letters he had received from well-wishers or to happily sing Ukrainian songs.

That John Demjanjuk was indeed concerned about his defense became apparent during the course of Professor Sheffler's testimony. Thus far, neither Gill nor O'Connor had had much success with Sheffler. And now Sheftel's questions were failing to hit the mark. The afternoon was getting late. It was the last day of the trial before the Passover break. Thursday sessions customarily ended at two-thirty, but Levin had said this one would continue as long as necessary for Sheffler to conclude. It was nearing four-thirty.

Demjanjuk's daughters had left the courtroom, on their way back to the United States; John Jr. had gone to take them to the airport. Sheffler had been on the stand the better part of a week in tedious, grueling sessions, difficult to endure except for the hopelessly addicted. Sheftel's questions were becoming more and more speculative and seemed tired too.

Suddenly, Demjanjuk raised his hand like an eager schoolboy. Without his family there, a feeling rushed through the room, as if anything could happen. Demjanjuk told the court he felt his lawyers had not asked Sheffler some important questions.

O'Connor apologized for Demjanjuk's intrusion, but it was clear the defendant had grasped exactly what was happening: Sheffler was about to leave the stand; the historical authenticity of the Trawniki card had met with no serious challenge.

Though the court said Demjanjuk would be allowed, if he wished, to ask the questions himself, O'Connor said *he* would: Could Sheffler comment on the jacket pocket button on the Trawniki photo? Sheffler answered that he wasn't a photographic expert.

Demjanjuk still was not satisfied. Gill rose to ask the same question. Again, Sheffler couldn't reply. Thereupon, Gill announced that "my friend and client," John Demjanjuk, still wanted to ask a few questions himself.

Shaked objected, but Levin was firm: "This is a most important trial, it is very important to the accused to ask one or two questions. The same questions it appears to the accused that the defense doesn't manage to formulate properly."

A microphone was set up for Demjanjuk: "These questions are very important to me," he said. "I'm a long time in jail now, and I don't know what the future may hold for me. . . . There are a few questions where I don't agree with the testimony that Professor Sheffler delivered.

"Professor Sheffler," Demjanjuk now asked, "you said these black uniforms were introduced into Trawniki later and that at first there were some sort of yellowish uniforms. That's what I heard. That is not true, and I would like you to clarify this."

"I never mentioned any yellow uniforms," Sheffler said. But he had, in fact, mentioned *khaki* uniforms.

But was he sure, Demjanjuk asked, that they were first black and then later another color? Sheffler said the whole matter of the color of uniforms was a tricky one. Generally speaking, Trawniki started out with the black ones and then used other colors; but at any one given time, there may have been several different-colored uniforms in the camp. At least, this was what he could answer, based on testimonies given at trials by others.

Then Sheffler added, "Maybe you can tell us what happened in this respect, in terms of the uniforms." Levin reacted quickly: "This last offer is not accepted." O'Connor lashed out in a stage whisper, "Impartial, huh?"

Demjanjuk now prefaced his remarks by saying that he was not speaking from personal knowledge but solely from things he'd learned from his trials. He asked Sheffler to look at the jacket breast button: Did it have anything to do with the uniform? Was it a field-jacket button or a shirt button? Sheffler could only speculate: he assumed it to be a tunic, a field jacket, he said, but it should be compared to other Trawniki jackets.

Demjanjuk asked him to examine the collar button under a magnifying glass. Sheffler scrutinized it, but said, "It's very difficult to see where the button belongs. . . . I don't see that as a historian, I can give information on this button." The judges also examined the photo. And if *that* was what was so crucial to Demjanjuk, he at least had brought it to the judges' attention.

"I would like to tell the court," Demjanjuk said with some satisfaction, though no one really knew why, "that it is eight years now in the U.S. that I've been seeing this photograph. I saw it first eight years ago, and I've seen a great many, many things that apparently would show that this is a forgery. For example, I was also wearing a pullover. Now, everything was done in this way in order not to show the identifying details. Now I would like here to say to the court that I am very grateful to them because they have acted justly, and today I have seen all of these details."

Demjanjuk thanked Sheffler, the court, and "everybody who has listened to me, and I would like to express my gratitude for this possibility of asking questions. I would like in this way to thank everybody who has taken part in this." He seemed genuinely happy.

But what did he mean when he said, *"For example, I was also wearing a pullover?"* That was something Demjanjuk would never explain.

Attorneys, and criminal attorneys, in particular, are not only free to take any sort of client, most feel compelled to do so by the very nature of the system. But O'Connor was unusual, in that he stressed in almost every press interview how he *personally* felt Demjanjuk was innocent.

With O'Connor, it was always, somehow, personal. Demjanjuk's life was in *his* hands; *he* was going to save John; he wanted to present *his version*. It was jarring. What was it about Demjanjuk's case that resonated in his own life?

Once during an interview with O'Connor, the conversation moved away from Demjanjuk, to O'Connor's personal experience as a captain in Vietnam.

O'Connor was asked if he had witnessed any atrocities. "All around you," he said. After the My Lai massacre, O'Connor related, he "looked around and talked to some of the people and got my own impression of what happened there."

Did what he see trouble him? O'Connor answered that what troubled *him*, was what was happening in America—the way the media treated the vets, "putting the guilt on them." It was, O'Connor said, "one of the most tragic things that had ever happened to America, what happened to the young men who had no options, nineteen years old, some of the bravest fighting men our country has ever generated. And to have that happen to them, where they were over there, and the times, and, of course, what they were doing was illegal and immoral. There was a mentality then, that if you have to kill another human being, you have to justify it. You have to reduce that human being to a level of an ant, otherwise you go crazy. . . . It was real tragic."

O'Connor may have been a psychology buff, but even a layman would have wondered if he was talking about grunts in Vietnam or the *Wachmanner* in Treblinka.

CHAPTER 20

German Participation and Cooperation

As the court delved into the minutiae of the Trawniki card, the courtroom crowds thinned. The trial proceedings seemed to take on an unremarkable air.

Yet something quite remarkable was occurring. Witnesses Helge Grabitz and Wolfgang Sheffler were German. They had been children during the war, and belonged to the immediate postwar generation. Grabitz had devoted twenty-one years of her life to the prosecution of Nazi war crimes in West Germany. She had traveled to Israel more than a dozen times to collect evidence and testimony. She had helped Israel locate documents and witnesses. Her daughter had spent summers in Israel on a *kibbutz*. Sheffler was, to a general observer, more German, an *echt* German: Saxon, haughty, arrogant in his expertise. Yet he had devoted the last thirty years of his life to the study of the Holocaust; for the last twenty years, he had testified as an expert at trials of Nazi war crimes. To hear their *hocht Deutsch* (high German) in the halls of the Binyanei Haooma, as prosecution witnesses, was remarkable in itself.

But the content of their testimony was remarkable, too. For it was Grabitz and Sheffler who, in answer to the questions of O'Connor and Gill, over and over again, repudiated the Nazi racial theories of Aryan supremacy. They did this particularly as O'Connor continued to pursue the psychological dimension of those who killed day in and day out at T4.

"I will repeat it once again," Grabitz said. "Those who were immune, looked on day in and day out and helped to gas the children and infants, those who had to participate against their will, they would have preferred to do something else, nevertheless they participated. And finally, there were those who did not know how to bring this into a balance with their own conscience, but they did not have the courage to refuse. . . . According to my own knowledge, I would say the greatest group was those who did it as a matter of course. They did it indifferently. Those who did it with enthusiasm, that is the second largest, and the least large is that group that had qualms of conscience." These opinions were based, Grabitz said, upon the testimonies of T4 personnel at the Trawniki trials.

It was Grabitz and Sheffler who testified about the crimes of Operation Reinhard, about the induction of collaborators into the program of death. And it was Grabitz and Sheffler who apologized when language failed them, and they had to resort to euphemisms of the Third Reich: "selection," "sorting," and so on. They presented this testimony not as penance for being German, but as historically accepted fact.

Their stance symbolized how Israel–West German relations had changed in the forty years since Israel had been established and even in the twenty-five years since the Eichmann trial. At the Eichmann trial, no German witnesses appeared, no help was sought from the German government.

Now in the court in Jerusalem, Reinhardt Altmann, a West German police officer, took the stand. How striking it was to hear him say: "The conclusion with regard to identity is based on the uniqueness of each individual. That is to say, each individual is unique in terms of his or her own characteristics. The uniqueness of each individual is the result of biological laws. . . . That is the theory of human biologists and human geneticists, and in any good biology textbook that deals with the development of man you will find that theory."

As if to mirror what was happening in court, on April 6, 1987, Chaim Herzog became the first President of Israel to travel in an official capacity to Germany.

Immediately upon his arrival, President Herzog went to the site of the Bergen–Belsen concentration camp, where he unveiled a commemorative rock quarried in Jerusalem. It was not his first visit to Bergen–Belsen. Herzog, who had served with the British forces during World War II, had been a soldier among the troops that liberated the camp. "I do not bring forgiveness with me, nor forgetfulness," he said. "The only ones who can forgive are dead. The living have no right to forget."

*   *   *

Prior to the Eichmann trial, Israel's relations with postwar Germany were complicated, at best. In its first days, Israel held to a strong anti-German line. Zionism demanded that Israel be seen as the proper response to the Holocaust.

But the Israeli government of Prime Minister David Ben-Gurion wanted allies in the Western world. Chancellor Konrad Adenauer's Germany was interested in allying itself with Israel, so as to distinguish itself from Hitler's Germany. In the 1950s, West Germany came to be Israel's economic development partner. Though many saw this as a devil's pact, Ben-Gurion's slogan was, "Let the murderers of our people not be their inheritors as well."

The opportunity for Israel and West Germany to confront their past and solidify their alliance came in 1960, when Ben-Gurion announced to a startled Knesset that Adolf Eichmann had been apprehended and was in custody in Israel.

World coverage of the Eichmann trial was great. But perhaps in no foreign country was the reaction stronger than in Germany.

The Eichmann trial could have been the opening of old wounds, but both sides were conscious of avoiding that. Germany publicly supported the trial of Eichmann. Adenauer hoped Israel would distinguish between Eichmann and current-day Germans.

Ben-Gurion obliged, saying, "My views about present-day Germany are unchanged. There is no Nazi Germany anymore." Afterward, Eichmann's conviction and execution was almost completely undisputed. The three major West German parties were unanimous in their assertion that justice had been done.

Subsequent to the Eichmann trial, West Germany entered into new loan agreements with Israel. And in 1965, both Israel and West Germany exchanged ambassadors.

But more significant was the impact of the trial on the young German generation. Writes historian Howard M. Sachar in *A History of Israel*:

> For the youth of Germany, particularly, the trial was a horrifying revelation. It supplied answers their parents had never given them. As they followed the court sessions in the press or on television, they sensed the truth at last of what their nation had done. Deeply penitent, thousands of them wrote the Israeli government, imploring them to be allowed to atone by working in Israel. For older Germans, too, it was suddenly much easier to talk about Israel, even to meet Israelis, than to face individual Jewish survivors in Germany with whom they had to

live side by side. It became the fashion to admire Israel, to laud its achievements, to urge the rising generation to visit it. And the young people did go, fully twenty thousand of them between 1961 and 1967. Some traveled in youth groups, some on their own. Not a few arrived to work in *kibbutzim* or in development projects. All of them were eager to witness the spirit that had made this Jewish nation victorious against its numerous enemies, and that had enabled it to capture Eichmann. It was ironic, then, that the Eichmann trial played a major role in fostering a new understanding between Germans and Israelis.

And it was that new understanding that was apparent, twenty-five years later in the Demjanjuk trial: the testimonies of Grabitz, Sheffler, and Altmann were testament to the normalization of the relations between the two countries.

Equally striking was the extensive use of documents from German archives to support and corroborate the authenticity of the Trawniki card. The job of spending countless hours in the German archives, and meeting with West German prosecutors, fell to one of the prosecutors, Michael Horovitz. And though searching out former Trawniki and Treblinka men in Germany was to Horovitz a personally repugnant task, he met with great success.

Vladas Amanaviczius, who was residing in Belgium, and Helmut Leonhardt, now living in Germany, had both served at Trawniki and agreed to be called as witnesses. Heinrich Schaeffer, also at Trawniki, and Otto Horn of Treblinka, had been witnesses at Demjanjuk's denaturalization trial and now lived in Germany. None of the witnesses were interested in traveling to Israel, but arrangements were made to hold hearings in June in their own countries.

In late May 1987, Horovitz left for Germany once again to make final preparations. As his plane was preparing to take off, someone came out of the pilot's cabin and said, "Is there a Mr. Horovitz aboard?" There was a radio call for him.

Amanaviczius, who was ninety-one, had died in his sleep.

A Lithuanian, who had served at Trawniki before being assigned to the Treblinka labor camp, Amanaviczius would have been an important witness. For while Leonhardt and Schaeffer could testify that Trawniki guards were issued service passes, Amanaviczius was a guard himself. He had said, in an earlier deposition, that not only did service passes exist, but he had been issued one himself and carried it at all times.

Undaunted, Horovitz hurried to Germany, more conscious than ever that time was running out. But upon arrival, he learned that Leonhardt would not see him. He was in the Black Forest and had no intention of cutting short his vacation. At seventy-one, he was not eager to testify; the whole subject was upsetting. But Horovitz got Leonhardt to agree that *after* his vacation he would testify.

The hearing was held on May 18–21, 1987, at a closed session of the Magistrate's Court in Koln, Germany, before Judge Becker. The public and press were not allowed because the hearing was not considered a court proceeding (technically, the court proceeding would be when the record of the hearing was presented in court in Israel). Prosecutor Horovitz appeared with Israel police investigator Etty Hai as his assistant; Mark O'Connor appeared for the defense, with Attorney Rudolf Strattman of Dusseldorf, who had been Treblinka commander Franz's attorney, assisting him.

Leonhardt, a retired policeman and resident of Koln, was balding, short, and red-faced. At times he became emotional during his testimony, but at the end of the day, Horovitz would recall, he always composed himself enough to ask for his day's travel expenses.

Before arriving at Trawniki in June 1942, Leonhardt had been a German police officer. He remained part of the camp personnel until July 1944, when he became a prisoner of war. He had worked in the administration office at Trawniki and was in charge of the file cards on foreign guards. When he arrived at the camp, the files were "in complete disorder." He couldn't recall how many weeks it took to organize them.

He didn't work in the battalion office, where the postings were done, so he had no personal knowledge as to whether they were always filled out completely.

Leonhardt was hesitant to say if he knew the purpose of the guards' training. He claimed no personal knowledge, but said he learned from others that the guards were sent to "clean up" villages of the Jews and were sent to the work camps Belzec, Sobibor, and Treblinka. Only later did he find out that the work camps were extermination camps.

Trawniki, Leonhardt confirmed, was an "instruction camp" for Russian war prisoners. He described the camp's induction procedures. The recording of the equipment was done not by Teufel himself, he revealed, but by a non-German guard. This accounted for the misspellings, the prosecution would contend.

As to other mistakes on the card, he later explained that, "When suddenly the many guards were recruited, one needed documents with which the guards could identify themselves. Such little details [as mistakes] were not considered."

Horovitz handed Leonhardt the photo album of Trawniki. Looking closely at the photographs, sometimes using a magnifying glass, he identified the details of the camp, officials, and the uniforms worn, even the window where he worked.

Horovitz placed before Leonhardt two photocopies of the Trawniki document and asked his opinion.

Leonhardt was certain: "The document is authentic." He recognized Streibl's signature and Teufel's distinctive signature in German Gothic script, which he had seen "countless" times.

Horovitz asked: "How did the *Dienstausweis* look in the original?"

An amazing thing happened: Leonhardt took the photocopies and folded them together in such a way that they were back to back, and that the photo appeared behind the first page with the inscription *"Dienstausweis."* It showed a complete familiarity with the document. While historians had spoken of the document, here was someone who had seen it in use.

The uniform of the person on the Trawniki card, Leonhardt said, was one of the early guard outfits. It could be clearly seen in the photo of Himmler's review.

Horovitz put before Leonhardt a transfer record of guards and asked what the numbers were next to each name. "This is a service number . . . that is put before the guard when his picture is taken." In a spontaneous, natural gesture, Leonhardt pointed with his right hand to a spot on the left side of his chest, to indicate the white rectangle that appeared on the photo and whose number had to match the *Dienstausweis.*

In his cross-examination, O'Connor tried to ferret out Leonhardt's feelings about the extermination of Jews at Treblinka and, toward the end, at Trawniki. Leonhardt said that he had learned of the exterminations at Treblinka from a guard named Arthur Raab, who had accompanied a transfer of guards to the camp.

Trawniki had a work camp attached to it where nine thousand Jews were held. Toward the end of the camp's existence, the Jews were forced to lie in pits, shot, and then incinerated. Leonhardt claimed to be in the hospital at the time the killings occurred, but his wife and young child were in a house near the camp. A guard had told her, in his broken German, "SS make bum-bum, all Jews *kaput.*" When she told this to Leonhardt, he secured a leave and took her and the child to his aunt's house. When Leonhardt returned, it was all over. "Only this stench was there, and also the ashes. . . ." Leonhardt started to cry. The deposition was stopped for a few minutes.

O'Connor wondered whether the exterminations might have had some impact on his sickness. At first, Leonhardt said he was not ill in that fashion. But, a few moments later, he said the killings affected him so much that "every day I drank between one and one-and-a-half liters of forty percent vodka." Leonhardt began to cry again, and at his request, a ten-minute break was taken.

O'Connor tried to imply Leonhardt's complicity by asking whether he knew the guards were being sent to "secret places" like extermination camps. But he answered that the postings were not secret; "every child in Poland knew about" the work camps, he said, and he learned from colleagues who traveled to the camps that mass murders took place there.

"But you indicated earlier guards fled from Trawniki?" O'Connor asked.

"Yes," replied Leonhardt. "If I had had to do the dirty work, I would have fled myself."

O'Connor wondered what Leonhardt made of the fact that the Trawniki card had no date of issue. He admitted that "normally every *Ausweis* [identity card] has a date of issue." Leonhardt said that when he was a police officer, if he had been shown an *Ausweis* without a date and didn't know the circumstances, he would have had to assume it was "a coarse falsification." But Leonhardt explained that on a Trawniki *Dienstausweis,* "one would only look at the sealed photo and whether the man coincided with the picture. Whether the *Ausweis* had a date of issue or not, nobody paid any attention, because for us they were inmates of the camp and no strangers."

Based on the card itself, Leonhardt said, one would have to conclude that the bearer was not at Treblinka, but was last in Sobibor.

But wasn't it possible the Russians captured blank forms? Leonhardt answered that he was already in Switnik, near Lublin, when the camp was taken over by the Russians; he had no idea how much time had elapsed between the guards' departure and the Russians' arrival. "Normally," he said, "all of the material would have been incinerated."

Horovitz later recalled that during Leonhardt's testimony, one of the translators, a young German woman in her twenties, broke into tears. She later asked Horovitz: "Is it true?" She had never heard a German speak about the murder and incineration of the Jews.

Although former Trawniki paymaster, Heinrich Schaeffer, had been a witness at Demjanjuk's denaturalization trial, Horovitz decided not to call him again. One former Trawniki man was enough. Leonhardt had been effective, more so than they had hoped. Schaeffer was more problematic: though he had given good testimony in the U.S., he had since signed a statement for the defense that directly contradicted his testimony. The prosecution was convinced that once the conditions under which the statement was obtained were explained, it would lose its importance and that Shaeffer did, in fact, recall seeing Trawniki service passes. But after Leonhardt, what did Schaeffer add?

If the defense thought Schaeffer so good for their case, *they* could call him as a witness. Horovitz telephoned O'Connor and said, "We waive calling Schaeffer." O'Connor said, "See you in Berlin."

The Israeli judges traveled to Berlin to observe the testimony of Otto Horn at the request of both sides. Judge Zvi Tal, arriving at the airport in Berlin, said he "never believed I would set foot on German soil." Tal went to the old synagogue in Berlin; Kosher food was provided for him throughout his stay.

That Jewish judges from the Jewish state traveled to Germany was heady: Who could have imagined this at war's end? Who could have even imagined it twenty-five years before, at the time of the Eichmann trial?

For Horovitz, meeting with the survivors had been heartrending and personally difficult. But spending time with the former Nazis was chilling. "It is very different meeting such a German; it does something to you," Horovitz would recall later.

Why did Leonhardt and Horn testify? Why would they cooperate with the Israelis? The answer was simple: because governmental authorities—American, German, and Israeli—had asked them to. They did not want to testify. But they were—they had always been—law-abiding citizens.

The testimony of Otto Horn began June 9, 1987, at the Teirgarten Court of Justice. Judge Hans-Jurgen Muller, in his early thirties, presided. The courtroom was small, more like a judge's chambers than a ceremonial courtroom. The three Israeli judges took seats along the side.

Otto Horn, eighty-three at the time, was retired and living in Berlin. With a full head of white hair, he seemed healthy and alert. Now called to testify, Horn set out, above all, to minimize his own role in the death process.

He coldly described his work at T4 as the ordering of jars—that the jars were for ashes, remains of the murdered, did not affect him. In his description of Treblinka, he was merely a wanderer, an onlooker of the process, never a participant. Judge Levin, exasperated, said finally: "What did you do?"

"*Saubermachen* [cleaning up]" was always Horn's answer. He was cleaning up at T4, cleaning up at Treblinka. He was free to wander in the death camp near the incineration process; sometimes he helped hang laundry; and if something happened at the camp, it was during the time he was on leave.

The extent to which Horn tried to distance himself, literally, from the extermination process, was obviously repugnant to the judges.

In Horn's account, the Jews were unloaded from the trains; transported to the *Schlauch;* at the gas chambers, the Jews had to wait until their turn came. "They were pushed into the entrance."

Levin asked what Horn meant by *"pushed"*?

"If they didn't want to, they were beaten. . . . They were beaten by Ukrainians and Germans with whips, there were those who moved them forward."

After being in the gas chambers, the Jews were *"taken"* out, *"placed"* on the ramp, and afterward *"put"* in the pit." This businesslike description of the horrors was given by Horn without the slightest sign of emotion. But one thing was clear: Horn knew Treblinka well, and was familiar with the people who worked there. He knew all the German officers, and he knew Ivan. "Ivan," he said, "he was friendly with Schmidt. They were always together. . . . He always worked with Schmidt. . . . He hurried the prisoners inside, together with Schmidt. He stood at the head of the gas chambers. . . . The people thought that they would be given a bath, and when they saw, they refused to go in, and began screaming. They would be beaten and while being beaten, were put inside."

When asked who did this, he answered: "Germans, Ukrainians, Schmidt and Ivan."

Asked to describe Ivan, he said: "He was big, and had a black uniform. He was big, tall, about 175–180cm approximately. . . . He had a powerful build. . . . He was twenty-three. . . . [His hair was] I don't know . . . dark blond."

"After the chambers were full," he testified, "Ivan and Schmidt would go together to the engines. . . . He was always together with Schmidt, he repaired cars with him. When the transports arrived, he was with Schmidt. . . . I stood above the *Schlauch* and could see everything.

"When no transports arrived, he was in the camp very little, he would get supplies. I was then in the Upper Camp. He would run by me, the distance was very small. . . . When no transports arrived, Ivan would be in the Lower Camp tinkering with cars. . . . He knew how to drive a car."

How often did he see Ivan? "I saw him almost constantly when I didn't have night guard duty or when I wasn't on furlough." And Horn testified that he saw Ivan after the uprising, when the gas chambers were operated to liquidate the final transports.

Horovitz showed him the first set of photographs. Horn picked the 1951 visa photograph and said: "Ivan's appearance was similar to that." Asked for further clarification, Horn stated, "He appears similar to him, there is a similarity. . . . He had a round full face, this is what can be seen here."

Horn also recalled that in 1979, a half-hour after he had selected Demjanjuk's visa photo, the investigators had shown him a second pack of photographs, one that included the Trawniki photo: "I said that possibly it is he. This is what he looks like. He looks similar to this." Now Horn picked out the photo of the young soldier and commented, "There is similarity. I can only say there are similarities. . . . I am as certain today as I was then."

"The Ivan you knew in Treblinka," Horovitz asked, "and the man whom you pointed out in the photographs at your home in 1980, as well as today, are they the same person?"

"Yes," was Horn's unequivocal answer.

Horn was aggressively cross-examined by O'Connor for seven-and-a-half hours. The former Treblinka man stood up remarkably well under the strain, but the young German interpreter asked to be replaced after five hours. Except for being hard of hearing, one observer noted, the wiry old man seemed extremely fit.

In 1979, Horn had said he only saw Ivan in the Upper Camp and never saw him commit beatings. Yet in 1986, he said he saw Ivan in the Upper and Lower camps.

Was his memory better in 1979 than in 1986 in Germany? He admitted freely that he had aged a great deal in the last eight years. But he still maintained that he had seen Ivan in both camps.

In 1983, Horn had signed a document recanting part of his testimony. For years, this recantation was part of O'Connor's "proof" of innocence. This was to be O'Connor's triumph. But during questioning by the judges, the circumstances surrounding the statement became clear. Horn had been visited by three persons who said they were from the Association for Freedom for Eastern European Prisoners. They were actually "associates" of the defense. They talked to Horn. They did not write down anything in his apartment. But the next day they took him to the U.S. Consulate, where they asked him to sign a typed document. Horn never read the statement; he assumed it contained what he had said. But it did not. In fact, he went to the German police in 1986 and set the record straight: Horn stood by his earlier testimony. Demjanjuk looked like Ivan.

O'Connor wanted to know why Horn remembered Ivan when he could no longer remember a German friend with whom he had gone on leave. Said Horn: "That was forty-five years ago that I saw Ivan. He was a young man. . . . I said that he looks similar. . . ."

"And in what is the similarity?"

"In the face. He has a full round face," Horn said.

"That is all?"

"Yes."

O'Connor was ruthless, and tried his best to intimidate Horn by dwelling on his actions at T4 and Treblinka, or to threaten him by showing that his actions today could also have deadly consequences.

O'Connor took a few steps away from Horn, paused, then turned quickly and asked him whether he knew John Demjanjuk could *hang* based on his identification.

Horn sat up straight. He was visibly affected. *"Hang?"* he said, anguished. "I didn't know that anyone did that anymore."

After forty-three years a person changes, Horn said. He could no longer say with complete certainty whether this was Ivan of Treblinka. But he could not change what he had said about the photograph: "This is approximately what he looks like," that there was a certain similarity in the round face.

But O'Connor pressed harder: "Do you have any doubts in seeing this photograph whether it is he?"

Horn, suddenly looking every year of his eighty-three years, answered with conviction, "It resembles him." After forty-three years, he could not be one hundred percent certain, but Horn concluded that he could not deny the resemblance, no matter the consequence.

CHAPTER 21

O'Connor's Mistake

Before the prosecution could rest, it had to address Demjanjuk's alibi. Demjanjuk's version of events, which he would soon take the stand to put forward, was known. But the prosecution wanted the court to hear it within a historical context, to show exactly what was true in it and what rang false with history.

Professor Matityahu Meisel of Tel Aviv University, an expert on Soviet history, had researched the periods before and after Demjanjuk claimed he was a POW at Chelm. First of all, Meisel said, not just anyone was chosen to drive a tractor—it was a privilege. Loyal party members were recruited for this and received better payment. They were required to have technical skills and qualifications.

O'Connor, in cross-examination, was more interested in asking Meisel about Stalin and the famine in the Ukraine, referring to it as "this *Shoah* [holocaust]" and speaking of the "large body of survivor testimony."

Blatman immediately objected to O'Connor's terminology. Judge Levin was inclined to let O'Connor use any term he wished. But Judge Tal voiced the opinion that O'Connor was improperly using a word with a specific connotation, transposing it to a situation that was also tragic but not parallel. "To my mind," Judge Tal said, "it leaves a very bad taste."

"I chose the statement '*Shoah*,'" O'Connor said, somewhat disingenuously, "because in the Western world, that term never refers to Holocaust. I shall not use it again."

Meisel continued, noting that when Demjanjuk was wounded as

a Red Army Soldier during the Soviet retreat, hospital records were not kept; the overall goal in treatment of the wounded was to return them to the battle front as quickly as possible.

The importance of this was that the Trawniki card listed Demjanjuk's distinguishing mark—the scar on his back. The Soviets would not have known this from their records; only Demjanjuk himself could have provided such information. This, of course, further enhanced the card's credibility.

As Demjanjuk himself provided no exact dates, the prosecution wanted to build a historic reconstruction of the events in his alibi. Demjanjuk had said that he was taken prisoner on the first day of the battle of Kerch. Kerch is a peninsula on the eastern side of the Crimean Peninsula. It was taken by the Germans in November 1941, and returned to Russian hands in a counteroffensive early in 1942. According to German war diaries, on May 8, 1942, the German 11th Army launched a renewed offensive in which the Kerch peninsula was again taken. More than one-hundred-twenty-five-thousand Russian prisoners were captured, Demjanjuk among them.

The Nazis were not prepared for their success. The transfer route for the POWs was along railway lines. Beginning the next day, POWs started to arrive at the Rovno camp. Transfers continued until early June.

Demjanjuk was paying close attention and had questions of his own: Were three Red Army units captured in the Kerch Peninsula? as he recalled. Were there historical accounts of forced marches from Kerch to Perikov? (as he claimed to have gone though). Meisel said that three Soviet armies were known to be fighting in the Crimea; but he had found no accounts of the march.

Dr. Shmuel Krakovsky, the director of archives at Yad Vashem and an expert on German POW camps, testified about the Chelm camp. He disputed Demjanjuk's scenario of the journey to Rovno taking more than a month because the POWs had to repair the railroad. German orders, Krakovsky said, were that soldiers taken prisoner at the front were to be taken rapidly to POW camps behind the lines—in weeks, not months. They were transported in trains in fine working order; they needed no repair.

Some 5.75-million soldiers of the Red Army were taken prisoner by the Germans. They did indeed live in inhumane conditions. There were eight-hundred-thousand auxiliaries recruited, of whom 60 to 70 percent were Ukrainians. Chelm was originally set up as a front-line camp for the German invasion of the Soviet Union. There were actually two camps, a southern and a northern one.

O'Connor wished to show conditions were so horrible that Soviet

POWs had no choice but to collaborate. Meisel and Krakovsky agreed that the conditions were inhumane, but both wanted to make it clear: though hundreds of thousands did collaborate, many more chose not to. O'Connor also argued that Ukrainians had a *right* to collaborate to fulfill their nationalistic ambitions. Krakovsky answered that collaboration was a crime that in no way furthered Ukrainian nationalism.

At Chelm, Krakovsky said, there were four different "selections." Jews and commissars were made to fall out immediately. Any Jews were killed immediately; those suspected of being Jewish were ordered to pull down their pants—if circumcised, they, too, were killed. And although Demjanjuk claimed that his Jewish foreman at Chelm was called *"Kapo,"* Krakovsky confirmed that the word *"Kapo"* was only used in concentration and extermination camps, not in POW camps.

Krakovsky introduced the German orders that chronicled the recruitment of POWs as auxiliaries; and he presented German Army statistical lists of POWs to show Chelm was a transit camp with a high turnover.

Beginning in the summer of 1942, Chelm's southern camp served merely as a transit camp; by spring 1943, there were no longer any prisoners there and the camp was turned over to civilian authorities. By the end of 1943, there were few POWs in the northern camp. Their place had been taken by Italians (Italy surrendered September 8). The Red Army entered Poland in January 1944, and Chelm began to evacuate its remaining few hundred prisoners. Contrary to Demjanjuk's testimony, no Rumanians were ever at Chelm, Krakovsky testified.

Demjanjuk had claimed over the years that after Chelm, he was at Heuberg and Graz as part of the Russian Liberation Army; that he served in the Vlassov army and received his tattoo there; and that the lies on his postwar forms were all conceived to hide his being a POW and a Vlassov army soldier. He said he lied because he was afraid of being repatriated to the Soviet Union: Red Army soldiers, he claimed, were to commit suicide rather than be captured; former Vlassov soldiers were traitors and were executed.

But during the time Demjanjuk said he was in Heuberg, the spring of 1944, there were no Vlassov units, Meisel testified. The Vlassov army was established in the fall of 1944; and the first unit was set up in Heuberg only in January 1945. An order was issued to establish a second division in Heuberg, and General Fedor Truckhin arrived in March to organize a division that had uniforms and arms. The second division was moved through Bavaria, only to be taken captive by the Americans and later handed over to the Red Army.

Dr. Shmuel Spektor, who also worked at Yad Vashem and was an expert in Ukrainian military formations, testified that in February 1945 there was an SS *Waffengrenadiren* division in Graz that a month later became known as the First Ukrainian Division. Lieutenant General Pablo Shandruk was in charge of the division and became Supreme Commander of the Ukrainian National Army. This force was independent of the Vlassov army. Spektor confirmed that death-camp guards served in the Ukrainian units.

Meisel, Spektor, and Krakovsky all testified that Demjanjuk could not have been at Chelm for eighteen months and then met up with the Ukrainian unit at Graz or the Russian Liberation Army (ROA) in Heuberg—there were ten months time between the closing of the Chelm camp and the start of the Ukrainian division, and an even greater time gap until the establishment of the ROA unit at Heuberg.

Finally, the prosecution's historians testified that tattooing at Graz or Heuberg was impossible because of the turmoil that existed. No tattoos could have been issued at Graz or Heuberg because blood-typing needed laboratories and special personnel and nowhere in the accounts of the Ukrainian divisions do they mention anyone being tattooed; rather, it became a defense to say they were not true SS, as they were not tattooed.

Demjanjuk could not have been in Heuberg or Graz when he said he was, Spektor said; if he served at all with the Ukrainian army, it was because he had been a concentration-camp guard—and his tattoo was no evidence of service in the Russian Liberation Army; to the contrary, it indicated SS service.

Professor Meisel said he had no knowledge of a Russian army suicide order, but Demjanjuk did have reason to fear being returned to the Soviet Union. The Soviet pardon issued to Vlassov army men in 1955, he said, did not apply to those who were war criminals.

Demjanjuk and his defense would have some explaining to do.

Throughout the trial, the press and the casual observer remained intensely interested in the Demjanjuk family, as if they provided the trial's "human element." Often they were served up by the media as victims of the trial process.

There would be no articles about the families murdered in Treblinka, and the families that would have existed had there been no murders at Treblinka. And, strangely enough, one never saw articles about the feelings of the children of the survivors who testified at the trial. Yochi Epstein Landau, Rivka Rosenberg, Tzvili Czarney, and Yoram Boraks attended the trial as well. They lived in Israel and were easily available.

No, it was the Demjanjuk family, as strangers in a strange land, that drew the attention. How did *they* feel? What had it been like growing up with *him*? Did they still believe in his innocence? What did they think of the trial? Demjanjuk would repeat his innocence, as would members of his family. There was no question that he had been a good father. And, conversely, it was no crime to love your father.

The family was always good for a quote and son-in-law Ed Nishnic could be counted on for stories: they had found the *real* Ivan, they had found Nikolai, they had filed a new suit against the OSI—but their revelations outside the courtroom rarely proved substantive in court.

The one way in which the Demjanjuk family did make a substantial impact on the trial, however, was through the defense purse strings, which they alone held.

Ed Nishnic had stayed in Israel in April to observe O'Connor in action. He was not pleased by what he saw. Sheftel and Gill wanted more say in defense decisions and strategy. O'Connor believed he, alone, should be in charge.

While O'Connor was away in May for the German hearings, the family decided that the defense should proceed by majority rule. O'Connor, though, would not acknowledge any power shift. He continued to project himself as lead counsel and bristled each time the prosecution talked about agreements reached with other members of the defense.

Tensions had run high between Sheftel and O'Connor from the trial's first days. At one point, O'Connor had announced that Sheftel would not stand to speak again; later he apologized and said they were smoothing out their disagreements. And so it seemed. But as the prosecution finished its presentation in May and early June, the defense problems resurfaced.

At the close of the prosecution's case, as per usual procedure, Sheftel made a "no case motion"—that the prosecution had not submitted enough evidence to support a guilty conviction. Sheftel did not really address the evidence as submitted, but rather argued how it should be viewed. The court told him those were the arguments he could make in summation; but not now. Before reporters and spectators, O'Connor tried to deride Sheftel's presentation to the press and before the spectators. But he was addressing the wrong audience.

The trial recessed in June. The defense was to begin its presentation on July 27. O'Connor's position with the family, and with Sheftel, became increasingly precarious. As he had often done in the past, O'Connor took to the press.

A June 25, 1987, story from the Associated Press quoted O'Connor as saying Sheftel "is under tremendous pressure from the Israeli media for representing an alleged mass murderer. He has reached a breaking point."

This played to Sheftel's advantage. He could pretend to take the high ground. He told the press that the public dispute was "an embarrassment. . . . We tried to keep it out of public view until Mr. O'Connor made it impossible." The die was cast.

A letter to O'Connor firing him, and one to the court, were drafted and brought to Demjanjuk in prison. Though Demjanjuk trusted O'Connor, he trusted his family more. He signed.

The letter to the court also stated that another attorney, John Broadley, would be joining the defense team. Broadley was a Washington lawyer who had been working, pro bono, on a Freedom of Information Act (FOIA) suit against the OSI for the Demjanjuk Defense Fund—a suit asking the OSI to release information about Demjanjuk from its investigatory files.

Sheftel drove back immediately from the prison to Jerusalem. A copy of the letter dismissing O'Connor was slipped under the door of the defense office, and the original was put under Mark O'Connor's hotel room door. Then the phone calls to and from the press began.

At first, O'Connor denied receiving any letter. He continued to maintain that he was lead counsel. "I still consider myself as Demjanjuk's lawyer," he said. "I feel personally responsible for the life of this man."

O'Connor visited Demjanjuk in prison. He wrote to the court, saying the family was pressuring the defendant to make decisions that were not in his best interest. He held a press conference at which he described Demjanjuk as confused and depressed.

On July 14, O'Connor wrote to the court. His letter was pure O'Connor, typos and all. Giving his Buffalo address, he wrote "Mr. Sheftel has submitted what purports to be a defense request yet omits the name of lead counsel on the document, thereby evidencing his continuing contempt for the Special Panel in this historic case."

O'Connor accused Sheftel of "bald allegations," then went on to make some himself, hinting at Sheftel's "close contacts" with Shaked and "life sentence bargains." He claimed to have dismissed Sheftel several months ago because of his "renegade" advocacy in and out of court, but the Demjanjuk family had retained him as "their personal attorney in this case." O'Connor then went on to list what he had done, what Sheftel had not. O'Connor signed the letter in his ornate, grandiose script.

The court held a special session on July 15, 1987, at the request of both O'Connor and Sheftel. At the hearing, Demjanjuk was as anxious to speak as O'Connor and Sheftel. But Levin announced that he would address the accused, and asked him to listen closely; he would then ask him if he had understood everything. Levin would discuss the requests before him in the order he had received them; and he would only allow the person he addressed to speak.

The judge pointed out that it was Mark O'Connor who had been granted the power of attorney to represent Demjanjuk. Sheftel and Gill had been appointed part of the defense team, according to court records, by O'Connor, not by Demjanjuk. Nonetheless, Demjanjuk had the right to appoint either of them independently, by doing so in writing or by declaring them to be his attorneys in court.

Demjanjuk said he understood everything thus far. Levin asked whether he would like Yoram Sheftel to serve as his attorney. Demjanjuk said he wished to consult his son-in-law without the presence of either defense counsel. Levin agreed. But he counseled Demjanjuk to do so with a certain understanding: John Broadley was not admitted to practice in Israel, so could not be appointed counsel; nor could Demjanjuk expect the court to grant any further delays. Finally, said Levin, public recriminations among attorneys was not an accepted, desirable, or honorable way of proceeding. He advised Demjanjuk to tell his lawyers he was not happy with their conduct.

A half-hour later, the court reconvened. Demjanjuk was asked to rise. He was asked if he wished O'Connor to continue to represent him. Demjanjuk answered that, "Since the beginning of the trial, the attorneys have not acted properly. . . . My family has decided to dismiss Mr. O'Connor, since this will not be in my interest to have him continue to represent me."

But it was not his family who was on trial, Levin said. What was *his* decision?

"My decision is to follow the advice of my family. I am in a cage. I am in jail. Therefore, I must follow the advice of my family. Whatever my family decides I must do." But his decision must be a voluntary one, Levin said.

Did he want Sheftel to replace O'Connor? Demjanjuk said he wanted Broadley to replace him. Levin informed him that Broadley had neither applied for nor had received permission from the Israeli

Bar to represent him, so the court could not appoint him. Demjanjuk then said that if "Mr. O'Connor is not on the case, then Mr. Sheftel replaces him."

Judge Levin explained that for an attorney to represent a person in court, a power of attorney must be submitted in court, or the accused can announce in open court that he appoints a certain attorney to represent him. Both of these are acceptable, but he must do one of them.

It was a decision, Demjanjuk said, that Broadley must make. Levin asked: "In other words, Mr. Sheftel is not regarded by you as your defense counsel?" "Apparently not," Demjanjuk said. He asked the same question about John Gill. Demjanjuk said Gill should be his attorney until Broadley was appointed.

There was no *until*, Levin said. He was his attorney at this trial or not. Then he was, Demjanjuk said.

Sheftel announced that Demjanjuk had already signed a power of attorney for Gill, which Sheftel asked to submit. Judge Levin asked Demjanjuk to read it over again. He confirmed it.

Demjanjuk had also drafted a power of attorney for Sheftel but didn't understand, Sheftel said, that he could not be his attorney without it.

Levin asked Demjanjuk again: "Are you asking Mr. Sheftel to serve as defense counsel at this trial?"

"Yes," Demjanjuk said.

Was he prepared to stand by his decision, even if the trial began less than two weeks later?

He stood by his decision, Demjanjuk said, without any doubt.

Levin asked again if he had dismissed O'Connor.

Demjanjuk could not answer directly. He wanted to dismiss O'Connor and appoint Broadley; but he felt that the court was trying to pressure him to appoint Gill and Sheftel instead.

This, in no way was the judges' intention, Levin said; they were only explaining what was happening. But the court needed to hear from him, in his own words, what *he* wanted to do.

Demjanjuk asked for a further recess to consult his family by telephone. The court gave him until the following Monday, July 20.

O'Connor's mistake was that he had assumed that as long as he maintained his personal relationship with John Demjanjuk, and kept both him and the case material at arm's length from everyone else, then he was in charge, irreplaceable—he could treat the family as he wished. But what he failed to understand was that the family had become the client. Because they were paying the bills, they wanted to call the shots; and Demjanjuk—his loyalty was to his family.

The day before the July 20 hearing, O'Connor wrote a letter, submitting his resignation. In the letter, O'Connor sought to "project" his version of events. Four pages single-spaced, again replete with typos, it was addressed to Levin from the defense office in Binyanei Haooma. It began, "I have finalized certain decisions regarding my status as lead counsel in the matter of John Demjanjuk."

O'Connor had advised the family, he wrote, that a study of the no-case motion would show Sheftel's "pattern of negligence and misconduct during the trial." Instead, O'Connor said, Sheftel had flown to Cleveland and convinced the family "that the scathing opinion of the court . . . [was] merely a reflection of the special panel's bias and prejudice in the case."

As O'Connor would have had it, Sheftel had pressured the family and Demjanjuk into firing him. Demjanjuk had tried to alert the court to his intentions, but Sheftel had acted as "the family enforcer," directing Demjanjuk in Russian.

"Mr. Demjanjuk had confided to me in prison," O'Connor said, "that although he desires my representation in the case, he must follow the direction of the family and they have placed their faith in Mr. Sheftel.

"Demjanjuk family members would naturally be particularly vulnerable to Mr. Sheftel's pressure. Because of my professional responsibility and human concern, however, I determined to make one last attempt to have the family take into consideration the unvoiced viewpoint of the man in the cell in Ayalon, the man who sits in court every day while the majority of his family wait on another continent for the outcome of the trial."

O'Connor felt his participation in the defense was necessary, for he alone had conversed with witnesses Rudolf Reiss and Heinrich Schaeffer, been present at the questioning of Leonhardt and Horn, knew Polish witnesses Samuels and Wuyek, and Garcia de Ribes of Spain, as well as Walter Dubovitz, who, O'Connor said, "had been prepared to testify that John Demjanjuk was serving with him at the time the prosecution alleges he was part of Operation Reinhard."

Now having done all he could, O'Connor bid his adieu.

At the hearing on July 20, Levin acknowledged receipt of the letter, but said the decision to release counsel from representing an accused was up to the court.

Levin asked Demjanjuk if he accepted O'Connor's resignation, even without a postponment.

"May it please the court," Demjanjuk answered, "you have given me four days of further thinking. I should like to inform you that I would like to release Mr. O'Connor without any consideration for the further continuation of the trial, regardless of that."

The court released O'Connor from representing Demjanjuk, but added, "we can not but express our appreciation to Mr. O'Connor for the efforts he has invested in the defense of the accused, the cross-examinations of the witnesses for the prosecution up to the present stage."

Though he was out of the case, O'Connor stayed in Israel, at the American Colony Hotel, putting on a public display, like a "government in exile." He appeared for the first days of the defense presentation, but later left the country and returned to Buffalo.

In a week the defense would make its opening statements, and call its first witness: John Demjanjuk would take the stand in his own defense.

CHAPTER 22

Dry River Beds

On the morning of Monday, July 27, 1987, Sheftel rose to present the defense's opening remarks. He was quick to distance himself from O'Connor, and to heap blame on him. "Your Honors," he began, "at the inception of my remarks, I see fit to apologize most sincerely to the survivors who testified at this trial, for the fact that they had to withstand cross-examination for days on end on matters that touched upon points the defense declared to be incontrovertible and had to answer questions such as what was the color of the flames in the pit where the corpses were burned, what was the distance from the gas chambers to the pits, and questions of that nature." Sheftel also apologized to the court "for the fact that the court was forced to deal with dozens of pointless objections, which had no legal grounds." Sheftel also apologized to the prosecution for wasting time arguing over documents that, if avoided, would have allowed the defense to prepare better.

"Let's get down to the crux of the matter," Sheftel said. In its opening remarks, the prosecution had presented historical facts with which the defense had no dispute. But what concerned him most, he said, were the facts that the prosecution did not mention, facts that pertained to the Trawniki card, which he claimed, the KGB had signed.

Sheftel argued that the annihilation of Eastern European Jewry was caused not only by the Germans but by the treachery of the Soviet Union, which signed the Ribbentrop–Molotov agreement a week before the invasion of Poland on September 1, 1939. This agreement, which allowed for the destruction of European Jewry, was itself based on a forgery, he argued. Ostensibly the agreement was for peace, but it covertly allowed the Germans to invade Poland on September 1, with the Soviets "keeping peace" on the Eastern front; in return, the Germans allowed the Soviets to invade the other half of Poland on September 17. This treachery, he said, was typical of the Soviets. Sheftel promised to call an expert who would prove that the Soviet Union was not a nation with a KGB but rather the KGB was a terrorist organization that ran the Soviet Union. And, therefore, the signatories of the Ribbentrop–Molotov agreement in effect were the same as the Trawniki card—the KGB. "It is the very same hand."

Sheftel made light of the prosecution experts who had testified that they had never seen a KGB-forged document. He promised to submit an entire book of KGB-forged documents from the war.

As for the identifications by the Treblinka survivors, Sheftel promised that a different picture would emerge from the one that Shaked had put forward. Sheftel said he would, in all probability, present the premier expert in the world on eyewitness identification, Elizabeth Loftus, whom he characterized as having been "barred from appearing in this particular case." (Loftus had been asked to testify but decided not to after an elderly uncle asked her not to appear.) She would show what weight should be attached to the survivor testimonies, based on her analysis and a comparison with the Frank Walus case, in which eleven witnesses, who, in Sheftel's words, "with the same good memory, the same self-assurance, identified the so-called Butcher of Pilsen, and turned out to be all wrong."

Sheftel also promised to present the UN war-crimes file on Alfred Bilitz, a Nazi criminal who was alleged to have been at Treblinka from June 1942 to September 1943, to have committed the same acts as recounted by the eyewitnesses, and to have been called "Ivan." The Bilitz evidence was based on the testimonies of three survivors who appeared before the Polish War Crimes Commission, one of whom was Leon Finkelstein, whom Reichman had mentioned in his testimony. Actually, the defense had only excerpts of their testimony. It had applied to the Polish War Crimes Commission and the Berlin Documentation Center for more data but had received no reply.

Sheftel also said that material just recently made available from a Demjanjuk Defense Fund suit against the OSI showed that twenty-one witnesses from Treblinka, including the barber Abraham Bomba who appeared in the film *Shoah,* could not identify Demjanjuk as Ivan. That made twenty-nine survivors, he said, who did not identify the defendant as opposed to the five who did. "What is more ponderous, the weight of five witnesses or the weight of twenty-nine witnesses?"

Sheftel said he would call experts who would not merely state the Trawniki card is a forgery but who "will shatter this document and leave nothing of it: neither the signatures of Teufel or Streibl, or the one that purports to be that of the accused, nor the picture, nor the stamps, nor any other element relevant to the document in this case. Nothing will remain of the entire document. We will shatter and pulverize this document. We will leave nothing of it."

"You will leave us the original, please," chided Levin. Everyone laughed, and Sheftel suppressed a boyish grin. "Definitely," he answered, "the original alone will remain intact."

Sheftel quoted Shaked as saying that though the Trawniki card did not place the accused at Treblinka, the eyewitnesses did. Therefore, even if the card was not proved a forgery, "and this is only for the sake of theoretical argument, even then, it remains for the identification witnesses to establish, whether or not the accused is, in fact, Ivan the Terrible, and we contend their testimony can not serve as grounds for this identification."

Saying that although Demjanjuk did not confirm or deny that the photo was his, witness Edna Robertson would show that the photo was, in fact, attached to another document, that the seals on the document were not the same as on the photo, and that the breast pocket number was, in fact, different from the number on the document.

Sheftel also said that he had received "some very interesting material" that Altmann, Cantu, and Gideon Epstein had been employed by the OSI to identify the body of Nazi war criminal Josef Mengele, and that their opinions had been found unreliable.

Levin asked why these questions were not asked when the witnesses were on the stand. The defense, he answered, didn't have access to those memos yet. "After all," he said, "we are not prophets."

Sheftel was working himself into an excited state, and his voice grew louder and more shrill. The judges asked him to calm down, lest he go hoarse.

As for the historical experts Sheffler and Grabitz, their testimony explained, Sheftel said, why Germany lost the war, and why Grabitz lost the Trawniki trial. Their contentions about forgery were baseless; as all you needed to forge successfully, Sheftel said, was well-oiled machinery.

Sheftel promised to call an expert to show how forgeries were perpetrated and to describe the chain of events leading *Stern* to publish the Hitler forgeries. He said he would produce a victim of the KGB who now devoted himself to its study and who ran a research institute.

Levin noted that examples of other forgeries by intelligence agencies in other countries would not serve to prove that the Trawniki document had been forged. "What may for the outside world seem of interest or relevancy is not relevant to this case and in this courtroom."

Shaked throughout this looked bemused, his face resting in his hands.

"When the accused takes the stand, he will show as part of his testimony, that none of the historical witnesses produced by the prosecution, can in any way disprove and refute his alibi." But Sheftel said they would not only have the accused's word, it would be supported by an expert from abroad, "the great-grandson of Tolstoy, an unquestioned expert of international reknown."

In conclusion, Sheftel wanted to take up the comments of Shaked and Blatman that Israel would not rest until Nazi war criminals had been brought to justice and that it was involved in tracking them down and enlisting other nations' help to do so. This was not the case.

"Next year, for what the Germans call 'humanitarian reasons.'" Sheftel said, "Kurt Franz will be released from prison. Under German law, he will be set free, but under the terms of the Nazi and Nazi Collaborators Law in Israel, he can still be brought to justice in Israel. But I can say with absolute certainty, that Kurt Franz will never be brought to trial." The reason? Said Sheftel: *Wiedergutmachung*, German war reparations. It was Sheftel's belief that the agreements had put an end to the trials of Nazi war criminals in Israel—at a time when many survivors were still able to testify and that since then, not one criminal had been brought to justice, with the exception of Eichmann. So Sheftel concluded: "I must determine that the statements of the learned state prosecutor and Mr. Shaked are utterly unfounded."

CHAPTER 23

Demjanjuk on the Stand

After Sheftel concluded his opening remarks, Judge Levin asked, "I gather that the accused will be testifying for the defense? Will the accused please rise." Demjanjuk stood.

Levin asked him to state his name.

"If it please the court," he said in Ukrainian, "I am John Demjanjuk."

Gill asked Demjanjuk to address the charges against him. "The Honorable Bench, I am accused here of being at Treblinka," he said. "This is not true. I was never either at Treblinka or at Sobibor nor at Trawniki nor at any other such place."

Next Gill led Demjanjuk through his personal history. By now the accused had told his tale many times, but never at such length or in such detail, and never for such high stakes.

Demjanjuk spoke calmly, in even tones. He started school, he said, when he was eight. He couldn't attend earlier because of his household duties. He was enrolled for *nine* years, but only passed the *fourth* grade. Until now he had spoken of having only a fourth-grade education; he had never said anything about nine years of schooling.

"In each grade, first, second, and fourth, I spent two years," he said. After two years in the fifth grade, he still had not passed. A third year was not allowed, so he received a disqualification report card.

It was not academic failure that held him back, he testified, but poverty. "The reasons are that my parents were very poor, and they had nothing to wear or no shoes to put on. If my father had any job whatsoever, I had to stay home, rather than going to school." Both his parents were invalids: his father had lost several fingers in World War I; his mother had caught a cold while pregnant with him, after which her right leg would no longer bend and she was bedridden for a year.

Demjanjuk was eager to recount to "all the people everywhere" the famine that befell the Ukraine in 1932 and 1933. "It was so horrible," he said, "it goes beyond anything that humanity had known up unto then. People ate anything they could lay hands on, including dogs and cats. . . . We and my relatives ate rats, and even our cat and bird. People were lying dead in their homes, in the yards, on the roads, exposed to the sunlight. Nobody collected them; nobody brought them to burial."

Demjanjuk's family sold their possessions and went to live with a relative on a *Kolkhoz* (collective farm) near Moscow; there, food was more abundant. But there was no work. The family soon returned to their village, he said, where "there was no longer any control. . . . People were scattered about, lying outside all around. We had no home of our own, and we went to our father's brother. But they were all dead by then."

When he was about seventeen, Demjanjuk went to work in a *Kolkhoz*. Starting as a plower, he ended up working with tractors. He was put in charge of the work team, and became an assistant to the tractor driver.

In 1938, he joined the *Komsomol*, the Communist youth organization; membership was not mandatory, but those who didn't join, he explained, risked becoming "an object of ridicule." He was given a small identity card with a photograph, he said, but he buried it in the ground when he was later taken captive.

When Russia declared war on Finland in 1939, tractor drivers were drafted immediately. The assistant tractor drivers took over. Demjanjuk was a driver, he said, until he himself was drafted.

In 1940, he and most of his fellow villagers received notice to report for service in the Red Army. Each man was required to have two pairs of underpants, a spoon, and a plate. As Demjanjuk was too poor to produce the required underpants, he was told to return home. In 1941, he was called for the second time. The clothing requirement had been abolished; he was inducted.

Gill asked whether a photo was taken. Demjanjuk could not remember. But he said his hair was cut. (One of Demjanjuk's objections to the Trawniki photo was that he said his hair was never that length.)

His recollection of his Red Army service was detailed. He recalled that the recruiting office was in a small town, Samgorodok, where all his hair fell out. He was sent from there to Besserabia, to the town of Bielce, to a unit where other members from his village were sent. They underwent artillery training, and were sent to the front; their first position was on the banks of the River Prut.

The Soviet army was in retreat. It passed through the rivers Prut and Dnieper. Near the Dnieper River, Demjanjuk said, he was wounded. He was taken to four Soviet hospitals, the names of which he recalled with precision: Melitopol, Berd'ansk, Stalino, and Tbilisi.

His wound left a scar on his back, but he said the scar that he still bore today was from surgery he underwent in 1948 to remove the remaining shrapnel.

After his recovery, he was sent to an artillery unit in the town of Kottaissi. Demjanjuk was there "perhaps a month or two." The unit was sent to Baku to complete the full force and from there it was sent to Kerch, where it remained some two weeks or so, before being dispatched to the nearby front.

There were a great many people at the front. He could not say how many were in his unit, but "there was talk of three armies." He arrived in Kerch in January or February 1942, he said. His unit received no training, it merely waited for its next posting.

"Once, and I remember this as if it happened yesterday, there was a very heavy rain, and we were all taken prisoner." He was now at a critical juncture: from here on, his version of events diverged from the prosecution's. Dates were critical.

Levin asked for a more precise date of his capture. But Demjanjuk would not be specific. He knew it was 1942, but said, "I can't tell exactly what month it was, but it was very hot and the grass was growing."

Demjanjuk said he was first taken to a small camp. A few days later, he joined a group of some seventy men who were preparing railroad tracks for German trains. He was engaged in this for six weeks to two months. Demjanjuk said he could not be more precise.

The prisoners pushed along a railroad car as they worked, and it was in this that they slept. "If the weather permitted, we had to get up and work; if the weather was not or did not make it possible, we stayed in the car." They wore their Red Army uniforms, and were served bread and coffee three times a day. Rumanian guards were there as well, he said.

Instead of completing the railwork, they joined other prisoners in a march along the canal. Those who stepped out of line to grab something to eat, or to jump in the water, were shot. Eventually, they came to a small camp near the canal. "We spent about a week, and they fed us once a day." Demjanjuk had never before mentioned this camp.

"Later," he testified, "they put us into cars and took us to Rovno. . . . The camp at Rovno was a very small one in which we could barely stand, so during the day we were taken outside of the camp into a clearing in the forest, where we could either lie down or sit down. We were fed once a day, a pot of some sort of pottage."

Demjanjuk denied being recruited at Rovno for Trawniki. "The prosecution can say whatever it wants, but I was there, and I am the one who knows that I went from Rovno to Chelm. At Rovno I spent only a week or two." Demjanjuk said he believed he was transferred in the fall.

The prosecution had placed him at Treblinka by autumn. Was he ever recruited, Gill asked, to serve in the SS?

"If it please the court and everyone present, I wish to state one thing and one thing only: that I am not the hangman or henchmen that you are speaking of. I was never at Trawniki or at Sobibor."

Because of a translation problem, Demjanjuk was asked to repeat his answer. "Since at the beginning of my trial," he said, "I have been sitting here looking at the shadow of death of the accursed Treblinka. My heart aches, and I grieve deeply for what was done to your people by the Nazis during the Second World War and only because of the fact that you were Jews. I wish to be believed, and please do not put the noose around my neck for things that were perpetrated by others."

Judge Levin reminded him that the question was more specific: Was he recruited and, if so, where was he sent?

But Demjanjuk would not answer directly. He pleaded: "Honorable Judge, I have just said that never in my life was I in Treblinka or Trawniki or in Sobibor. I wish to be believed, and please do not put the noose around my neck for the deeds of others."

But was he *ever* recruited into the SS auxiliary forces?

"Never," Demjanjuk said.

Gill asked him to describe conditions at Chelm.

"First of all," Demjanjuk said, "after we were taken there, there weren't enough barracks, and we had to sleep on the ground. These circumstances, the conditions, were atrocious. We helped to build the barracks. We carried railway tracks from the camp, and we didn't understand what they were for. Later, we understood that these railway tracks that we had carried were to be used to build trenches in the ground."

Judge Dorner wanted to know the time frame. From the fall of

1942, Demjanjuk replied, throughout the winter of 1943—which was precisely the time he was accused of being at Treblinka and Sobibor.

At Chelm, Demjanjuk said, the POWs gathered wooden railway ties and placed them on carts that were taken to the camp. Even after he was transferred to a barracks, there were no beds, only three-tiered slates or pallets to sleep upon. Some prisoners still had to sleep outside, in the winter. In each barracks, there was someone in charge whom the Germans called a *"Kapo."* The head of his barracks was said to have been Jewish. Reminded that Dr. Krakovsky had said that it was impossible for the person in charge to be Jewish, Demjanjuk answered that in Vlassov's army there were many Jews.

Levin asked him to reply to the specific question about the POW camp, not Vlassov's army. "I don't know who was in charge in other barracks, but the one in charge in my barracks was said to be Jewish."

Gill asked whether there were Jews in the other camps in which he had been held.

"In the other camps, there were so many of us and we were so cramped together that it was impossible to know who was who. Second, we never took any interest in the nationality of anyone; we were all prisoners, and all of us were just thinking of when we could get something to eat."

Did he see anyone taken away?

Red Army officers, he said, were taken away immediately and never seen again. Accordingly, officers tried to conceal their rank; some succeeded. Likewise, Jews tried to hide their religion. And, he repeated, in Vlassov's army, there were many Jews.

Demjanjuk now returned to Chelm: "In 1943, we were working at various tasks and in the spring I was added to a group that would leave the camp and conduct diggings of turf outside the camp. . . . Throughout the summer and autumn and even as snow began to fall we were still digging the turf [peat]. . . .

"When snow fell and covered everything, we stopped, and we did not go out to any more diggings. But we were put on duty for different jobs, such as, for example, unloading trains of whatever products they might have held, such as turnips, potatoes, and coal. . . . Whenever it was turnips or even potatoes, we tried to eat them, but, of course, on the condition that nobody was watching us."

Gill asked if he had ever seen POWs being removed from the camp. "I saw that many of them were put on trucks but I don't know where they were taken to. . . . I cannot say whether those same trucks returned. The trucks took prisoners away and brought prisoners. I don't know whether they were the same ones. That I couldn't say."

Asked by Gill how many POWs were transferred, Demjanjuk answered, "I can't say. It was none of my business, and, in fact, I didn't take an interest where people were taken to, whether they were taken for other jobs elsewhere or whether they were taken to other camps."

Was he ever taken to another camp? Yes, he replied: "In the spring of 1944, we were told to get out of the barracks and line up in rows, not only from my own barracks, but from other barracks. A German appeared and pointed with his finger at those who were to fall out and line up in a second row. All Ukrainians were ordered to leave the ranks. We were about three-hundred-and-fifty to four-hundred people. The others were told to disperse. We were all registered and were sent to other barracks."

Judge Levin asked, "Could the witness tell us how long, to the best of his knowledge or his estimation, he spent at the Chelm POW camp?"

"All in all, I think it must have been some eighteen months." And that, in effect, was Demjanjuk's alibi.

Some three or four days passed in the new barracks at Chelm, he said. His Soviet uniform was taken away; he was issued an old but clean Italian one. More days passed before he and others were taken by train to Graz. Demjanjuk said he had no idea where he was being taken.

In Graz, the POWs were housed in stables. They underwent a medical exam, which included a blood test; each man's blood type was then tattooed onto his left arm; Demjanjuk still bore the scar from removing it.

Gill asked when and why he had removed the tattoo. "I began removing it when I was in Heuberg, and I continued doing so when I was in Landshut. I began removing it when I found out that the SS division wore the same tattoo."

Levin wanted Demjanjuk to tell when the transition from POW to a soldier occurred. The defendant said he was still a POW at Graz, locked up in the stables except at meal times, but when he was tattooed, he was informed he would be joining a division. Demjanjuk refused to make clear whether the choice was his.

Demjanjuk said he was among some three-hundred POW recruits who were taken from Graz to Heuberg, which he said was in the Austrian part of Germany. Gill asked if and when he understood why the Germans were enlisting him. "In Graz we understood something, and in Heuberg we understood exactly," he answered.

In Heuberg, he recalled, "we were told to line up in three rows, and an officer appeared who chose the men. My own posting was to a unit of guard officers, generals, in fact." This unit, he said, was known as the Russian Liberation Army. General Fedor Truckhin commanded the army; his commander, he said, was one Lieutenant Topkar, and the leader of his guard unit was a man named Dubovitz. Recruits could move freely about the camp, he recalled, but were not allowed out of it.

The next day in court, Demjanjuk had changed his mind as to when it was that he first realized he was no longer a POW: it was, he now said, when he was transferred from Chelm to Graz.

He also revised his statement that he had received no military training, now saying that at Heuberg "we were taught how to use ammunition, automatic ammunition, rifles, and grenades. . . . In the very same room where they have this ammunition we were taught how to use them."

He remained at Heuberg, he insisted, until three weeks before the war ended. "Thereafter, the whole army left. I wouldn't know where. But I, together with ten other people, were taken to a certain station. At that station there were some GHQ equipment and cars for the generals." After a few days they were given gasoline and commandeered a car and drove to Salzburg.

Once in Salzburg, the car was taken away by a General Malishkin. From thereon, Demjanjuk said, he was on his own. With some fellow soldiers he walked to Bishophoffen, arriving on "the day of capitulation." American soldiers had gathered there.

Demjanjuk and the other soldiers were now American POWs. One American guarded them, but did not stop those who wished to escape. Later, Demjanjuk was among those POWs taken by train to a farm outside Munich. There they spent two months with German farmers, and no one stood guard over them.

Eventually, Americans arrived with trucks; the POWs were taken to Landshut where they were held captive by one guard. "I and another three people left to work with a German farmer." Later on, a United Nations representative appeared and registered them.

When did he remove his tattoo, Gill asked, and how long did it take? "I can't say how long it took exactly," Demjanjuk said, "because you have to wait a long time for the wound to heal and then you start again. And then you start again, waiting for it to heal."

Gill led Demjanjuk through his postwar life—his years in the DP camps; his job as a truck driver for the U.S. Army; his marriage to Vera; the birth of their daughter, Lydia; his application and arrival in the United States; his residence in Indiana, then in Cleveland, where he found work at the Ford plant.

Demjanjuk was evasive about his work at Ford. He would not say whether he'd needed any special training to work on engines there. Basically, Demjanjuk said, he had learned on the job how to test and repair the four-cylinder engines.

The engines at Treblinka were diesel. Gill confirmed that the engines at Ford were gasoline-operated.

When Gill asked him about his promotions, Demjanjuk was dismissive: "There was no such thing as a mechanic being promoted. A mechanic is a mechanic."

Demjanjuk made the statement matter-of-factly, but the remark was haunting. The survivors and even Otto Horn had described Ivan in the same way, with the same words, in the same tone. "He was a mechanic," they'd all said.

Gill wanted to flesh out the picture of Demjanjuk: home-owner in Seven Hills, churchgoer, union member; father of three and recent grandfather.

But what about his immigration forms? Why had he lied? Why had he stated that he'd been at Sobibor, Pilau, Danzig? Here, too, Demjanjuk had something new to relate: At his first screening by the International Refugee Organization (IRO), he had told the truth. It was only at a *second* screening that he lied. The deputy director of the United Nations War Relief Agency (UNWRA), who spoke Russian, told him that if he did not wish to return to the Soviet Union, he must hide any details that would reveal him to have been a Soviet national or Soviet soldier.

"We were told," he said, "that you must find yourself a place either in Poland, or in Czechoslovakia, or anywhere else, but don't put it down that you came from the Soviet Union and give these details at the time of questioning, and that is what we did.

"At the time, I did not know any Latin-printed language, but we found an atlas and we found a map and randomly picked a place, and I gave that place to the secretary, and later I tried to find that particular place on the map. Now I find on the map only the name Sombor, and I think that was the place."

"Were you ever in Sobibor?" John Gill asked.

"No."

"Never in Pilau?"

"No."

"Or in Danzig?"

"No."

"During that period of time, 1937 to 1943, were you in any other place, other than you have testified yesterday and today?"

"No."

"Why then did you tell that you were in these various places?"

"I said just now that these places were chosen in order to hide the fact that I was a citizen of the Soviet Union, that I had been a member of Vlassov's army."

Judge Levin wanted to give Demjanjuk every possibility to explain himself. He asked, "Are you rejecting the possibility that you may have been at Sobibor?"

"Your Honor . . . these . . . places were chosen for me by somebody who could read German and he chose them for me."

"In other words," said Judge Levin, "you insist on the fact that you were never at Sobibor at any time at all and that that possibility just does not exist?"

"No, never in my life."

"And the mention of the names is [a coincidence]?"

"I know that we found this on a map and as I am now looking at the map, I find Sombor only."

Levin said, "So in other words, you were not in Sombor either?"

"No."

But Judge Dorner said that she did not understand his version. "What did you have to hide?"

Demjanjuk repeated that he wanted to conceal his Soviet citizenship. But didn't the forms he filled out say he was born in the Soviet Union?

Yes, the forms said he was born there, but they also stated that for a number of years, he had lived in Poland.

But he had written that his wife had been in the Soviet Union throughout the period in question.

Demjanjuk at first claimed that his wife had a separate form, but when shown it was one and the same, he said, "My wife wrote what she thought she should have written on that form."

That didn't make sense; they were married, and she had the same fear of repatriation. Demjanjuk said his wife wasn't in the army; she wasn't in any danger. Anyway, he said, he and his wife filled these things in because they knew they could change their statements when they applied for American citizenship.

The police assumed he was at Sobibor, Gill said, because the camp appeared on the form. Demjanjuk would not answer directly but offered: "The police or the prosecution say this, but I know where I was; and I was never in Sobibor or in Sombor or in anywhere else, not in Treblinka. Otherwise, I, myself, wouldn't have looked like a skeleton, as if I, myself, had been taken out of Sobibor . . . as though I, myself, had been in Sobibor, or in Treblinka or in Trawniki. When I was in the camps, I would have given my life in order to get a loaf of bread and survive."

Judge Levin wanted to get to the bottom of this: "You insist most adamantly that you were never in Sobibor. Is that true?"

"I am speaking the truth, no matter how many times you ask. It is the truth as it was." He waved his right hand for emphasis.

"There is a document," Judge Levin said sternly, "around which this trial, to a great extent, is focusing. This is what we call the Trawniki document or the service card. . . . On that document, it says that you, sir, were for a certain length of time at Sobibor. I would like to know, in light of your very definite, categorical answers, that this entry can, by no stretch of the imagination, be true? Is that what you are saying?"

"I was never at Sobibor, nor at Treblinka. Why it says it there, I don't know. I kept writing letters to my family, and in those letters, I described where I had been. I explained that I had been injured, but I don't know why that entry appears here."

But Judge Tal wondered: "Isn't it a very strange coincidence that on [the Trawniki card], which you say you have never seen in your life, it says Sobibor? And on the form that you submitted to the immigration authorities of the United States, it also says Sobibor?"

"Maybe it is surprising," Demjanjuk answered, "but I have never been in those places in my entire life."

And how did he explain his comment that Eichmann was big, and he was small? Now, in the courtroom, he claimed that Eichmann was a terrible Nazi, while *he* was innocent and should not have been brought to trial.

Demjanjuk said it was only in 1947 that his fear of repatriation ended. But in the 1960s, when his wife traveled twice to the Soviet Union, he stayed behind. He did not go, he said, because he had to care for the children, and because he would still have been seen there as a traitor. "I think they would have arrested me, judged me, and executed me, because that was the law," he said, citing again the order to commit suicide rather than be captured.

It had long been the defense position that Demjanjuk was the victim of a KGB plot that arose because his mother, living in the Ukraine, had been receiving a pension—awarded because her son had been presumed killed in the war. The packages the Demjanjuk family sent her, and Vera's visits to the Soviet Union, had made her decide to renounce her pension. Once the KGB found out Demjanjuk was still alive, it had concocted the charges against him.

Gill submitted no documentary evidence to support this contention; rather, he asked Demjanjuk to confirm it. Surprisingly, Demjanjuk was not helpful. He insisted he did not write to his mother for many years, but that his wife wrote *her* family. Demjanjuk said that he never expressed his fear of repatriation in letters; that the packages were not sent to his mother but his mother-in-law; that he did know his mother was receiving a pension. It seemed that Demjanjuk would not help his case.

Gill came now to his final question: "In conclusion, the question that only you can answer: Are you that terrible and dreadful man from Treblinka, Ivan Grozny?"

"Please listen, Your Honors," said Demjanjuk. "That I should be the man that you claim I'm supposed to be, and that you claim that I was, at Treblinka and Sobibor, I would never, ever, put down these names."

Levin broke in to remind him that it was not the court accusing him. The court was simply trying him.

"I apologize. I said these places, and even if I only had four years of schooling, I'm not all that stupid as to write Sobibor. I said I have never, ever, in my life been to such a place and I would never, ever, put it down anywhere. . . . I reply I never was, and I am not Ivan the Terrible."

"Have you ever killed any person in your life?"

"Never. I cannot even kill a chicken; my wife invariably did it."

Judge Levin had a question, one that he thought the defense counsel should have asked: Was the signature on the Trawniki card his? "How can it be my signature, if I have never been to Trawniki? I never saw such a document, nor did I ever sign such a document."

Lydia Demjanjuk complained to the press about the mood of the courtroom. During Demjanjuk's testimony, members of the prosecution team had smirked. There was too much joking around, she believed. Her father was not being treated with the same respect accorded the Holocaust survivors. But Demjanjuk, who had been testifying for a day-and-a-half now, seemed positively ebullient, unconcerned that the cross-examination would follow. On his way out of court, he spotted a little boy, bent down and waved at him saying, "*Shalom, shalom. . . .*"

CHAPTER 24

Caught in Contradictions

Demjanjuk's cross-examination lasted a week. The prosecutors sought to take apart his story piece by piece until there was nothing left in the court's mind save one word: "liar."

Blatman started by asking Demjanjuk about his tattoo. During questioning by the defense, Demjanjuk had said for the first time that he began to remove it in Heuberg and finished in Landshut. He said he had always admitted the existence of the tattoo.

But that wasn't the question. Blatman tried another tack. Why did he remove the tattoo in the first place?

Demjanjuk replied that when he arrived in Heuberg, he found out that the tattoo he had received in Graz identified him as an SS soldier. So he removed it.

This, too, was new: that Demjanjuk had admitted his tattoo was the same as an SS soldier's and that he had realized it long ago. In Cleveland, he had not mentioned the SS, but said that in Vlassov's army they had no such tattoos and that he wanted "to be like the other boys."

Why had he never mentioned the SS? "Because nobody asked me," he said.

Wasn't it more likely that he removed the tattoo because he had been in the SS and wanted to hide that fact?

"Never," he insisted.

But *why* was he tattooed? Was there an SS division in Graz?

Demjanjuk said he knew nothing about an SS division and

avoided any answer other than he had received a tattoo and had decided in Heuberg to remove it when he found out it signified SS.

In Heuberg, Demjanjuk had previously testified, he guarded generals, General Truckhin in particular. Blatman now asked if Truckhin was tall.

"Yes, very tall," Demjanjuk said.

"Taller than you?" Blatman asked, peering over his professorial glasses.

Demjanjuk sensed the trap, and admitted he really couldn't say. Contrary to his earlier testimony, he now said he never saw the general, never guarded him, "because I didn't have the proper uniform."

Demjanjuk said he arrived in Heuberg in the late spring of 1944, and remained for weeks, maybe months. But in 1981, Demjanjuk had said that it was snowing when he arrived in Heuberg.

Demjanjuk corrected himself now, "In Graz it was snowing, but in Heuberg it wasn't."

But if he was only there for a few weeks, how could he have been there, as he had said, until just before the capitulation in May 1945?

Demjanjuk said he was there for eight or nine months.

Wasn't it strange that he would be asked to guard generals in his Italian uniform?

Demjanjuk now said that he did *not* guard; he had the wrong uniform, and he was too emaciated. "I was skin and bones at the time."

If he was skin and bones, how could he serve at the front?

"Who said anything about the front?" asked Demjanjuk.

Demjanjuk had, of course. At his deportation hearing, he said that he was tattooed in case his division was sent to the front and that it had been drilled at Graz.

That was what members of the unit thought at the time, he now said, but in fact they were taken to Heuberg. If he said there were drills, he must have been thinking of Heuberg.

If there were no drills, and no Ukrainian divisions waiting to be called up—who was at Graz and what had Demjanjuk done there?

At Graz he had no duties, Demjanjuk said. All he did was play cards and stay in the stables, except when an officer came to take them for meals. There was no SS division there, no Ukrainian division—no Ukrainians at all, save the person who brought him his meals, and the person who accompanied him to Heuberg. But, in earlier testimony, he had said that the Ukrainian National Army was stationed at Graz.

Having to explain so many inconsistencies was stressful for Demjanjuk. He told the court, "I have a pain in my side and could we perhaps conclude for today because I am very tired."

If Demjanjuk then spent the evening trying to get his stories straight, it clearly didn't help. The next day, he told Blatman that, at Heuberg, in Vlassov's army he had no weapon and he didn't guard. He explained that he had been trained in weaponry but he'd had to leave the weapons in the training room.

This sounded much like Sheffler's explanation of weapons training at Trawniki. Demjanjuk was reminded that he had testified he *did* guard with a gun.

"Maybe that is so," he reflected.

Why the discrepancy?

"I didn't remember at the moment . . . I just recalled it."

Demjanjuk explained that there was a handful of officers at Heuberg, each of whom commanded a different unit. A man named Dubovitz was in charge of the guard section, and was with him every day. Demjanjuk said Dubovitz would testify on his behalf (he never did, see Notes).

The generals arrived at Heuberg, he said, after he did. Though in previous testimony, Demjanjuk had said General Malishkin was among them, he now said he was not; instead Malishkin was the general who commandeered the car from him in Salzburg.

Under Blatman's questioning, Demjanjuk said he had learned a great deal about the Vlassov army while living in Cleveland. He had seen a video that said Jews served in the Vlassov army. Blatman asked if he had ever placed ads to locate persons who might substantiate his alibi. He said he had not; he had never thought of it. But his daughters may have, he admitted, as "they did a great deal for me."

Perhaps the explanation for all this, Blatman suggested, was that Demjanjuk had come to Graz or Heuberg as part of a unit of concentration-camp guards.

Demjanjuk denied this; he was never in a concentration camp.

Blatman turned next to Demjanjuk's account of his Red Army service and capture by the Germans.

Here, Demjanjuk's memory was no longer so faulty. He recalled everything—the retreat; the small towns they passed through; the fighting on the day he was wounded; that night and his time at various hospitals; his return to the front; the days preceding his surrender.

After his capture, he was taken at first to work on the railway. Conditions were harsh. "I was even punished, I was whipped," he said. But he could not remember how long he spent at the railway. Here dates were important, but Demjanjuk's memory became hazy again. In his direct testimony, he had said he was there eight weeks; to Israel Police he had said a month, more or less. Until his questioning by the defense, he had never mentioned the camp where he spent five days. Why?

Demjanjuk said that in prison he had begun to recall more details and that no one had ever asked him how he got to Rovno.

In his deposition in the U.S. in 1978, and at his deportation, why had he said his capture occurred at the end of 1942, beginning of 1943?

"I can only say that if it says that, then I suppose that is what I thought; but actually I can't say when it took place. I don't remember when it happened."

Judge Levin explained to him that the purpose of the questioning was that he was being asked to tell the truth, and to give truthful explanations for previous inconsistencies.

"I try to tell the truth," Demjanjuk said. "I don't want to mislead anyone."

Blatman suggested that he wanted to hide the years 1942 and 1943, the time he was at Treblinka. "I have nothing to hide," Demjanjuk said. "I was never at Treblinka, and I have no reason to seek refuge behind some figment of imagination."

He said he was at Rovno for two or three weeks; there were no roll calls or parades, no selections of Jews, commissars, or officers. There was no inquiry into his background.

"It was a very small camp. We spent only the nights there, where we could only stand up. Throughout the day we were permitted to leave and spend time in the clearing of woods, and at night we were taken back to the camp and made to remain standing."

Given the terrible conditions, Blatman asked, didn't everyone want to get out of there as quickly as possible? Demjanjuk answered that no one thought of escape because it would have been impossible. Though he conceded that trucks did come and take people away, he knew nothing about POWs being taken to perform duties for the Germans. Asked whether trucks left the camp full of Ukrainians, Demjanjuk said, "This wasn't Rovno, it was from Chelm. At Rovno, the people were taken generally."

Demjanjuk left Rovno, he said, in a covered truck. But at his denaturalization trial, he had said that he and others went from Rovno to Chelm in railroad cars. "That's how it is written, but it isn't true," he said.

Blatman homed in: "Perhaps the lorries you were talking about brought you to Trawniki?"

"That's not true," Demjanjuk said.

"You continue to maintain that you came to Chelm?"

"I am not maintaining, I am speaking the truth."

Demjanjuk arrived at Chelm, he said, with other POWs. "There may have been seven hundred, or eight hundred, maybe six hundred." At the time, there were only a few barracks. "We remained sleeping on the ground outside . . . even when there was rain, we had to remain out of doors." At Chelm, he said, there were no roll calls, no "selections."

But had he ever been asked who he was?

"Registration was conducted when we got to Graz. . . ." Blatman said he was speaking about Chelm. "Well, it was at Chelm," Demjanjuk said. At Rovno, he said, there was no such registration, neither upon arrival nor when he left. But at Chelm, a month after they arrived, once they had moved into barracks, the POWs were registered: "Name, place of birth, where you came from, everything." It sounded much like the Trawniki card information.

But in his earlier U.S. deposition, Demjanjuk had said nothing about giving personal information. "No one asked," he now said.

Demjanjuk said there were no barracks at Chelm (earlier he had said there were a few). But the POWs soon built them, with wooden slats from railroad tracks. Demjanjuk lived with other prisoners in a barracks. He recalled it was not heated, but the winter was not especially harsh.

Demjanjuk recalled seeing people being taken away in trucks, but he did not know what became of them. No one in his barracks was removed: "Our entire barracks got out to dig peat. Every day we were taken there, and then they took us back." He worked at this "for a long time," he said, "maybe nine or ten months. That is all we did."

The POWs dug for peat at a site two-and-a-half kilometers away, to which, he said, some days they hiked, and some days they were driven.

The subject returned to food. People in his own barracks died of starvation, "especially those who smoked." But his own health, he said, "was fairly good, but I was losing weight for lack of food."

Demjanjuk worked for ten months with about sixty people from his barracks. "I can see them before my eyes," he said. But he could not remember their names.

Earlier Demjanjuk had said there were only Russians at the camp. Now he said there were Italians, too; that explained why he had the Italian uniform. But pressed for details of these "Italians," Demjanjuk retreated: this was a rumor, he said. He didn't see any Italians himself.

Demjanjuk found himself increasingly confronted with contradictions in his testimony. In the United States, he had mentioned building barracks, but not digging peat for nine to ten months or more.

Blatman kept at him. In his Israel Police investigation, Demjanjuk had mentioned that there were *Kapos* at Chelm. Why had he never mentioned this before? "Nobody asked me about it," he said.

"*Kapo*" was the Germans' word, he said; not his. The POWs called him "by the name of his father plus his first name." Blatman asked the name of his *Kapo*. "I don't remember," he said. "I don't want just to throw out any name. I want to speak the truth. I just can't remember now."

There were more inconsistencies. Earlier, he had told investigators he was guarded by Rumanians at Chelm. That must have been a mistake in translation, he now said. He meant the Crimea.

Did Demjanjuk know Chelm was a transit camp? He couldn't tell. Maybe that was because, Blatman suggested, he had been at Chelm only for a short period, if at all.

"No, I don't agree with you. You want to prove now that I am a liar, and that is not true!"

Blatman: "Actually you are claiming that one couldn't forget the events that you suffered through in 1942, '43? Is that what you are claiming?"

Demjanjuk: "Yes, that's right."

Blatman: "It is impossible for you to have forgotten what you went through in the battles of Kerch, and it is impossible for you to have forgotten what happened to you in Rovno. Is that correct?"

Demjanjuk: "It is impossible to forget just as it is impossible to forgive what was done to me over the past ten years. This is why I am fighting."

Blatman: "Just as you cannot forget the events of the famine when you were young, so, too, you cannot forget the horrors of the camp at Chelm. Is that correct?"

Demjanjuk: "Yes."

Blatman: "You are saying, you are claiming that at the camp at Chelm, you spent a very long period, eighteen months. Most of the period of the Second World War. Is that correct?"

Demjanjuk: "Yes."

Blatman: "And you are claiming that you were made to work at hard labor without food, without decent living conditions, with people dying nearby?"

Demjanjuk: "Yes."

Blatman: "And you claim that you came out of this camp, skin and bones."

Demjanjuk: "Yes."

Blatman: "And that it was an atrocity that you cannot forget, neither the horror of it nor the camp itself."

Demjanjuk: "Yes, those were atrocities that I want to forget, but one can't forget them. You can't forget it, just as one can't forget anyone who survived the Holocaust, cannot forget."

Blatman: "And, in fact, you couldn't forget what you went through after you came out of Chelm either; all of the events were still fresh in your mind when you received this indictment. Is that what you are saying?"

Demjanjuk: "When I was given the indictment, I read it. We looked for a defense counsel. I started to fight, just as I've fought to this day, and I will continue to fight to my dying day."

Later, Demjanjuk would tell his defense counsel that when he first heard the charges, "It was a tremendous shock both for me, my family." In court, he felt "all the time very harsh, very difficult experiences, emotions." The last decade of trials, Demjanjuk said, "is very difficult to go through . . . for someone who is innocent. But I am enduring it. I am experiencing all of this because I want to prove I am an innocent man."

But why, then, in his first deposition on April 20, 1978, his first defense of the horrible charges against him, did he say he was a POW in two camps, and was able then to recall Rovno but not the name of the other camp—Chelm. Demjanjuk said, "Yes, I forgot. I just could not, I just couldn't say it at the time."

Blatman found it strange that he recalled the place where he had been for a few weeks, but not the one where he had suffered for a year-and-a-half under conditions that were, by his own account, impossible to forget.

Demjanjuk found himself in a trap.

Three times in his 1978 deposition, he was given a chance to give his alibi, but he could not recall the Chelm camp.

"I didn't think of it because it did not come to mind . . . what could I do?"

But he had remembered every small town and hospital.

"Everything that happened in the Soviet Union," Demjanjuk said, "I could remember." Blatman pointed out that he had recalled the names of the various DP camps where he had lived in Germany. Demjanjuk said he had been in Germany for a long time. But he had been at some of these camps only six months. The question was: How he could forget Chelm and his eighteen months there?

"I can't say why I forgot. I forgot."

Judge Levin tried to explain to Demjanjuk just how serious a matter this was: *Chelm, in effect was his alibi.* "The very same camp that serves as your alibi," the judge said, "that precise camp, you failed to mention. How is that possible?"

Demjanjuk: "I said that I had been in two camps in Poland. One I forgot."

Demjanjuk asked to see the original deposition. Blatman objected, but Levin allowed it: "This is a very difficult and severe trial. The charges are very grave. The witness is in a certain quandary, a predicament, and in order to dispel any doubt, however slight, in order to make it perfectly clear that it is not the case that he was not allowed to give a proper answer, let us give him a chance."

Blatman: "Showing the witness these documents is not what is going to alter the fairness of this questioning."

Judge Levin replied with a Talmudic saying, "Justice must not only be done, it must be seen to be done."

Demjanjuk now reviewed the documents. At the first interrogation, eight months after the complaint against him was filed, he did not recall the camp's name. At the second, in December 1979, a year-and-a-half later, in his own attorney's offices, he recalled the name of the second camp as Chelm. But when asked what he did there, he said he built barracks. At his denaturalization trial in 1981, when asked what he did at Chelm, he said that he dug trenches and hauled railway tracks. Asked if he had done other work, he answered that he had built barracks. Asked again if he had done other work, he answered that he had been part of a group that cleaned the camp.

But he never mentioned digging the peat bogs, which was how he now claimed he'd spent most of his time there. Why didn't he ever mention it before?

"If I didn't mention peat bogs, so what could I do about it?"

But it was important to his alibi, Levin reminded him.

"I agree with you, Your Honor, but take into account, please, that I am answering in that manner because no one prepared me the way they prepare witnesses in Israel to give replies."

Levin: "You don't have to be prepared to tell the truth."

Demjanjuk tried not to answer, then insisted he had told Judge Battisti in Cleveland about the peat bogs. But he had not. Said Demjanjuk: "I explain, and I explain over and over, that forty years had gone by and then when I have to answer quickly, hastily, I can't think of everything, but no one wants to understand that."

Blatman returned to his seat. Shaked now rose.

How was it, Shaked asked, that Demjanjuk managed to get a job at the Ford plant only a month after arriving in Cleveland? A friend from a DP camp, who worked at the Ford plant, found the job for him, Demjanjuk said. For the first year, he worked on engine parts; then he became a motor balancer.

Shaked assured him he knew exactly what the job involved. He gently led Demjanjuk though the details of his life in Cleveland—a life that was, by anyone's standard, quiet and unassuming.

So why did the KGB choose *him*, of all people, to attack? Because of his mother's pension, or his wife's visits to the Soviet Union? Shaked doubted that. In earlier testimony, Demjanjuk had said that once his mother received aid from him, she renounced the pension. But at the denaturalization trial, he had testified that his mother had to inform the authorities when she found out he was alive.

In either case, he acknowledged that he had begun to send packages in 1953 or 1954; and that his wife had been in correspondence with her family even earlier and that his wife's first visits to the Soviet Union were in the 1960s. How strange that the Soviet Union would wait twenty or even ten years before concocting charges. Demjanjuk's answers began to flip-flop as to when it was that his mother had renounced her pension.

Judge Levin was disturbed: "Look, you are the accused in this case. You must be believed. You can't say things that run counter to your testimony in the United States and expect to be believed. . . . But it is your own reckoning."

Why was it that he waited until 1953 to contact his family? They had not heard from him since 1941. Didn't he wonder whether his parents were alive? Wouldn't they be worried about him? When he and his wife arrived in the U.S., Demjanjuk said, it was as if they were born anew. He was too worried about providing for his wife and family to worry about his parents.

So when exactly did this fear of the KGB begin? After receiving the complaint, he said, and after another accused collaborator was assassinated in New Jersey.

Shaked wondered why, if he so feared the Soviets, Demjanjuk had written to a niece in the Soviet Union to ask her to request his birth certificate and military record from the local authorities. Why put *her* at risk?

"I sent her, yes," he admitted. By way of explanation, he said, "Actually, you might say my tragic mistake was that I can't think properly and I don't know how to answer accordingly."

How, if he was so afraid of the Soviets, could he let his wife travel to Russia? "It's not that I wasn't afraid," Demjanjuk answered. "We were always afraid of the Soviet Union, but my wife wanted to go, and I couldn't convince her not to, and in the end I told her to go ahead." If the Soviets were so interested in him, how was it that she came and went, without fear, and without any inter-ference from the Soviet authorities?

Shaked brought forth the Trawniki card and went over the infor-mation on it. There were certain disagreements. The province listed on the card, Zaporishce, was the wrong one—his village, Dub Ma-charenzi, was first part of the province of Kazatin, and later, of Samogorodov. The card put his height as 175cm. Demjanjuk said he estimated his height then as 185cm. Shaked showed him forms where his height was listed as 6', 6'1", and 188cm, to show that mistakes could occur in the recording of his height.

Shaked handed him the original of the card. Demjanjuk thanked him; in Cleveland, he said, he had not been allowed to hold it. Asked about the signature, he confirmed it said Demjanjuk in Cyrillic but insisted it was not his signature. But he agreed that in 1942 he did sign his name in Cyrillic, and that in a 1980 deposition, he had said the signature *looked* like his. "It is like I wrote my name," he had said, but now he claimed what he meant was that it was *spelled* correctly.

Shaked turned his attention to the photograph on the card. "He resembles me, yes," Demjanjuk conceded. Yet the haircut wasn't right, and he had never worn such a uniform.

Shaked went on to consider Demjanjuk's mechanical skills. Dem-janjuk had said that he did not know how to drive a vehicle other than a tractor until 1947.

Yet Shaked brought forth an enlarged copy of his 1948 IRO form and pointed to an entry saying that Demjanjuk had been a driver for UNWRA–IRO in Landshut from May 1945 to July 1947. Dem-janjuk conceded that Shaked had read the entry correctly; but he denied it was true.

It was inconceivable to Shaked that Demjanjuk would have sup-plied the IRO with incorrect information. To a DP, this was too important a form. Wouldn't the IRO know whether he had worked for it for two years?

Demjanjuk would say only that he did not work as a driver in the IRO.

"So what?" Shaked said contemptuously. "Were you lying here?"

Why was he so afraid to admit that he knew how to drive before 1947? He was a tractor driver before the war, wasn't he? Didn't he tell the Israeli investigators that at one point in the Red Army he drove an ammunition truck? They must have misunderstood him, he said. In the Soviet Union, you needed seven grades of schooling to be a driver; he had only four.

But that wasn't so, Shaked said. Fedorenko, in his own testimony, had said he was a truck driver in the Ukraine before the war; he only had three years of schooling.

What was the matter with knowing how to drive a truck? Shaked thought he knew: Fedorenko had said that when the Germans came to recruit at Chelm, they asked all drivers to step forward. Didn't Demjanjuk say that the conditions at Chelm were so terrible he would have given his life for a loaf of bread? So why not tell them he was a mechanic and save his life?

Even if he could operate a tractor, Demjanjuk said, he knew nothing about driving a car.

But he did know about them. And that was why his 1948 application, filled out only a few months after he received his German driving license, listed him as a "skilled driver." He had been driving for two years for the IRO. And he had driven before 1945, Shaked said. At Treblinka.

"I was never at Treblinka," Demjanjuk said, "and I never drove a truck."

"Look," Shaked said, "there is somebody who was in the SS and who was at Treblinka. His name is Otto Horn. He is the one who identified your picture as Ivan the Terrible, the Ivan who operated the gas engines, and he says that you, together with Schmidt, were employed on trucks and engines."

Demjanjuk insisted, again, that he was never at Treblinka, and could not drive before 1947. But Shaked, too, insisted: He drove at Treblinka and along the roads in Poland. Shaked showed him a map of Poland. He pointed out where Treblinka was, and where Sobibor was. And he pointed out the two towns, Kosow and Miedzyrec Podlaski, that Inspector Russek had asked him about. Demjanjuk had replied to Russek, "You are pushing me toward Treblinka."

"I may well have said it, but I can't remember," Demjanjuk now responded.

"Maybe every once in a while," Shaked said, "you happened to be on the road between Treblinka and Sobibor, driving along there. Maybe that's why you know these two places?"

Demjanjuk denied he had ever driven there. If that was so, then why on his IRO application did he say that he was at Sobibor from May 1937 to July 1943, and that while there his occupation was "driver"?

Demjanjuk insisted that the same person who found Sobibor in the atlas told him it was an agricultural area and to say he was there on a farm. But he could not recall being told to write "driver," and said he was surprised to see it written because he could not drive then.

Perhaps, Shaked asked, he wrote "driver" because he had been one all his life, from two years before the war until Ford pensioned him.

Demjanjuk: "I know that I was a tractor driver, before the war, and I only became the driver of a vehicle after the war, after I finished the driving school, and you have a document to this effect in your possession, and I can't say anything more about it."

Demjanjuk's desire to hide his mechanical skill, for fear of it being incriminating, Shaked said, was perhaps the reason behind another set of inconsistencies in his testimony: his schooling.

Shaked made Demjanjuk account for his schooling on a year-by-year basis. By their calculation, the only grade Demjanjuk completed in one year—third grade—occurred during the worst year of the famine. Wasn't it surprising that he had attended school or that this was his best year? Demjanjuk said that food was given at school, and that that was the year he did not repeat. By his account, Demjanjuk was not allowed to complete the fifth grade at age seventeen-and-a-half. But Shaked said that such a poor student could not have received a Komsomol membership.

In all of Demjanjuk's previous testimony, he had said that he completed four grades and did not complete the fifth. No mention was ever made, before his testimony in Israel, of his schooling having taken nine years. His 1948 IRO form read: "primary school education 1927–1930"—four years, not nine. Demjanjuk said he had answered how many *grades* of school. But Shaked pointed out that the form asked: from year X to year Y.

The same form also stated that he was a student in Kazatin from 1935 to 1937. "During that period," Shaked asked, "you didn't study anything that had to do with mechanics or tractors in Kazatin?"

"No," Demjanjuk said.

"Very well," Shaked said skeptically.

Demjanjuk had also told Kaplan that he could not have been at Treblinka because he was "skin and bones." Shaked suggested he had said this because he knew well that only the healthy and fit were recruited for Treblinka.

Demjanjuk denied ever seeing POWs recruited at Chelm except when they were chosen to go to Graz. But to be recruited for Graz, wouldn't he have had to be healthy, too? "In actual fact," Demjanjuk now said, "I was thin and think I just *looked* like skin and bones."

Demjanjuk had maintained that a person who collaborated with the Nazis because he had no choice, was not guilty. But someone who volunteered, or went beyond the Germans' orders, deserved to be punished. A person forced to carry out a death sentence did not, he said now: "If he could not refuse then, what should he be punished for?" But he was quick to add in his defense: "I could never in my life have done that. I could not have carried that out. I would have run away."

Earlier Shaked had thrown Demjanjuk off balance by pausing, in passing, to ask him to identify a man sitting in the front row. Demjanjuk said he knew him, his name was Mr. Brentar; but he played down their relationship. Shaked asked him not to pretend that he didn't know Brentar well: Brentar ran a travel agency and had traveled the world over in his defense; had testified in his defense in Cleveland; and represented an organization that assisted Eastern Europeans who found themselves in difficulty—"of the kind you find yourself in." Demjanjuk said he did know him, but that he didn't know about his organization. Shaked left it at that. By the next day, Brentar had left Jerusalem.

But it was Brentar who had testified in Cleveland that the IRO screenings were conducted scrupulously, and that had the truth of Demjanjuk's war-time activity been known, he would have been sent back to Russia.

Demjanjuk knew this before he went to the IRO office, and he also knew that the form would be completed not by him, but personnel there. He knew the clerks would perform the rescreening and would question him. Therefore, the questionnaire was important. The form was important. To all this, Demjanjuk assented readily.

Shaked: "Okay, now would you agree with me that everyone and you, too, knew that anyone who was caught lying—in other words, if a clerk caught anyone including a falsehood here—that person would no longer be entitled to a visa, to travel to the West."

Demjanjuk: "I want to say, as you see when I asked for citizenship in the United States, that I changed all the particulars, and I gave the real facts, I said I was born in Dub Macharenzi . . . you simply don't want to understand this."

Levin: "Again, I am sorry you are not answering the question. The questions are fairly simple, and I do not accept that you haven't understood the questions. If I thought the questions were too complicated, and if I thought that you, given your intelligence, couldn't understand them, I would simplify them. But the questions are simple, and for some reason, you are not answering them. Please listen to the question. And give an answer to the question that was put to you."

Demjanjuk told Shaked that he knew of no cities or towns outside the Ukraine. He'd looked in an atlas to come up with one for the IRO screening. Shaked wondered why he had chosen such a remote place as Sobibor. Why not Warsaw or Cracow, even Byalistok? Why not mention Rovno or Chelm, places he had been to—they are large towns—or a town nearby the camps? Demjanjuk said he didn't know any of the surrounding towns; but admitted perhaps that he should have put down Chelm; it just didn't occur to him, he said, because he had been there as a POW.

Shaked suggested that perhaps he didn't say Chelm because he was never there.

"I was in Chelm," Demjanjuk said, "and even when the prosecutor asked me, I could tell about the camp even if I had forgotten its name. I'll never forget Chelm to the end of my days, even if I did not think of the name at the time."

But what was it, Shaked asked, that he told the official, Sobibor or Sombor?

"I can't remember what I told the official," he said, "whether it was Sombor or Sobibor, but it's what is written down. It's a fact that it says Sobibor in the form . . . I am saying it from my view. That's all I could find on the map. I can't find the place now, so it's not Sobibor, it's Sombor . . . I didn't see anything like that on a map, I didn't see Sobibor on the map. I saw this place on forms, but I just didn't know what it was. And until they began to bother me in the States, I just didn't know what it was about, or what this place represented. . . . The person who helped me, he had a small map, and in this atlas he found this place, he said this is a good place, mention it."

Was that how on previous occasions, in other places, he said he'd found the name Sobibor? "Everywhere," he insisted, "that's what I told, because it happens to be the truth, the whole truth."

Yet, as Shaked demonstrated by reading from his earlier testimony, Demjanjuk had said first that someone had *told* him the name; it was only later that he mentioned seeing an atlas. Demjanjuk said he could no longer recall what it was he said, or what the official wrote down, but when he first saw the *News from Ukraine* article, which said he was in Sobibor, he looked at a map and could find only Sombor.

Demjanjuk said that he knew there would be a rescreening and that he would have to conceal where he was during the war.

"It was as though," Shaked said, "you would have to invent an alibi for the period of the war."

"That is what we were told, yes," Demjanjuk replied.

Demjanjuk knew that to hide his Soviet citizenship he would have to prepare an answer. He knew he was going to choose some place in Poland, but he had no specific place in mind until he walked into the office. "I thought I would get to the office and would get someone to help me, and this is what happened."

Shaked asked if he had told the official anything other than Sobibor. "Nothing except for the fact that I worked there as a farmer."

But he *had* written something quite different. The form read that between 1937 and 1943, he was in Sobibor and Chelm where he worked as a driver for an auto firm for pay of forty zlotys. Judge Tal asked him to account for that. Demjanjuk claimed he said he was a farmer; he couldn't be a driver at seventeen, because he couldn't drive until 1947. What was written on the form, Demjanjuk said, was the problem of whomever wrote it down.

As to why he wrote Chelm, Demjanjuk was evasive. "I was in Chelm, but I wasn't in Sobibor, and I don't know how far they are from one another."

Shaked reminded Demjanjuk that in his earlier testimony he'd said he had to conceal his Soviet citizenship to avoid repatriation to the Soviet Union. Instead he claimed to be Polish. "I thought this would be so," agreed Demjanjuk.

Then why did he tell the IRO that, as of January 1943, he had moved to Pilau, Germany?

Demjanjuk: "All I can say is that all this was done in order to hide and to show that I had been living in a number of places. . . ."

Demjanjuk said he was never in Pilau and knew nothing of the geography of either Poland or Germany. But how did he come up with Pilau? He could not recall; perhaps someone had told him to say it. As for the next entry, Munich, Demjanjuk said he had once worked near there. Shaked accepted this; but asked why he didn't just say he was in Munich the whole time. Why put Pilau, a place he said he'd never heard of? "Probably somebody told me. . . ." was his only reply.

Shaked said Fedorenko went to the Stutthoff camps after Treblinka, and within part of the Stutthoff complex, there were camps at Danzig, and there were known to be executions on the seashore near Pilau. Said Shaked: "Don't you think it's a strange coincidence?"

Demjanjuk: "What you are telling me here about Fedorenko— that's Fedorenko's affair, as I said yesterday already. He was at Treblinka, and he's on the list of those that had been at Treblinka; but my name is Demjanjuk, and I am not on the list of any camps. If I were the man who had been at the places that you say I had been, I wouldn't be sitting here, because I wouldn't have got to the

United States . . . I am here today in order to show the truth, the real truth, and that I am decent person."

Shaked had spent many a sleepless night preparing the cross-examination; and as it unfolded, as the prosecution jumped from subject to subject, keeping Demjanjuk off guard—but painting him into corners where he had to face the inconsistencies in his testimonies—it was a dramatic confrontation.

Once again, all Israel was glued to its radios and TVs. Blatman had come at Demjanjuk with a formal, diffident style; Shaked a more relaxed, almost intimate approach—walking over to Demjanjuk and pointing out entries on his forms, like a spider weaving its web around a fly.

And throughout Israel, people were saying: How come we had never heard of Shaked before? He had become a hero. For if Sheftel was the "bad Israeli," Shaked was the "good Israeli"—well spoken, polite, proud, righteous, the best and the brightest.

Judge Dorner asked Demjanjuk whether the same person who told him to write down Sobibor suggested that he write down Pilau. No, Demjanjuk said, he wrote down Pilau at the first registration.

But, Levin said, you told us you spoke only the truth at the first registration.

Demjanjuk agreed.

"Therefore," the judge reasoned, "if you put down on the first occasion, Pilau, that would be the truth."

Demjanjuk was adamant: "I was not at Pilau."

So either he told the truth and was at Pilau, or he was lying. Demjanjuk responded: "But I was not at Pilau, and I wrote down a lie because this was at the time when I was wearing an Italian uniform, and was a member of Vlassov's army, and I had to hide that fact, and that is why it says what it says. I had to say that I had been working elsewhere, that I was not a member of the Vlassov army."

Shaked pointed out that Demjanjuk had given this excuse at a late date, in 1984. Why not in 1978? Said Demjanjuk, "But that was my first testimony when they began harassing me, and that was a very harsh blow for me, and I didn't know what I was answering." He said he had always mentioned his Red Army service.

Shaked agreed that he had reason to fear the Soviets, but it was not because of repatriation. Shaked wondered what instances of Soviet repatriation he had witnessed. Demjanjuk admitted he had not seen any with his own eyes.

Demjanjuk said he feared repatriation until he settled in the U.S.

But Shaked read from earlier testimony that indicated otherwise: "When the war ended, I was afraid," he had said. "But as time passed, and things settled down, the fear disappeared."

But Demjanjuk said, "Even now I am afraid of the Soviet Union." Levin suggested his present fear may be for different reasons.

But after several questions, Demjanjuk conceded that the fear of forced repatriation had ended before he moved to Regensburg in May 1947.

Shaked wondered: If he feared repatriation in the rescreening, why had he written that he was born in Kiev? Demjanjuk answered that he wanted to present himself as an ethnic Ukrainian, born in Kiev but living in Poland. Yet why, on the same form, does it say his new wife was a Soviet citizen?

"I am not responsible for what she writes," Demjanjuk said. But it was *he* who had signed the form. Surely, having been married for only six months, he didn't want to see his wife returned to the Soviet Union? Demjanjuk said it was different for a woman. As long as he was a soldier, he had to fear repatriation.

But Shaked felt that the reason he had to fear repatriation was because he was a war criminal. The survivors who had come to court had described all the terrible things they had seen him do. Yet the only thing he had seen fit to say during all of their testimony, was to shout "liar" in Hebrew at one witness.

"I do not know how to say 'liar' in Ukrainian," Shaked said. "But as the situation looks now, after all the testimony was heard here against you, and after all those long days of the cross-examination, there is no way of not concluding that you are, in fact, Ivan the Terrible from Treblinka."

"Prosecutor," Demjanjuk said, angry and tired, "witnesses who gave testimony here, and who have claimed to have seen me there, these witnesses never saw me in their lives. You said that they called me Ivan the Terrible. That, too, is a lie, because nobody in my whole life has called me Ivan the Terrible . . . I would ask you that if you say that I am Ivan the Terrible, you show me where it says so. . . . Where is your information? You are trying to trip me up, because I gave the confused answers, but of course I am not an educated person, I don't have a tutored mind."

Judge Levin asked if Demjanjuk had anything to add.

"I think, later on," he said, "you will see who I really am."

CHAPTER 25

Defense Experts

John Gill was the defense team's documents expert, but his questions appeared to puzzle forensic documents examiner Gideon Epstein. "I understand that graphologists who attempt to identify personality through handwriting go through something like this," Epstein said, "but it's not considered scientific and not within our procedures."

Gill's approach was radically different from the prosecution's: What he stressed was the differences in the *size* of each letter and the *degree* of slant among the signatures.

As both Israeli analyst Bezalelli and his American counterpart Epstein stressed, the key to signature identification was looking for the unconscious habitual characteristics of the writer: the fluidity, the confidence of the signature. A person who signs his signature many times does so in a characteristic manner each time, but if the letters are exactly the same size and same slant, the signature is more likely to have been traced or forged.

The defense was unable to shake the opinions of Sheffler or Grabitz as to the historical authenticity of the Trawniki card, or those of Bezalelli and Epstein as to its signatures. Gill had extracted one concession: Dr. Anthony Cantu, the U.S. chemist and paper and ink expert, did not dispute that his analyses could not uncover a forgery if it had been made from 1941 materials. But this meant that the forgers had preserved the paper and ink since then, and that the forgery was so good it would go undetected.

To prove the card was a forgery the defense called Edna Robertson, a Florida documents analyst for whom Gill submitted an eight-page resumé. She had been an expert since 1974, she told the court, and was president of the World Association of Documents Examiners (WADE). She had worked on more than one-thousand different cases, on about ten-thousand questions of signature comparison, and had testified in court more than fifty-five times.

Robertson was a diminutive, gray-haired woman from Panama City, Florida, with thick glasses. She spoke in a flat, folksy twang. Court observers were ready to cast her as Miss Marple, come to save the day for the defense.

And if that was to be her role, she was ready to play it. She had first become involved in the case in January 1984 at the request of John Gill. At that time she examined photographs of the Trawniki card; the original, she inspected for three days that past May. Gill prepared to hand her the original. But Robertson hesitated: "I don't have my gloves."

"I'll solve that problem for you," Judge Levin said. Wanting to show that the Trawniki card was no precious icon, he removed it from its clear protective case and flipped it toward the translator, Mrs. Batya Frost. The frail document, of which so much had been made, seemed to flap in the air as it traveled the short distance. Frost passed it along to Robertson.

It was no identity document, she concluded, and was not as worn as it should be. She was troubled by the rust stain of a paperclip under the Streibl signature. She discussed extensively how she had tested the card's stamps, using various methods. She had found that a certain circular stamp that was half on the document, half on the photo, when viewed under special light, did not luminesce in the same way on both parts—therefore, they were not the same stamp and were proof of forgery.

"I have reached a conclusion," Robertson said, "that the document is an altered document and it is not authentic." She cataloged the card's deficiencies: "I say the photo has been removed and replaced. My finding is that the signature of Demjanjuk does not compare with the known standards of his signature. I cannot give a firm opinion about the signatures of Trawniki commander Streibl and SS supply corporal Teufel. There is the unresolved question of rust stains under the photo. I could not prove that the ink used in the rubber stampings was the same, nor could I discover the origin of a red stain on the card."

She thought the red stain might be a solvent used to take off the original photo. An examination of the number on the white breastplate in the photo led her to conclude that the number on the photo was not the same as the document, 1393, it was 1693—more proof that the photo had been taken from another document.

The card was not authentic, she said. That sounded good for the defense; and it would have been, had there been no cross-examination.

Shaked began with an aggressive and uncharacteristic slight, saying, "Dr. Robertson or Professor Robertson, which is it?"

"Mrs. Robertson," was the answer, as Shaked let her lack of professional credentials hang in the air. She was the first defense witness, and Shaked wanted to send a message to others who would appear: *Be willing to stand your ground, for nothing will remain when I am finished.*

Shaked tore into Robertson's credibility as an expert. A documents expert, Robertson agreed when asked, does not give opinions based solely on photocopies. But *she* did so in 1984 with the Trawniki card. *That,* she said, was a provisional opinion.

But Shaked had done his homework. He reminded her about another case where she had given an expert opinion based on a single photocopy. "I should have been more careful," Robertson now said, admitting she had acted against a basic tenet of her profession.

Shaked proceeded to demonstrate that her organization, the World Association of Documents Examiners (WADE), did not require forensic document experience as an admission criterion; that U.S. courts had found their members not qualified to be experts; and that she did not qualify for membership in recognized American professional organizations (which require having worked for a law enforcement agency) like the American Academy of Forensic Documents Examiners, to which Gideon Epstein belonged.

Shaked said that she had not conducted an objective analysis: "I think you decide on a theory first, and try to find proof for it." Robertson denied this.

She had stated that the card was not an identity card. But Shaked suggested flatly that the card's heading, "identity card," was contrary proof. Robertson countered that her opinion was based on the card's lack of wear. But it was not wear or tear, Shaked said, that defined an identity document.

Shaked then casually asked if she had seen or known of the existence of similar identity documents.

In a case of many surprises, perhaps the greatest shock was that surprises continued. Shaked paused. Lightbulbs went off in the startled minds of court observers: "Is Shaked saying there are other Trawniki cards?"

In fact, he was. Just ten days before, the Prime Minister's office had received a call, out of the blue, from Armand Hammer: he would be delivering three other Trawniki service cards from the Soviet Union.

They were striking. The three Trawniki cards were: card no. 847 of Ivan Juchnowski, born in 1913 near Vinnitsa, who was posted to the Lemberg (Lvov) ghetto; card no. 1926 of Nicholas Bondarenko, born in 1922 and posted to the Poniatova concentration camp. Both Juchnowski and Bondarenko had listed their nationality as Ukrainian. Ivan Wollenbach, who was listed as a Russian, had card no. 1211—it listed no posting whatsoever, and the photo from it had fallen off.

To behold them was astounding. The inks, the typewriting, the cardboard, the stamps, were unmistakably the same. They, too, had mistakes. One had the same orange stain on its back. The cards presented a strong visual argument for the Trawniki card not being unique, or as the defense had long claimed, "a one-of-a-kind KGB forgery."

Though the defense had been notified about the cards and Gill had visited the prosecution office to take photocopies of them over the weekend, Robertson did not want to examine these cards outside her laboratory. Both Gill and Sheftel vigorously objected to their introduction, coming in "through the back door."

"Cross-examination is not a license to do away with discovery," Gill said. He later told reporters that the timing of the cards' appearance was suspect—coming after the prosecution had rested, and during the testimony of the first defense witness to challenge the Trawniki card's authenticity. Their submission, he said, was "unconscionable."

The court, however, said that the cards could be used for the limited purpose of confronting defense experts and challenging their testimony.

Robertson was still hesitant to answer. "I do not wish to look at these documents. . . . My credibility will be diminished. This testimony is broadcast worldwide."

She must answer, the court informed her. But Mrs. Robertson tried to evade giving, in her words, "expert" testimony about the new cards.

Actually, she was no expert, Shaked contended. Without any knowledge of chemistry, how could she speak about the chemical composition of ink or rust, or stains, glue, and solvents? But she held firm, saying that she had taken courses on paper and ink.

Judge Levin commented, "An expert should know his disciplines. But you want to convince us that a little knowledge of inks, papers, and of instruments is sufficient."

"You have spent the entire afternoon on what I am not," Robertson said peevishly. "I would like to mention what I am." But the court reminded her that cross-examination was the time to answer questions, not to make statements.

She conceded that her conclusion that the document was altered was based on her opinion that the photo had been removed. She did not believe that the photo itself was faked but rather that it had been taken from another document. Shaked said, So what?

As to the stamps' luminescence, Shaked brought into the court the machine she had used in the police lab, the visual spectral comparator (VSC), and asked her to repeat her experiment for the court. At first she could not repeat the effect.

When she was able to show that there was a slight difference between the ink on the photo and that on the card, Shaked asked her to try the same test on Demjanjuk's 1947 driver's license. The identical effect occurred. Are you saying, Shaked asked, that this card is a forgery, too?

That the ink of the stamp luminesced differently on the photo than on the card was only testament to the fact that the ink was absorbed differently into the cards than the photos. It was no evidence of forgery.

Shaked found in Robertson's opinions of the Streibl and Teufel signatures more ammunition for his claim that her testimony was neither objective, nor expert. He ascertained that she had not stopped in Germany to see the original exemplars. She had given her opinion based on copies, something she already had established was problematic.

Robertson also revealed that she always reviewed the acknowledged signatures, and chose a "standard" from among them because she found inconsistent elements among them. Judge Tal was surprised by this: if she doubted accepted signatures, how could she arrive at a credible result?

Shaked intimated that this was a good example of how she invented new ideas to support her conclusions.

Shaked had left Robertson's critique of the Demjanjuk signature for last. Robertson had said that she had examined original Demjanjuk signatures. But in court, the album she presented had no evidence of originals, only photocopies. "It was not practical, so I brought the photos." This did not sit well. Shaked exposed her background as more graphology—personality analysis—than forensic analysis.

As his parting shot, Shaked asked whether she was willing to retract any part, or all, of her expert opinion. Robertson had been cross-examined over a three-day period, but to the last, she remained stubborn, defiant. She said: "I stand by my opinion." There was not much left to stand by.

"You must feel relieved that you have concluded your testimony," Judge Levin said.

Afterward in the defense office, Robertson looked pale, tired, and shaken. Gill tried to excuse her performance by saying she was suffering from jet lag and diarrhea. But the next day an article appeared in *Yeddiot Akronot,* in which Robertson said, "I was broken. . . . My career is finished." She believed the judges had abused her, but she had nothing but admiration for Mickey Shaked, whom she called "brilliant."

Just then, Anita Pritchard, the next witness, stopped by the defense office. She looked at Robertson and did not like what she saw. Pritchard spent the night unable to sleep, chain-smoking.

The next morning, she seemed nonetheless in good spirits. She told the court she was a member of WADE, and described herself as a grapho-analyst—that is, that by looking at someone's face, she could ascertain personality traits. She was a doctoral candidate at the University of the Columbia Pacific, she said.

She had been called by the defense to assess whether the photo on the Trawniki card was of Demjanjuk; to counter and critique Altmann's and Smith's photo comparisons; and to testify as to how suggestive photographs may be and how optical illusions can be created in facial montages.

She spoke of how "part of the perception is in the perceiver," which, roughly translated, meant that superimposition is open to misinterpretation. She believed that Altmann's work showed that he had altered the photos by the way he'd mixed them.

There was a psychological dimension, she said, to how people looked at photos. In Pritchard's opinion, by exploiting this, one could bias people toward certain conclusions. As a demonstration, she had taken the pictures of twelve male models, randomly selected from newspapers. She halved them and reassembled them to prove that you could "match" different people. Pritchard seemed to be enjoying herself, laughing.

The court asked her to relate specifically to the work conducted by Altmann and Smith but she did not, explaining that her expertise was not in forensic matters, but in psychology. This was the opening for Shaked's cross-examination.

Shaked said he would ask her questions about certain fields of knowledge. If she was not familiar with them, Shaked suggested, she could answer: I don't know. He did and she did. Anthropology, anthropomorphy, morphology—all, "I don't know." That there was no scientific underpinning to her analysis, quickly became evident. She retracted her statement about Altmann's work being "altered"; and apologized for any offense implied. She admitted, with regard to her rematched male models, that her "random" selection was done without scientific criteria.

She also admitted that she had not done a scientific study but, rather, as she termed it, "a private study," in which she never went beyond "the purely visual."

In what, then, was she an expert?

She said that she was an expert in visual perception. But Shaked challenged this too: Did she know anything about neurology? Physiognomy? The optics of the human eye? The retina?

She did not.

"You're creating the illusion," Shaked said finally, "that you're an expert." He suggested, "Maybe you should take back what you told the court earlier about vision; tell the court you're not an expert."

"I'm not an expert on the physical implications of vision," Pritchard said with increasing strain. "I'm an expert only as far as the general influence of vision on personality is concerned."

But this would not withstand attack. Shaked tore into her credentials: her only book, it turned out, was self-published; her doctorate degree, which she had not yet received, was from an institution which had not been accredited when she began her studies there. Her master's in psychology wasn't from a psychology department but from the human relations department of the University of Oklahoma. Her knowledge of graphology was principally from a correspondence course. She was not familiar with other professional publications, journals, or associations. Her voice had become a whisper.

Finally Shaked asked her, as he had Robertson, whether she wished to withdraw her statements.

"I was under the impression that I could give my opinion and it was not up to me to decide if I'm the expert." But Shaked asked her to assess herself. She couldn't answer.

Sheftel tried on redirect to rehabilitate her, asking her to restate her qualifications. But Judge Levin said, "Why torment the witness further, after she has admitted she is not an expert?" He asked Sheftel to excuse her, which he did shortly thereafter. Shaked offered her his hand by way of farewell. To reporters Pritchard seemed a blip in the case, a witness soon to be forgotten. But that was not so.

At eight P.M. that night, Sheftel called upon her room in the American Colony Hotel. He found her passed out. Pritchard was reported to have said, "I did a stupid thing." She was rushed to Bikur Holim Hospital. Dr. Shmuel Banai, the emergency-room doctor in charge, said Pritchard had swallowed more than fifty pills, mostly painkillers and tranquilizers, and had slit her wrists.

"She said she didn't want to live," said Dr. Banai. "She didn't want us to help her. She pulled out the intravenous tubes that we put in." The hospital pumped her stomach and treated her cuts.

She was released the following evening. As she awaited a flight home, she told an Israel radio reporter that testifying at the Demjanjuk trial had been a nightmare, but she believed she had recovered.

CHAPTER 26

Experts and Their Opinions

Avraham Shiffrin, called to the stand by the defense in late October, was to be an expert in two areas: the forgery abilities of the KGB, and its posture toward the Ukrainian community.

Shiffrin, at first, made a good impression: a decorated Red Army soldier, after the war he had worked as a Soviet prosecutorial investigator, working hand in hand with the KGB. In 1953, he was arrested, tried as a Zionist agent, and sentenced to thirty years in prison. He served ten years, and then was exiled to Odessa. He emigrated to Israel in 1973. Since then, he had run an institute devoted to the study of the KGB, staffed by many researchers, and responsible, over the years, for twenty publications. He had testified about the KGB to the U.S. Congress.

Shiffrin now was handed the Trawniki card, whose Russian translation in purple ink bore the initials NGB. The NGB, he explained, were the former initials of the KGB.

The KGB, he said, has a special department for forgeries, equipped with materials, inks, papers, and even a special machine to age paper. He personally had seen KGB-warehoused paper and blank German war forms. The examples of KGB forgery of German documents were countless, he said.

Shiffrin said every former Soviet citizen living in the West was considered a defector by the KGB. Someone who had been in Vlassov's army *had* to be persecuted. He saw a further motive for the KGB in the Demjanjuk case: a provocation between the Ukrainians and Jews, the two most dangerous minorities in the eyes of the KGB. The KGB wished, he said, to sow dissention between them, rather than have them work together against the Soviet Union.

So far, so good for the defense. But on cross-examination, Yonah Blatman brought out that Shiffrin's "institute" was, in fact, his apartment; that he had no serious academic publications; that his researchers were part-time contributors.

Shiffrin had been quoted in newspaper articles as having made some wild claims, Blatman revealed, saying over the years that the KGB was using radiation and "psychic" forces to cause heart attacks, control the minds of Western politicians, and cause electrical blackouts. Shiffrin dismissed the articles as ridiculous and his comments in print as misquotes.

But Shiffrin did admit that he was involved in parapsychology, which he deemed a serious science. The KGB *was* interested, he stated, in harnessing paranormal forces, and had recruited sorcerers and witchdoctors throughout the world to study them; while in prison, he testified, he had seen people using parapsychological force to cause trances or fits in others.

So much for Shiffrin's credibility as an expert witness. He had nothing relevant to add to the case and could produce no evidence of Soviet forgery of Nazi wartime documents. But Sheftel had high hopes for his next witness, "Count" Tolstoy.

Born in England in 1935, Nikolai Tolstoy was the author of many books: children's novels, historical novels, and historical nonfiction. He had written several works on Soviet history, including *Stalin's Secret War;* and two on forced repatriation, *Victims of Yalta* and *The Minister and the Massacres.* He held bachelor's and master's degrees in modern history. He had no Ph.D., he said, but understood his research to have been at a postdoctoral level.

Tolstoy was willing to be expert on all things for the Demjanjuk defense: on the forced repatriation, which, he said, never formally ended but went on even in 1950; and the fear of repatriation, which continued even after that. On the Vlassov army, Tolstoy testified that there were hundreds of thousands of Vlassov's soldiers wandering through Western Europe at the time Demjanjuk claimed to have been there; Sheftel then submitted photos of soldiers bearing ROA (Russian Liberation Army) badges from 1943.

Tolstoy also testified about the KGB's history of forging documents. He disputed the findings of the prosecution's historians, in particular, Professor Meisel, whose research, he said, he had never come across in his fifteen years of study; and whose statistics he found "in the first instance, easily falsifiable and, in the second, unverifiable." As to Demjanjuk's having lied on his immigration forms, Tolstoy told the court that British officials encouraged Soviet DPs to conceal their Soviet birth and say they were Polish citizens.

He found "nothing inherently implausible" about Demjanjuk's version of being brought to Heuberg and conscripted into a unit of former Soviet POWs who wore ROA badges in the spring of 1944. He knew of no such units before 1945, but it was possible. He confirmed Sheftel's claim that Vlassov's chief propagandist, Zikoff, was thought to be a Jew and that some Jews were known to be concealed in Vlassov's army. It was possible, he said, that Demjanjuk was assigned in Heuberg to guard generals but was given no weapons because the Vlassov army's function then was, for the great part, propaganda; and all the Russian soldiers there were still prisoners.

Sheftel showed Tolstoy the Trawniki document. It was the regular procedure of the KGB, Tolstoy confirmed, to obtain an authentic document and then doctor it; the correct information on a card is of minimal value. What is crucial, said Tolstoy, is the context of the card. The Trawniki card's provenance was questionable, he felt, not only because of the closed nature of the Soviet archives, and the fact that it was handled by the KGB, but also because of how it came to Israel via Armand Hammer. There was no context to establish the card's authenticity.

Sheftel asked for his overall comment on Demjanjuk's alibi.

Tolstoy obliged him: "His account is fully consistent with historical events as they are known to me."

Blatman began the cross-examination by asking Tolstoy his political views about the Soviet Union, the Second World War, Ukrainian-Jewish relations, and the prosecution of Nazi war criminals.

Tolstoy, the English gentleman, seemed flustered by Blatman's inquiries into his personal opinions. Later Tolstoy would make it seem as if the prosecution were interested in his opinions on World War II *at the time*—when he was ten years old. But Blatman's interest was neither idle nor general.

In short order, Blatman demonstrated these were not private matters, but subjects on which Tolstoy discoursed publicly in articles, lectures, pamphlets, and letters to the English papers. And perhaps, Blatman suggested, Tolstoy's historical analysis and "expert" opinion were not so neutral, if his publications were any indication: at the time of Canada's Deschenes commission deliberations on whether to investigate and try Nazi war criminals, Tolstoy had authored a pamphlet called "Trial and Error." In it he argued that the Soviet Union's crimes were as serious as Nazi war crimes, and the latter should not be prosecuted if justice was not administered to the former. Now Tolstoy distanced himself from the publishers of the pamphlet and the groups that distributed the pamphlet.

But in a letter published in England's *Jewish Chronicle,* which Blatman produced, Tolstoy had written, "Some Ukrainians persecuted some Jews, some Jews persecuted some Ukrainians, some Ukrainians again persecuted some Jews, and so it went on." This was not the unbiased view of a historian.

Blatman also attacked Tolstoy's expertise as a historian. Tolstoy conceded that he did not conduct any research in German archives for his book *The Long Knives.* On *Victims of Yalta* (published in the U.S. as *The Secret Betrayal*) Blatman introduced negative reviews of his works from historical academic journals (as opposed to the more positive reviews Sheftel had introduced from the press).

The net effect was that Tolstoy was revealed as a popular writer on historical subjects, not as a historian. His research technique, in terms of presenting an expert opinion, left a great deal to be desired; they were acceptable for a writer, but not from an academic, historical point of view.

Tolstoy's academic connections and credentials also left much to be desired. His Ph.D. was never really undertaken (even though a book jacket claimed that he was working on a thesis); his M.A. was not a master's degree involving study but rather one available to anyone with a B.A. who paid an extra ten pounds; and his B.A., it turned out, did not involve the study of modern European history.

Tolstoy complained to the court that his personal views rather than his expert opinion were being attacked. He asked that the proceedings be stopped; he threatened to leave the stand. Without the court's assurance of "fair play in accord with standards of Western justice," Tolstoy declared, he would be "unable to participate further."

The court informed Tolstoy that it was not for *him* to set conditions for his testimony. *He* had agreed to be a witness. If he did not wish to testify, he could be compelled to do so; or if he left the witness stand, his testimony would be struck as if never given; and if he wished to insult the court, as was the innuendo of his comments, then he could be held in contempt, and tried for slander.

Further, defense counsel had not objected to the questioning, and there was good reason: the questions were legitimate and appropriate. There would be, Judge Levin said, no limitations and preconditions placed upon the court. Tolstoy's "subjective feeling," he said, "is not our business." Tolstoy remained on the stand.

Under Blatman's cross-examination, Tolstoy began to make a hasty retreat from his "expert" opinions. Tolstoy admitted that he was not an expert on the Gallician division. As to recruiting in the Graz area, he admitted "to the best of my knowledge there was no such recruiting."

The cross-examination continued along this same line, with Tolstoy admitting: "I have no knowledge of such a camp. . . . I am not an expert on the German army at that time . . . not an expert on German military records. . . . I do not know to the best of my recollection of forced repatriation after May 1946." Tolstoy admitted his research was more extensive as to the British Zone than the American, though he said he had researched the American archives. "I have a general interest in Vlassov . . . what studies I have conducted . . . [are] not very far from exhaustive."

As to the business of ROA badges at Dabendorf, the photos and the thousands of ROA soldiers in 1943, he admitted they were only propagandists. Tolstoy again stressed that he was not expert in this area, and conceded there was no evidence of any unit in Heuberg during the summer of 1944. Finally, he conceded that Sheffler's method for determining the historical authenticity of the Trawniki card was valid.

All in all, there was very little left of Tolstoy's testimony that went unqualified. Tolstoy tried to excuse his lack of preparation by time constraints, admitting that he had prepared his testimony from his personal library, not actual archives. He was an expert, perhaps, on repatriation in the British Zone. But as Shaked had asked of other defense experts: So what?

As were the previous witnesses, Tolstoy was more opinion than expert.

CHAPTER 27

A Forgery So Good, It Can't Be Detected?

In August, the court took a two-week break, which was extended after Judge Tal suffered a mild heart attack during another proceeding. During the break, the defense was able to recruit Dr. Julius Grant, one of the world's best-known forensic documents examiners, as well as Arizona documents examiner William Flynn, who had helped uncover the Hofmann Mormon letters forgery.

Grant was born in London in 1901, and received his doctorate in 1926. Between the years 1929 and 1951, he worked in a paper manufacturing plant, first as senior chemist and later as general manager. He developed a method for identifying fingerprints on paper and published many books in his area of expertise. In 1952, he joined with an expert on manuscripts to found an office for forensic investigations. "He wanted to know more about the paper," he said, "and I wanted to know more about the manuscripts, and so we acted in concert."

Since 1952, Grant had become a forensic investigator with notable success. He'd solved the forgery cases of the Mussolini diaries and the Hitler diaries. In both cases, other experts had adjudged the documents authentic and then Grant discovered them to be forgeries by examining the paper.

Grant examined the Trawniki card in mid-October and again at the beginning of November. At the same time, he also examined the three Trawniki cards that Hammer had delivered. He found them all to be of similar paper composition and printing, and were probably, he wrote in his expert opinion, made in the same mill at the same time. He also found the printed type faces on all three cards to be identical.

Grant had four categories, as a scale for judging evidence: 1) *high probability* was the top determination, equal to 99.9 percent certainty; 2) *probable,* sufficient for identification in criminal law— "probable" was the highest rating he gave when examining only photocopies; 3) *possible,* the category was neutral, neither affirmation nor negation; 4) *unlikely,* a negative determination.

He, however, stressed that a final conclusion could be given only on the comparison of original documents.

Grant was a spry witness. Though eighty-six years old, and seemingly frail, he came alive on the stand. Sitting behind the witness lectern, he drew himself up and spoke in a strong voice, with often cheeky answers to Shaked's cross-examination. He held beside him a green British West Indies Airlines flight bag, which contained his notes and files, as a sort of portable office. Sheftel led him through his direct testimony.

On the Streibl signature, Grant made a determination of "high probability." But the rust line in the shape of a paperclip gave him pause. He had been told that paperclips of this type did not exist at Trawniki. Therefore, he suggested, it may be such a good forgery that it can't be detected. Grant found Teufel's signature very convincing, but because he had examined only photocopies of it, he could rate it only "possible."

As to the Demjanjuk signature on the Trawniki card, Grant did not dispute the prosecution's analysis of its elements. But his doubts of its authenticity arose in comparison to the other signatures he had studied.

Grant was asked if he had seen originals of Demjanjuk's signatures; and if so, were they in Cyrillic or Latin characters? Grant was positive he had *not* seen originals. He said he had examined only the questioned signature and the 1947 signature (in German Latin characters). All the others were photocopies. The court re-asked the question several times to make sure this was the case; Grant confirmed that it was.

But the following day, in response to a "technical question" from Sheftel, Grant said, "I was inaccurate when I said I had not seen [originals]." And he listed a long list of signatures that he had seen in the original; he also now claimed that at the police station he'd also examined original Cyrillic signatures.

Finally, Sheftel asked: "Is this the service pass of the accused or not?"

"The indications [are] that it could not [be]," Grant answered. "I am greatly influenced by the signature—I believe it not to be that of the accused." But he would not base his opinion solely on the basis of the signature. He asked to examine the photo again overnight.

The next day, Grant said that the card was *not* authentic. The signature was not enough by itself for him to make his conclusion; the photograph troubled him as well.

The fact that an expert of Grant's caliber doubted the card was not to be underestimated. In a decade of trials, Grant was the first reputable examiner to dispute the card's authenticity in court. And unlike Robertson or Pritchard, Shaked could not undermine his opinion by attacking his credentials. Shaked would have to take Grant's opinion, in all its elements, apart and see how he had come to the conclusion he had.

Grant's testimony about the card, in effect, formed an equation: doubts about Demjanjuk's signature *plus* doubts about the photo *equaled* the card not being authentic. His concerns about either the photo or the card were not by themselves great enough for him to doubt the card's authenticity.

To attack Grant's equation, Shaked first set about examining its components. Grant had testified that he found that the signature was "unlikely" to be Demjanjuk's based on three characteristics: the D, M, and the pen lifts. But Demjanjuk himself, in all his earlier testimony, Shaked pointed out, had never objected to the D or the M (which in Cyrillic looks like a "u"). In fact, Demjanjuk had said in 1980, "It is like I wrote my name [in 1942]."

Did this affect his opinion?

"If what I have been told now is true," Grant said, "then my deduction that the signature was not written by the defendant is not of the same security value, and loses some of the security of its certainty, [it] loses from its certainty."

Shaked now turned to the second half of the equation, the photo. Grant's problems were that in comparing the Trawniki card to the three other supplied, only the Trawniki photo had two holes in it; that purple ink similar to that of the Russian translation on the card was found in the holes; and that the stamp on the photograph did not fit with that part of the stamp on the document. All this suggested a KGB forgery—purple KGB ink linking the photo to the document.

But Grant had examined only the upper of the photo holes, Shaked revealed, not the lower one; Grant's own examination found that the ink came *after* the hole, not *before*. And his examination found the adhesive used was not a strong one. This information, Shaked said, did not necessarily lead to the conclusion that the card was forged by the KGB.

Shaked asked Grant to consider a different scenario: that at

Trawniki, Demjanjuk's photo was first affixed to another file document (hence the two holes), *then* attached to the Trawniki card and stamped, and then *at a much later date,* fell off (explained by the poor quality adhesive) and was reaffixed (why the stamp doesn't match).

"I admit the possibility," said Grant.

Without the photo, could he still conclude that the card was not authentic?

"I cannot," said Grant.

Still, Grant's testimony was disturbing. First there was the matter of the paperclips: Grant had questioned the Streibl signature because of the presence of a paperclip rust stain, which troubled him because paperclips were not in existence, or so he said, in 1942 at Trawniki.

In cross-examination, Grant revealed the sources of his knowledge: it was from Robertson that he'd learned it was rust from a paperclip, and from Sheftel that there were no paperclips in existence at Trawniki at that time. Why would an expert of Grant's caliber rely on secondhand information?

Equally troubling was the question of whether Grant had examined original Cyrillic Demjanjuk signatures made at the behest of the police. One day, he said clearly that he had *not;* the next, he said he had. What had happened? Grant had explained that as the signatures Demjanjuk gave the police were unquestioned, he had not thought to mention them. But the court, in its verdict, did not accept his explanation.

Other questions remained: Why didn't Grant take into account the differences between the Latin and Cyrillic alphabets? Grant's objections about the photo were subjective, not objectively ascertainable. All together, the information revealed on cross-examination left one wondering about Grant.

William Flynn had all the proper credentials of a documents examiner; not only that, but he had been a pupil and colleague of Gideon Epstein. He had gained recognition with regard to the Hofmann forgeries case.

Hofmann, a rare documents dealer, had over the years "uncovered" and sold a number of manuscripts about the Mormon Church to dealers, collectors, and even to the church itself. The contents of the documents were often controversial, but their authenticity was unquestioned.

But after a series of bomb-related deaths in Salt Lake City, the police began investigating a possible link with the documents and called in George Throckmorton, a forensic documents examiner. He, in turn, called in William Flynn from Arizona to help. After examining the questioned documents for a short time, Throckmorton became convinced that they were forgeries; not too long after, Flynn was able to uncover how Hofmann had achieved a certain ink effect.

In September 1986, William Flynn arrived in Israel and conducted three days of tests on the Trawniki card at the forensic laboratories of the Israel Police.

The following month, he convened a meeting of U.S. documents examiners in Palm Springs, on the subject of historical documents.

The Hofmann case had taught him, he told the convention, that just because one couldn't detect a forgery in a historical document, didn't mean it was authentic. As an example, he brought along a copy of the Trawniki card. It appeared authentic beyond doubt, he said. But the Hofmann case had taught him that one still couldn't say it wasn't a forgery.

Now, in the courtroom in Jerusalem, Flynn said it was impossible to give a conclusive opinion about the signatures on a historical document. He had not found in Streibl's or Teufel's signatures a fact "that will confirm or negate the ability to say it is a forgery."

Although Flynn was of the opinion that the card was in some respects a forgery so perfect it couldn't be uncovered, he now saw some obvious faults.

"It is definitely unreasonable," he said, that Demjanjuk's signature on the card was his own; further, he was troubled by the holes in the photo, the purple ink in those holes, and the discrepancy in the parts of the stamp.

Flynn had prepared forgeries of the signatures of Streibl and Teufel as well as a photomontage of himself in SS uniform to demonstrate how easily these documents could be forged. Shaked objected: the issue was not whether *Flynn* could commit a forgery; the question was whether the Trawniki card was forged. As Flynn's evidence was not relevant to the card, the court disallowed it.

Sheftel jumped up. If the witness could not present this evidence, then Sheftel asked that he leave the stand and that his testimony be struck from the record. The court refused. Sheftel said the witness had no further testimony.

But Flynn was not yet free to leave. The prosecution insisted on its right to cross-examine. Again Sheftel asked to withdraw Flynn's testimony. The court again refused. Flynn was hesitant to go on. His client, he said, the John Demjanjuk Defense Fund, did not wish him to testify. The court explained that he must answer the questions of the prosecution or be held in contempt. Flynn agreed to continue his testimony.

The prosecution then read from his comments at the convention in Palm Springs: "Forensic tests will be conducted, the certificate will be all right, but she [sic] still will not be original." He still agreed with the statement.

But how could the card be, at the same time, a forgery so good it couldn't be detected, yet be found by Flynn to have obvious flaws? Wasn't this a contradiction?

Flynn said that part of the document was orderly, but other things indicated forgery. He asked to listen to the tape.

The next day, Shaked played the recording of his speech: "I have examined the card firsthand for three days," Flynn could be heard saying. "I have examined the thing microscopically, and there's nothing about the card that I can see that would not have passed muster."

Flynn, clearly uncomfortable, refused to answer any further questions. He told the court that he was in a quandary. He had a "contractual agreement" with the Demjanjuk Defense Fund. Ed Nishnic, who ran the fund, he said, had ordered him not to reply to questions of the prosecutor; and had threatened to file suit against him in the United States if he did so. Even if he won the suit, it could prove costly.

The court was not familiar with experts who had "contracts"; but they understood that he was in a dilemma. The court would compel him to testify only if the prosecution requested it. It did not and Flynn left the courtroom.

The court asked the Israel Police to question Nishnic to see whether he had intimidated Flynn by threatening litigation, and thereby had attempted an obstruction of justice. Nishnic was visited by the police at the American Colony Hotel for two hours, but no charges were ever filed. Nonetheless, Nishnic left the country soon after, not returning for the rest of the trial.

Once back in the United States, Flynn told the press in Arizona that his testimony had been conclusive, but the "biased" court had disregarded it.

A clue as to why he gave this version of actual events can be found in a comment he made to an Arizona columnist. Asked about the card, Flynn responded, "I've staked my reputation on it." Clearly it was a reputation better defended in Phoenix, than in Jerusalem.

CHAPTER 28

A Memory Problem

There were always doubters among the general public who were eager to dismiss "eyewitness testimony" as faulty and Holocaust survivors as "too emotional." After forty years, they argued, what really could be remembered?

Inside the courtroom, it would be far more difficult to discredit the survivors' testimonies, but the defense promised to do so with their own experts—on memory.

The defense's first choice for testifying was Dr. Elizabeth Loftus, an experimental psychologist on the faculty of the University of Washington Law School. The author of many articles and books on eyewitness testimony and memory testing, Loftus had championed the cause of experimental psychology and its value to the courts. Although she had testified in many cases, she declined to testify in the Demjanjuk case for personal reasons. Loftus did, however, recommend a colleague with whom she was in frequent electronic-mail contact, Dr. Willem Wagenaar, a professor of experimental psychology at the University of Leyden in the Netherlands. She also agreed to travel to Jerusalem, at the defense's expense, to consult and advise during Wagenaar's testimony.

Professor Wagenaar took the witness stand in mid-November, 1987. A dapper man, with sandy hair and graying mustache, he appeared in a gray suit and bow tie. He submitted a list of eighty-seven publications in which his articles had appeared, and he said he had testified in many cases, more than half concerning memory problems.

To the press, the defense had said that their expert would testify about "memory forty years after," but in the court the story changed. Wagenaar said the reliability of the survivors' memory was precisely what he was *not* going to talk about. Rather than focus on the survivors and their memories, he would concentrate on the photospread; based on the statements of the survivors, he would critique the identification test, not the survivors.

Wagenaar would also demonstrate how, after forty years, mistakes and slips of memory were common and normal, but he was not talking about the survivors—he meant Demjanjuk, whose memory gaps made his alibi that much less credible. When the final verdict was read, the opinions of Wagenaar would not figure in the calculation of guilt or innocence; but his testimony, at a certain level—a psychological one—was the one that most strengthened the prosecution's case.

Wagenaar's fundamental precept was that a memory problem existed, illustrated by the fact that not all the witnesses were perfectly certain, or perfectly accurate in their police identification statements.

The great majority of scientific studies on such matters involved subjects who'd had limited contact with a person and who were asked to recall him a short time thereafter. Nonetheless, Wagenaar believed the studies relevant. On the one hand, the Treblinka survivors had had a prolonged and intense contact with Ivan, but Wagenaar felt that this was counterbalanced by the more than thirty-year interval since the survivors last had seen him.

Wagenaar put forward the proposition that, given certain factors, a witness faced with an identification parade (live or photo) may experience a "positive response bias"—he or she may feel compelled to point someone out, even if the "target" suspect is not present. And among those who feel such a compulsion, there may be a "specific response bias"—factors by which a person, once having decided to point, will choose one individual over another.

Wagenaar contended that all the survivors had described Ivan as having a round face, short neck, and incipient baldness. He had conducted an experiment at the University of Leyden with students and the very same photographs. Two photospreads were presented, the one used by the Israel Police, and another that placed Demjanjuk's picture among those persons with the same identifying characteristics. Students were asked to pick out the criminal with the round face, short neck, who was balding.

When shown the Israeli photospread, 100 percent of the students chose Demjanjuk; but when using the prepared one, only 8 percent did. The conclusion, Wagenaar said, was that the Israeli photospread would *not* "for purpose of scientific research . . . be considered to constitute valid tests of memory."

Would it be true, Sheftel asked, that the more severe the crime, the more atrocious the act committed, the higher the probability of such mistaken identifications? "I think that would be a perfectly logical conclusion," Wagenaar answered, but "no practical studies had been done to confirm this . . . that sort of very much applied literature does not exist."

Wagenaar then turned to Demjanjuk's forgetfulness. First he explained that he could not assess the reliability of the survivors because their experiences had been so emotionally laden; and the court had other ways of cross-referencing the accuracy of their statements. But Demjanjuk's experiences, he said, were not so emotionally laden, he felt; and Demjanjuk alone was the basis for judging the accuracy of his testimony. Of course, Wagenaar said, the final decision as to reliability was the court's.

Demjanjuk could not recall, when first asked, the name of the POW camp, Chelm, that was his alibi; he had not mentioned he dug peat there under arduous conditions. Wagenaar advanced several theories for this: Demjanjuk never knew the camp's name; he could have confused episodes; perhaps he did not receive the right memory cue for this episode.

Demjanjuk nodded, paying close attention.

Sheftel then showed Wagenaar a newly uncovered photo of Demjanjuk in a hat and uniform bearing an IRO badge on the arm. For six months in 1946, Sheftel explained, Demjanjuk had been an IRO police officer in the Landshut DP camp but had forgotten the episode until he saw the photo.

To Wagenaar, this was another example of the same phenomenon: if one doesn't receive the right cue, one may not recall a specific episode. He concluded, "There is no scientific basis to interpret these errors as signs of deliberate lying."

Shaked began his cross-examination. What was so impressive about Shaked was his ability to become an expert in each field as he discussed it, be it handwriting, forensic documents examination, or experimental psychology.

Wagenaar begrudgingly agreed that memory of faces was a subject not fully understood, but it was known that the quality of the contact, its duration, and the associations with that face all lent to its being etched in the consciousness of the beholder.

The situation of the survivors remembering Ivan, he had to admit, was vastly different than that of his students who had never known the subject. So Wagenaar's test was really no test at all.

As to Wagenaar's theories that the photospreads were "biased,"

Shaked brought out that the scientific basis for both "positive response basis" and "specific response bias" were *experimental* studies. But there was no scientific basis, whatsoever, for the notion that extrapolating these results to a real-life situation would be valid. None of the studies used was based on police investigations, or actual police lineups.

So what bearing did they have on the Demjanjuk identifications?

There had never been an experimental re-creation of the conditions in a death camp, Wagenaar conceded, nor of the same intense contact, for the same prolonged contact. So much for his experiments.

Now as to Demjanjuk. How was it, Shaked wanted to know, that Demjanjuk's memory was only *selectively* defective? That Demjanjuk could recall all the hospitals he was taken to when wounded, and the small towns they were in, with only a regular cue—"Where were you?"—but that he forgot the months of his alibi?

Why did he forget the ten harsh months he spent digging peat? Perhaps, Wagenaar suggested, to Demjanjuk they were not so harsh.

But Judge Tal wondered if Wagenaar meant that because a person has had harsh experiences in his past, he was less likely to recall other subsequent harsh experiences? Were there any scientific studies to confirm this? Personality psychology, Wagenaar said, was not really his area.

Wagenaar's contention had no solid footing, Shaked pointed out. Demjanjuk himself had said that he had known the name Chelm; Demjanjuk had said his experiences there were so harsh that he could never forget them.

Wagenaar clung to the explanation that Demjanjuk didn't forget it; he merely skipped over the episode and forgot to bring it up at the right time.

But, as Demjanjuk only first mentioned the name Chelm years after his first questioning, Shaked said, the possibility existed that he'd learned that name only after being questioned.

Wagenaar could not exclude this possibility.

"We have no means of finding this out, do we?" Shaked asked.

"I would say then, you have a problem," Wagenaar said.

"I suggest that you too, Dr. Wagenaar, have a problem," Shaked said. For when Demjanjuk was on the stand, he never claimed that he didn't know the name at the time; he took it for granted that this place was called Chelm. Wagenaar said that based on the papers he had received, he could not come to that firm conclusion.

Shaked then asked Wagenaar what he knew about Demjanjuk's photo in IRO uniform. Sheftel had told him, he said, that for a period of at least six months and no more than twelve months in 1946, Demjanjuk was an IRO police officer.

Was he sure? Couldn't it have been from when Demjanjuk was an IRO driver in 1946?

Shaked wanted to play a tape for Wagenaar. What had the prosecution come up with now? It was an interview Wagenaar had given a Dutch journalist several months before. Wagenaar was surprised. On the tape, he spoke of a picture of Demjanjuk when he was an IRO driver.

How, Shaked now asked, had he come to the police officer story?

Wagenaar claimed that the mistake was all his: Sheftel had told him that Demjanjuk had been part of the camp's internal order service, but having known Demjanjuk had been a driver, he'd confused the two when talking to the journalist.

Shaked suggested another possibility, that Sheftel *had* told him that the picture was of Demjanjuk as a driver for the American forces in 1945–46, which is what Demjanjuk had said on his IRO application. Wagenaar said, no, he knew nothing about other forms.

At the break, when asked by the press how the prosecution had got hold of the tape, Wagenaar said, "The journalist was Jewish. He was probably asked to do service to his country."

Shaked had been critical of Wagenaar's findings because they were based on experimental studies that bore no relation to the case. Now he went a step further. He asked Wagenaar what "expert" opinion could an "experimental" psychologist offer?

Wagenaar said he believed that there was no real controversy on this subject; he felt he did have "expert" testimony to offer to aid the court.

But even that statement was not "expert," Shaked said, it was partisan: the in-court value of experimental psychology was a much debated and much contested subject in the United States; one on which Wagenaar had a clear stand. But he should have informed the court about the controversy—and of his viewpoint, Shaked said.

Levin said this, if true, was important: courts must move prudently into new areas of science. Experimental psychologists had never testified in court in Israel. If the rules of experimental psychology were accepted by the international scientific community, fine; but if they were not settled, still vague and unreliable, the court must say that the time was not yet ripe to accept them. And if Wagenaar had taken a partisan stand in the debate, it was his duty not only to inform the court of both sides of the debate, but also of his position.

Shaked contended that even if the court were to accept expert testimony from experimental psychologists, they could not accept it from this witness.

Wagenaar said he had appeared in forty cases, of which twenty dealt with gambling and the remaining twenty with memory. But Shaked interrupted: How many of the memory cases concerned an identity parade, a suspect among photos, or a live lineup? The answer: "Of such a case, where a suspect was placed among other people and had to be recognized as suspects—I know of only one. . . ."

Shaked revealed that Wagenaar's in-court presentation was not based on his own material but on articles and experiments of others; that Wagenaar had not written a single article concerning identification parades or any aspects thereof.

Shaked also suggested that his testimony was not based on impartial facts. He had given many press interviews before his court appearance. In those, with which he now confronted Wagenaar, he always put forward the defense version of events. Wagenaar said he had presented both possibilities, but he admitted he was ignorant of many of the facts of the case.

Had Wagenaar entertained the "banal possibility," as Shaked put it, that Demjanjuk's forgetfulness could be lies?—"that he was not at Chelm at all."

"Of course," Wagenaar said, "that's what this case is all about."

Wagenaar had stated earlier that the survivors avoided Ivan, but Shaked informed him that they were in constant contact and could not avoid him. This was an example, Shaked said, of the misinformation by which Wagenaar constructed testimony that was not "expert."

"I can't understand," Shaked said, winding up, "how you can testify about this subject without knowing anything either from the standpoint of experiences, or experiments, or the literature, or any experience in this area."

"My field of experience," said Wagenaar testily, "is how memory is tested in general and whether such a test provides a valid picture of the contents of memory. And the task I've set myself is to evaluate the memory tests that have been set before the witnesses—just the way I would evaluate memory tests in scientific situations, and the question I put myself is, Are the outcomes of such tests acceptable as valid representations of the contents of memory?"

But Shaked asked Wagenaar to recognize the lopsidedness between his experiments, in which he examined the "memory test," and the person whose memory was tested. The essential difference was that here, the witnesses knew the suspect. When you are attacked by someone you know, there is no need for a lineup, he said.

You are not selecting the person who looks most like your attacker. Rather you are identifying the person with whom you are familiar. As Shaked analogized, if his neighbor broke into his apartment and stole his VCR, he would not need a lineup to identify the neighbor.

In all of scientific literature, Shaked said, there was only one study in which memory was tested more than forty years later. This was the Bahrick study, in which persons were confronted up to fifty years later with photographs taken from their high-school year-books.

Wagenaar agreed that in more than 90 percent of the cases, they made correct identifications. And that the Bahrick study was scientific evidence for the proposition that a photograph was a good cue to trigger the memory of a person one knew, even forty years later. Just like this case.

So why do you need a lineup?

Wagenaar believed you still needed a "test of the accuracy of the memory of the witnesses" to get at information "that can help a court make its determination."

But the court itself was finding that Wagenaar's approach lacked expert underpinnings. "Let me give you an example," said Presiding Judge Levin, "that in a given graduating class of a high school, there were, let us say, ninety students. They spent some time together. A murder was committed by one of the students who disappeared and was not found. The police kept on working on the case. Thirty-five years later, it turned out that the suspect had moved to an enemy country and, therefore, he was inaccessible. Then he is extradited to Israel, and he says I never went to that school. I never spent any time there. I don't know what they want from me. I didn't commit any murder there, either. And then the students from his graduating class are interviewed and they are told, 'Look, here you have a picture that we found, and it is—if he was in high school when he was seventeen years old—this is a picture of him when he was twenty-one,' and when the witness is shown this picture, he says, 'Oh, yes, this is the boy who was with me in the graduating class.'" Levin then asked what the witness thought the probability was that a single student would correctly identify the accused.

"There is a ninety-percent chance that indeed this is the person you are looking for, a ten-percent chance that this is not the person," Wagenaar answered.

Following on Levin's question, Judge Tal asked what were the average results of accuracy in criminal identifications when the victims were exposed to the accused for even less time?

"There is in general an upper limit of eighty percent correct for one single eyewitness," Wagenaar said.

"I'll let you in on a secret," said Judge Tal. "I did not ask this as an idle question, but to the best of my knowledge, and what I have learned so far, the degree of accuracy is, in fact, eighty percent, and your answer, in fact, confirms this. We wanted to be clear in our own minds on this point."

Later in the session, Judge Tal had a few more questions. He asked what the odds were of someone by chance picking out an individual from a group of eight photographs?

"One to eight," the professor answered.

"If there are five identifiers," continued Judge Tal, "and all of them point to the same photograph, then the chance of their doing this by sheer coincidence, is one to eight to the fifth exponent . . . which is a very small chance. Is that correct?"

With some misgivings, Wagenaar agreed.

Shaked was asked if he had any further questions. He did not. He had got what he wanted, more than what he wanted. He had chosen to leave a certain impression in the judges' minds, without giving the defense time to realize what had happened.

In that room, on that day, it was clear that the defense attorneys, who were smiling, and Demjanjuk himself, who was smiling at his son-in-law Ed Nishnic in the front row, and the wire-service journalists who were leaving their balcony perch to file their stories, and the hundred or so persons who were scattered through the hall, which was only a third filled—it was clear that few of them realized, as the prosecutors had, that Wagenaar had illuminated *the opposite* of what he had set out to present.

A few weeks later, Demjanjuk returned to the witness stand to testify about the IRO photo. He began by denying that it was taken, as Sheftel had said earlier, in 1946, at the Landshut DP camp. Demjanjuk now claimed that in 1951 he worked for a few weeks as a policeman in the Felderfink DP camp; that he was then diagnosed as having tuberculosis and although no longer officially a policeman, he continued to do the same duties and was paid with a carton of cigarettes, or some small pay.

Shaked suggested that perhaps the photo *was* taken in 1946. But that he wasn't a police officer then, but a driver for the IRO—as written on his 1948 IRO form. Demjanjuk maintained that he couldn't drive until 1947, no matter what the IRO form said.

He also denied he had ever said that the photo was from 1946.

Yes, his son had told him about finding it, but he denied he had ever told Sheftel the photo was of him as an IRO police officer in 1951.

But if that was the case, why didn't he say something in court?

He claimed that he was sick, and not in court that day; that he wasn't in court during any of the time it was discussed—during Wagenaar's testimony and his cross-examination; that only when he read in the newspaper that it was from 1946 did he inform his attorneys it was really from 1951; that he knew nothing of the photo until he saw it in the newspaper.

But Demjanjuk *had* been there: in court; in front of the judges, the attorneys, the spectators; on TV. He had sat there, nodding, as Wagenaar and Sheftel spoke about the photo.

Sheftel's defense strategy was one of tit for tat. If the prosecution had called two experts; he would call two—and claim his "experts" were more "expert" than theirs, his experts were more prestigious, regardless of the content of their testimony. If there was one aspect of Demjanjuk's testimony he could substantiate; or one of a prosecution expert's he could repudiate, he would call a witness—as if one flaw would invalidate a whole testimony.

Before the defense finally rested at the end of December, it called Yitzhak Almagor, an Israeli, to testify that Jews *had* served in the Vlassov army. Almagor himself had never served in the Vlassov army, but while in a detention camp in 1948, he had met two Jews who had served as army interpreters.

To respond to Patricia Smith's photo and video matchup of the Trawniki photo and Demjanjuk, the defense brought in a Florida anthropolgist, Dr. Yascar Iscan. Iscan's expertise was not in morphology, the study of the human face, but in determining the age and sex of skeletons. In cross-examination, Iscan conceded the validity of the scientific basis for Smith's comparison technique.

The defense also called its own German witness, Rudolf Reiss. Reiss, who also testified at Demjanjuk's deportation hearing, had worked at Trawniki. His hearing was held in Germany in October 1987 (as he was not an identifying witness, the judges did not attend).

Reiss had worked in Trawniki's administrative section as a paymaster. He claimed to be a document analyst—though he was no such thing. When presented a copy of the Trawniki card, he said he had never seen one at the camp. He then examined it and cited what he claimed was evidence of forgery, all matters previously explained by prosecution experts.

During the course of the hearing, Reiss was difficult and impudent. Several times he refused to answer Horovitz's questions—he called the entire process a "circus." But when Reiss was asked about identity documents in the camp, his descriptions seemed to support everything the prosecution experts had said about the card, save its actual existence.

Reiss admitted there were two types of camp documents that were not kept in his office but in the office of the battalion command. He recalled that photographs were taken with the rectangle on the left breast and that the photo was first stapled to personal records, then put on a cardboard ID document.

Reiss then described an ID that was similar to the Trawniki card, except that Reiss said it was contained on a metal disk. Finally, Reiss confirmed the existence of paperclips at the Trawniki camp, thereby ending "the great paperclip war" and further diminishing the strength of Grant's opinion.

The defense, in its opening remarks, had said it would not rely upon "Nazi" witnesses like the prosecution's—Horn, Leonhardt, Amanaviczius. But then it called Reiss, a thoroughly repugnant, and unrepentant Nazi sympathizer. Horovitz confronted him with a letter he'd written to the American authorities. In it he spoke of: "the singular and unprecedented miscarriage of justice in the history of legal proceedings by the Tribunal at Nuremberg" and "the continued illegal detention of Rudolph Hess, who was acquitted at Nuremberg."

The defense called no more witnesses, although over the next few weeks it would submit documents and recall Eliahu Rosenberg during the summations. But the bulk of its case had been put before the court. There was a month's recess to prepare for arguments, for each side now would have to tell the court the significance of the more than ten thousand pages of trial transcript that had accumulated over almost a year.

CHAPTER 29

Summation and Surprises

"The Lamentation of the Slaughtered Jewish People" is a poem written by the Polish poet Yitzhak Katznelson. In its fifteen stanzas, he gave an eyewitness report of the deportation of the Jews from Warsaw. It was a poem he wrote over several months and then hid in three bottles, which he sealed and buried beneath the root of a tree in Warsaw shortly before his own death. The poem was disinterred after the war.

"This is the state of affairs in this lamentation, too," Shaked said. "The memories of the witnesses have lived on in the hearts of those who survived," he said. In court, the survivors had unfolded the atrocities they'd witnessed and the terrible suffering they'd endured.

A court is often asked, in cases of a more routine nature, to visit the site of the crime; Shaked proposed to revisit Treblinka through the witnesses' special knowledge. In their accounts, Ivan was the walking weapon upon which they'd focused. No lineup was necessary: his face was etched into their memories.

In the prosecution's opening remarks, Blatman spoke before Shaked; the summation followed the reverse order. The closing arguments began January 25, 1988. Each side spoke for nearly two weeks, reviewing each piece of evidence and submitting their contentions of how the court should view it.

The Trawniki card, Shaked said, had been shown to be authentic in all its respects. Every question raised by the defense or their experts had been dismissed.

The defense experts, Shaked said, fell into two categories: those who were true experts, Grant, Flynn, and Iscan, but their testimony was not beyond reproach; and those who set themselves up to be experts and turned out not to be, Robertson, Pritchard, Shiffrin, Tolstoy, and Wagenaar.

Blatman, forceful, rhetorical, and emphatic, examined the threads by which Demjanjuk's alibi had unraveled. For Chelm, Graz, and Heuberg, Demjanjuk had tried to stretch dates and facts to pull a cover over the period in question, without any historical support.

The accused had told tales without foundation, he said, and the tales he told were fabrications. Tolstoy had showed no expertise in any area except repatriation, Blatman said, and there he'd had nothing to prove. When Demjanjuk filled out the IRO forms in 1948 he'd had nothing to fear, that is, unless he was a war criminal.

Blatman dismissed Demjanjuk's fears of the KGB, and the Rudenko plot. Fedorenko had traveled to the Soviet Union three times in the 1970s. Demjanjuk's wife visited the Soviet Union twice. Where was this fear? Where was this plot?

Fedorenko himself had demonstrated the route taken from the Ukraine through Trawniki to Treblinka. The Trawniki card was the link. It said Demjanjuk was a *Wachmann*, an SS guard.

Blatman said the accused had totally denied the charges, so there were no grounds for mitigation. Given the seriousness of the charges, it was worth noting, he said, that regardless, no grounds for mitigation existed. "We have proven the heinous deeds of the accused over a period of several months; they involved continuous brutal indefatigable activity . . . as well as the taking of personal initiative. . . . All this serves as grounds for saying that the deeds of the accused reflect a deliberate intent to act against the Jewish people . . . it is apparent that the accused knew these were Jews. He wanted this to take place. He was party to the knowledge . . . and his intentions are manifested clearly in the deeds he performed. . . .

"Even a cog in the machinery, even a driver, can be a party to the crime. . . . And when it comes to the hierarchy of the Nazi machinery, the accused can indeed be viewed as a small cog in the hell. . . . However, when one examines and reviews the actual deeds he performed, one sees that he was not merely a guard . . . nor did he play a marginal role. . . . He was, in fact, an active partner in the very act of carrying out one of the greatest acts of murder ever in history. . . ."

The defense, Blatman said, had presented contentions that might lead one to believe that Demjanjuk acted as "a member of his people, as many of the members of his people joined the Nazi forces, and that this in itself is not to be regarded as something to find fault with."

To the contrary, Blatman said, the prosecution experts had demonstrated that the majority of Ukrainians refused to collaborate with the Nazis, and even of those who at first did, many withdrew or defected.

The idea of extermination was the Germans', Blatman said, but they could not provide the manpower to carry it out. They needed collaborators and they recruited them from the civilian population of the Soviet Union as well as from the POW camps.

It was these collaborators, Blatman said, whom the Israeli legislature had in mind as war criminals. They have escaped twice—first to the West; and second, "they are still trying to escape their past by denying it."

"The world today," Blatman said, "is going through a transition period. The survivors of the Holocaust are steadily dwindling in numbers. The Holocaust, as such, seems to have been forgotten from the collective memory. And the generations that have grown since the end of the war and that never knew the Holocaust are tired and weary of the Holocaust and Nazi war-crime trials.

"Here in Israel, [this 'forgetting' of the Holocaust] may have been sharpened because the existential problems that the State of Israel and its people face tend to push out of one's consciousness whatever is not to be found in the day-to-day reality. Moreover, this is fed by a phenomenon that is to be condemned outright, the denial of the Holocaust. There are those who would wish to rewrite history and relieve the conscience of certain people and make it possible for them to live out their days quietly. But the world has rejected this approach. Since the war, the Allies have agreed to track down Nazi war criminals; that is why, in Israel, there is no statute of limitations and why criminals like Eichmann and Demjanjuk are brought to justice.

"Here in court, decisive evidence was produced that shows unequivocally that the accused is Ivan the Terrible, who killed scores of thousands of men, women, and children while showing extreme bestiality and torturing his victims and who later found refuge in the United States. . . . It is our contention that [Demjanjuk's] quiet and peaceful countenance should not be misleading, because behind it lies the face of Ivan the Terrible. We ask that the accused be found guilty of all the charges."

During Eliahu Rosenberg's testimony, almost ten months earlier in March, he had told O'Connor that the 1947 Friedman statement was not the first he had given. Rosenberg said that in 1945 he had given a statement, handwritten in Yiddish to a Polish government representative, that had not been seen or heard of since. The defense had found the statement in the archives of Warsaw's Jewish Historical Society. In the midst of the summations, Rosenberg was recalled to the witness stand to be cross-examined by Paul Chumak, a Canadian attorney of Ukrainian descent, who had joined the Demjanjuk defense team after O'Connor was fired.

Chumak, in his mid-forties, was a former prosecutor in Toronto. He had the bearing of a litigator, and he approached Rosenberg with confidence. He showed him the document. Rosenberg confirmed that it was the one he had written in Poland in 1945.

The statement is a far grislier account of Treblinka. But what was of interest to the defense was that it, like the 1947 Friedman statement, spoke of the death of Ivan.

Chumak, impatient with Rosenberg, asked him to read in Yiddish and translate the passage: "We went out of the barracks and fell on the Ukrainians who were guarding us. Mendel and Chaim, who had pumped water from the well, jumped the *Wachmann*. . . . After this we broke into the engine room toward Ivan, he was asleep then. Gustav, [who] was the first, hit him on the head with a spade. Thus he was left lying there forever. . . ."

"You wrote this and is it correct?" Chumak asked.

"What I said there I didn't see. I heard," Rosenberg said. "There is a very big difference."

Chumak's voice grew louder: "Did you see that? Mendel and Chaim?"

"No," Rosenberg said. "I didn't have a chance to see. My role, along with five other people, was . . . to take blankets and throw them over the fences."

"But on December twentieth you wrote. . . ," Chumak said.

"That's right. I wrote—but I didn't see it." Rosenberg explained that he was too busy escaping to see those other things. "Escape. This was my purpose. The bullets were shrieking all around us," Rosenberg said.

Judge Tal asked, "Why didn't you point out what you did write and what you saw?"

"Perhaps it was a mistake," Rosenberg said contritely. "I wanted to believe and I did believe. It was a symbol for us. For us, it was a wish come true. It was a success. Can you imagine such a success, where people who were the victims could kill their executioners? I believed it, and wish that it were so."

Chumak was frustrated: "How can you come to this court and possibly point the finger?" He was building to a pitch.

"But he's there," Rosenberg pleaded, pointing at Demjanjuk. "He's alive; I'm seeing him there."

But why believe he was dead, Chumak said, and repeat the story?

"It was my fondest wish," Rosenberg answered. "I wanted to believe, to believe that this creature . . . Unfortunately, to my great sorrow, he managed to survive. What luck he had!"

Chumak continued to ask Rosenberg to explain the narrative of the document. But the document was not meant as his personal memoir, Rosenberg said. He'd told what he believed to have happened *chronologically,* first inside the camp, then outside, regardless of what he personally saw and when he learned it.

Proof that he didn't see it himself, Rosenberg said, was that his 1945 account of Ivan's death was different from his 1947 one; and still different from that he had heard from survivor Chaim Steir. But he'd never corrected any of them, he said, because until 1976, he believed that Ivan was dead. But *there* he was. Now, sitting across from him, alive!

"Mar Rosenberg," Demjanjuk suddenly shouted, grabbing the microphone, *"atah shakran, shakran, shakran!"* Demjanjuk repeated, the words he had said to Rosenberg before: "You are a liar, liar, liar."

Chumak's questioning had taken almost two hours, yet it had failed to prove anything for the defense. To the contrary, Rosenberg was all the more convincing.

The next week, Sheftel led off the defense summation, saying that the prosecution's three streams of evidence—the survivors, the card, their historians—were, upon examination, *wadis*—dry river beds.

The first *wadi,* the testimony of the survivors, he argued, was flawed in a far-reaching manner and should not be given any weight. The same held true for the depositions of the three eyewitnesses who had since died.

Sheftel went over the statements of each survivor, sometimes arguing at length about each sentence, to show why they were insufficient. He contended that the photospreads were an identification procedure—like a lineup—and not based on recognition. The photospread would not pass muster as a lineup under Israeli law, he said, and as there was no single unequivocal identification that was not tainted, Demjanjuk could not be convicted.

The testimony of the survivors was contradictory: some said Ivan had been killed in the uprising, some said he was at Treblinka until the day of uprising. How, then, could he have been posted to Sobibor in March 1943? The survivors had said that when they arrived at Treblinka in September 1942, Ivan was already there—and that they saw him everyday thereafter; the Trawniki card said that on September 22, 1942, the bearer was posted to L. G. Okzow. How could he be in two places at once? And finally, Sheftel said, the list of Treblinka survivors who did not identify Demjanjuk as Ivan was longer than those who did.

Moreover, the witnesses were biased and had obviously colluded. At the Fedorenko trial they were accused of such and had admitted that they had traveled, stayed, and dined together during the trial.

The second stream that failed was the Trawniki card. It was proved to be a forgery through Grant and Flynn. Grant, Sheftel said, was an expert of far higher caliber than Bezalelli. Flynn's testimony, he said, should be treated just like Boraks's—selectively. Sheftel suggested that the judges accept only those areas of Flynn's testimony that he was cross-examined on.

He derided prosecution experts, Grabitz and Sheffler: "Grabitz is a lawyer, does that make her an expert? I'm more an expert on Meyer Lansky than she is on Streibl, does that make me an expert on the Mafia? Is a prosecutor of drug cases, an expert on drugs?" He called Sheffler "a German who lives off testifying about the destruction of the Jews." Sheffler was no expert: he had seen only one *Dienstausweis* ever, and had never been in the Soviet archive from which it came. Sheftel believed this was critical, as Tolstoy was of the opinion that custody was the decisive factor in determining its authenticity.

As to the postings, Sheffler and Arad had said that Trawniki was the base camp. For Demjanjuk to have been posted to Treblinka, as the prosecution claimed, and intermittently sent to Okzow and Sobibor, as the card claimed, he would have had to have passed through Trawniki several times, and the card should have listed Treblinka several times.

There were at least three Ivans, according to Sheftel: Ivan of Treblinka, Ivan of Sobibor and the Trawniki card, and Ivan Demjanjuk. Later Sheftel would introduce still more Ivans.

The link between the card and Demjanjuk, Sheftel argued, was the photo. As Demjanjuk himself could not say whether it was his photo or not, Sheftel said, one couldn't accept that it was his photo. That's why the prosecution had called experts. And when the court chooses among the expert opinions, he said, the court should prefer the testimony of an anthropologist, Iscan, over that of Smith, a dentist.

The third dry river bed was the prosecution historians Meisel, Krakovsky, and Spektor, who were no experts, he said, when compared to the world-famous Nikolai Tolstoy.

More interesting than the arguments, which were long-winded and revealed nothing new, were the judges' questions. Judge Levin had spent the three-week break before the summations at his desk every day poring over the transcripts, making notes, organizing the points that needed to be addressed by both sides.

Levin asked the prosecution to address the fact that Treblinka was not listed on the Trawniki card. What was Demjanjuk's route after Treblinka? Did he, like Fedorenko, travel north to the Stutthoff complex of camps? Or did he travel south to Trieste, as SS man Gustav Munzberger had said? Did one contradict the other? Could he have been at both?

"We don't know," Blatman said. The best he could offer was "What matters for us, is that he survived the uprising. . . . We are saying," he said, pointing at Demjanjuk, "you were elsewhere. You were at Treblinka."

Demjanjuk shook his head.

The court also asked the defense to address the postings. But they asked them: Did the posting to L. G. Okzow and Sobibor provide the defendant with an alternative alibi?

"It should not be used as grounds for anything," Sheftel said. He argued that the witnesses and the card contradicted each other. It was the prosecution's job to make the two meld; as far as the defense was concerned, both were false.

Sheftel's theory was that the original KGB conspiracy was to accuse Demjanjuk of having served at Sobibor via the card, and then return him to the Soviet Union. This plan was derailed when the survivors, due to the suggestive photospread, accused Demjanjuk of being Ivan of Treblinka. But the two could not coexist.

The court was still unclear as to Sheftel's position on the photospread: the survivors who identified were biased, and the ones who didn't, were not? And as to the photo on the Trawniki card, if it wasn't Demjanjuk, who was it? And who were the survivors identifying in the Trawniki photo: Was that person the real Ivan of Treblinka or were they mistaken there too?

Sheftel said that the position of the defense was this: Not all the survivors were influenced by positive bias; and as for the person on the Trawniki card—he looks like the accused, Sheftel said, but Demjanjuk could not say it was him, because he never had such an ID, dressed in that uniform. But Sheftel avoided directly addressing the prosecution's contention that Demjanjuk was both in Sobibor and Treblinka.

Chumak now rose to speak. The identifications were flawed, he argued, because Demjanjuk had no identifiable morphological feature—he was arguing, in effect, that all Ukrainians look alike.

Chumak now asked the court to consider the political motivations of the USSR and the KGB, the anti-Semitism of the USSR and the anti-Ukrainian unit of the KGB. The KGB, Chumak said, wished to foster inimical feelings between Ukrainians and Jews through this case. They chose an ordinary person, because famous people have friends. It was the ordinary man whom the KGB wished to scare. Frank Walus, Chumak said, was lucky that the exonerative evidence he'd needed was in the West and could be obtained. The material that could help Demjanjuk was in Soviet hands and the defense could not get at it. Perhaps it would in five or ten years, but Chumak asked the court not to act now, out of fear, and make a hasty judgment.

The court would not be acting out of fear, Judge Levin assured him.

"There have been few trials in the history of a nation," Chumak said, concluding, "that are so profoundly affected, where the heart of each and everyone is proceeding. The horrors of Treblinka, very few men have stood trial for such enormous crimes. The court must act with great caution. Captain Dreyfus was convicted at the beginning of this century on false charges. This trial has all the earmarks of the Dreyfus trial. . . ."

Levin interrupted, explaining, "in the history of the Jewish people, the Dreyfus trial has a clear meaning." He asked Chumak to reconsider his comments. Chumak and Gill conferred, while Sheftel kept his head down and shrugged.

Chumak started again: "At stake in this trial is not only the name and quality of Israeli justice. . . ." But Levin interrupted again, to explain that Chumak was, in effect, threatening the court. Levin said it might be best for everyone if a recess was called. Perhaps Chumak would consider the matter in a different light tomorrow.

Sheftel turned to Chumak and said: "You have been on your feet all day. You spoke so brilliantly and so well. They use an opportunity to fuck you, to shame you. What you've passed here, now, I've been through since the beginning, every day or two. I told you not to say this. The Dreyfus case has a connotation." Chumak said, "I really don't understand. . . ."

The next day Chumak began: "I innocently referred to the Dreyfus case. . . . I meant no criticism and disrespect to this honorable court and if there was any such inference I apologize." He said he'd only meant to refer to the Trawniki card and the anti-Ukrainian Unit of the KGB.

But he clearly had not taken the message to heart. He reminded the court that its verdict must stand the test of time, "so that five, ten, or fifty years from now it will be said, justice was done in Jerusalem, Demjanjuk was acquitted according to law. Israeli law will stand as a beacon." He hoped "the three Israeli judges would have the courage to say not guilty."

Gill said, for his part, that the survivors who had made their identifications were not reasonable—they were motivated by pure emotion. He reiterated his theory that the survivors could not know Ivan so well and that the *Kapos* provided a layer of insulation between Ivan and the Jewish workers; he read from Ryan's book about Reichman avoiding Ivan's gaze, about their working and running with their heads down.

He reminded the court about the frailty of eyewitness testimony and the danger of a conviction made on that basis against an accused who has an ordinary face with no outstanding morphological features. Mere suspicion, he said, was not enough.

Gill was interrupted by an old man, Yisrael Yehezekeli, who had screamed out at various points in the trial and began to do so again. The court ordered him to be led outside. He continued screaming in the hall: "I can't keep it inside any longer. I'll tell you all about what the Ukrainians did." He had a picture of himself as a boy with his family. "You can still recognize me," he said. Though he had spoken out before, there was greater passion today: the trial would soon end. The police restrained him, and the journalists barraged him with questions.

Gill continued: The Trawniki card could not belong to Demjanjuk. He reminded the judges that Leonhardt had testified that the bearer of such a card—if found outside a camp—would have been arrested and returned to his last posting, Sobibor. Based on the card, Gill said, Demjanjuk was not posted to Treblinka. And Rudolf Reiss, he said, had also found many errors in the Trawniki card, including the lack of proper postings.

Dorner asked about *Reiss's* posting to Trawniki.

"I did not find it in his pay book," Gill said.

"I did not find it either," Dorner said.

But proof beyond a reasonable doubt, Gill said, is what separated this society from others that were not democratic. Gill told a parable about a man who held a bird in his hands. The fate of that bird was in the man's hands. So, too, the fate of John Demjanjuk, he said, was in the judges' hands.

Gill concluded with an Irish proverb: "May the sun rise to meet you, may the wind always be at your back, may God hold you in the palm of His hand as you decide the fate of John Demjanjuk. . . ."

He asked that the defendant be allowed to make a statement. Levin informed him that a statement would not be appropriate at the moment. Earlier, Chumak had argued that the defense was hindered by not having access to archives in Eastern Europe and the Soviet Union, and to the full OSI investigative reports. So much so, Chumak said, that the prosecution had an unfair advantage that amounted to an "unfair prosecution." This was a serious charge. Shaked was offended that such a claim should come on almost the last day of trial—and that it should come from Chumak: "Your two colleagues," he said, "who have been with the trial much longer, can't look us in the eye and make such a claim. They know better."

Levin hoped Chumak would reconsider and withdraw the charge, and "strike from the record this dismal event." If not, the prosecution would have to respond.

"I'm sure," Chumak said.

Shaked rose. The prosecution had not only fulfilled its duty to the defense in this case, he said, but had gone beyond that duty by providing documents, summaries of documents, indexes, and translations of documents in German, Yiddish, and Polish.

The prosecution had provided all this, above and beyond the call of duty, even though the defense had its own researchers and investigators, who for years had searched throughout the world for evidence. The prosecution believed that what was important was that there be a good defense, Shaked said, and had aided these researchers. Some of the researchers—Brentar, in particular—had used unsavory methods and were aligned with repugnant organizations that spoke of "the myth of the gas chamber. . . ."

John Demjanjuk Jr. stood up suddenly, brusquely, and walked to the rope at the front of the courtroom to let himself out. His hand was trembling with anger. He walked up the stairs of the proscenium. At the top of the stairs, he stood a few feet from Shaked. They looked at each other. The son of the accused marched offstage.

His sister, Irene, suddenly also stood, and said in a shrill voice, two octaves higher than her normal dulcet tones: "You're lying, that's what it is."

Vera Demjanjuk stood up as well, shouting: "You're liars, you're liars. Shame on you. Shame on you. You have no shame, no heart, no nothing." They made their way to the stairs.

Irene helped Vera up. For a moment it seemed that Vera might faint, but they all exited. The room had fallen silent. Shaked turned back to the court. And then from the wing, the voice of John Demjanjuk Jr. cried out a final salvo: "You lying son-of-a-bitch."

Demjanjuk appeared unfazed throughout this episode. He did not react when his son stood up, or when his daughter and wife walked out. He acted as if nothing had happened.

Shaked finished his argument. Levin ruled that no unfair prosecution had occurred. The judges retired.

The visitors left the room. The hall went silent. Some guards went to take each other's pictures, onstage, before everything—the judges' bench, the witness dock, all the tables—was disassembled. It was anticlimactic. On a bus a college student talked about the Demjanjuk family's outburst, "They wanted to leave a bad taste in our mouths."

The trial ended on February 18, 1988, a year and two days after it had begun. Amazingly, at this late date, the public was unsure of the trial's outcome—How would the court weigh the evidence? Was there a reasonable doubt? No one could say. Court observers were divided. But no one doubted that the judges would address every piece of evidence and every argument raised so far.

In mid-March, Sheftel called for an "extraordinary session of the court" to consider new evidence: twelve reports of interviews with Treblinka survivors from Camp One, and the 1979 deposition of a Soviet citizen Ignat Terentyevich Danylchenko—the same Danylchenko whose name appeared in the *News from Ukraine* articles.

The material had been released in the Demjanjuk Defense Fund's Freedom of Information Act (FOIA) suit against the OSI. Levin decided to accept the evidence under Section 15 and reopened summations for both sides to address what weight it deserved.

Shaked said that the prosecution had chosen its witnesses only from that small circle of survivors who had seen Ivan day in, day out. The persons from the investigatory reports, which Shaked analyzed one by one, were all from Camp One—some had been there for only a few hours.

Some of the Camp One survivors had identified the visa or Trawniki card pictures, but they were not the kind of witnesses the prosecutors had wished to call. The reports did nothing to advance the case of the defense, Shaked argued, and could serve only to enhance the prosecution's case.

But Sheftel believed that the reports of those who did not identify the photos should carry great weight. Also, the fact that the identifiers described Ivan variously as a watchtower guard, a train driver, a ranking officer, and as being five foot five, all served to confirm the mistaken identification of the survivors. There were at least six

Ivans at Treblinka, Sheftel argued, none of whom was John Demjanjuk.

The Danylchenko statement was testimony from a former
Wachmann who said he'd served as a guard with an Ivan Demjanjuk in March 1943 at Sobibor and later at the Flossenburg camp.
Given in the presence of Soviet prosecutors in 1979, Danylchenko
explained that at Sobibor there were four platoons in the camp,
formed according to height, and he said that he belonged to the first
platoon—of guards at least 180cm tall. "Of the guards who served
with me in the first platoon," he said, "I remember Ivan Ivchenko,
who was our cook, and Ivan Demjanjuk."

"When I arrived at Sobibor [in March 1943]," Danylchenko said,
"Demjanjuk already served in the camp as a private in the SS
guards. I do not know Demjanjuk's patronymic. From conversations with Demjanjuk I do know that he was from Vinnitsa Oblast.
He was roughly two to three years older than I, had light brown
hair with noticeable bald spots at that time, was heavyset, had gray
eyes, and was slightly taller than I, roughly 186–187cm tall. I remember Demjanjuk's appearance well, and I could possibly identify
him. I do not know directly from where and when precisely Demjanjuk arrived at Sobibor. From what Demjanjuk said I know that
like all of us [the guards] who served in Sobibor he had been trained
at the SS camp in Trawniki. . . ."

"Demjanjuk, like all guards in the camp," Danylchenko continued, "participated in the mass killing of Jews. I also participated in
this crime and I was convicted and punished for it. While I was at
the camp I repeatedly saw Demjanjuk, armed with a rifle, together
with other guards and, in many cases, myself, guard prisoners in all
areas of the camp, from the unloading platform to the entrance of
the gas chambers." Danylchenko said he saw Demjanjuk push Jews
with his rifle butt and hit them, but this was a common occurrence
during the unloading of the Jews. He did not see Demjanjuk personally shoot anyone, although he said this occurred regularly if anyone showed any resistance along the way to the gas chamber.

"Demjanjuk was considered to be an experienced and efficient
guard. For example, he was repeatedly assigned by the Germans to
get Jews in surrounding ghettos and deliver them in trucks to the
camp to be killed. I did not receive any such assignments, since I did
not have sufficient experience. Demjanjuk also guarded the outside
of the barracks for the special detachment, which serviced the gas
chamber. I saw him at this post many times, carrying a rifle. I do
not know whether he served guard duty inside the gas-chamber
zone. As I remember, Demjanjuk was frequently granted leave because he conscientiously carried out all orders from the Germans."

Danylchenko reported that in March or April of 1944, "Demjanjuk and I were sent from Sobibor to the city of Flossenburg in Germany, where we guarded an aircraft factory and a concentration camp for political prisoners. In case we were wounded, all of the guards at this camp, including Demjanjuk, were given a tattoo on the inside of the left arm, above the elbow designating the blood type.

"In late autumn of 1944 in October or November, Demjanjuk and I [among other guards] were sent to the city of Regensburg, or rather from the concentration camp located in the city of Flossenburg, we escorted two hundred political prisoners to another camp located 18–29 km from Regensburg. Until April 1945 we guarded the prisoners in this camp, who did construction work. In April of 1945, due to the approach of the front, the entire camp was evacuated and marched toward Nuremberg; I escaped along the way but Demjanjuk continued to accompany the prisoners. I suggested that he escape with me, but he refused. I have never seen Demjanjuk since then and his fate is unknown to me."

According to the documents submitted to the court, the day after his deposition Danylchenko returned to the Soviet Procurator's office. There, he was shown three sets of photographs. The first set had three young men in Red Army uniform and caps—Danylchenko selected Demjanjuk's 1941 Red Army photo. The second was of young soldiers without caps—here Danylchenko picked out the Trawniki card photo. And finally, the third set was of men in civilian dress. He selected Demjanjuk's 1951 visa photo as the Ivan he had known. Danylchenko told the Soviet prosecutors that, in each case, he'd singled out Demjanjuk based upon the distinctive facial characteristics he recalled: "oval face, chin, shape of eyes, and protruding ears."

Judge Levin asked the prosecutors for their reaction to the statement. Shaked answered that the statement "may be a fabrication, it may be that it is not." The Trawniki card's authenticity need not, and should not, he said, be judged by Danylchenko's statement. The prosecution knew nothing about Danylchenko or the circumstances of his questioning. There also were glaring historical problems with the account: Sobibor was dismantled in November 1943, but Danylchenko said he had served there until spring 1944.

It would be convenient for the court, Levin said, to pretend that the document did not exist; but it did, and the court had to relate to it in the verdict—So what was the attorneys' position? How did they reconcile Danylchenko's testimony with that of the survivors?

The defense need not prove anything, Sheftel argued. The statement only cast further doubt on the prosecution's case, he said, and showed Wagenaar was correct—a memory problem existed.

Judge Dorner suggested that the two *could* be reconciled: after January 1943, the transports and gassings decreased, and the survivors would have had little contact with Ivan; in March, he could have been at Sobibor.

Sheftel disagreed. There could be no reconciling the two. Even Horn had testified that Ivan was in the camp after the uprising.

Danylchenko, Shaked said, certainly did know Demjanjuk; that was evident from the identification. But Danylchenko may have recalled him, not exclusively from the time they had spent in Sobibor, but from the total time they'd spent together.

It was Shaked's view that Danylchenko had spent more time with Demjanjuk *after* Sobibor—at Flossenburg—than previously. He found Danylchenko's testimony about Demjanjuk more telling about when they were apart than when they were together: they were posted to different duties, Danylchenko had testified; Demjanjuk was given leaves, and sent out of the camp on various assignments. How long these assignments took, Shaked said, is not clear.

Danylchenko, who said he'd met Demjanjuk in March at Sobibor, Shaked pointed out, remembered him as an excellent *Wachmann*. But the Trawniki card placed Demjanjuk there only after March 27. "[Demjanjuk] must have gained his experience elsewhere," Shaked said. "We say it is Treblinka."

Demjanjuk may have been at Sobibor in April briefly, Shaked offered, before returning to Treblinka. Later he spent time with Danylchenko at Flossenburg. Though this was different than the exact route the prosecution had drawn for Demjanjuk before, it did not contradict it: Demjanjuk could have been at both Flossenburg *and* Pilau. The evidence submitted revealed, Shaked said, that *Wachmanner* were being shunted back and forth throughout Central Europe, depending on the situation along the front lines. Demjanjuk, a skilled driver, may have served at several postings.

But Sheftel maintained that it still did not tie in with Otto Horn's and Munzberger's statements that Ivan had been at Treblinka in late August 1943; and Munzberger's claim that after Treblinka, he had served with Ivan in Trieste.

Judge Tal also wanted to offer an observation, asking Sheftel to forgive him for the analogy he was about to draw. If in another thirty-five years he was asked about the trial, he would say yes, for a whole year, I saw day in and day out the prosecution and the defense. But, of course, there were gaps in the trial. So, too, was it not possible that Danylchenko, in 1979, recalling events almost forty years before, had telescoped several months into one chunk?

Yes, of course that was possible, Sheftel admitted. But with only the statement to go on, Sheftel believed that you couldn't really tie Danylchenko's testimony to the case.

But that was exactly what the court would do.

CHAPTER 30

The Human Face of Evil

On April 18, 1988, Demjanjuk was brought out of Ayalon Prison at 5:30 A.M. Camera crews were waiting. "I feel good," Demjanjuk announced. One journalist shouted, "Today's your big day." "Today is *your* big day," said Demjanjuk heartily. He got into the police van, and as it made its way through the hills up to Jerusalem, Demjanjuk could be seen in the back in good spirits. The sky was bright blue.

The van was brought to the rear of the courthouse rather than the usual front entrance. But when the doors opened, Demjanjuk would not leave. Sound came out of him in a high-pitched whine. The cry sounded more animal than human. The guards tried to talk to him: "John, come on, John . . . John . . ." Then they begged him. Finally, four of them carried Demjanjuk into the building. He was kicking and struggling, and continued to cry. He was carried quickly through the courtroom before the spectators entered and put on a cot in the courtroom's holding cell.

The first spectator had arrived at midnight. Most began to gather outside at 6:00 A.M. Teenage students from Jerusalem joined the line a half-hour later. By 8:30 A.M., most had found seats inside.

The court attendant put his cap on, fixed his tie, pulled himself to attention, and then spoke the by-now familiar call to order: *"Beit Hamishpat!"*

Demjanjuk would not leave his cot; the court agreed to proceed in his absence. Levin then announced that the verdict was more than four hundred pages (in Hebrew; seven hundred in English), so it would not be read it in its entirety. Only main points would be read aloud, but even this would take the entire day. Each judge now opened a black binder.

"We have before us an indictment," Levin read, "a vast and bleak and horrifying one. It is worded in scathing terms. It describes unspeakable acts. It appears that the facts that constitute the basis of this indictment have been depicted with pent-up anguish, with a tearful eye and a quaking hand. For this indictment unfolds . . . the most horrifying chapter in the history of the Jewish people, which has suffered such torment throughout its chronicles. It is an unspeakable and indescribable as well as unforgivable chapter in our history of the annihilation of eight-hundred-seventy-thousand men, women, and children, who were led as sheep to the slaughter from throughout Poland and other Jewish communities in Europe and were exterminated with indescribable brutality in the slaughterhouse of the Camp of Treblinka. . . .

"In this indictment, the state attributes to a mortal being the perpetration of brutal and savage acts against hundreds of thousands of human beings until death. These acts as depicted in the indictment were perpetrated, according to the indictment, by the accused zealously and with a thirst for murder. . . .

"It is this bitter and terrifying truth that we are being asked to expose and clarify, so as to determine whether the accused has had any part in these crimes.

"This is a challenging and difficult task that we have been called upon to perform, with a sense of awe, cognizant of the heavy responsibility that rests upon us.

"With a sense of awe, because we are being asked to review the terrible history of the Jewish people in Europe in the most dreadful period of the Holocaust, as our people found itself drenched in blood and shedding tears, and as we remember the eight-hundred-seventy-thousand human beings who were killed, who were slaughtered, who were asphyxiated, burned, and forced to die in the sanctification of the Holy Name by the German murderers and other collaborators from other peoples.

"We are cognizant of the heavy responsibility, because it is incumbent upon us to determine judicially the historical truths with regard to events that beset our people in one of the most difficult periods in the history of mankind and, in particular, in the history of the Jewish nation.

"It is our responsibility to seal a man's fate, a man who, when he was young as a member of the Ukrainian people, suffered famine and persecution by a tyrannical and despotic ruler. Later, he served in the army and fought against the invading German army. He was wounded, hospitalized, then recruited back into duty. He was taken captive. He experienced the horrors of being a prisoner of war. He survived. He emigrated to the United States, built up his home, and lived peacefully with his family, and was a member of his community, until such time as suspicion fell upon him of having perpetrated the terrible crimes attributed to him. It was then that he was extradited to Israel and was put on trial before us.

"Our sense of responsibility makes it necessary for us to examine and weigh these facts, commonly, prudently, and judicially without emotion and in disregard of anything that has been written or said outside of the walls of this courtroom, whether in the media or in the public-at-large. . . .

"Though the events took place over forty-five years ago," Levin said, "the question arises: Can one remember and describe faithfully things that happened so very long ago? Because, seemingly, the passage of time clouds the memory, advancing age dims the senses. . . . How can an individual, then, recall precisely events to which he was witness or which he experienced? How can a person remember people whom he knew closely, or more superficially, in those horrible and unforgettable days?

"One might ask, is it possible to forget? How can people who were in that field of carnage, who experienced its atrocities, who lived in the atmosphere of repression and terror of persecution, in the confinement of a death camp—people who witnessed death and humiliation and brutalization day in and day out—who saw the taskmasters and henchmen perform their work at the death camp of Treblinka—how can they forget all these? People who were forced to perform humiliating and degrading tasks, with the fear of death looming over them day in and day out—could such people possibly repress such heinous events?

"One cannot but ask, is it possible for an individual who experienced the dreaded reality described in the indictment, is it possible for him to remember the deeds while forgetting the perpetrators?

"One might also ask, is it conceivable, can one possibly grasp, that a mortal human being, a person who is a civilized human being, would be capable of planning, realizing, and putting into effect as satanical and diabolical a plan as the one designed to annihilate a whole people?

"Is it, in fact, possible that a nation that has sprouted people of intellectual and spiritual stature, would set for itself the uppermost goal to destroy, to kill, and to cause to perish all Jews, both young and old, little children and women, as stated in the Book of Esther?

"Is it possible for a person like the accused, and other Ukrainians who had experienced famine and suffering, who themselves were victims of persecution and killings of masses of human beings, is it possible for such people to assist the death units of the SS to serve as their auxiliary forces in putting into effect the plan of annihilating the Jewish people?

"Would anyone who had such experiences be capable of perpetrating such deeds? Is it possible for everything described in the indictment to have happened? Did it, in fact, happen?

"These questions, and the very difficult dilemmas that they raise, obligate us to offer a clear and unequivocal answer beyond a reasonable doubt. . . ."

"We must make reference primarily to the testimony of those survivors who actually experienced the atrocities, who were personally involved, and witnessed firsthand that which took place, people who observed the perpetrators of the crimes in the field of carnage of Treblinka and actually came into contact with them. It is for this reason, naturally, that the testimony of the survivors is so important and powerful. It is they who bear in their minds and hearts the terrible history of these events. But it is precisely because of the great emotion that this involves that we must examine their testimony most prudently and carefully, while at the same time bearing in mind the information that they are capable of sharing with us.

"It is important that we gain an impression of their reliability. We must try to examine whether they may not be swayed, God forbid, by any prior conviction or by hearsay. We must also pay heed to the possibility of a memory that may have betrayed them, a sincere and genuine mistake in identification and other hindrances that are liable to impede a witness as he described such terrible events, etched in their very flesh, albeit fifty years, or forty-five years ago.

"The description of these facts in their entirety, on the historical plain, as well as with regard to the identity of the accused, is, in fact, part of the same entity. These are links in a single chain that is closely interconnected. One matter depends on the other.

"We attribute the utmost importance to the question of the physical proximity, or as this has often been described in the course of the testimony, the actual friction, the actual contact between the survivors and Ivan when, in that period, they lived in close proximity and would come into contact with one another day in and day out, in an atmosphere of continual fear and anguish. . . ."

Judge Levin drew the Final Solution as one bloody trail leading from the speeches of Adolf Hitler as early as 1930, through the racial theories and laws of the Nazi regime, the Wansee Conference, the euthanasia program, the mass killings by shooting, to killing by gassing, and the establishment of the extermination camps, Treblinka among them.

"Treblinka, with the terrible tragedy that it embodies, is, in fact, the very end of a very long, bitter, and tortuous road at the end for millions of Jews, and it was described and it was meant to lead to a single goal, to exterminate the Jewish people and Jewish communities throughout Europe.

"As we hear the survivors unfold before us with emotion, yet fluently, just what happened to them, we feel how deeply these events and experiences are etched in their souls. The atrocities live on with them. The spectacles are part and parcel of their memory. Not everything could be told. Not everything has been told."

The deeds committed at Treblinka could not have been accomplished without the full cooperation of the Ukrainian guards, Levin said, among whom was Ivan, nicknamed Ivan Grozny (Ivan the Terrible). His deeds were known from the testimonies of that handful of survivors who survived the uprising. Levin asked: Could they remember Treblinka and Ivan?

Based on the testimonies before them, he said, the court wished to state: "Yes, one can remember the horrible deeds and the dreadful events that make up the Holocaust and through which the Jewish people passed, even though it is almost fifty years ago.

"We also wish to state that: It is impossible to forget what happened. It is impossible to forget, too, Ivan the Terrible and his misdeeds.

"The witnesses' direct appearance here, their testimony, which was suffused with frankness and honesty, the living eyewitnesses to what went on, and to what is deeply etched in their memories, none of it will they ever forget. And to the person who wonders, even though the mind boggles at what happened, even though it cannot take it in, even though it is inconceivable that this could have happened, it *did* happen.

"There was the bestiality, there was this horrendous train of events. There was its inception and its perpetration. It is one tiny detail from the overall story of the extermination of the whole of European Jewry, of which the eight-hundred-seventy-thousand Jews in Treblinka was just a tiny part. The memory and the lesson shall be learned, lest it ever be repeated."

Levin said that the court had reviewed the Final Solution, first from the German point of view, from the documents and historical submissions: the declarations, the laws, the programs of confiscation, ghetto-ization, deportation, extermination. All served two purposes, he said, the extermination of the Jewish people and the enrichment of the Nazis. "Not only evil was behind the actions of all the instigators and perpetrators of the Final Solution program, but also the lust for money and avarice." Then Levin reviewed the same events from the survivors' point of view, using their own words to recount the path of degradation and the series of deceptions that took them from their homes and families and into Treblinka.

To watch the survivors listen to their own words, as read by Judge Levin, was painful for observers, but more so for the witnesses. Czarny wore aviator glasses, but dabbed at his eyes, brushing away large tears; Epstein sat on the edge of his seat, nervously, his fingertips at his lips; Rosenberg was tightly wound, and his wife held his arm to calm him.

The judges had put all of the pieces of the diabolic puzzle together. There were no more distractions—only the evidence—which grew, gaining weight, weighing deeply upon each listener. The details of the "work" of the Jewish forced-laborers, of the barbers and the dentists, were gruesome; the description of the pits, each known by the name of the Jewish communities whose corpses filled it, was revolting.

The overall setting was far more horrific, far more extensive and emotionally heartrending than any one scene that had been drawn in court. The verdict was no dry legal opinion. It was as if the judges wanted, after fifteen months, to bring the accused back to the crime. And it was succeeding.

Levin continued to read, without break, for three hours, until 11:45 A.M. Then, after a short break, Judge Tal confronted the question, Did Ivan die in the uprising?

None of the accounts of Ivan's death during the uprising, by Rosenberg in 1945 and 1947, by Goldfarb and by Hellman, Judge Tal said—none was an eyewitness account. There were extreme discrepancies within the accounts and among the versions. Rumors heard in camp were later found to be wishful thinking, as when some of the murderers were confronted in Dusseldorf.

Accordingly, the judges found no grounds, he said, whatsoever, to establish that Ivan was killed in the uprising. On the contrary, there was the testimony of Otto Horn, who saw Ivan after the uprising, as well as the deposition of Danylchenko. "The proven truth," Tal said, "is that Ivan Grozny was not killed."

Shortly after this, the Demjanjuk family left the hall. They saw no reason to sit and listen anymore.

Turning to the alibi, Judge Tal explained that it was critical to Demjanjuk's defense: "Proof of this contention, even if it were merely to amount to reasonable doubt, would amount to grounds for an acquittal. However," Tal said, "refuting this contention lends support to the positive proof brought by the prosecution."

Demjanjuk's alibi centered on the contention that while Ivan was perpetrating his monstrous deeds, the defendant was being held captive by the Germans in a POW camp called Chelm. The defense did not cite any evidence to support the alibi, Tal said, which rested on the reliability and credibility of Demjanjuk's testimony and on the question of whether he'd created a reasonable doubt that he, in fact, had spent the entire period in Chelm.

Tal sat hunched over his copy of the verdict, and adjusted his glasses. Demjanjuk did not, when first asked, Tal said, recall the name of the camp that was his alibi or what he did there. Chelm, the camp where Demjanjuk had said he spent eighteen months under conditions so terrible that he could never forget them. Demjanjuk gave no reason for his forgetfulness. The defense advanced several explanations for Demjanjuk's defective memory, including the testimony of Wagenaar. But "Out of respect for Professor Wagenaar," Tal read from the verdict, "we can only say that these explanations do not have a leg to stand on. . . ."

Moreover, Tal said, the judges did not believe that Demjanjuk was at Chelm. "The accused cannot describe the camp or any part," he read. "Neither can he describe those who lived with him in the shed, or anyone else. He cannot name anyone or describe anyone. He cannot describe any of the office-holders in the camp. If anyone spent eighteen months in a given camp, it is inconceivable that he would be unable to give details about the place.

"At the same time, where German records tell us that Chelm was only a transit camp, the accused's version, as if he had spent some eighteen months at Chelm, is totally unacceptable and implausible, in view of the transient nature of the camp."

The rest of Demjanjuk's war-year timetable was also unbelievable, Tal said. "There is an inexplicable gap of over a year, which exists between the day he claims to have left Chelm and his arrival in Graz."

Demjanjuk's tale of Graz and Heuberg and service in the Russian Liberation Army also was not credible, he said. Even Tolstoy admitted that at the time Demjanjuk claimed he was in Heuberg, there was not a single Russian regiment there. Demjanjuk's claims that he was tattooed while serving at Graz or that there were Rumanians and Jewish *Kapos* at Chelm were equally unbelievable.

Judge Tal paused. Demjanjuk's alibi, he said, was simply untrue: "It is a lie. The Chelm version is simply unacceptable to us and is not credible. It is very poor. It is not substantiated by anything, and a few details that he brought forth in order to bring it to life have been proved false."

The removal of the tattoo, a long and painful process, Tal said, was incriminating. So, too, were the forms he'd filled out that spoke to Demjanjuk's mechanical abilities. "All the facts known about

Demjanjuk," Tal said, "added up to a picture of a young man who, through the collective farm in the Ukraine and his Soviet army service, right down to postwar Germany and the American army, knew how to handle a car, knew something about engines. Even on the 1948 PCIRO form, Demjanjuk was listed in several places as a driver. . . . But when he spoke before us, he tried to distance himself from anything remotely connected with mechanics, motors, and engines."

There was also, he said, the question of why Demjanjuk listed Sobibor on the forms, an entry he denied making, and then claimed he meant Sombor, but later retracted that.

Why write Sobibor and Pilau but hide Treblinka? Shaked had noted a similar example in the case of Fedorenko. The answer, Tal read was that "Fedorenko as well as the accused knew that their applications would be scrutinized. They would be asked to provide exact details as to how they were exiled from Poland, whether they were deported, what happened after the war, and so on. The details had to live up to the expectations of the interrogators. Therefore, they deliberately gave names of small, unknown places. *Wachmanner*, of course, take leaves to nearby towns, as Fedorenko testifie[d] . . . so that they would have been capable of providing full descriptions of these places. . . . At the same time, they did deliberately conceal the main sight of the crime about which there is information and there are survivors and witnesses."

Tal paused again, looking out at the hushed room. "Did the contention that Demjanjuk was at Sobibor," he asked, "suggest an alternative alibi—that he was there and not at Treblinka? And even so, if the accused himself did not raise it, did the possibility of such an alibi place upon the court the responsibility to suggest it?" Tal said the judges felt they were under no responsibility to consider it; but they were nonetheless convinced, he said, that the evidence "do[es] not cast any doubt as to indicate that the accused was only at Sobibor and not at Treblinka."

A short recess was held. Upon the judges' return, Judge Dorner announced she would read the section of the verdict concerning the Trawniki document.

Demjanjuk contended originally, Dorner began, that the card was a one-of-a-kind document, forged by the KGB. But this was not so, she said. There was evidence that similar service cards were drawn up routinely at the camp, and Leonhardt had seen many such passes. There was also the evidence of the three other service cards. Additional support was found, Dorner said, in the official correspondence about the loss of a Trawniki service card. Reiss's testimony, she said, was such that he would have said anything to help the accused.

Dorner said the defense had taken two positions with regard to the card: either that it was such a good forgery that it could not be detected; and/or it was forgery as proved by their experts. The first contention, she said, was based on the testimonies of witnesses Tolstoy, Shiffrin, and Flynn. But Tolstoy and Shiffrin could not provide one example of a Soviet forgery of Nazi-era documents; and the sum total of Tolstoy's opinion was that the document should be carefully checked, and this, Dorner said, had been done. Shiffrin was not an expert but an eccentric, she said. Even William Flynn had found many faults with the card. So it was not "perfect."

Now as to proof of forgery, she said, the defense had two points to fall back on: the photograph on the Trawniki document and certain slips, or irregularities, in the personal details of the person on the card.

The photograph on the Trawniki card, she said, was of a young man. Demjanjuk was now sixty-eight. But, Dorner read, "one would say that the accused belongs to that sort of people who have not been affected with the passage of years in their features."

An entire series of authentic photographs of Demjanjuk, spanning the years 1940 to 1986, had been placed before the court, she noted. In the course of seeing those photographs, the judges could observe, she said, "how the accused is getting older, [but] certain outstanding features of his face, certain landmarks remained unchanged." On the basis of the judges' own perception, Dorner said, they could compare these features to his face today and to the face on the Trawniki card.

"In the case of the accused before us," Judge Dorner read, her voice starting to strain, "we can, therefore, establish unequivocally that the photograph in [the Trawniki card] is that of the accused. Both Professor Patricia Smith and, also to a lesser extent, Mr. Altmann bear this out. In brief, the photograph of the Trawniki document . . . is that of the accused."

Smith impressed the judges, she said: "She had carried out very thorough investigations and described it in the tiniest detail to us, and her conclusions are based on very thorough research, and they are acceptable to us." But since Altmann's method was not based on measuring, the court found the objective dimension missing, she said. His identification attempt could not be the sole basis for identification, but could be underpinned by means of other evidence.

The defense contention that the card was not authentic, Dorner said, rested in great part on the testimony of Julius Grant. Grant's conclusion rested on two matters, the photo and the signatures. But his contentions about the photo were unexplained, she said, and his reservations about the signatures were insufficiently founded. And as for witness William Flynn, Dorner read: "Here in court the witness was subject to threats by those who had a contract with him, and he himself admitted that he did not feel at liberty to reply to questions, because of what he called a contractual agreement with the Demjanjuk Defense Fund."

Dorner reminded the courtroom that Flynn's statements in court contradicted what he had said at the documents conference in the United States. "Once the witness refused to explain it in cross-examination," she said, "clearly no weight whatsoever can be attributed to his testimony in court insofar as it runs counter to what it says in the conference in the United States."

Judge Dorner paused and looked over at Judge Tal. He said one word, "postings," and started to read again. The postings were the card's major fault, he said. But the question, Tal said, was not whether the testimonies of the survivors were contradicted by the fact that the Trawniki card had no posting to Treblinka. Rather, he said, the question before the court was "Did the accused serve in Treblinka?"

Tal read: "The main pieces of evidence against the accused is not the document [the Trawniki card]. His guilt is not proved on the basis of this document in itself, although in the course of the discussions and deliberations, days and even weeks were devoted to this document. Although the experts for both parties dealt in minute detail with each and every facet, starting with the staple perforations and the rust marks, it is not, after all, technical details that will seal the fate of the accused, but rather the testimony of the survivors, which is etched in their memories."

Shaked had argued, he said, that without complete knowledge of the manner in which postings were listed on the service cards, it was possible to assume that main postings, such as Treblinka, were not entered. This contention, Tal said, was unacceptable: "The fact was that the accused's posting to Treblinka should have been entered on the card, and it was not. . . . Nonetheless, the nonentry of this information does not necessarily rule out the possibility that the accused was at Treblinka, nor does it in any way detract from the authenticity of the document."

On the contrary, he said, the omission refutes the charge that the card was part of a KGB plot. Why fake a document that runs counter to the testimonies of the survivors? Why forge a document that lists Demjanjuk as a rank-and-file guard at Sobibor rather than being Ivan of Treblinka?

The only explanation, Judge Tal said, was that the card was authentic, that it was the identity card of Ivan Demjanjuk.

There was another short recess. The courtroom was crowded and had become very warm. But many stayed in their seats rather than risk losing them.

After a half-hour, the clerk called the room to attention and the judges took their seats. Levin said he would now read the sections of the verdict concerning identifications.

Sheftel had argued, Levin said, that under Israeli law a proper identification lineup was not held. But Israel case law was more variegated, and less inflexible, he said, than Sheftel would have it. "Each and every case must be judged upon its own merits. . . ." Levin said that the judges found Sheftel's argument that the number of nonidentifiers outweighed those who had identified Demjanjuk, "somewhat simplistic."

"It is not just a question of arithmetical calculation," Levin read. "It is not just a poll that was conducted—so and so many for's, so and so many against. . . . Every statement, every testimony must be examined according to its independent weight as well as the circumstances, and the factual conclusion can only be formulated on the basis of the sum total of this material, the cumulative weight from different perspectives."

Levin said that it was established that any proximity between the identifier and the suspect may do away with the need for an identification parade. This was true in drug cases, or when neighbors lived close together; there was no need here for an identification parade. It became a mere formality, he said.

"How, then," Levin read, "can we compare the extent of the forced familiarity between Ivan and the survivors, and I draw all the necessary differences here, between him and SS officer Otto Horn? How can we compare? There is no ground for comparison." But, he said, "despite the uniqueness of this case, the traumatic intensity as well as the close proximity, we still hold that it is necessary to examine the intensity of the identification, the accuracy of the identification, as well as its weight in keeping with the identification tests, since, after all, a great many years have elapsed between those events and the time when the witnesses appeared before us . . . as many as thirty-five to forty-five years."

The court must do, he said, "everything possible to avoid committing the grievous error of convicting a human being because of misidentification." Although it appeared that the identification parade was not necessary, the fact that identity parades were held could only aid the court in making the correct decision.

Levin divided the parades into three groups: the ones conducted by Radiwker in 1976 ("a preliminary step for tracking down suspects"); by Kollar ("an ordinary photospread identification procedure, because he, in fact, was dealing with someone who was already a suspect and was a candidate for denaturalization. . . . On the other hand, let us not forget that at that stage Kollar was acting according to the guidelines issued by the American authorities, and was fulfilling their requirements to a "T"); by the Americans, for Reichman and Horn ("a more advanced stage in the interrogation of the accused in the United States").

Contrary to the criticisms and innuendos of the defense, Levin said, Radiwker's testimony was "utterly credible." He said the judges were deeply impressed by her honesty, integrity, and remarkable memory. They categorically rejected any innuendo that Radiwker "ostensibly was working to bring about the conviction of the accused, even at the expense of the actual truth," or that she did not act in good faith, or gave hints to the witnesses or coached them. Levin was emphatic: "There is absolutely no leg for this criticism to stand on."

But the court, Levin continued, did note that when Kollar reinterviewed Rosenberg and Epstein in 1979, showing them the Trawniki photo, the survivors may still have recalled the 1951 visa photo. This, he said, detracted from that identification procedure. But Kollar himself, Levin said, "acted with integrity and honesty in questioning the identification witnesses and followed all of the rules established in this regard. His reliability is beyond a shadow of a doubt."

To establish the weight of these identifying testimonies, Levin said, "both the methods and the philosophy of Professor Wagenaar is not acceptable to us." Instead, "the specific weight of each and every one will be considered, concerning also the certainty that it entered." The specific language in the statements was not, Levin said, the determining factor—each and every statement was weighed on its merits, in light of the manner in which the identification was made and the circumstances surrounding it.

The court, he said, had observed Rosenberg on the stand for many days. Levin read: "Although there were certain inaccuracies in his testimony, we do not hesitate to establish that Rosenberg was a reliable witness who had a long-ranging memory for everything that went on at Treblinka as well as the persons involved in the wholesale massacre. Rosenberg is a hard person, a very forceful person. At the same time, he knows what he is talking about, and for us he was a reliable witness in anything to do with this case.

"What is important for us, in terms of the weight, is the immediate spontaneous reactions of the survivors when they had the photographs of the accused before them. It is the instantaneous, spontaneous reaction that shows the perception, the ability to discern, and the ability to falsify, and this is what counts in identification processes."

In the case of Rosenberg, Levin said the court had determined that Rosenberg's identification on May 11, 1976, was "an identification of a high degree of probability; and his qualifying remarks merely indicates his desire to be very, very sure of himself." Rosenberg had argued with Radiwker when she said the man was not from Treblinka. And Rosenberg was not content just to identify the picture: he gave, Levin said, a description that the court found "a very interesting, very edifying description"—and one very similar to Demjanjuk.

"Rosenberg described the ears that stand out and the beginnings of a bald patch"—features, Levin noted, not very common in a twenty-three-year-old. Demjanjuk himself had said his hair had begun to fall out in the Red Army. When Kollar put the Trawniki photo before Rosenberg in 1979, he observed "this may be a photograph from the time before Treblinka and at Treblinka he was already a little fuller. It may be that already he had better food in those days." This precision, Levin said, added to the high quality of Rosenberg's identification.

And so high was the quality of Czarny's identification, Levin now said, that the court would have been willing to convict on the basis of it alone. But it did not need to. There was the added weight of the identification by Rosenberg, which was of a high level of certainty; there was Epstein's identification of the 1951 picture and his identification of Demjanjuk's walk, which the court found of a "high standard"; Reichman's, which was of great significance; even Boraks, who, Levin said, had certain problems with dates on the stand, gave what was, in the judges' opinion, a forceful and clear identification of the accused. The cumulative weight was further enhanced, Levin said, by the recorded testimonies of the deceased survivors Turovsky, Goldfarb, and Lindvasser. Finally as to Hellman, it was true that he should have recognized Demjanjuk, but did not. His recollection was vague, and his memory failed him.

As to Otto Horn, the court, out of extreme caution, Levin said, would not make an incriminating finding solely on the basis of his identification—but it attached great weight to it. And even Danylchenko's deposition from the Soviet Union added cumulatively to the evidence: the man Danylchenko remembered was the same Otto Horn remembered; the same as the survivors remembered.

But, Levin said, Danylchenko's testimony highlighted another problem: how to reconcile the conflicting accounts of Ivan's where-abouts after March 1943. He read: "If Ivan Grozny was stationed in Sobibor from late March until this camp was demolished, how is this reconciled with the testimony of Horn, who says that after the uprising in August 1943, he saw Ivan there?"

Levin continued to read with energy: "In fact, it can be recon-ciled. Danylchenko says that Ivan, who excelled in his assistance to the Germans and who was extremely efficient in performing the labor of annihilation, was sent to hunt out Jews from the ghettos in the vicinity and to supply them by vehicles to the extermination camp.

"During the uprising, something happened. There was a change in the overall situation. Several Ukrainians had been wounded or even killed. Several of them disappeared, and Treblinka was in the process of being done away with. It stands to reason that Ivan was sent to Sobibor, as Danylchenko describes it, and later back to Treblinka, to help do away with the last traces of the camp."

Could there have been two Ivans? Levin asked. "It might have been contended that perhaps there were two Ukrainian Ivans who bore a remarkable resemblance to one another," he said. "One was Ivan Grozny, who operated at Treblinka, and the other was Ivan Demjanjuk, who operated at Sobibor. However, this would be a highly unlikely coincidence. When one speaks of an individual who has many salient features, such as being tall, balding at a relatively young age, protruding ears, a special build of nose and eyes—there has to be an extremely rare kind of coincidence in order for this to happen.

"The Ivans are indeed one and the same," Levin said con-clusively. "Demjanjuk who operated at Sobibor from late March 1943 and Ivan Grozny who operated in Treblinka during the sec-ond half of 1942 and early 1943, the Ivan identified by Danylchenko and the Ivan identified by the other identification wit-nesses are one and the same. Otto Horn said that Ivan was there in the camp, but occasionally he would go out on leave for extensive periods in time. When there were no shipments of Jews for annihila-tion, Ivan was not in Camp Two. Rosenberg, too, responded to our question and said that perhaps he didn't see Ivan a few weeks be-fore the uprising, even though, initially, he sounded like a person who was saying that he did see Ivan right up until the uprising.

"It may be remembered," Levin said, "that when it comes to the concept of time, on that different planet Treblinka, Treblinka was different from time as we know it now. One day was the same as another, day after day without change, and we read in Deu-teronomy chapter twenty-eight about the fact that when one's life is

in a continual state of threat and that one is continually afraid of
death, in which case, one cannot know just what reality is. Under
these circumstances, when the survivors said that they had seen Ivan
throughout that period, it means that Ivan was there and was involved in the work of extermination.

"Be that as it may, as to the question of whether he was there
until the uprising itself, we have grounds to believe that the survivors were wrong in stating this and that their testimony has nothing to rest on. Their descriptions of his evil deeds all relate to the
period of the gas chambers, which in the main came to an end toward February 1943. . . ."

During the day, as afternoon gave way to evening, the room felt
increasingly crowded. There were no more people than earlier—the
room had been full to capacity all day—but the air became thicker.
There was tremendous sadness filling the room.

As the facts piled on each other, each like the corpses in the pit,
the crimes became more and more real. There was an equation un-
derlying the conviction: as long as Demjanjuk was not guilty, one
could avoid the crimes Ivan had committed; they had been the work
of a demon on that other planet, Treblinka.

But if Demjanjuk was guilty, the crimes were real. Each murder
was a separate death, a corpse, a ghost that now came to life. The
sadness set in because it was all true, the deaths were real. This
man, Ivan, he did all this. It was true.

Levin was now coming to what would be the climax of ten hours of
reading—the judgment—yet his voice betrayed no change of emotion when he read, that the court "having weighed and considered
the evidence in its entirety, most painstakingly, cautiously, and with
the utmost care, we determine unequivocally and without the
slightest hesitation or doubt that the accused, Ivan John Demjanjuk,
standing trial before us, is Ivan who was called Ivan Grozny."

A few persons clapped. Levin looked up from his binder, surprised. Sternly, he asked the spectators to quiet themselves, and
then continued to read: "We therefore find him guilty as charged, a)
of crimes against the Jewish people; b) of crimes against humanity;
c) of war crimes; d) crimes against persecuted people. . . ."

Levin suggested that the sentencing hearing be held in a week.
Gill asked to argue it the next morning. This was an affront to the
court. Clearly, there was no way that in one night the defense could
study the verdict; and the defense argument should be based on it.

The prosecution requested a week to prepare. Its request was granted. The judges adjourned until then.

Many were milling outside the hall. The day had been draining. Numbing. Among the many lost in thought was Colonel Menachem Russek. For him, this moment had been a long time in coming. He had been the one to first suggest Demjanjuk be extradited to stand trial in Israel. He said: "It's been ten years. I had felt confident [about a conviction]. But to hear it pronounced is a complete satisfaction. It was revenge for all those who didn't make it."

The spectators left the hall. A little later, Demjanjuk was led from his back holding cell through the courtroom. Taking small steps, he raised his arms to the reporters and said, "I feel good. I am innocent. The wrong man. This is ridiculous what has happened Ha'yom [Hebrew for today]."

A week later, on Monday, April 25, 1988, the sky was still blue, but there was a chill in the air. Seating in the courtroom was by invitation only. John Demjanjuk Jr. arrived but was asked not to sit in the first rows. The security forces didn't want him too near his father. No other Demjanjuk family members were there. Demjanjuk, who said he was in too much pain to walk, appeared in a wheelchair, and blew kisses to the spectators while he was maneuvered into his dock.

Gill began by saying that the defense had been promised a translation of the verdict, but had never received one. Judge Tal corrected him; Gill conceded that, in fact, he had received a translation of the spoken parts and of the parts not spoken. It was not a good way to start.

Blatman stood. As the crimes committed showed an utter disregard of the conventions of human morality, and were done excessively, voluntarily, and zealously, he requested the death penalty.

Although editorial cartoonists had portrayed Demjanjuk as a small bolt in the swastika, a cog in the Nazi wheel, and Demjanjuk had tried to characterize himself as such, Blatman called him a major criminal, a central part of the death process, someone who acted "willfully, fervently, and with a show of initiative."

It was unimaginable, he said, that such a creature, who had physically murdered hundreds of thousands of Jewish persons, might be allowed to continue to walk the Earth.

All the while, Demjanjuk was nodding his head "no" vigorously, occasionally crossing himself, staring upward, his lips mumbling.

Gill argued that there was an irrevocable aspect to the death sentence, and in cases based on eyewitness identification, there was always a possibility of error. Gill asked the court that it not allow "the second horrendous crime to happen, the execution of an innocent man." Gill went further: "The taking of any innocent human life is a Holocaust." Gill asked that in such case, each individual eyewitness would have to be sufficient, not the cumulative weight of them.

Gill said Demjanjuk wanted to speak. He had no other submissions. The defense would not argue mitigation, Sheftel said, because to do so would imply guilt and the defendant admitted none.

Demjanjuk told the court: "Your Honors, it was very painful to hear the great tragedy that befell the Jewish people." His voice was deep and strong, "Not everyone survived, six million did not survive. They were killed in the Nazi camps, and they died a horrible death. . . . I hope they have all reached heaven.

"I believe the atrocities took place, and Ivan existed. It was not the prisoners who gave me the name Ivan Grozny, that human was not I, Ivan Demjanjuk.

"Last week you pointed to me. That's a mistake, a very grave mistake. . . .

"I have no doubt in my head, my heart is pure. Today, I do know, you must sentence Ivan the Terrible. But your sentence will not be against him but a person not guilty. I am innocent, and it's most unfortunate. I am filled with admiration at this democratic, cultured country, Israel. But in the twentieth century, how can it be possible for such an injustice to be done? I'm referring to the conviction. I am innocent, innocent and God," he said, pointing his right index finger upward, "is my witness. Thank you."

The judges retired.

People milled about, pacing, walking. It was hot in the courtroom, smoky in the foyer. The tension was thick; the pressure exhausting.

After a three-hour recess, the judges returned. Demjanjuk was wheeled in, and shouted in Hebrew, "I am innocent." Someone else shouted back, "*Atah shakran* [You are a liar]."

Judge Levin, with a haggard face and a tired voice, announced that Judge Tal would read the decision.

Tal's voice was equally sad, as he read: "Almost fifty years have elapsed since Treblinka. The accused has opened a new chapter in his life, far away from the scene of his crimes. He has established a new home. He has built himself a home and a family, and today when we must sentence him, we ask ourselves whether the time that has elapsed can in any way alleviate the sentence that must be imposed upon him. Most crimes that may be committed are forgivable. Time dulls the pain. Time desensitizes to a certain extent, and they fall subject to limitations. A person who has changed his course in life need not necessarily be sentenced because of crimes committed a long time ago. This holds true for most crimes. However, there are crimes against the Jewish people and against persecuted human beings that must be excluded from this. The same holds true for crimes against humanity and war crimes. These categories of crimes can never be forgiven, either within the letter of the law or forgiven in the hearts of men. The law, here and elsewhere, abrogates all prescription that would apply to such crimes.

"They can never be obliterated from memory. Any limitations, any statute of limitations on such crimes, would imply that they should be regarded as transcending time, as though Treblinka continues to exist, as though Jews are still being strangled and crying out in pain, as though the blood of the victims still cries out to us, like the blood of Zechariah the prophet. And Ivan the Terrible goes on to stab and to slaughter his victims indiscriminately, the old and the young, slashing off breasts and stabbing people, drilling in living flesh. We have not heard any arguments from the defense concerning extenuating circumstances. . . . The learned counsel, Mr. Gill, has cautioned us against the terrible possibility whereby sentencing the accused to death would amount to shedding an innocent man's blood in vain. . . . In fact, we are aware of the peril of an irrevocable sentence. This is one of the major reasons cited by those who are against the death penalty in principle. In Israel, too, this sentence may not be imposed for murder, but so long as the legislator has allowed to do so, the court, regardless of the personal views of the judges concerning capital punishment, may uphold it when it sees fit. The question is whether the present case is such a case.

"In our verdict, we established unequivocally and without the shadow of a doubt that the person before us, the accused, is Ivan the Terrible of Treblinka. Unlike the contention of the learned counsel, Mr. Gill, the fact that we did not make do merely with identification, which could, in fact, have existed in its own right, and we have seen fit to add to it cumulative evidence, which as a whole reinforces the identification, this fact in no way detracts from our certainty in determining that the accused is Ivan the Terrible.

"What punishment can be imposed on Ivan the Terrible, a person who killed tens of thousands of human beings and brutalized so many of his victims on their way to their deaths? What can he be sentenced to? A thousand deaths will not exonerate him or be weighed against his crimes. We may cite from Eichmann's appeal to the Supreme Court: 'We were fully aware of the fact that any sentence that we may mete out upon the accused will not measure up to the terrible deaths that he sentenced his victims to. Just as there can be no word in human language that would apply to the crimes of the type perpetrated by the accused, so, too, there can be no punishment in the books of any legislator that would be tantamount to these crimes. However, knowing that any punishment cannot be considered fitting or appropriate, we must nevertheless not be deterred from imposing punishment, meting out judgment against the accused.'

"True," Tal said, "the accused is not Eichmann. He was not the initiator of the annihilation. He did not organize the extermination of millions. However, he served as an archhenchman, who with his very own hands killed tens of thousands, humiliated, degraded, victimized, and brutalized, persecuted innocent human beings zealously.

"It is for this reason that we sentence him for the aforementioned crimes, to the punishment of death as stipulated."

The room was gray. The silence thick. Levin said, "This concludes our deliberations," and informed the defense it had forty-five days to lodge an appeal. The clerk called the courtroom to order once more. The judges rose and disappeared down their exit for the final time. The spectators rose to their feet and many broke out in spontaneous applause. The survivor witnesses who were sitting in the hall embraced. Then all turned, stunned, at the sight of teenagers near the back rows, standing on the chairs, hurling epithets at Sheftel, and singing "*Am Yisroel Hai* [Israel Lives]." They were led by an elderly survivor, visiting from Florida, who egged them on like a coach at a soccer game. The TV cameras, which had been turned intently on the audience, now focused on the youths—and more joined in.

A half-hour later, the courtroom emptied, Demjanjuk was led out again to a gaggle of reporters. Carol Rosenberg of United Press International shouted, "Are you going to hang?"

Demjanjuk shouted back: "I don't care what the judges say, I feel innocent." Reporters politely refrained from pointing out that *feeling* innocent is not the same as *being* innocent.

Tabloids around the world would proclaim his guilt and his death sentence. Editorials about "Justice in Jerusalem" and for/or/against the death penalty immediately would follow. Defense pundits would make their comments in columns and letters to the editors.

The Eichmann case, Hannah Arendt wrote in *Eichmann in Jerusalem*, "was built on what the Jews had suffered, not on what

Eichmann had done." Here the opposite was true. The crimes of Eichmann were easier to understand and believe true; it was harder to grasp the crimes of Ivan, because they were committed with such zeal by so simple, so human a criminal. But once proved, they became all the more real. Demjanjuk had given abstract evil a human face.

EPILOGUE

Demjanjuk's appeal to the Israel Supreme Court began on May 14, 1990, more than two years after he was found guilty and sentenced to death by the Jerusalem District Court. Arguments for both sides took seven weeks, one of the longest appeals in Israel's history.

Hearing the case were the president of the Supreme Court, Meir Shamgar, its vice-president, Menachem Elon, and three other senior justices, Yacov Maltz, Aharon Barak, and Eliezer Goldberg. Both Shamgar and Barak were former attorneys general.

The appeal was originally scheduled for December 1988. A week before it was to begin, on November 29, 1988, former Israeli district court judge Dov Eitan, who, the previous August, had joined the Demjanjuk defense team for the appeal, committed suicide by jumping from the fifteenth floor of the Eilan Tower in Jerusalem. The police ruled out foul play based upon witnesses in the hotel and the physical evidence, such as the shoe polish marks on the windowsill.

Though no satisfactory explanation for Eitan's death was forthcoming—there was no suicide note, and there had been no signs of depression to any friends, family, or colleagues—in hindsight, a picture of profound dissatisfaction emerged. Eitan had resigned from the judiciary several years before because of his disappointment with Israeli politics. No one knew what had drawn him to the Demjanjuk case, or to approach Sheftel and offer his services, as he did several months prior to his death. But one friend reported that Eitan had found no solace in the case.

At Eitan's funeral on December 1, 1988, seventy-year-old Yisrael Yehezekeli suddenly lunged at Sheftel, hurling a hydrochloric-acid solution at him. "This [Eitan's death] is because of you," he shouted. Sheftel was rushed to the intensive-care unit of Hadassah Hospital. Although there was no scarring to his face, the vision in his left eye was blurry. Upon examination, doctors discovered that the protective cover of his cornea was seriously damaged. Sheftel underwent one operation in Israel to remove the damaged tissue and another in Boston to transplant healthy cells from his right eye to his left to help the regeneration of tissue. Sheftel has now regained full eyesight, but he occasionally wears sunglasses to protect his sensitive left eye.

Yehezekeli was immediately arrested. An occasional visitor to the trial, on its last day the police had to escort him out of the hall for disturbing the proceedings with an emotional outburst. A Jerusalem old-age-home resident who worked part-time at the Ministry of Education, Yehezekeli had spent the war years in the Soviet Union and had lost many family members in Treblinka. Friends were quoted as saying that he was distressed by Eitan's death. He was subsequently convicted of aggravated assault and given a five-year jail sentence (two years of which were suspended), a $6,000 fine to cover the cost of surgery, and a further fine of 10,000 new Israeli shekels ($5,000) to compensate for Sheftel's suffering.

The appeal was delayed a year to allow Sheftel to recover and prepare. Sheftel then received a total of another year's delay to investigate material he had received from the Demjanjuk defense FOIA suit as well as other sources. Sheftel needed time because he was now on his own—Gill and Chumak had bowed out for the appeal.

Generally, appeals are dry matters where the rulings of the lower court are challenged; facts are not presented. But it is the task of every appellant to get the appeals court to see the case as new. In this, Sheftel was fortunate because the Israel Supreme Court has great discretion both in what they can review, and in what they can decide. The Supreme Court had the power to affirm the conviction and the sentence, or only the conviction and award a different sentence, return the case to a lower court, or acquit Demjanjuk.

Sheftel had discovered that the lower court had employed a press-clipping service to monitor coverage of the trial for violations of the *sub judice* law. This was, in and of itself, he argued, a violation of the law. The judges could not decide the case, he argued, when influenced by the harsh, circuslike media attention. The judges' attitude toward the defense in general, and him in particular, was manifest throughout the entire record and the verdict, according to

Sheftel. As a result, he said, the verdict should be void because of their obvious bias and prejudice.

During the two-year delay before the appeal was heard, many doubts about the case were raised in the media. A whole area of inquiry centered on Demjanjuk's whereabouts after he was accused of being at Treblinka. Gitta Sereny became particularly concerned about this. The testimony of SS man Gustav Munzberger in Dusseldorf, and a letter Sereny had uncovered from SS man Franz Suchomel, put Ivan of the death camps at Trieste. Sereny had traveled to Trieste to interview several persons who might have known Demjanjuk there. Though she found no proof positive of Demjanjuk having been in Trieste, she became convinced that Ivan of Treblinka had served in that locale.

But the court in its verdict had accepted the testimony from Danylchenko that made Demjanjuk's presence at Trieste unlikely. Danylchenko said Demjanjuk had served with him at Flossenburg. As Sereny saw it, only one of two scenarios could be true. Ivan Demjanjuk might have been at Trieste. In that case, Demjanjuk was Ivan the Terrible, the court had made a mistake by accepting the Danylchenko testimony, and having made a mistake, the hearing should be reopened. This would mean that Demjanjuk should not be executed. Alternatively, there could have been two Ivans: one who was the gas-chamber operator at Treblinka and served at Trieste; the other, an Ivan Demjanjuk who served at Sobibor with Danylchenko and accompanied him to Flossenburg. In this case, Demjanjuk's life should also be spared, so Sereny might argue.

Sereny even traveled to the Soviet Union to find out more about Danylchenko. She went to the Siberian city of Tobolsk and found his last-known apartment. She didn't find Danylchenko—he had passed away in 1985. But she did interview his widow, who knew little about his wartime activities; she also spoke with Madame Natalya Kolesnikova, the Soviet war-crimes procurator who confirmed that Danylchenko indeed had been tried and sentenced for his service at Sobibor, and had identified Demjanjuk. But Sereny uncovered no evidence that contradicted the testimony of the survivors and that gave Demjanjuk an alibi for the crimes at Treblinka.

This notion of a Sobibor alibi, provided by the Trawniki card and by Danylchenko, was conclusively dismissed in the Israel District Court's opinion. But it bears repeating that both Danylchenko and the card place Demjanjuk at Sobibor *after* March 1943. The crimes for which Demjanjuk was convicted mainly took place before then, between September 1942 and February 1943. By March 1943, due to the Nazis' success in their program of Jewish extermination, the trains to Treblinka from the ghettos slackened, and the gassing slowed down as well. Then Ivan, who was by all accounts an experienced guard favored by the Germans, was dispatched to where his services were needed—to Sobibor, less than a hundred miles down the road—from there to neighboring ghettos to round up Jews, or back to Treblinka for the final gassings in August. The notion that after Treblinka he may have been posted to Trieste, and/or to Flossenburg, does not contradict the conclusion that he was the gas-chamber operator at Treblinka. There was no evidence from Munzberger, Suchomel, or from Danylchenko to attest to when or for how long he was in Trieste or at Flossenburg, and no evidence that being at one rules out the possibility of being at the other. To the contrary, evidence was presented that after Treblinka was closed, *Wachmanner* were shunted around Central Europe.

Sheftel was also allowed to conduct a rogatory in Germany of a seventy-year-old German woman, Josephine Dolle, to prove there were Russians at Heuberg before November 1944 as Demjanjuk had claimed. Unfortunately for Sheftel, the prosecution was able to demonstrate in its cross-examination of her that her evidence was not firsthand.

Sheftel also submitted newly released material from the Demjanjuk defense: another account of Horn's 1979 OSI interview, this time from George Garand, the translator (this account varies slightly from Dougherty's 1979 account by having Horn single out the 1951 picture before the Trawniki photo). In each case this new evidence was trumpeted in the media as exonerative proof, though clearly it was no such thing. It was easy to make claims in the media, but much harder to support them in a court of law.

"60 Minutes," for example, found a Polish witness, Mrs. Maria Dudek, who claimed she knew intimately an Ivan Marshenko from the Treblinka death camp whom she called "Ivan the Terrible." CBS did not mention how it came to her, or why she had never been called to court by prosecution or defense attorneys. It is not because she was "suddenly" uncovered. Jerome Brentar told a Columbus, Ohio, newspaper that he had spoken with the woman in question six years before.

But days before the appeal was to begin, Sheftel asked for a delay to examine her evidence. Sheftel revealed that he had traveled to Poland and that Mrs. Dudek had repeated her statement to him but refused to come to Israel or give a signed statement. Sheftel also said the OSI had been withholding a document from Poland that had the name of SS auxiliaries at Treblinka including the name Marshenko.

Shaked countered for the prosecution that the document had not been withheld—in fact, it had been part of the court proceedings against Demjanjuk in the U.S. The list had been compiled by Polish authorities and based on what one Polish individual said he had been told by other Ukrainian guards. As for Mrs. Dudek, Shaked had no problem with the introduction of Sheftel's report of her statement—but he insisted that it be submitted together with a statement her husband had given Polish authorities. Although Mrs. Dudek had been unwilling to speak to Polish authorities, her husband, Kazimierz Dudek, had given a signed statement to Polish investigators in 1986. In it he recounted knowing the Treblinka guard who operated the gas chambers and who was known as Ivan the Terrible. Dudek explained that he lived in the nearby village of Wolga Okralnik where he ran a tavern Ivan visited regularly. He, too, said the gas-chamber operator's name was known to be Ivan Marshenko. But there was an interesting addendum. The police then placed eight pictures of Ukrainian guards before him. He pointed to Demjanjuk's Trawniki photo and positively identified it as Ivan Marshenko, the one who was known as Ivan the Terrible.

Shaked also pointed out that Marshenko was Demjanjuk's mother's maiden name! "When we questioned him [Demjanjuk] on this later, we got the impression that he instinctively felt that a connection with this name could be dangerous for him."

A decision is pending.

SELECTED BIBLIOGRAPHY

BOOKS AND PAMPHLETS

The books listed below were consulted for this work. For books on the Holocaust in general, or for further reading as to specific elements brought up in the narrative, I refer you to *The Holocaust in Books and Films: A Selected Annotated List* prepared by the Center for Studies on the Holocaust and available through the Anti-Defamation League.

Arad, Yitzhak. *Belzec, Sobibor, Treblinka*. Bloomington and Indianapolis: Indiana University Press, 1987. (cited below as *Arad*)

Arendt, Hannah. *Eichmann in Jerusalem*. New York: Penguin Books, 1977.

Bauer, Yehuda. *Anti-Semitism in the 1980's (Louis A. Pincus Memorial Lecture)*. New York: United Jewish Appeal, 1983.

Bellant, Russ. *Old Nazis, the New Right and the Reagan Administration*. Cambridge: Russ Bellant and Political Research Associates, 1988. (cited below as *Bellant*)

Blum, Howard. *Wanted! The Search for Nazis in America*. New York: Quadrangle/The New York Times Books Co., 1977.

Boshyk, Yury, ed. *Ukraine During World War II: History and Its Aftermath*. Edmonton: Canadian Institute of Ukrainian Studies, 1986.

Conot, Robert E. *Justice at Nuremberg*. New York: Carroll & Graf Publishers, 1986.

Deriomov, Mikhailo. *Let Justice Be Done*. Kiev: Politvidav Ukraini Publishers, 1987.

Donat, Alexander, ed. *The Death Camp: Treblinka*. New York: Holocaust Library, 1979. (cited below as *Donat*)

Drew, Margaret, ed. *Holocaust and Human Behavior, Annotated Bibliography*. New York: Walker & Co., 1988.

Friedlander, Saul. *Some Aspects of the Historical Significance of the Holocaust (The Philip M. Klutznik International Lecture)*. Jerusalem: Institute of Contemporary Jewry, the Hebrew University of Jerusalem, 1977.

Friedlander, Saul. *Reflections of Nazism*. New York: Avon Books, 1982.

Friedman, Tuviah. *The Hunter*. Haifa: Institute for the Documentation of Nazi War Crimes, 1961.

Gibson, John, Chairman; O'Connor, Edward M.; and Rosenfield, Harry, members. *The DP Story: The Final report of the United States Displaced Persons Commission*. Washington, D.C.: U.S. Government Printing Office, 1952. (cited below as *The DP Story*)

Hanusiak, Michael. *Lest We Forget*. Toronto: Progress Books, 1976.

Harel, Isser. *The House on Garibaldi Street*. New York: Viking Press, 1975.

Hausner, Gideon. *Justice in Jerusalem*. New York: Schocken Books, 1968.

Hilberg, Raul. *The Destruction of the European Jews*. New York: New Viewpoints, 1973.

Lanzmann, Claude. *Shoah*. New York: Pantheon Books, 1985.

Liebman, Charles S. and Don-Yehiya, Eliezer. *Civil Religion in Israel*. Berkeley and Los Angeles: University of California Press, 1983. (cited below as *Civil Religion*)

Marrus, Michael R. *The Holocaust in History*. Hanover and London: University Press of New England, 1987.

Myers, Ken. *The Rhetoric of Holocaust Denial Literature*. Evanston: unpublished master's thesis, Northwestern University, 1983.

O'Bryan, Conor Cruise. *The Siege*. New York: Simon & Schuster, 1986. (cited below as *The Siege*)

Ryan, Allan A., Jr. *Quiet Neighbors*. New York: Harcourt Brace Jovanovich, 1984. (cited below as *Ryan*)

Sachar, Howard M. *A History of Israel*. New York: Alfred A. Knopf, 1986. (cited below as *Sachar*)

Sereny, Gitta. *Into That Darkness*. New York: Vintage Books, 1974. (cited below as *Sereny*)

Sillitoe, Linda and Roberts, Allen. *Salamander*. Salt Lake City: Signature Books, 1988.

Simpson, Christopher. *Blowback*. New York: Weidenfeld & Nicholson, 1988. (cited below as *Simpson*)

Tolstoy, Nikolai. *Trial and Error*. Toronto: Justinian Press, 1986.

Troyat, Henri. *Ivan the Terrible*. New York: Berkley Books, 1984.

Trunk, Isaiah. *Jewish Responses to Nazi Persecution*. New York: Stein and Day, 1979.

Wagenaar, Willem A. *Identifying Ivan*. Cambridge: Harvard University Press, 1989.

West, Rebecca. *The New Meaning of Treason*. New York: Penguin Books, 1985.

"Holocaust 'Revisionism': A Denial of History—an Update." New York: The Anti-Defamation League. ADL Facts, winter 1986.

Liberty Lobby and the Carto Network of Hate. New York: The Anti-Defamation League. ADL Special Edition, Oct. 1987.

CASES AND STATUTES

"Immigration and Nationality Act," relevant sections re: deportation of Nazis living in the U.S.:

8 USCS sec. 1182 pp. 169.53
8 USCS sec. 1251 pp. 262.86
8 USCS sec. 1252 pp. 311.312.95
8 USCS sec. 1253 pp. 99.100
8 USCS sec. 1254 pp. 358.102

Also of interest: hearings before the subcommittee on Immigration, Citizenship and International Law, Committee on the Judiciary House of Representatives, 95th and 96th Congress. (cited below as *Hearings*)

United States v. *Demjanjuk,* 518 F. Supp. 1362 (N.D. Ohio 1981), *U.S.* v. *John Demjanjuk,* Civil Action # C77–923; "Trial Transcript Testimony" (Feb. 18, 1981): 1. Chiel Mayer Rajchman [also known as Yehiel Reichman], pp. 408–33; 2. Eliahu Rosenberg, pp. 499–521; "Trial Transcript Testimony" (Feb. 19, 1981): 1. Eliahu Rosenberg, pp. 523–27; 2. Georg Rajgrodski, pp. 574–89; 3. Sonia Lewkowicz, pp. 605–16; "Trial Transcript Testimony" (Feb. 20, 1981): 1. Pinhas Epstein, pp. 636–59; "Trial Transcript Testimony" (Mar. 4, 1981): Edward M. O'Connor, pp. 1020–58 (see also testimony of Edward O'Connor in *U.S.* v. *Kairys*); "aff'd," 680 F. 2d 32 (6th Cir. 1982), "cert. denied," 459 U.S. 1036 (1982).

United States v. *Demjanjuk,* 103 F.R.D. 1 (N.D. Ohio 1983) and C77–923 (N.D. Ohio filed Feb. 12, 1985), "aff'd," Nos. 85–3212 and 84–3106 (6th Cir. filed June 28, 1985).

Matter of Demjanjuk, File No. A8 237 417 (Imm. Ct. filed May 23, 1984), "aff'd," File No. A8 237 417 (Board of Immigration Appeals filed Feb. 14, 1985), "aff'd," No. 85–3198 (6th Cir. filed June 28, 1985), "cert. denied," U.S. No. 85–845 (Dec. 16, 1985).

Convention on Extradition between Israel and the United States, T.I.A.S. 5476, 14 U.S.T. 1717 (1963).

Matter of Extradition of Demjanjuk, 612 F. Supp. 544 (N.D. Ohio 1985). See *Demjanjuk* v. *Petrovsky,* 612 F. Supp. 571 (N.D. Ohio 1985) (denial of habeas corpus relief to extraditable respondent), "aff'd," 776 F. 2d 571 (6th Cir. 1985), "cert. denied," U.S. No. 85–1068 (Feb. 24, 1986). "See also *Demjanjuk* v. *Meese,*" No. 86–5097 (D.C. Cir. filed Feb. 27, 1986).

United States v. *Fedorenko,* 455 F. Supp. 893 (S.D. Fla. 1978), "rev'd," 597 F. 2d 946 (5th Cir. 1979), "aff'd sub nom. *Fedorenko* v. *United States,*" 449 U.S. 490 (1981).

See, also *Demjanjuk* v. *U.S.* Case No. C88–0864, Complaint for declaratory and injunctive relief. U.S.D.C. N.D. Ohio. (this is the Demjanjuk Defense Fund FOIA suit), and other related materials and exhibits (includes report of OSI investigator Harold Jacobs, cited below as *Jacobs*).

Attorney General of the Government of Israel v. *Adolf Eichmann,* Israel, District Court of Jerusalem (special panel: Landau J., President; Halevi and Raveh JJ.), Dec. 12, 1961; Supreme Court, sitting as a Court of Criminal Appeal (Olshan J., President; Agranat J., Deputy President; Silberg, Sussman and Witkon JJ.). May 29, 1962. E. Lauterpacht, International Law Reports, Vol. 36 (1968) pp. 18–226: District Court judgment; pp. 227–342: Supreme Court judgment. Report: (1962) 16 Piske Din, p. 2033 (in Hebrew). Report: (1965) 45 Pesakin Mehoziim 3 (in Hebrew).

After conviction, Eichmann appealed to the President of Israel for clemency, but this appeal was rejected. On May 31, 1962, Eichmann was executed by hanging; his body was cremated, and the ashes were scattered over the sea.

State of Israel v. *Ivan (John) Demjanjuk,* criminal case 373/86, verdict issued Apr. 18, 1989 (Government Printing Office); sentencing, Apr. 25, 1989.

ARTICLES

It is not possible to list all the articles, relevant and irrelevant, consulted in researching this book. I was fortunate to have had at my disposal the clip services and articles archives on Demjanjuk and Nazi war crimes prosecutions of the Columbia Graduate School of Journalism, *The New York Post* (thanks to Eric Fettmann), *The Plain Dealer* (Michele Lesie), the Anti-Defamation League in New York (Elliot Welles), Jerusalem (Harry Wall), and Cleveland (David Friedlander), and a complete set of *Ukrainian Weekly*'s for the past five years. In addition, one can not overlook the resources of YIVO, the New York Public Library, 42nd St. and Mid-Manhattan branches, which were a great help and a pleasure to work in. Suffice it to say that articles appearing between 1976 and the present in *The Plain Dealer, The Jerusalem Post, The Ukrainian Weekly, The New York Times, The Cleveland Jewish News, The New York Post,* and, as translated for me from *Davar, Maariv, Koteret Rashit,* were all consulted. A few other articles of specific interest are listed below:

Adams, Susan. "Ivan the Terrible's Terrible Defense." *The American Lawyer,* Oct. 1988, pp. 145–57.

Bahrick, H.P., Bahrick, P.O., and Wittlinger, R.P. "Fifty Years of Memory for Names and Faces: a Cross-sectional Approach. *Journal of Experimental Psychology: General,* 104, pp. 54–75, 1975. (cited below as *Bahrick*)

Boutwell, Jane. "Letter from Trieste." *The New Yorker,* Dec. 26, 1988, pp. 76–80.

Cardinale, Anthony. "Inside the 'Trial of the Century.'" *Buffalo,* Jul. 10, 1988, pp. 6–29.

Clements, William and Nicodemus, Charles, with reporting by Bushinsky, Jay. "Past Traps 'Cruel Ivan.'" *Chicago Daily News,* October 29–30, 1977. pp. 1, 6. (cited below as *Bushinksy*)

Cohler, Larry. "Bush Campaign Committee Contains Figures Linked to Anti-Semitic and Fascist Backgrounds," *Washington Jewish Week,* Sept. 8, 1988, pp. 3, 46–47. (cited below as *Cohler*)

Gottlieb, Mark. "The Hunt for Ivan." *Cleveland Magazine,* Nov. 1979, pp. 52–59, 156–66. (cited below as *Gottlieb*)

Loftus, Elizabeth. "Trials of an Expert Witness." *Newsweek,* June 29, 1987, pp. 10–11.

O'Connor, Edward M. "Our Open Society Under Attack by the Despotic State." *Ukrainian Quarterly,* spring 1984, pp. 17–49.

Ophuls, Marcel. "Letter from Lyons." *The Nation,* June 27, 1987, pp. 884–87.

Rosenbaum, Eli M. "Nazi War Criminals and the Law." *Patterns of Prejudice,* summer 1987, pp. 17–24.

Sereny, Gitta. "The Two Faces of Ivan of Treblinka." *The Sunday Times Magazine,* Mar. 20, 1988, pp. 20–38.

Tolstoy, Nikolai. "J'Accuse." *The Sunday Telegraph,* Dec. 13, 1987, pp. 15, 16.

State of Israel v. *Ivan (John) Demjanjuk,* criminal case 373/86 opened on Nov. 26, 1986, was immediately recessed and began in earnest on Feb. 16, 1987. The verdict was delivered on Apr. 18, 1988; the sentence on Apr. 25, 1988. There were 110 days of trial; 170 sessions of court, excluding the reading of the verdict, which took a full day; and the sentencing hearing and decision, which took another day.

The Demjanjuk trial was conducted in Hebrew. The proceedings were recorded verbatim, and were simultaneously translated into English. Witnesses speaking in German, Yiddish, or English were translated into Hebrew, and then into English for the benefit of defense counsel and observers. Translation was provided for Demjanjuk into Ukrainian; and when on the stand, from Ukrainian into Hebrew. Verbatim transcripts were available in Hebrew and English on a daily basis. The official record is in preparation and is to be in Hebrew. The available verbatim record in English is not completely accurate. I relied on my personal notes and the verbatim transcript. The exhibits were in a variety of languages, not always submitted with translation. The extensive U.S. proceedings also provided a wealth of material.

Spellings of places and names were a problem, as they vary from German to Polish, Yiddish, or Russian; and change again when transliterated from these languages into Hebrew or from Hebrew. For proper spellings, I have relied on court documents and on the resourceful staff of the YIVO.

What follows are not footnotes, in the traditional sense, but information related to the relevant text. Unless otherwise noted, all material in this book comes from court records and exhibits, as well as from interviews with the participants. Where the information was supplemented by other sources, the source is referred to—the full citation being in the bibliography above.

CHAPTER ONE

p. 3   **According to Israeli law and procedure . . .** Based on the British common law, the Israeli legal system is similar to the American legal system, more so in criminal cases than in other matters. However, there is no jury. Israel believes that appointed judges make for a more professional judiciary than elected ones. All judges are selected by a majority vote of a nine-member panel comprised of Supreme Court justices, lawyers, Knesset members, and two Cabinet members including the Minister of Justice. All judicial appointments are for life. There is also no constitution— so arguments, motions, and opinions are detailed.

p. 5   **Treblinka . . .** Information about Treblinka comes from *Arad* and testimony: See *Sereny; Donat; Ryan.*

CHAPTER TWO

p. 20   **Israel did not rush to commemorate the Holocaust . . .** See *Civil Religion; The Siege; Sachar.*

p. 21   **A trial of former Treblinka SS men . . .** See *Donat; Sereny.*

CHAPTER THREE

p. 25   **Those cases involving U.S. citizens would still be filed . . .** No statutory basis exists under current U.S. law for the assertion of federal criminal jurisdiction in Nazi cases, particularly since the crimes were committed beyond the territorial boundaries of the United States. Many experts believe that any attempt to amend the federal criminal code to cover such cases would run afoul of the Constitution's proscription against ex post facto legislation (Art. I, Sec. 9). As a result, the OSI's only recourse has been to petition the courts to denaturalize those suspected war criminals who have acquired citizenship and then, if successful, to institute separate deportation proceedings against them (if the individual never obtained naturalization as a U.S. citizen, the government may proceed in the first instance with deportation proceedings). See *Rosenbaum.*

p. 26   **The OSI . . .** By the end of 1989, the OSI (including its predecessor unit) had brought legal proceedings against sixty-four suspected Nazi criminals, obtained thirty-one denaturalization orders and eighteen deportation orders, and actually deported ten suspects, two of them to the Soviet Union. In addition, fifteen individuals are known to have fled the United States rather than face or complete such legal proceedings. The OSI has also participated in proceedings that resulted in the extradition of three Nazi suspects previously prosecuted by OSI (Andrija Artukovic to Yugoslavia, Bruno K. Blach to West Germany, and John Demjanjuk to Israel).

p. 26   **The list was compiled by . . .** We will perhaps never really know the true source of the allegations. Whether the information came his way through an agent of the KGB is something even he does not know. But there is a connection between the organization of the Society for Cultural Exchange, the newspaper Hanusiak works for, and the Ukrainian newspaper that first published articles on Demjanjuk and that first published the Trawniki card. The card itself contains on its face the information that, in fact, may be the prime source for the allegations against Demjanjuk. However, all of the above does not explain how the Soviets, even if they found the Trawniki card, and then leaked the information on it, to Hanusiak, knew Demjanjuk was alive and living in Cleveland.

Hanusiak can no longer recall where he found the Demjanjuk charge. It is clear that he did not uncover the information, firsthand, for Hanusiak never went to Dub Macharenzi, Demjanjuk's village, nor ever saw or was shown the Trawniki card. It seems more likely that he found the allegations in a Soviet publication. This is supported by journalist Mark Gottlieb, who interviewed Hanusiak in 1979. At the time, Hanusiak claimed he found Demjanjuk's name in a European Ukrainian-language newspaper. We will probably never know how the allegation came to Hanusiak's attention. But we do know how it came to the attention of the Immigration and Naturalization Service.

p. 27   **Early in November Senator Javits wrote . . .** Sen. Javits's letter of Nov. 6, 1975, confirming receipt of Hanusiak's list and its forwarding to the Justice Department's special task force, is to be found in the Department of Special Collections of the State University of New York at Stonybrook, Jacob Javits Archives, SUNY Stonybrook.

CHAPTER FOUR

p. 32   **Early in May 1976 . . .** See *Gottlieb*.

p. 33   **The INS also contacted the witnesses on Demjanjuk's naturalization . . .** See *Gottlieb, Bushinsky,* and *Jacobs;* author interviews Mark Gottlieb, Jay Bushinsky.

p. 38   **In January 1977, Jay Bushinsky ...** See *Bushinsky*. Hellman died on Aug. 21, 1984; Lindvasser in Mar. 1977.

CHAPTER FIVE

p. 41   **The overwhelming majority ...** See *Ryan*.

p. 42   **The DP Act. ...** See *The DP Story; Hearings; Gottlieb; Bushinsky*.

p. 46   **John, Vera, and Lydia arrived in the United States ...** See *Gottlieb, Bushinsky*.

p. 49   **The allegations shocked ...** same as above.

CHAPTER SIX

p. 50   **interview with Bob Franken ...** See *Gottlieb*. Journalist Matthew Rinaldi reports in *The Jerusalaem Post* that in Feb. 1979 he visited Demjanjuk and had a brief interview. "Asked why he thought the charges against him were filed, Demjanjuk answered: 'It's the Jews,' he said bitterly. 'The Jewish organizations are all telling lies about me.'" (Mar. 6, 1979)

p. 51   **In two separate photographs ... "the Trawniki card." ...** The picture of the Trawniki card as it appears in *News from Ukraine* is different from the original in two respects: the original bears purple ink translation into Russian from 1948, and the name of the translator appears followed by the initials "N.G.B."—the old name of the KGB; neither translation nor translator is visible. On the original, the entry "Sobibor" is slightly obscured by the translation; in the newspaper, the letters have been filled out.

p. 52   **Kollar ...** Kollar retired in 1984.

p. 53   **Kollar reread Radiwker's files ...** In reading Rosenberg's file, Kollar found no statement as to Fedorenko, so he invited him to come in again. Rosenberg was shown the same collection of photographs. And though there is some conflict as to whether he immediately pointed again at Demjanjuk's photo, Rosenberg did point to Fedorenko's photo and said: "This reminds me of a Ukrainian guard from the Ukrainian staff in the Treblinka camp. When I saw the man from the guard detail, then I recalled him as one of the guard staff who accompanied our transport from Warsaw, from the concentration place and on the train to Treblinka."
In the Israeli district court's verdict, they found it interesting to mention, with regard to the accuracy of Rosenberg's memory, that Fedorenko's own testimony revealed that he arrived at

Treblinka as part of a unit of Ukrainian guards, accompanying a transport from Warsaw at the end of summer 1942—which, the court noted, conformed to the period of Rosenberg's arrival in Treblinka on Rosh Hashanah.

p. 54   **The United States Court of Appeals, Fifth Circuit . . .** The U.S. Court of Appeals in a three-to-none ruling on June 29, 1979, told Judge Norman Roettger Jr. in Ft. Lauderdale to cancel the naturalization certificate of Fedorenko. "Immigration law does not allow a defense, in a naturalization case, that a material misrepresentation was motivated by fear of what might have resulted if the applicant told the truth." In effect, because of Fedorenko's admission, the truth of the survivors' testimonies was not in question.

p. 56   **Horrigan and Moskowitz were determined that even without the original . . .** Horrigan received a photocopy of the Trawniki card and on Nov. 8, 1979, he filed papers in federal court disclosing to the defense that he could produce a photo and document pertaining to Demjanjuk.

p. 61   **There was even a notation that the OSI had received . . .** OSI did receive summaries of several Soviet protocols. There was a report of five Soviet citizens who did identify Demjanjuk from photos (I. N. Ivchenko on Sept. 18, 1979, in Vinnitsa, Ukraine; I. T. Danylchenko on Nov. 22, 1979, in Tiumen RSFSR; P. S. Bondaruk, July 9, 1979, in Vinnitsa, Ukraine; P. S. Garbruk, July 9, 1979, in Vinnitsa; I. M. Bazeluk, Sept. 25, 1979, in Vinnitsa—all conducted in the presence of procuracy counsel and in the presence of two witnesses) and one who did not (N. P. Malagan in Novo Petrova). The fact that not all identified Demjanjuk was seen as proof that they were not coached—otherwise why include it? Allan Ryan later said that these statements were thought to be of little value in a U.S. proceeding because the statements were not taken in the presence of defense attorneys and no cross-examination took place. They were never used or produced in court, said OSI attorney Bruce Einhorn in a later memo, because "these protocols did not relate to Demjanjuk's service at Treblinka. Moreover, OSI is unaware of exactly how Soviet authorities located the subjects of those protocols." Its existence, though, was disclosed to the Demjanjuk defense as part of the interrogatories prior to the denaturalization trial.

In Mar. 1981, during Demjanjuk's denaturalization trial, *The Plain Dealer* reported that the statements were submitted of five Russian witnesses who served at Trawniki, one of whom, Nikolai Dorofeev, said he had heard the name Demjanjuk while at Trawniki and he identified the photographs of Demjanjuk as resembling the facial characteristics of the person he knew with that name.

CHAPTER SEVEN

p. 64   **There was no jury** . . . There is never a jury in a denaturalization proceeding. Congress does not include it in the category of civil cases where jury trials are allowed.

p. 64   **Twenty federal marshals** . . . See *Ryan*.

p. 65   **Otto Horn did not actually appear** . . . Demjanjuk's attorneys were flown to Germany at government expense to cross-examine Horn.

p. 68   **Fedorenko denied ever seeing** . . . It is not so surprising that Fedorenko would not claim to recognize Demjanjuk; he was not looking for more people who would identify him—or to show himself as having had any contact with the death camp.

p. 68   **Joseph Tholl never rendered an opinion** . . . Tholl, a forensic documents examiner for the Cleveland Police Department, died a few years after the trial.

CHAPTER EIGHT

p. 71   **Menten and Wagner** . . . Wagner committed suicide in 1979. Menten died in 1987, at the age of eighty-eight, in a nursing home. Tried by the Dutch and sentenced to ten years, he steadfastly maintained his innocence, claiming that he was the victim of a KGB plot.

p. 72   **Col. Russek** . . . Menachem Russek retired from the Israel Police at the end of 1989.

p. 72   **The "right case" for the first extradition** . . . Valentin Trifa had been denaturalized in the U.S. for having been head of Rumania's Iron Guard and having incited crowds to murderous riots against Jews in Bucharest. As he was awaiting deportation, pressure was brought on Israel and cries went up from Holocaust survivors that Israel should take Trifa and try him. But for Israel, Trifa was not the right case. Said Gouldman, "There were no witnesses who we felt could show his actual participation in the mass murders. It was very difficult to get a direct link between some rather anti-Semitic speech that he may have made on the radio and the fact that some mobs went out and committed atrocities there. There obviously was a connection but it would have been much harder to get a conviction, than a case [like Demjanjuk] where you've got witnesses who say, 'Yes, I saw him killing. I saw him pushing them into the gas chambers. He shot my friend.'" And for the first case since Eichmann, Israel wanted a direct connection to the murders of their people.

p. 73   **Fedorenko . . .** Fedorenko was deported to the Soviet Union in Dec. 1984; sentenced to death, after a ten-day public trial, in June 1986; and his execution, by firing squad, was announced in July 1986.

p. 74   **[O'Connor had] testified . . .** Edward O'Connor testified that although repatriation was supposed to have ended in 1945, it did occur in some isolated instances; more important, fear of repatriation continued. At a later date, he said, those who had lied on their visa forms were given an opportunity to correct such misinformation; and if the sole cause was fear of repatriation, they still would have been eligible for admission under the DP Act. He agreed, however, when asked, that anyone who lied on their application to conceal Nazi service, would not be admitted.

p. 74   **Mark O'Connor . . .** O'Connor, born in 1943, attended Connisius College, of which his father was a trustee, and he is a 1968 graduate of State University of New York at Buffalo Law School. O'Connor's trial experience was limited. The case he often speaks of as a "precedent-setting international case regarding sovereign immunity," *Grey* v. *Republic of Congo,* was a landlord-tenant dispute that he settled, eventually, out of court. An official at the Embassy recalls that they came to O'Connor because of his father's connections to the Organization of African States, and to the Kennedy administration. The Embassy was, he said, pleased with O'Connor—they did remain in the building, though he recalls there was a dispute over the fees.

Mark O'Connor also appeared in the press in 1985 as the lawyer for Arthur Rudolph. Rudolph, a former NASA rocket scientist, was questioned in connection with alleged war crimes at the Mittelworkl V-2 rocket complex. In 1984, Rudolph had signed an agreement with the OSI whereby he gave up his U.S. citizenship and moved to Germany. However, a year later, O'Connor was saying Rudolph was railroaded by the KGB, and that he took the case voluntarily. No case was ever filed by O'Connor.

p. 74   **He promised he'd stay involved . . .** Edward O'Connor died in 1985 at age seventy-seven. Brentar would later comment that in hiring Mark O'Connor, the Demjanjuk defense thought they were hiring the father, but that they got the son. "And Mark turned out not to be the man his father was," Brentar said.

p. 74   **John Gill** . . . Gill, a native of Cleveland, won a basketball scholarship to Baldwin Wallace College. Following service in Italy during the Korean War, he attended law school at night while working for the Cleveland Fire Department by day. He served for four years as a prosecutor in Brookpark, Ohio.

Gill met O'Connor on a prior related matter: shortly after the decision was issued denaturalizing Demjanjuk, a meeting was held at the Lakeside Holiday Inn in Cleveland to discuss "the use of Soviet evidence." The meeting was sponsored by CAUSE (Committee Against the Use of Soviet Evidence). Frank Walus flew in from Chicago to address the meeting, his air fare paid by CAUSE (for more about Walus see *Ryan* and note on Walus below). At the request of Jerome Brentar, he stayed at Brentar's home. In his speech, Walus spoke of a "Wiesenthal forgery factory" and also said Wiesenthal had been behind the false charges against him. The comments were picked up by the Cleveland press. Wiesenthal sued Walus for libel.

As the suit was filed in Cleveland, Walus's counsel in Chicago retained the firm of Kelley and Gill as local counsel. According to an article in *The American Lawyer,* they chose the firm from Martindale Hubbel, in part, because it was a litigation firm with a non-Jewish name. Though Tom Kelley initially was involved in the case, by the time it was to be argued, his partner Gill handled it.

As the Walus libel suit was tangentially related to the Demjanjuk matter, O'Connor contacted Kelley and Gill and asked to be involved. Chicago counsel was contacted and they agreed to let O'Connor be cocounsel. Walus countersued Wiesenthal, claiming he was behind his own false prosecution. O'Connor was of the opinion that they could reap millions on the case, Gill recalled at a later date. Gill thought that they should settle. The case proceeded nonetheless. The pleadings of the Walus libel defense and countersuit are full of hyperbole, spelling mistakes, nonsequiturs, and run-on sentences. Eventually, the case was settled out of court, with a letter of apology from Walus, and a payment for Wiesenthal's attorney fees and court costs.

During the course of their work together, O'Connor told Gill about the Demjanjuk case and about the Trawniki card. Gill told O'Connor of his interest in graphology. O'Connor was impressed and suggested that he could use someone who knew about document examination in the Demjanjuk case. Gill accepted.

p. 75   **Vlassov army** . . . Andrei Vlassov was a general in the Red Army who was taken prisoner by the Germans in July 1942. He was considered one of the Soviet Union's most brilliant and successful generals, having distinguished himself in the defense of Moscow and in military engagements outside Leningrad. Upon his capture he revealed himself to be strongly anti-Stalinist and anti-Communist and willing to collaborate with the Germans under certain conditions. Germans saw good propaganda value in Vlassov and set him up in Davendorf, a suburb of Berlin at the propaganda center of the supreme German command. There he remained for two years trying to fulfill his wish of establishing a Soviet army. In summer 1944, as the Germans were suffering increasing defeats, and the internal struggles among the German leadership intensified, Himmler was ready to conscript persons of all nationalities into SS forces. On Sept. 16, 1944, Himmler gave Vlassov the approval to set up what had been known till then as the ROA—the Russian Liberation Army.

p. 76   **Ties to Holocaust revisionists** . . . See *Cohler*. Both Brentar and Nazarenko would be asked, in 1988, to resign from the Ethnic Nationalities Committee of George Bush's presidential campaign, because of their views and affiliations. Brentar has denied he is a Holocaust revisionist. But he has said that "the whole truth is not known," and spoken of the "alleged gassings." In a 1985 Cleveland radio interview, he said that the only Jews who survived the camps "collaborated" with the Nazis. Brentar told the *Pittsburgh Press* in Feb. 1987 that Demjanjuk's conviction in Israel would "be a curse on them [the Jews] and their children and grandchildren, just as was the crucifixion of Jesus Christ." A Holocaust revisionist newsletter referred to Brentar as "the energetic Cleveland Revisionist." Reiss's views were made known in a letter he wrote to American authorities condemning the Nuremberg proceedings.

See *Simpson, Bellant* for a discussion of the political alliances between far-right supporters of Baltic-American and other ethnic nationalities now incorporated into the USSR, anti-Communists, and Holocaust Revisionists—this was one of the more troubling resonances of the Demjanjuk case. The link to all of these for the Demjanjuk defense was Edward M. O'Connor and Brentar. The fact that Mark O'Connor and the Demjanjuk family relied on these persons would continue to taint their defense.

CHAPTER NINE

p. 80   Eugen Turovsky . . . died on Nov. 29, 1980; Avraham Goldfarb on July 19, 1984.

p. 81   **Modern security and surveillance** . . . Demjanjuk was isolated from the prison's six-hundred other prisoners, watched by three guards by day, two at night, and observed on closed-circuit TV.

p. 82   **For his first detention hearing** . . . Under Israeli law, a suspect can only be held in prison by police authorities for fifteen days, a period of time that may be renewed by a remand hearing. After ninety days, a prisoner can only be held by permission from the Supreme Court president.

p. 83   Demjanjuk also told his investigators that: "People from Vlassov's army—including Ivan himself—were transferred from the Heuberg camp to Flossenburg before the end of the war. He said they lived in barracks there and did nothing. In the course of the conversation, Ivan was asked to detail the precise dates and he retracted that he had reached Flossenburg before the end of the war, and said he reached Flossenburg *after* the war."

In a later conversation, Demjanjuk said, "I told you I was at Flossenburg, but I was mistaken because I looked at a map and didn't find such a place. I asked many people and they said there was no prisoner-of-war camp there at all. There was a concentration camp there." And in his testimony in court in Jerusalem, he denied he was ever at Flossenburg.

p. 84   **Ish Shalom knocked Demjanjuk's hands off him** . . . After the trial, Ish Shalom told an Israeli Police magazine that Demjanjuk had tried to choke him before he pushed his hands away.

p. 86   **James McDonald** . . . McDonald reportedly worked for Edward O'Connor in Germany from 1950 to 1953. He said he screened persons, and later said he was a background analyst to evaluate CIC reports to screen out spies and criminals. He is at work on a book on the Demjanjuk case. James McDonald wrote recently "I continue to marvel at the parallel between the Demjanjuk and the Dreyfus cases. Why do we visit such atrocities on innocent people?"

McDonald also was the sponsor of a VFW resolution at its national convention in 1984 asking for an investigation of OSI; and claiming that extradition for war crimes should not be allowed or else U.S. citizens may be apprehended for alleged war crimes in Southeast Asia. McDonald also has been featured, interviewed for, and has authored articles for *Spotlight*, the newspaper of the anti-Semitic Liberty Lobby.

p. 89   **Dov Levin would preside** . . . Dov Levin, born in Tel Aviv in 1925, fifth generation in the country. He served in the Israel Freedom Fighters. Appointed to Tel Aviv Magistrate's Court in 1966; appointed Tel Aviv District Court Judge in 1972; was made vice president of that court in 1979; and was appointed Supreme Court Justice in Feb. 1982. Levin would not be without sympathy for the defense: as a young attorney, Levin had assisted in the defense of Malchiel Greenwald in the Kastner case. This controversial case, ostensibly a libel matter, questioned whether Rudolf Kastner, as one of the leaders of the Jewish community in

Budapest, saved Jewish lives by his dealings with the Nazi authorities or collaborated in the death of many more. The case, and Levin's role in it, are described in Ben Hecht's controversial work, *Perfidy*.

p. 89   **Zvi Tal** . . . Zvi Tal was born in Poland in 1927, emigrated to then Palestine in 1935. He graduated Hebrew University Law School in 1953, practicing law until 1978 when he was appointed to the District Court.

p. 89   **Dalia Dorner** . . . Dalia Dorner, born in 1934 in Turkey, came to then Palestine in 1944. She graduated from Hebrew University Law School in 1956. Recruited to the Israel Defense forces in 1960, where she served in the Judge's Advocate-General's unit, she later served from 1973–79 as a military judge and was appointed a district court judge in 1979. She has served on the Military Court of Appeals.

p. 90   **Frank Walus** . . . In 1977, Frank Walus, a Polish immigrant living in Chicago, was charged as a Nazi war criminal. He was identified from a grainy enlargement of his 1959 visa photograph by eleven Holocaust survivors who testified in court about the SS man they recalled as "the butcher of Kielce." The case would have seemed to go for Walus. The man the survivors recalled was, they said, twenty-five or twenty-six; Walus at the time was eighteen. Further, Walus had an alibi, and documentary proof to support it. But Judge Julius Hoffman would not let the evidence be introduced; Walus was denaturalized. Subsequent to the decision, Walus was able to find other documentary proof to support his alibi. The Court of Appeals found the irregularities and the alibi evidence sufficient to warrant a new trial; but instead, the OSI withdrew and apologized to Walus. For many, the Walus case has come to symbolize that testimony by Holocaust survivors can not be trusted. Actually, the case is testament to the fact that a credible alibi is always more persuasive than eyewitness testimony. For more on Walus's case, see *Ryan*. Walus joined the Demjanjuk defense team, speaking at rallies and traveling to Europe at Brentar's expense to search for evidence.

p. 92   **Sheftel was not an unknown** . . . As a law student, Sheftel formed the Meyer Lansky Committee, four students who protested the cancellation of Lansky's visitor visa in Israel—or, as Sheftel put it, "the U.S. meddling in the most important right a Jew has—the law of return." They kept in touch. In 1981, Sheftel, by then a practicing attorney, garnered headlines when he won Meyer Lansky the right to a visa to visit Israel. It was a right Lansky never exercised because Israel asked him to put up a bond—and, according to Sheftel, Lansky replied, "My word is my bond." Sheftel has said, "If Meyer Lansky had been in Treblinka, those Ukrainians wouldn't have lasted a month." On another occasion, he said, "If there were six million Jews like Meyer Lansky, there never would be a Holocaust in the world."

CHAPTER ELEVEN

p. 107 **Transforming the trial into an event . . .** At first, the trial was not televised, because the government didn't think there would be sufficient interest; by the second week, though, the Communications Ministry had arranged to broadcast the entire proceeding on the country's experimental second channel.

p. 108 **With the testimony of survivors . . .** Sheftel made reference to the statements of three survivors: Goldfarb and Rosenberg, who are discussed in the book, and that of Chaim Staier. Arad had met Staier in Australia, but was not familiar with his testimony. Chaim Staier appeared in the courtroom in Jerusalem in June 1987. Ernie Meyer, of *The Jerusalem Post,* interviewed the seventy-eight-year-old Treblinka death-camp survivor. "Staier says during the revolt he met Ivan the Terrible in the camp's yard, picked up a shovel and hit him. The blow did not kill him, because when Staier returned to the same spot minutes later, the Ukrainian was gone. . . . He said that later, with the help of other prisoners, he killed other Ukrainian guards including Ivan's partner, Nikolai, with the blade of a large pair of tailor's scissors." The prosecution interviewed Staier as well but did not call him as a witness. Neither did the defense, who originally said he would appear at their behest.

CHAPTER TWELVE

p. 119 **Nahalat Yitzhak . . .** The cemetery, Nahalat Yitzhak, is in Givat Haim, a suburb of Tel Aviv. In the cemetery are several memorials to the Holocaust. The Treblinka monument itself consists of mock tombstones three feet high intertwined with barbed wire at the end of which there is big rendering of an oven made of large stones piled one on the other.

CHAPTER FOURTEEN

p. 143 **If he could name his children . . .** In 1967, an investigator from Yad Vashem visited Boraks and interviewed him but decided not to record his testimony because, according to her notes, Boraks had become confused and forgotten the name of his youngest son. But, in fact, as Boraks explained later, he was confused by *her* question as to which family she was asking about—the one he lost in Treblinka or the one he made in Israel. And the notes she took are an accurate record of his experience at Treblinka.

CHAPTER SIXTEEN

p. 155 **Reichman would not look Demjanjuk in the eye . . .** After the trial, Reichman said that Ryan had misunderstood him. He did not want to look Demjanjuk *in the eye,* lock eyes with him, at Treblinka, because to draw attention to yourself could mean death. But that did not mean that he never *saw him.* Or, for that matter, never *looked* him in the face. As for the Cleveland trial, looking Demjanjuk in the eye made him tremendously angry, so angry that he took a tranquilizer after his testimony. But this didn't mean that he didn't look at him, see him, recognize and remember him.

CHAPTER EIGHTEEN

p. 167 **Innocent until proven guilty . . .** Under Israeli legal doctrine, so-called ancient documents—documents that are over twenty years old—and so-called public documents—documents that are official documents of a competent authority—are presumed authentic, and the defense must show them to be unauthentic.

p. 167 **Trial of Trawniki commander Karl Streibl . . .** The Streibl trial began in 1960 as part of a complex of trials—it was separated from the others in 1969. The indictment was issued in 1970; the trial ran from Dec. 1972 until June 1976—when Streibl was acquitted. The appeal, which lasted three years, was rejected.

p. 168 **July 19, 1942 . . .** July 19, 1942, was also of historical significance, Sheffler said, because it was the date on which Himmler ordered that all Jews should be deported from the general gouvernement (i.e., killed) by the end of the year.

p. 169 **L.G. Okzow . . .** Professor Sheffler told the court that L.G. Okzow was an agricultural enclave, a farm, at which there were forced-laborers. The agricultural estates were part of a "utopian dream" of the creation of SS defensive bases at the frontiers of the Reich territory. A current Polish atlas lists a village named Ochowsa, outside Chelm. Given that entries at Trawniki were written phonetically by *Volksdeutscher,* this may explain Demjanjuk's insistence on Chelm as his alibi, even if he was never there as a POW; and why he listed Chelm on his 1948 IRO form even though he can't describe anything about the Chelm camp itself.

p. 169 **But whose Treblinka posting was not listed** . . . Other documents submitted, which supported the fact that service passes did not always accurately list entries, included:

1. A letter dated Dec. 12, 1942, from Streibl to Globochnik, protesting that *Wachmanner* were being posted from one camp to another without his knowledge.

2. The *Personalbogen,* the camp's individual personnel record, of Amanaviczius lists two postings: commando Lublin and prisoner camp Lublin, whereas from another document—personnel strength in Treblinka—it is apparent that Amanaviczius was stationed at labor camp Treblinka.

3. In the *Personalbogen* of Fritsch, it was entered that he was posted to labor camp Treblinka, while from his index card, it was shown that he was posted to Orinburg and death camp Treblinka.

4. In the service certificate of Ivan Wollenbach, one of the three new Trawniki *Dienstausweis* later submitted, no postings are listed, although it is unreasonable that he was not posted anywhere.

5. In the payment ledger of Rudolf Reiss, who testified that he served at Trawniki training camp from Dec. 20, 1941, until Aug. 1943, there is no record of that.

6. In the *Personalbogen* of Tchernievski, it was listed that on July 27, 1942, he was posted to labor camp Treblinka whereas, in the index card, it is listed that on the same date he was posted to death camp Treblinka, and from a third document, a promotion letter, it is evident that indeed he was at death camp Treblinka.

p. 172 **Cantu used a hypodermic-needle probe** . . . In each case, the samples were shared with the expert for the defense. And when other samples from the other documents were taken, the same samples were also sent to the defense so that their expert might examine them.

CHAPTER NINETEEN

p. 179 **Derogatory posters of Sheftel** . . . A poster set up alongside a black-and-white picture of the Holocaust read: "Lawyer Sheftel, 6 Million Holocaust Victims Are Accusing You As A Traitor."

p. 181 **Edward Nishnic** . . . Edward Nishnic was born June 6, 1955, in Cleveland. His official biography lists him as of "Third generation Carpatho-Rus background"; attended high school and community college in Cleveland; worked for employment agency where he met Irene in 1977 (she was a secretary); married in 1983; son, Edward Nishnic, Jr., "Eddie," born Dec. 10, 1985; formed John Demjanjuk Defense Fund Apr. 86. The John Demjanjuk Defense Fund was incorportated as a not-for-profit corporation in June 1986.

CHAPTER TWENTY

p. 192 **If the defense thought Schaeffer was so good a witness, they could call him** . . . Under Israeli criminal procedure, when the prosecution waives calling a witness, they automatically give the defense the right to summon the witness after the prosecution rests and even cross-examine the witness on the stand.

p. 192 **Horn** . . . With regard to Horn's identification, several documents and accounts that vary slightly were before the court. The initial meeting took place Nov. 14, 1979. Present were Horn, Moskowitz, Dougherty, and translator George Garand. Dougherty submitted a report to the OSI that was received less than a week later on Nov. 20, in which he describes the events that took place. This is thought to be the most reliable account. Horn himself gave a deposition at the American Consulate in 1980; he testified in 1981. In 1983, as described, he was visited by defense aides. In 1986, he gave a statement to the German police describing the circumstances of the 1983 statement; and reaffirming that he saw Ivan from close up every day and recalled his facial features distinctly; and in 1986, George Garand gave an affidavit to his recollection of events.

CHAPTER TWENTY-ONE

p. 196 **Prof. Matityahu Meisel** . . . A lecturer in history at Tel Aviv University who specializes in military history, in particular the military history of the USSR and WWII. A graduate of the Hebrew University of Jerusalem, his doctorate is from the University of Rochester, N.Y. He also studied for two years at the Center for Russian Studies at Harvard.

p. 197 **Dr. Shmuel Krakovsky** . . . A Holocaust survivor, he wrote his doctorate on the Jewish armed resistance in Poland, and has also published a book on the same subject. Dr. Krakovsky is the head of the Yad Vashem archives and a lecturer at Tel Aviv University and is considered an expert on POW camps in Nazi Germany.

p. 199 **Dr. Shmuel Spektor** . . . A graduate of the Hebrew University of Jerusalem, he wrote his doctorate at the Institute for Contemporary Judaism there. Dr. Spektor is the head of the Center for Holocaust Studies, and he specializes in the subject of the Holocaust of Ukrainian Jews, the problems of the Ukrainian people, and the Ukrainian army divisions. He has also written a book about the destruction of the Ukrainian Jews. Dr. Spektor has worked for thirty years at Yad Vashem and has visited numerous archives, including many visits to Poland.

p. 201 **John Broadley** . . . Broadley was a partner in the Washington, D.C., office of Chicago's Jenner and Block. He told Susan Adams of *The American Lawyer* in Oct. 1988, that he spent approximately $160,000 of pro-bono lawyer time on the FOIA litigation. The decision not to join the Demjanjuk defense was one made by Broadley in consultation with the firm's partnership. Though many partners had strong feelings about the case, financial considerations were the deciding factor. The case had been tendered as a paying matter and the firm thought the Demjanjuk family's funding problems too great. Broadley, though, continued his involvement in the ongoing FOIA suit.

p. 204 **Witnesses Samuels, Wuyek, de Ribes, Dubovitz** . . . Though O'Connor and other Demjanjuk defense supporters would continue to cite these witnesses to the media, the Demjanjuk defense never submitted their testimony.

CHAPTER TWENTY-TWO

p. 207 **Bilitz** . . . Sheffler testified that Bilitz was known to be an SS man, not a guard—and he was never referred to as Ivan, except for the notation in the UN war-crimes archives, whose files are known to be riddled with misattributions.

CHAPTER TWENTY-THREE

p. 214 **There were many Jews in Vlassov's army** . . . Demjanjuk, when mentioning Jews in his testimony, used the word *"yivrai,"* not *"zhid."*

p. 216 **[Walter] Dubovitz** . . . Dubovitz never appeared in court. I spoke with him once; he hung up on me. I wrote to him on several occasions; the letters were returned. There is a "Dubovitz affidavit," which Dubovitz would neither confirm nor deny. As it has never been confirmed, its contents are, at best, suspect.

In it, Dubovitz recounts that as a Soviet soldier, he was captured by the Germans in July 1941 and was held in a POW camp in Germany until the end of the summer, when he joined the Russian Liberation Army and was trained at its propaganda center in Dabendorf. In Feb. 1945, he accompanied the general staff to Heuberg. Dubovitz describes the camp, its surroundings, its officers, in detail. He was in charge of a security detail for General Truckhin. He then says:

"Soon after my arrival in Feb. 1945, one day I walked in the grounds around the barracks and talked to soldiers that looked suitable. I selected fourteen or fifteen men from the second divi-

sion to serve under my command. In this group were Ivan Demjanjuk and his best friend, another Ukrainian by the name of
Alexei Podhorny. I remember these two were dressed the same
but I cannot be certain in what uniform. I recall about six men in
this group were wearing dark outfits lacking any insignia, with
short jackets ending at the waist and trousers gathered at the bottom. These were not Soviet or German SS uniforms, but looked
like tank crew outfits. . . ." Dubovitz goes on to say he remem-
bers Podhorny better than Demjanjuk. "Ivan was quiet. I chose
Demjanjuk because he had a likable face and good physique. He
was fairly tall and of normal weight. . . . I would not have selected any soldier for my unit who was weak or in bad shape."
He says that although he knew nothing of his past, he assumed
that Demjanjuk and Podhorny had served in the Red Army together and been POWs together. He goes on to say that he was
not friendly with Demjanjuk, only commanded him once a week.
"Demjanjuk was a nice fellow and a good soldier. He carried out
his duties well. He spoke Russian well, but with a Ukrainian accent."

The unit stayed in Heuberg until the end of Apr. when they
evacuated and made their way to a town called Kalden, where
they surrendered to the Americans. Dubovitz was in the Regensburg DP camp between 1945 and 1947. He saw Demjanjuk
and Podhorny several times in the camps. He said that Demjanjuk
was not working; and that neither before or after the war did he
ever see Demjanjuk drive. He says he lost track of Demjanjuk in
1947 when he went to work in Belgium in a coal mine. Finally, he
says he ran into Demjanjuk once in the early 1960s at a summer
resort in Cassville, N.J., where they talked for fifteen minutes
about unimportant matters.

Finally Dubovitz says, "I think that the Ivan Demjanjuk I knew
at Heuberg and Landshut looked somewhat like, but somewhat
unlike, the face in the Demjanjuk ID Card photo. I am not convinced it is the same person. . . . The man I knew in Vlassov's
army and after the termination of the war, was Ivan Demjanjuk.
He is the same man as John Demjanjuk, whom I have seen on
television as being on trial presently in Jerusalem."

On the one hand, Dubovitz does seem to know Heuberg. On
the other, it isn't clear that he knows Demjanjuk, other than the
fact that he knows him by name. There is no special information—his patronymic, his place of birth, his age—no distinguishing features or talents—Dubovitz's description is bland.
Demjanjuk himself never mentioned Podhorny; and he was always working after the war; and he never, as far as we know,
visited New Jersey in the early 1960s. But even if true, the statement is neither exonerating, nor incriminating. He knows nothing
of Demjanjuk's past prior to Feb. 1945. Some of the men in the

unit were wearing uniforms that sound like guard outfits, but Dubovitz does not say Demjanjuk was one of them.

p. 218   **Sombor . . .** There are actually towns called "Sombor" in the Soviet Union and at least one called "Sambor" in Poland. Sambor was a town south of Lvov where in Aug. 1942, 4,000 Jews were deported; and on Mar. 14, 1943, 900 Jews were shot in the main square. There may be another key to Sombor. "Sombor," as any Soviet child knows, has a very specific meaning in Russian history: it was the conference that unified the various medieval Russian leaders under the authority of none other than Ivan the Terrible. Was Demjanjuk, subconsciously, making a slip?

CHAPTER TWENTY-FOUR

p. 229   **[Demjanjuk's] mother . . .** Demjanjuk's mother, Olga, died in 1970.

CHAPTER TWENTY-SIX

p. 250   After his testimony, Tolstoy wrote a lengthy article published in the *Sunday Telegraph* as "J'Accuse!" arguing that "the man called 'Ivan The Terrible' is Israel's Dreyfus," showing his talents as a writer by presenting his version and continuing to insult the court. This self-rehabilitation in the press long favored by defense attorneys, would become popular among defense witnesses.

CHAPTER TWENTY-SEVEN

p. 251   **Judge Tal suffered a mild heart attack . . .** Judge Tal was one of three judges in the closed-door hearing of Mordechai Vannanu, the Israeli nuclear technician who was tried, and eventually convicted, of treason relating to revealing Israeli nuclear secrets to a British newspaper.

p. 253   **Purple KGB ink . . .** Grant was asked whether he believed that if purple ink was found beneath the photo, it would be a further indication of KGB forgery. Grant said that he could answer that only if he had taken the photograph off and examined the back of it. The defense has since often made the claim that Grant "was not allowed" to remove the photograph and examine the back. But the fact is that Grant never made such a request, and only raised its possibility during his testimony.

p. 254   **Paperclips . . .** Rubik Rosenthal, in *Al Hamsishar,* Nov. 15, 1987, wrote an editorial called "Banalities of Another Kind," saying that because of trivialities such as a paperclip, the trial of Holocaust atrocities had become, "as though you'd gone to view Dante's inferno but instead found yourself at a live broadcast of a TV series. . . ." The response came two weeks later on Dec. 4, in *Davar,* from Knesset member and Holocaust survivor Sheva Weiss, who wrote in "Who's Afraid of the Demjanjuk Trial," that the crimes for which Demjanjuk was accused, merited the most serious prosecution Israel could undertake, and it was to Israel's credit that it, through its system of justice, had responded to the charges against this man; and that if the paperclip could help in proving the card authentic and convicting him, or in proving the card a forgery and exonerating him—then Israel had to spend day and night and assume every cost to arrive at a result. "If this person is acquitted he will be free to return to his family and tell the world that 'there be judges in Jerusalem.' . . . Is there another nation anywhere on earth that lost one third of its sons to systematic murder and that tries its murderers thus?"

p. 256 **Nishnic was visited by police . . .** "I had no intention of breaking Israeli law," Ed Nishnic told the Associated Press. "But if Mr. Flynn is in violation of a contract, I intend to uphold it. He got the message," he said.

CHAPTER TWENTY-EIGHT

p. 262 **Wagenaar had not written a single article . . .** Since appearing at the trial, Wagenaar has several new publications, including a volume, *Identifying Ivan,* in which he repeats the same arguments, based on the same assumptions as presented in court—the book does list several new articles.

p. 263 **Bahrick . . .** See *Bahrick.* Wagenaar sought to distinguish the present situation from Bahrick by saying that the persons involved were remembering not their friends from fifty years ago, but rather the yearbooks that they may have viewed recently. However, it emerges from the article that those being examined were asked about the frequency with which they viewed their yearbook, frequency of meeting with their schoolmates, when they last looked at the book, etc., and these data were taken into account in weighing the study results.

CHAPTER TWENTY-NINE

p. 277 **Danylchenko . . .** The protocol revealed that on Nov. 21, 1979, Danylchenko, who was retired and living in the city of Tobolsk, appeared at the offices of the Procuracy of the USSR in the city of Tyumen. He was cautioned and asked about his wartime activities and knowledge of Ivan Demjanjuk. Questioning began at 10:00 A.M.

and was concluded at 6:15 P.M. with a break, and was undertaken by senior legal counsel N. P. Kolesnikova (who is now the chief Soviet war-crimes prosecutor). Danylchenko was born in 1923.

p. 277 **FOIA** . . . Nishnic and Turchyn had filed two FOIA requests in May 1986 asking for the investigative reports from OSI. Nothing happened. In Aug. 1986, they had a meeting with the Justice Department where they took along TV cameras to ask why nothing was being done. In Oct. 1986, they filed suit and Broadley took over responsibility. The suit produced a determination that the reports were the OSI's protected "work product." Nonetheless, the OSI released much material. Nishnic continued to file related motions in the FOIA suit. Most recently, on Jan. 26, 1990, U.S. District Court judge Louis F. Oberdorfer denied Nishnic's request for the OSI to produce certain documents gathered in investigating Demjanjuk's denaturalization case, and rejected Nishnic's allegations of improprieties on OSI's part.

p. 278 **Sobibor** . . . Many seemed to believe that if Demjanjuk were found not to have been at Treblinka by virtue of having been at Sobibor during the entire period in question, he would be "innocent." But Israeli law provides both at the trial and appeal level for an accused to be convicted of crimes if the facts become known in the course of the hearing (in Demjanjuk's case, this might require the consent of the party from whom Demjanjuk was extradited; but there is no reason to believe the U.S. would not grant it).

CHAPTER THIRTY

p. 289 **Pilau** . . . The court would remark on the entry of Pilau, where exterminations of Jews took place, on Demjanjuk's form:
"We, for whom the Holocaust of our people is part of our existence, did not know of this place. The accused knew, and placed himself there, just as he placed himself at Sobibor, also a place of extermination of Jews."

p. 289 **The Trawniki card** . . . The mistake on the Trawniki card as to the province of Demjanjuk's birth is explained by the fact that the cards were filled in by ethnic Germans unfamiliar with the geography of the Ukraine. This is supported by the fact that Demjanjuk's village, Dub Macharenzi, while correctly entered, is misspelled as "Duboimachariwzi."

p. 294 **Otto Horn** . . . As to Horn's identification and the various affidavits submitted, the court said, "Nothing emerges from them . . . that shows collusion or fabrication of evidence. . . . There is nothing in these affidavits that can detract from the force of the identification by Horn."

p. 296 **We therefore find him guilty** . . . The court found added support in some of Demjanjuk's utterances—"You are pushing me to Treblinka," for example, which the court found to be the beginning of an admission that constituted incriminating behavior on his part; so, too, his comments during his interrogations such as "Eichmann was big, Ivan was little . . ." or, "When the Germans order to collaborate, who could refuse?" And his many comments to Kaplan explaining himself, such as, "there is nothing to try him for . . ." The court said that if not for his qualifying each statement by saying that, of course, he wasn't talking about himself, it would have constituted a clear confession. So the court viewed the beginning of an admission part of the incriminating fabric brought up in the course of the trial.

WITNESS CHRONOLOGY

The witnesses at the trial appeared as follows:

FOR THE PROSECUTION:

Dr. Yitzhak Arad, Holocaust historian	Feb. 17, 1987
	Feb. 18
	Feb. 19
Pinhas Epstein, Treblinka survivor	Feb. 23, 1987
	Feb. 24
Eliahu Rosenberg, Treblinka survivor	Feb. 25, 1987
	Feb. 26
	Mar. 2
	Jan. 27, 1988 (additional cross-examination)
Yossef Czarny, Treblinka survivor	Mar. 3, 1987
Gustav Boraks, Treblinka survivor	Mar. 4, 1987
Alexander Ish Shalom, police officer	Mar. 5, 1987
Yehiel Reichman, Treblinka survivor	Mar. 9, 1987
	Mar. 10
	Mar. 11
Arye Kaplan, police officer	Mar. 11, 1987
	Mar. 12
Miriam Radiwker, police investigator	Mar. 17, 1987
	Mar. 18
	Mar. 19
Dr. Yaacov Ziegelboim, prison doctor	Mar. 19, 1987

Martin Kollar, police investigator	Mar. 24, 1987
	Mar. 25
Helge Grabitz, Hamburg State Attorney	Mar. 25, 1987
	Mar. 26
	Mar. 30
	Mar. 31
	Apr. 1
	Apr. 2
Prof. Wolfgang Sheffler, Holocaust historian	Apr. 6, 1987
	Apr. 7
	Apr. 8
	Apr. 9
Amnon Bezalelli, documents examiner	Apr. 21, 1987
	Apr. 22
	Apr. 23
Reinhardt Altmann, criminal identification	Apr. 27, 1987
	Apr. 28
	Apr. 29
Prof. Patricia Smith, identification expert	Apr. 30, 1987
	May 5
	May 6
	Dec. 28 (reexamination for the defense)
Gideon Epstein, documents examiner	May 7, 1987
	May 11
Prof. Matityahu Meisel, historical expert	May 11, 1987
	May 12
	May 13
Dr. Shmuel Spektor, historical expert	June 22, 1987
Dr. Shmuel Krakovsky, historical expert	June 23, 1987
	June 24
Dr. Anthony Cantu, documents examiner	June 25, 1987

By Rogatory: Helmut Leonhardt—former Trawniki policeman; Otto Horn—former SS Treblinka man

Deposition by Section 15: Eugen Turovsky—Holocaust survivor, deceased; Avraham Goldfarb—Holocaust survivor, deceased; Avraham Lindvasser—Holocaust survivor, deceased

FOR THE DEFENSE:

John (Ivan) Demjanjuk, the accused	July 27, 1987
	July 28
	July 29
	July 30
	Aug. 3
	Aug. 4
	Aug. 5
	Dec. 29 (reexamination)

Mrs. Edna Robertson, documents examiner	Aug. 6, 1987
	Aug. 10
	Aug. 11
	Aug. 12
	Aug. 13
Mrs. Anita Pritchard, documents examiner	Aug. 17, 1987
	Aug. 19
Avraham Shiffrin, expert on KGB	Oct. 26, 1987
	Oct. 27
	Oct. 28
Nikolai Tolstoy, historical expert	Nov. 2, 1987
	Nov. 3
	Nov. 4
	Nov. 5
Dr. Julius Grant, documents examiner	Nov. 9, 1987
	Nov. 10
	Nov. 11
Dr. Götz Pollzien, German attorney	Nov. 12, 1987
Willem Wagenaar, psychologist	Nov. 16, 1987
	Nov. 17
	Nov. 18
	Nov. 19
William G. Flynn, documents examiner	Nov. 23, 1987
	Nov. 24
	Nov. 25
Prof. Yascar Iscan, anthropologist	Dec. 14, 1987
	Dec. 15
	Dec. 16
	Dec. 17
	Dec. 21
	Dec. 22
	Dec. 23
Yitzhak Almagor, former Jewish POW	Dec. 29, 1987

By Rogatory: Rudolf Reiss—former Trawniki man

By Section 15: Shlomo Hellman—Treblinka survivor, deceased; I. T. Danylchenko—Soviet citizen, former *Wachmann;* reports of investigations conducted by the OSI

TIMELINES

HISTORY

Sept. 1, 1939 German invasion of Poland.
Jan. 1941 Wansee Conference.
July 1942 Treblinka begins operation.
Aug. 2, 1943 revolt in Treblinka.
May 1945 Germany surrenders.
May 1948 Israel founded.
1961–62 Eichmann trial.

DEMJANJUK TIMELINE

Apr. 3, 1920 Ivan Demjanjuk born to Nikolai and Olga Demjanjuk in village of Dub Macharenzi in Ukraine.
1937 Demjanjuk employed on collective farm (*Kolkhoz*), first as assistant, then as tractor driver.
1941 Demjanjuk enters Red Army.
1941 Photo of Demjanjuk in Red Army uniform with friends Ivan and Petrov.
Demjanjuk wounded in back, treated in four hospitals, returned to front.
May 1942 Battle of Kerch; Demjanjuk becomes German POW.

PROSECUTION VERSION 1942–43

May 1942 Demjanjuk taken immediately to POW Camp Rovno.
No later than July 19, 1942 Demjanjuk arrives at Trawniki training camp;

336

his photo is taken in guard uniform. Demjanjuk is trained as a *Wachmann*. Trawniki card no. 1393 is issued to Ivan Demjanjuk.

By Sept. 1942 Demjanjuk is transferred to Treblinka death camp.

Sept. 1942–Feb. 1943 Demjanjuk serves at Treblinka, working in the death-camp area as the operator and mechanic of the gas chamber's engine. He is, on occasion, briefly posted elsewhere.

Sept. 22, 1942 Demjanjuk is at L.G. Okzow, a work farm near Chelm.

Feb. 1943 From then on, there are fewer gassings at Treblinka; Demjanjuk is used where services are needed.

Mar. 27, 1943 Demjanjuk is at Sobibor. Statement of Danylchenko, submitted by the defense, that he first met Demjanjuk at Sobibor in Mar. 1943.

Aug. 1943 After the revolt Demjanjuk is again at Treblinka to operate the gas chamber for the final transports.

DEMJANJUK VERSION 1942–43

June–July 1942 Demjanjuk arrives in Rovno camp. After a few weeks is transferred to Chelm POW camp.

Late summer 1942–spring 1944 Demjanjuk is at Chelm.

AFTER TREBLINKA

Sept. 1943 Treblinka is dismantled.

PROSECUTION VERSION 1943–45

Evidence was submitted that: Demjanjuk was assigned to Trieste in fall 1943 (Munzberger's statement); Demjanjuk's own IRO and visa forms that said he was in Pilau; Danylchenko's testimony, submitted by the defense, puts Demjanjuk at Sobibor until Nov. 1944, although Sobibor closed in Nov. 1943, and then has him at Flossenburg and Regensburg.

Prosecution argues that Demjanjuk could have served at Trieste, Flossenburg, and Pilau. Demjanjuk was a skilled *Wachmann,* and evidence was submitted that during this period, *Wachmanner* were shunted around Central Europe.

DEMJANJUK VERSION 1943–45

Demjanjuk testified that he was a POW at Chelm until spring 1944. Next taken to Graz, where he was tattooed and from there to Heuberg, to join the Russian Liberation Army in Feb. 1945. Demjanjuk then went to a series of other POW camps before the war ended and he was registered as a DP in Landshut, Germany. This is in direct contradiction to forms Demjanjuk filled out beginning in 1948 saying that during the war years he was at Chelm, Sobibor, Pilau, and Munich.

POSTWAR CHRONOLOGY

May 1945 Demjanjuk becomes a DP at Landshut DP camp.

May 1945–Feb. 1952 Demjanjuk lives in various DP camps in Germany: Landshut, Regensburg, Ulm, and Fedalfing.

Sept. 1, 1947 Demjanjuk marries Vera Kowlowa. Shortly thereafter, Demjanjuk files for affidavit of lost identity papers to IRO.

Oct. 1947 Demjanjuk enrolls in driving course, a prerequisite for becoming a truck driver for the Americans.

Nov. 1947 Demjanjuk receives driving license with photo on it; he signs in Latin script.

Mar. 1948 Demjanjuk fills out IRO assistance form. He writes that from 1937 to 1943 he was a driver at "Sobibor–Chelm–Poland"; and from 1943 until Oct. 1944 he was in Pilau, Germany, and from then until the end of the war in Munich. He says that his first choice for immigration is to Argentina, his second to Canada.

Demjanjuk works for American army as an truck driver, driving the length of Germany, sometimes alone, by his own account, driving as much as eight hundred miles a day.

1950 Daughter Lydia is born.

1951 Demjanjuk applies for immigration to the U.S. On the form he again says that he was in Sobibor and Pilau and was employed as a driver. He submits passport-sized photo in coat and tie.

Feb. 1952 Demjanjuk, wife, and daughter arrive in U.S.; travel to Indiana.

July 1952 Demjanjuk settles in Cleveland.

Aug. 1952 Demjanjuk starts work at Ford as an engine mechanic.

Nov. 1958 Demjanjuk becomes U.S. citizen; changes first name to John.

Jan. 1960 Daughter, Irene, born.

Aug. 1965 Son, John Jr., born.

Nov. 1975 Demjanjuk name first submitted to INS as alleged Nazi collaborator at Sobibor.

May 1976 Israeli Holocaust survivors first identify 1951 visa picture of Demjanjuk as Ivan of Treblinka.

Aug. 1976 Ukrainian article accuses Demjanjuk of having been a guard at Sobibor; mentions a Trawniki identity card and quotes another former guard, Danylchenko, who claims to have served with him there.

Fall 1976 Demjanjuk appears at U.S. Attorney's office answering to INS request but, under advice of attorney, postpones interview.

Aug. 1977 Complaint filed charging Demjanjuk with being Ivan the Terrible of Treblinka and asking that he be denaturalized.

Sept. 1977 *News from Ukraine* first publishes pictures of the Trawniki card; and mentions Danylchenko again.

Apr. 1978 Demjanjuk's first deposition. He says that during the war he was a POW at Rovno and another camp whose name he can't recall.

Nov. 1979 Justice Department receives Soviet protocols including Danylchenko's; information is communicated to defense attorneys in interrogatory answer.

Dec. 1979 In answer to interrogatory, Demjanjuk gives written reply that he was at Rovno and at Chelm building barracks, and afterward joined the Russian Liberation Army and was in Graz and Heuberg.

Feb. 1981 Demjanjuk's denaturalization trial begins. Trawniki card appears and is found authentic. Demjanjuk is found to be Ivan the Terrible of Treblinka. His citizenship is revoked.

1982 Appeals of decision denied.

1983 Mark O'Connor is hired. O'Connor in turn hires John Gill.

Sept. 1983 Deportation hearings begin.

Nov. 1983 Israel requests extradition of Demjanjuk.

1984 Demjanjuk ordered deported.

1984 Appeals of deportation denied.

Apr. 1985 Demjanjuk's bail is revoked; he enters prison.

1985 Appeals continue; extradition hearings are held.

Nov. 1985 Extradition of Demjanjuk to Israel upheld.

Feb. 27, 1986 Demjanjuk is put on El Al Flight to Israel.

Feb. 28, 1986 Demjanjuk arrives in Israel and is taken to Ayalon Prison, outside Tel Aviv.

Sept. 29, 1986 Israel files indictment against Demjanjuk to be tried under Nazi and Nazi Collaborators Law of 1950.

Nov. 1986 Demjanjuk trial opens; Feb. 16, 1987, trial begins in earnest.

Apr. 18, 1988 Demjanjuk found guilty.

Apr. 25, 1988 Demjanjuk sentenced to death.

INDEX